ORPHAN ROAD

ORPHAN ROAD

The Railroad Comes to Seattle, 1853-1911

Kurt E. Armbruster

WSU
PRESS

Washington State University Press
Pullman, Washington

Washington State University Press
PO Box 645910
Pullman, WA 99164-5910
phone: 800-354-7360
fax: 509-335-8568
e-mail: wsupress@wsu.edu
web site: www.publications.wsu.edu/wsupress

Library of Congress Cataloging-in-Publication Data

Armbruster, Kurt E.
      Orphan road : the railroad comes to Seattle, 1853-1911 / Kurt E. Armbruster.
          p. cm.
      Includes bibliographical references (p.).
      ISBN 0-87422-185-4 (hdb.). — ISBN 0-87422-186-2 (pbk.)
      1. Railroads—Washington (State)—Seattle Region. 2. Railroads—Washington (State)—
Puget Sound Region. 3. Seattle Region (Wash.)—History. 4. Puget Sound Region (Wash.)—
History. I. Title.
TF25.S44A76 1999
385'.09797'722—dc21   99-37058
                                                                          CIP

Cover: Poised for a fast run to Oakland, the Shasta Limited awaits the highball for departure on the opening day of the Oregon-Washington Station, March 15, 1911.

Museum of History and Industry, #83.10.6758

Dedication

For my father, Frederick Robert Armbruster,
who took me to watch the trains go by.

ACKNOWLEDGMENTS

I wish to thank David Anderson of Cranbrook, B.C., Dan Cozine of Seattle, Jim Fredrickson of Tacoma, Doug R. Phillips of Calgary, Alberta, and Larry Schrenk of Minneapolis for their assistance. Special thanks go to Paul Dorpat, Rick and Tom Mendenhall, and Warren Wing for opening their fine photo collections to me. Finally, special thanks to the WSU Press staff for encouragement and support.

Contents

FORGERS OF CIVILIZATION, CREWMEN POSE PROUDLY WITH COLUMBIA & PUGET SOUND
No. 7, *Hyak*. BUILT IN 1872 AS THE WALLA WALLA & COLUMBIA RIVER'S *Walla Walla*,
THE LOCOMOTIVE WAS RENAMED THE *Hyak* AFTER PURCHASE BY THE C&PS IN 1881.

Renton Historical Society

Introduction

"My motto in life was to never go backward." —Arthur A. Denny

SOUTH OF DOWNTOWN SEATTLE, along a vagrant and unlikely looking streak of rust in the backwater of the city, one may meet the pioneer ghosts of old Seattle. Feeble and arthritic is this railroad track, straggling between nondescript buildings and giving every appearance of living on borrowed time. This is the oldest track in Seattle. Here, on May 1, 1874, wagons plodded to a halt beside a fork of the Duwamish River, rickety river steamers disembarked men in varying states of sobriety, and Henry Yesler and the Denny brothers pitched in with their neighbors to begin hacking a railroad into the forest.

Many worked as they hadn't in years, and next morning felt it in their bones. But all could reflect happily upon being present together in what they knew was a defining moment in their city's history. Blisters were perhaps fondly remembered three years later when a shiny new locomotive named the *A.A. Denny* rolled down this homemade track. After a fashion, Seattle had arrived. But it remained unconnected.

On November 13, 1851, Arthur A. Denny had stumped down the schooner *Exact*'s gangplank to found a city. Denny lugged his family's belongings ashore—grim determination set upon his already stern features. He peered through the rain to see his wife, Mary, sitting on a trunk, weeping.

The stolid midwesterner commiserated as best he could, but no shadow of doubt clouded his vision: "My motto in life was to never go backward."

Denny saw the future clearly, and that meant connection with the East: "I came to the coast with the belief that a railroad would be built across the continent to some point on the northern coast within the next fifteen or twenty years, and [I] located on the Sound with that expectation."

Rude cabins went up, and the settlement was optimistically named New York. Surely, connection would not be long in coming. Indeed, within two years of Denny's landing at Alki Point, Washington Territory's first governor, Isaac I. Stevens, dangled the prospect of a railroad to Puget Sound within five years. But "New York" gave way to a strange-sounding new town—"Seattle"—and it took much longer, and much more of a struggle, to get that railroad than Denny ever imagined.

Instead of a natural partnership with a transcontinental line, Seattle found itself in a long and bitter feud with the railroad company it hoped would bring prosperity. Even after trains finally reached Seattle, keeping them coming proved to be problematic.

The hunger for connection grew, and in the words of Seattle's pioneer historian Clarence Bagley: "Imperial Richard on Bosworth field yearned no more fervently for a horse than did Seattle for a railroad."

Railroads—real and imaginary, blessed and cursed—would accompany Seattle through all the stages of its rise to maturity, and make a grand spectacle along the way. ■

"MILEPOST 0" OF SEATTLE RAILWAYS. THE AUTHOR STANDS AT THE SPOT WHERE, ON MAY 1, 1874, THE CITY GATHERED TO BUILD THE SEATTLE & WALLA WALLA RAILROAD.

GUSTAVUS SOHON'S DEPICTION OF RAILROAD SURVEYORS CROSSING
THE HELLGATE RIVER (CLARK FORK, MONTANA), MAY 5, 1854.

Isaac I. Stevens, Reports of Explorations and Surveys

CHAPTER 1

Isaac Stevens and the Northern Pacific Survey

"You can see in imagination cities and villages." —Isaac I. Stevens

THE NOON HOUR was almost over on June 17, 1884. The workmen at the Stetson & Post mill and the Columbia & Puget Sound Railroad shops were closing their lunch boxes and tapping out their pipes. But what was all the commotion? An unusually large number of people seemed to be gravitating toward the wide, planked-over railroad trestle, even women and children. Someone muttered something about a train coming. Odd; the track had lain there for months, now, but no train from the direction of the Columbia River had ever come down the trestle into Seattle.

Just then, a wagon cluttered by bearing a tall gentleman in a stovepipe hat—and a cannon. "McNaught," someone muttered.

The appearance of the well-known Seattle lawyer in the company of artillery guaranteed that something was definitely "up"! The crowd grew thick, and even the mill foreman was out there along with his laborers, their work forgotten.

Someone yelled: "There she comes!"

A mile away, at the far end of the trestle, a puff of gray smoke curled up from the trees, then a locomotive emerged from the woods and started across the long trestle toward the waiting crowd. A whistle screeched thinly, and the arm of the tall gentleman dropped. The cannon boomed once, twice . . .

The first standard gauge passenger train into Seattle had arrived.

From the infancy of American railroads in the 1830s, men dreamed of running trains to the Pacific Northwest. Lewis and Clark brought the region into the national consciousness, and the opening of the Oregon Trail in 1843 invited settlers into the great, green land stretching from the Willamette Valley to the Puget Sound country. The provision for free land under the Oregon Donation Land Act of 1850 further stimulated migration to the Northwest.

However, by wagon overland or sailing ship around Cape Horn, getting there was a three-to-six-month ordeal fraught with every conceivable discomfort and menace. The new "steamcars," able to rush along at twenty miles an hour, were the only possible means of truly opening the West and tying it to the rest of the nation.

Visionaries of every stripe enlivened the pre-Civil War years with transcontinental railroad schemes: Many had the Pacific Northwest as their destination. As early as 1835, Samuel Bancroft Barlow was writing treatises in favor of a line to the Columbia River, but the 1845 proposition of New York entrepreneur Asa Whitney was the first to garner widespread support. Whitney stressed the need to tie the far Northwest to the Union before it either became part of the British Empire—still very much active north of the Columbia—or struck off on its own, with its abundant resources and fast-growing population.

He warned, Oregon "may become an independent state, and establish free trade with Japan, China, India, Mexico, and South America. It may control the fisheries of the Pacific, and become our most dangerous and successful rival in the commerce of the world."[1]

Cornerstone of Whitney's plan was a vast grant of public land along two thousand miles of line from the Midwest to the mouth of the Columbia—more than seventy million acres. This he deemed essential to invite settlement, generate cash for construction, and provide a basis of credit for investors.

Though opinion in favor of a Pacific railroad quickly grew, many balked at handing over the national largesse to private individuals or corporations. More serious an impediment was sectionalism. Southerners such as Jefferson Davis, James Gadsden, and Sam Houston were strong in their opposition to Whitney's northern route. Thomas Hart Benton, the powerful senator from Missouri, led the southern faction, scorning Whitney and other private railroad schemers as "jobbers" intent on plundering the national treasury. Benton favored instead a "national highway" between St. Louis and California, following the footprints of animals that had migrated between East and West since time immemorial, and built and operated by the government:

"All propositions to have this [transcontinental] road made as a private road by individuals or companies are utterly condemned by the magnitude of the undertaking, by the question of Indians' title and possession and by the impolicy and illegality to treat with Indians. All these things require national means, national authority."[2]

These railroad visions attracted wide support, but none got past the talking stage. Despite the fact that the Whitney plan had by 1848 garnered resolutions of support from eighteen states (including five southern ones), Congress was unwilling to commit such unprecedented amounts of land and money to a bold thrust into a region which, for most, was as unknown, remote, and wild as Africa.

It fell to a Vermont civil engineer, a man who had never ventured west of St. Paul, to provide the vital spark for a transcontinental railroad. Edwin Ferry Johnson had been captivated by the reports of Lewis and Clark and other early explorers, and spent much of the 1840s and 1850s distilling all available data on the Pacific Northwest's topography, climate, rivers, and resources into his own prospectus. Johnson's study was found by subsequent surveyors to be remarkably accurate, and it provided a definitive plan for a railroad to the Pacific through the territories between the 47th and 49th parallels.

The northern region offered more resources to sustain greater numbers of settlers than the sections to the south, he declared, and its climate was generally benign and conducive to agriculture. Precipitation, including snowfall, was moderate. Coal, silver, and iron ore were to be found in abundance. Running almost due west from the St. Lawrence River and the Great Lakes to Puget Sound, connecting with shipping lanes at both ends, Johnson's route offered the shortest line to and from the vast, untapped markets of Asia. A northern railroad, Johnson proclaimed, would create the most productive realm of commerce and settlement in the world.[3]

Johnson enlisted the support of another Vermont engineer, Thomas Canfield, and laid his proposition before Secretary of War Jefferson Davis. Davis read Johnson's recommendations with alarm: He was a devout southerner, with no interest in promoting any northern schemes. Still, the demands of the public had to be heard, and, in the antebellum years, those demands were waxing loud for a transcontinental railroad. Roused by Whitney and Johnson, communities from the Potomac to the Columbia held town meetings and fired off resolutions to Congress.

By 1853, lawmakers' desks were groaning under a flood of constituent mail all asking the same question: Where is our railroad?

The politicians themselves were by this time all but convinced. That February, they appropriated $150,000 to fund reconnaissances of four potential rail routes from the Mississippi to the Pacific—a northern line between the 47th and 49th parallels as outlined by Edwin Johnson and Asa Whitney; a route along the 37th and 39th parallels from the Arkansas River to the Great Salt Lake; a line following the 35th parallel from Arkansas through New Mexico to California; and a fourth route through the Tulare and San Joaquin valleys to connect lines along the 35th and 32nd parallels. Jefferson Davis had contrived to obtain War Department jurisdiction of the survey. If there was to be a Pacific railroad, he would do his best to see that it would be a southern one. He therefore added a fifth route, to follow the 32nd parallel across Texas and Arizona.[4] But he did not reckon on Isaac Stevens.

As a young army officer, Major Isaac Ingalls Stevens had made a name for himself in the Mexican War. In 1849, he became assistant director of the U.S. Coast Survey in Washington, D.C., where he developed a strong reputation for diligence and devotion (and also as something of a martinet). Believing fervently in Manifest Destiny, Stevens was a vigorous exemplar of the "Young America" movement, which looked to the great and yet to be developed West for national fulfillment. A railroad to the Pacific was a central component of that dream, but Stevens assumed that such a vast project lay years in the future.

The year 1853 saw any such reservations swept away. Congress' Pacific railroad appropriation electrified Stevens, and he quickly began to formulate a program that might bring the great railroad dream—and his own career advancement—closer to reality. Providentially, Stevens had only the year before campaigned for his friend, Franklin Pierce, in the 1852 presidential campaign. Pierce's presidential bid was successful, and Stevens promptly applied to him for a position that appeared to offer just the opportunity Stevens was looking for—appointment as the first governor of newly created Washington Territory. The grateful president-elect was happy to honor this request, and, on March 17, Stevens resigned from the army and took up his new commission.

Stevens next asked Jefferson Davis for command of the northernmost of the five War Department Pacific railroad surveys, which was to follow Edwin Johnson's prescribed route to Puget Sound. This was a task Stevens could handily perform en route to his new post, and he assured the war secretary that he could have the survey done by the

congressionally mandated deadline of February 1854, for the sum of $48,000. Davis agreed, and Stevens threw himself into an intensive six-week preparation rounding up men, maps, and supplies for what he intended would be the greatest and most comprehensive American exploration yet.

Stevens assembled an impressive team of army and civilian talent, including civil engineers Abiel Tinkham and Fred Lander, topographical engineers John Lambert and J.K. Duncan, geologist Dr. John Evans, naturalists Dr. George Suckley and Dr. James G. Cooper, artist John Mix Stanley, and a multi-talented young aide, James Doty (and, at a later date, soldier/artist Gustavus Sohon). At the Smithsonian Institution, Professor Spencer Baird would

oversee the cataloguing of zoological and botanical specimens. Stevens spent his few free hours immersing himself in the works of Lewis and Clark, Father De Smet, and Sir George Simpson of the Hudson's Bay Company.

He also took the time to write to the leading men of Puget Sound, among them Arthur Denny and Dr. David S. Maynard of Seattle: The "Northern Pacific Railroad Exploration and Survey" was coming; any information they could furnish on the Puget Sound country and the Cascade Range would be gratefully received.[5]

Stevens divided his reconnaissance party into three groups. His own, main force would proceed across western Minnesota, and through what are now North Dakota, Montana, Idaho, and Washington (then parts of Nebraska and Washington territories) to Olympia. Lieuten-

ant Rufus Saxton, Jr., who had worked in Stevens' Coast Survey office, would lead a second force from Fort Vancouver, Washington, and explore the Bitterroots and Rockies. The third group was placed under the command of a young major in the Army Corps of Engineers whose work Stevens had much admired during the Mexican campaign: Major George Brinton McClellan.

McClellan's commanding officer, General Joseph Totten, had reservations about placing a U.S. Army officer under civilian authority, and suggested splitting the expedition into two independent eastern and western surveys led by Stevens and McClellan. Stevens demurred, insisting that it was necessary to have a unified overall command under one leader; McClellan would not only be treated with all due deference, he assured Totten, but he would undoubtedly relish his assignment. Totten acquiesced, and McClellan was given the task of traveling by sea to either Fort Vancouver or Puget Sound, and, from there, exploring the Cascade Range in search of prospective railroad routes. This last task, Stevens quickly perceived, was crucial to the adoption of a northern route. The Columbia River gorge was the Northwest's main artery, but little was known of the mountains to the north, though Stevens had seen reports that Indians and Hudson's Bay Company traders had long utilized crossings along the Naches and Yakima rivers. To open up the Puget Sound region to the nation, it was imperative to find a way through one or more of these passes.

Stevens cautioned McClellan: "The amount of work in the Cascade Range and eastward . . . will be immense . . . We must not be frightened with long tunnels or enormous snows, but set ourselves to work to overcome them."[6]

Flying a banner emblazoned "Westward Ho" (which also prophetically portrayed a locomotive chasing a buffalo), Stevens led his main expedition out of St. Paul at the beginning of June 1853. Despite withering heat, recalcitrant mules, and stampeding buffalo, the governor made good time. Tinkham and Lander ranged north and south from the main body to observe the lay of the land, and Stevens patiently lectured wary Indians that the coming of the railroad would bring greater, not lesser, prosperity.

McClellan had already embarked for the Northwest, and planned to penetrate the Cascades obliquely from the east: "Supposing that there would be less timber on the eastern than the western slope of the range, and that the elevation of the plateau between the Rocky and Cascade mountains would facilitate our progress."[7]

McClellan and Saxton landed at Fort Vancouver in late June. Saxton quickly requisitioned the best of the available supplies and pack animals, and headed for the Bitterroots to replenish the main Stevens party when it should arrive. McClellan took the leftovers—meager rations and played-out mules—and on July 18 led a 61-man party northeast up the Cathlapootle (now Lewis) River and over

BISON HERD ON THE NORTHERN GREAT PLAINS, BY JOHN MIX STANLEY.
Isaac I. Stevens, Reports of Explorations and Surveys

Klickitat Pass south of Mt. St. Helens and Mt. Adams. The animals may not have been first-rate, but McClellan's assistants were: ethnologist George Gibbs, surgeon-naturalist Dr. James Cooper, meteorologist Lt. Sylvester Mowry, and assistant engineer J.F. Minter. The weather was pleasant but the underbrush thick, the trail almost nonexistent, and the scenery obscured by smoke from forest fires. The mules began to give out from lack of proper forage, and clouds of mosquitos made men and beasts miserable.

The party trudged into the Yakima Valley, which impressed McClellan as barren and worthless, and stopped at Ahtanum Ridge and a tiny Oblate (lay) missionary outpost. Father Charles Pandosy informed him that some fifty miles to the northwest there was an easy mountain crossing much used by Indians and trappers: Snoqualmie Pass. McClellan met also with Yakima

Indian chief Kamiakin and his brother, Skloom, who were skeptical of McClellan's pronouncement that he sought a route to be used by settlers only in passing through this area. Kamiakin was apparently mollified by McClellan's assurances that Governor Stevens would not lie or cheat them, and he provided a guide to lead the party into Naches Pass.

On the 22nd of August, McClellan halted at the summit of Naches Pass, fifteen miles northeast of Mt. Rainier and 5,000 feet above sea level. The air was thin, and the climb up had been rocky and steep. McClellan perceived that Naches Pass was lofty indeed—perhaps too lofty. He noted, too, the snow marks on the trees, from eight to twenty feet in places. That much snow would undoubtedly be a serious problem for trains. McClellan frowned, and turned his horse east. McClellan hoped to receive fresh mules from Fort Steilacoom. When word arrived on August 31 that none were available, his mood blackened. Deciding that there was nothing to do but reduce his party by half and make the best of it, McClellan established a depot camp near present-day Ellensburg, and with a small detachment followed the Yakima River west, toward its source: Snoqualmie Pass.

On September 6, the explorers arrived at the south end of Lake Keechelus and continued west up a steep mountain path to the summit. Climbing steadily, they skirted jewel-like Lake Willailootzas, now known as Lost Lake, at the headwaters of the Yakima River, and were soon at the top. This was the pass of the "main Yakima," leading to the westward into the valley of the Nooksai Nooksai, the Cedar River. McClellan gazed around at a panorama prickly with peaks and pinnacles; a brown pall of forest fire smoke obscured the details of depth and distance, and an Indian guide gestured to a ridge that marked the divide between the Yakima and the Snoqualmie River. At 3,500 feet, Yakima Pass was substantially lower than Naches. It still seemed an awful height; the climb up from the valley was sharp, and the horses had to be led. How would locomotives fare? How deep would the snow get in winter?

McClellan and his men rode another three miles down the west slope, then—having no orders to continue further west—turned around. Back at Lake Keechelus on September 9, the guide pointed to a faint track disappearing into the heavy underbrush to the northwest. This, he stated, was a footpath through the divide they had seen from the summit, a trail that led to the headwaters of the Snoqualmie River and continued all the way to the great falls at the foot of the west slope. The Indians did not use it much, the guide averred; it was usually choked with brush and blow-downs, and no good for horses. The trail they had just ridden was the one they preferred. McClellan wondered if the choked-up footpath was not indeed the easy, low-level pass that Stevens hoped he would find. Time was running short, however, and McClellan was anxious about rendezvousing with a relief party bringing rations from Steilacoom. At any rate, the distinction between Snoqualmie Pass to the north and Yakima Pass located six miles south was now clear, and McClellan would report to Stevens that Yakima Pass was "improperly called the Snoqualme Pass."

Later, he would note: "It should be stated that there is a foot trail leading from the head of Lake Kitchelus to the head of the south fork of the Snoqualme. The Indians represent this as practicable on foot with the greatest difficulty, and that it is seldom used, although much nearer the Snoqualme Falls than by the ordinary horse trail; in fact, there is no trail, properly so-called—merely a possibility for an unencumbered and active man to get through there."[8]

There was much more ground to cover. Guided by Yakima chief Owhi, McClellan pushed swiftly northward over Colockum Pass to the confluence of the Wenatchee and Columbia rivers. The upper Wenatchee Valley was bypassed, possibly because the Indians did not use the pass at its head. McClellan made cursory and inconclusive forays up the Chelan, Methow, and Okanogan valleys, then ranged as far north as Lake Okanagan, in British Columbia. At the beginning of October, he turned south to meet up with Stevens.

While McClellan was finding the Cascades problematic, Isaac Stevens was making gratifying progress in the Rockies. In two months' time, Stevens and detachments under Andrew Donelson, Cuvier Grover, Frederick Lander, John Mullan, and Abiel Tinkham had located promising rail routes along the Marias, Teton, Sun, Clark Fork, Dearborn, Jocko, and Coeur d'Alene rivers, and through Stevens (Lookout), Hell Gate (Mullan), Lewis and Clark, and Cadotte passes.

On the 26th of October, all three elements of the Northern Pacific Expedition and Survey were reunited at "Camp Washington," near Spokane Falls, and enjoyed a spirited bivouac leavened by abundant liquor, courtesy of the Hudson's Bay Company. Stevens delivered a rather tipsy encomium to his diligent men, and singled out McClellan for special praise. Good feelings dissipated somewhat the following day when Stevens ordered McClellan to proceed to Olympia over Snoqualmie Pass. It was a prospect the tired officer was in no mood for, and he excused himself with the handy circumstance that his mules were worn out and his barometers broken. Stevens relented, and the parties again split up for the journey to Puget Sound via the Columbia gorge.

Stevens rode south to the Hudson's Bay Company's Fort Walla Walla, then turned west down the Columbia. On the 25th of November, he arrived at Olympia, suffering from a hernia and miserable in rain-sodden buckskins. Pausing at the new capital barely long enough to set up his desk, Stevens embarked on a bone-chilling cruise of Puget Sound aboard the sloop *Sarah Stone*, accompanied by ethnologist George Gibbs, who would make a general survey of the region's native population. In a week, Stevens confirmed to his own satisfaction that promising railroad terminal sites were to be found at Steilacoom, Bellingham Bay, Fidalgo Island, Skagit Head, Port Townsend, Penn Cove, Port Gardner, and Seattle.

Stevens returned to Olympia and began distilling the data of seven months and two thousand miles into a report to the war secretary, casting the northern transcontinental route in the most positive possible light. Cumula-

tive ascents and descents of mountain passes, gradients and curvatures, probable speeds and timings of trains, and geological and meteorological data were all duly noted. The Cascade crossing presented the greatest challenge, and options for tunneling under the Cascade summit were presented—a 4,000-yard bore at Lake Willailootzas, and a two-mile tunnel south of Lake Keechelus. Easier grades prevailed in the Rockies, and, just as Edwin Johnson had said, the climate along the whole northern line was much milder than generally assumed. The Northwest was rich, fertile, and begging for settlement, Stevens concluded, and a railroad could be built from St. Paul to Seattle, via Yakima Pass, for $105,076,000. Another $7,000,000 would take it via the Columbia, and for $129,806,000, the "entire system" of Columbia gorge, Yakima Pass, and a connecting line up the Cowlitz Valley could be built, adding $5,000,000 for "engineering and contingencies."[9]

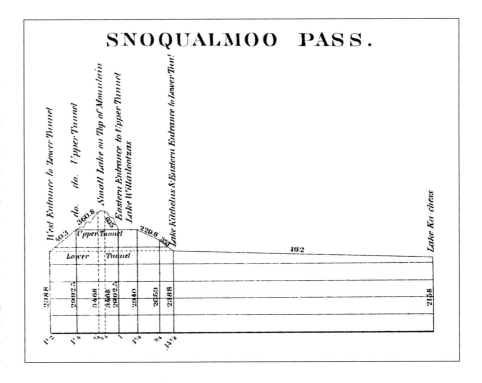

SNOQUALMOO PASS.

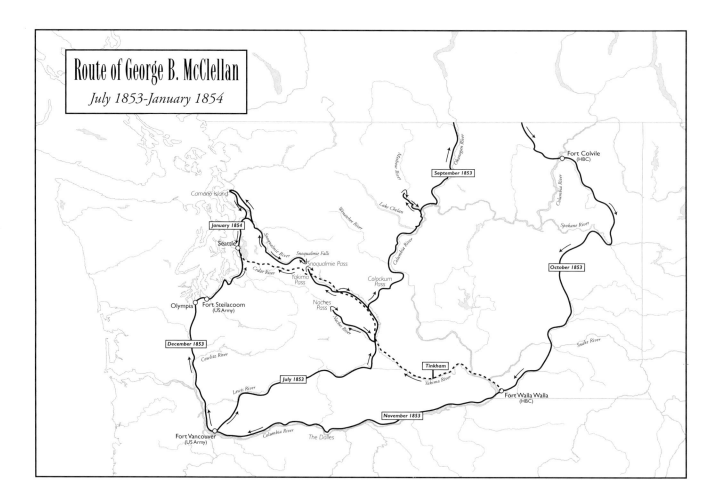

To Stevens' vexation, though, his counsel on overcoming "enormous snows" was thoroughly forgotten by McClellan. After parting company at Camp Washington, the two met again at Fort Walla Walla on November 2. Within a couple of days, the weather had improved so markedly that Stevens asked McClellan if he would not have another go at Naches Pass, "if I can get you twenty good, fat horses."

By this time, McClellan had had enough; enough of hardtack, inadequate clothing, barometers that did not work, sickly mules, and "lonely and dispiriting" country. McClellan "objected so strongly to such a performance"

that Stevens again backed down and assigned the task to Fred Lander. The governor then departed for Olympia, leaving McClellan in charge. Lander was no more eager to go mountaineering than McClellan, and he made convenient use of fresh rumors that an immigrant train was marooned on Naches Pass in twenty-foot drifts. McClellan took this at face value and canceled Stevens' orders; nobody would cross Naches or any other Cascade pass.[10]

McClellan, Lander, and Donelson rode west toward Fort Vancouver, shivering in the wind of the Columbia gorge and keeping their blood warm trading jibes at the niggling, bothering, stupidly optimistic "politician,"

Stevens. McClellan's bitterness was now compounded by the knowledge that he would be required to venture again into the mountains from the west once he reached Puget Sound.

"Thoroughly disgusted with the whole concern," he scribbled in his diary, "and can only pray that I may be relieved from duty with the Survey at the earliest practicable moment."

To his mother, he wrote: "We have to pass the winter at Olympia on Puget's Sound, a flourishing city of some 10 or 12 houses—fine prospect that. In addition I have to start again for the mountains as soon as I reach there . . . As I never saw a snowshoe in my life (except in a museum or a picture book) I don't anticipate much pleasure during the jaunt & am desirous of finishing it as soon as possible . . . we don't expect to see the sun anymore until next summer . . . I don't think much of it [Puget Sound]—it is surely overrated in every respect."[11]

On December 16, McClellan dragged into Olympia, complaining that he had been delayed because his horse had fallen on his foot. Standing before Governor Stevens, he made gloomy recitation: Naches Pass was too steep, too rocky, and too snowbound for rails. Yakima Pass also was steep; both slopes were rocky and narrow, the horses could barely hobble up the road, and the snow depth reached twenty feet or more—the Indians said so.

Stevens did not believe it; McClellan would have to try again. Muttering, he shrugged, gathered men and hard-tack, and in two canoes paddled up Puget Sound to Port Gardner and entered the mouth of the Snohomish River, then proceeded to its Snoqualmie fork. As 1854 began, the reluctant captain poked warily into the frowning, mist-shrouded approach to Snoqualmie Pass. At Snoqualmie Falls, he met a small band of Indians who confirmed his worst suspicions: The snow was twenty-five feet deep at the summit, and even snowshoes were useless in the powdery white stuff; to go up there now was courting death!

Seven miles east of the falls, McClellan turned back, "being forced to the conclusion, that if the attempt to reach the pass were not really impracticable, it was at least inexpedient under all the circumstances in which I was placed."[12]

Stevens had also ordered McClellan to explore the harbors on the east side of Puget Sound, but, as the worst winter in living memory gripped the territory, he got no further than Camano Island. Cursing snow, cold, and most of all Stevens, McClellan retreated to Olympia.

McClellan held fast to his opinion of twenty-five foot snows on Snoqualmie Pass, and Stevens was bound and determined to prove otherwise. In December, Stevens had taken the precaution of directing Lieutenant Abiel W. Tinkham, nearing Fort Walla Walla with the eastern division, to cross Snoqualmie Pass: "If you and your party are not too much exhausted by your protracted labors."

Tinkham must not be fooled by the locals, Stevens warned: "On the route you must be on your guard not to be misled by wrong information. It is believed here that the priests at the Yakima mission . . . are in the habit of representing the country and the climate in the worst possibly light, in order to discourage settlements; and the Indians, you well know, are prone to story-telling."

A case in point was the tale of the Naches Pass blizzard that had so scared Lander and McClellan: "On the 8th of November certain Indians came into Wallah-Wallah with the report that the emigrants were obliged to abandon their wagons and animals in consequence of snow in the Naches Pass, and the week previous two Indians turned back, the snow being up to the breasts of their horses, whereas the emigrants saw no snow whatever in the pass, and none fell till the 3rd of November, and that to the depth of only four inches."[13]

On January 21, the intrepid Tinkham forced his way over Yakima Pass. A seasoned civil engineer, Tinkham had done well in scouting the Rockies, and his enthusiasm had held up rather better than McClellan's. He was pleased to report to Stevens that snow "would cause very little detention to the passage of trains" in Yakima Pass; the white stuff was only six feet deep at the summit.

An elated Stevens emphasized the good news in his report to Jefferson Davis, marshaling every statistic to

GENERAL MCCLELLAN AND HIS WIFE DURING THE CIVIL WAR. MCCLELLAN GAINED FAME AS THE COMMANDER AND ORGANIZER OF THE ARMY OF THE POTOMAC DURING THE FIRST YEARS OF THE REBELLION, BUT WAS DISMISSED BY PRESIDENT ABRAHAM LINCOLN IN LATE 1862.

University of Washington, Special Collections

convince the secretary that snow was not the problem that Davis and most others seemed to think; "genial rains" kept the pack moderate, and Snoqualmie (Yakima) Pass was certain to be the gateway to Puget Sound. Nonetheless, "to satisfy the skeptical," he proposed that a winter observation post be set up to resolve the matter once and for all.[14]

McClellan would not be swayed. Tinkham found only six feet? It was only the result of a "remarkably dry season." Steamcars in the Cascades? "I am of the opinion that the Yakima Pass is barely practicable, and that only at a high cost of time, labor, and money." This final verdict was passed on to the war secretary; Stevens could not have been pleased.[15]

George McClellan's role in the northern survey has long invited controversy. Historians have portrayed him as a ditherer. Stevens' son and biographer, Hazard, was bitter in his criticism: "Deterred as usual by the reports of Indians and magnified difficulties," McClellan raised "obstacles which existed chiefly in his own imagination" and sabotaged the northern route with his negative conclusions.

McClellan's credibility has been called into question by his selective use of local information—accepting rumors from Indians about blizzards, but then complaining to Davis: "Not the slightest faith or confidence is to be placed in information derived from . . . the inhabitants of the territory; in every instance when I have acted upon information thus obtained, I have been altogether deceived and misled."[16]

As to later charges that his work was less than rigorous, McClellan put it thus: "The examination of the passes of the Cascade mountains was necessarily limited to a hasty reconnaissance of the region, for the reason that that range was almost wholly unknown, and as I was under the necessity of completing the examination as far as the northern limits of our territory, I had no choice but to ascertain, with the least possible delay, the most important facts with deference to each pass, and then rush on in search of others." The cursory nature of his exploration did not stop McClellan from concluding that Yakima Pass was the only one between the Columbia and the Canadian border that was usable by a railroad.[17]

Blessed with energy and endurance, the sanguine Stevens offered a glaring contrast. "The major [Stevens] is crazy, actually crazy, or he never could work as he does," marveled the expedition's astronomer-secretary, George Stevens.

Isaac Stevens believed strongly in the northern route, and as governor had much at stake in its adoption. Where McClellan came to view the locals with disdain, Stevens courted them: "I was struck with the high qualities of the frontier people, and soon learned how to confide in them and gather information from them." The Indians, whom McClellan DID believe, were dismissed by Stevens as incompetent judges of snow, "lying in their lodges as they do all winter."

Character differences aside, neither McClellan nor Stevens had sufficient resources to do the job as thoroughly or as comfortably as they would have liked. The deficiency rankled, as did saddle sores, chilblains, hardtack, and decidedly ungenial weather. By the conclusion of the survey, relations between the erstwhile friends were as icy as the frozen Snoqualmie River. McClellan curtly refused to let Stevens have his journals for inclusion in the summary—for one reason, they contained less than complimentary references to the governor—and demanded that his name be mentioned "as seldom as possible" in the final report.[18]

Stevens had nonetheless been pleased with McClellan's work overall, and gamely praised his "lucid and able" observations.

And both agreed on Seattle: "I have mentioned Seattle as the proper terminus of the road, whether it crosses the mountains by the main Yakima or by the Columbia Pass," McClellan wrote in his summation. "This place . . . is by far superior to any other harbor on the eastern shore of Puget Sound . . . It is easily entered with any of the prevailing winds, is secure from heavy seas, and has a most excellent holding-ground of blue clay, and good depth of water . . . The banks are suitable for a town; the deep water

comes so near the shore that but very short wharves will be required. Semi-bituminous coal has been found within fourteen miles by water up the D'Wamish. The harbor can be defended by permanent fortifications."

Stevens concurred, and reported to Davis that "Seattle combines the greatest number of advantages" of all the Sound locations. It was the ideal railroad terminus.[19]

Diverting the Far East trade of Europe through America had been a prime objective of all Pacific railroad schemes. Stevens affirmed: "The trade of this vast region, including China, Japan, and the Asiatic archipelago, has been the great commercial prize in ancient and modern times . . .

Nature has clearly indicated the northern pathway for the commerce from the future mart of Asiatic trade to this country and Europe. The road communicates on a direct line with the northern lake trade. It intersects the Mississippi River, thus communicating with the Southern States; it is on the line of the great wheat producing regions of America and on a direct line of shortest distance between centers of European and Asiatic population. A portion of European trade and nearly all travel to Asia must take a course across the continent and on the northern road, as the shortest route."

The Northern Pacific route would be ideal, too, for

perishables: "Teas, as well as other animal and vegetable substances destined for human sustenance, are heated and greatly injured by exposure to a continued high temperature . . . all merchandise which is deteriorated by exposure to a tropical climate will take the northern route across the continent."

As for regional needs: "There will be a great thoroughfare of business and travel from the sound to the Columbia river. The interests of the two Territories of Oregon and Washington will soon require a railroad."[20]

Much more survey work remained to be done, but Stevens' allotment was spent. He asked Davis for another $40,000 to continue the survey until the coming June. The secretary responded as if lecturing a wastrel son: Arrears of $25,000 would be paid, but, "The department very much regrets that, with a full knowledge of the extent of the means at the disposal of the department for the survey intrusted to you, you have so made your arrangements as to absorb all your funds so long before the completion of your work. I have no means of meeting any further demands for the expenses of your party."

The secretary then applied the coup de grace and informed Congress that the southern route, along the 35th parallel through Texas and Arizona to California, was the one that best fulfilled the survey mandate of being the "most practicable and economical." Davis laced his summation liberally with McClellan's gloomiest observations—that the "general sterility" of the northern plains, the "severely cold" climate, the great cost of climbing several mountain ranges, and the "proximity to the dominions of a powerful foreign sovereignty" all made the northern route a poor choice.[21]

As for the critical Cascade pass: "The information now possessed is sufficient to decide against this route . . . In the opinion of the officer making the reconnaissance— Capt. McClellan, Corps of Engineers—the pass is barely practicable, and only at a great cost of time, labor, and money." Davis offered faint praise: "The work upon this route, under Governor Stevens, embraced a wider field of exploration than that upon any other route explored." He

then inflated Stevens' cost estimate by $38,000,000 and handed his report to Congress. The South had spoken; the Northern Pacific was nixed.[22]

If the northern survey failed to convince the secretary of war, and failed to prevail in Congress, it succeeded fully in being the greatest survey done in the West since the Lewis and Clark expedition. It was indeed far and away the most exhaustive of the five surveys.

Altogether, the thirteen volumes of *Reports of Explorations and Surveys to Ascertain the Most Practicable and Economical Route for a Railroad from the Mississippi River to the Pacific Ocean, 1853-1854* stand as a landmark of nineteenth century science, and added greatly to knowledge not only of geology and topography, but of plant and animal life, weather, and native cultures. In the Stevens' volumes, the ethnographic work of James Doty, George Gibbs, and John Mullan provided some of the first detailed knowledge of the native peoples of the Pacific Northwest; George Suckley furnished pioneering data on salmon; artists Sohon and Stanley captured evocative views of Indians, landscapes, and buffalo herds before the white onslaught; and aided by his topographical specialists, Stevens made a significant inroad in countering the prevailing belief (though not, unfortunately, Jefferson Davis') that the Northwest interior was merely an arid wasteland unfit for habitation and cultivation.

Isaac Stevens never gave up. Addressing the first session of the territorial legislature on February 28, 1854, the governor conjured up a prosperous future dependent on railroads: "Our commerce doubles in seven years . . . the necessities of the times imperiously demand that the roads now running westward should not be stayed in their course till they reach our western shores."

More surveys were needed, and more money. Stevens and Tinkham journeyed to Washington, D.C. and the governor appealed to Congress, saying: The Northwest was filling up fast; Puget Sound's population had doubled in the year since the territory was born; the United States could run rails there, or see the trade go out in Hudson's Bay Company ships—English ships!

Edwin Johnson published his own study the same year, declaring: "Within the mouth of the Columbia or upon the waters of De Fuca [strait] will yet arise the Queen City of the Pacific."[23]

In the wake of Stevens' epic survey, the first of several Northern Pacific Railroad schemes emerged on paper. It was presented for approval in the Canadian legislature in 1854 as a joint U.S.-Canadian effort to build from Montreal to Puget Sound and the Columbia. The proposal went nowhere.

In January 1857, the Washington territorial legislature made a second attempt. Stevens and Seattle's Arthur Denny took their places among a long list of Northern Pacific incorporators representing interests in Washington, Oregon, Minnesota, Wisconsin, Iowa, Illinois, Nebraska, and Maine. The railroad would start in Nebraska and extend north through Minnesota before turning west through what is now the Dakotas, Montana, and Idaho. In Washington, the road would branch into two lines, one down the Columbia River to Fort Vancouver, the other over the Cascades to tidewater; a west-side connection would link the Columbia with Puget Sound.

The press on both coasts hailed the venture as "one of the most gigantic and magnificent projects of the age," but this second Northern Pacific project also remained a paper railroad. The nation entered a recession in 1857, and money was tight. After 1848, too, California was the place to be. Newly freed from Mexico and flourishing on Sierra Nevada gold, the state was a magnet for settlers who quickly began clamoring for a railroad to the East. Tensions were growing, also, between the North and South over slavery and other issues. Both wanted a California railroad, but the disputed route would either be tied to the industrial North, or to the cotton-and-slave economy of the South.[24]

Elected as Washington's territorial delegate to Congress in the fall of 1857, Isaac Stevens used his new office to spread the Northern Pacific gospel. In San Francisco, Boston, and New York, the handsome and eloquent trailblazer captivated audiences with Puget Sound images—inexhaustible stands of timber . . . coal, a greater element of wealth than all the gold in California . . . wonderfully fertile soil . . . a climate perhaps superior to any in the world . . . limitless salmon and cod runs . . . one of the most magnificent bodies of water in the world!

He strove to overcome eastern impressions of the Northwest as a bleak, inhospitable wilderness: "Why sir, the climate of Puget's Sound is milder than that of New York! . . . Do not great national interests urge the accomplishment of this enterprise at the earliest possible moment?"[25]

The following spring, Stevens presented a territorial memorial to Congress requesting an official sanction, subsidy, and land grant for a railroad. Again, the government declined to act, but Stevens persisted in his lobbying efforts. Three years later, Stevens, then in his second term as delegate, joined with representatives from Vermont, New Hampshire, Wisconsin, Minnesota, and Oregon to enter a bill in the House of Representatives for congressional incorporation of a Northern Pacific line from Lake Superior to Puget Sound. A public subsidy of $25,000,000 and a liberal land grant were requested.

This third Northern Pacific proposal got no further than the speaker's table. In a worsening tug of war between sectional interests, proponents of a southern or central railroad to California were prevailing. The South and the central states hoped to strengthen or maintain their economic base, and San Francisco was by far the West's biggest city, the nation's Pacific anchor, and a logical railroad terminus. With the opening of the Civil War and the exodus of the southern bloc from Congress, the proponents of an Omaha/San Francisco line finally garnered majority support in the capitol. In July 1862, the Pacific Railroad bill won congressional approval, and the Union Pacific/Central Pacific became the first authorized transcontinental line.

By then, Isaac Stevens had gone to war for the Union, soon advancing to the rank of major general. On September 1, 1862, regimental colors in hand, he fell at the Battle of Chantilly. ∎

TRAILBLAZING OFFICIALS FROM THE
NORTHERN PACIFIC RR CO. AND
JAY COOKE & CO. POSE IN HELENA,
MONTANA, AFTER HAVING TOURED
PUGET SOUND IN THE SUMMER OF
1869. LEFT TO RIGHT: WILLIAM
MOORHEAD, SAMUEL WILKESON,
THOMAS CANFIELD, AND WILLIAM
MILNOR ROBERTS AND HIS PRIVATE
SECRETARY.

University of Washington, Special Collections, #3612

CHAPTER 2

The New Northwest

"Our enterprise is an inexhaustible gold mine." —Samuel Wilkeson

DESPITE THE EMERGENCE of the Central Pacific/ Union Pacific as the first transcontinental railroad to be built, numerous factors ensured that the Pacific Northwest would be next in line for a railway connection. The strategic and commercial importance of the Columbia River and Puget Sound regions; the desirability of a rail line far removed from the secessionist South; gold strikes in Oregon, Washington, and the Fraser Valley of British Columbia; the continuing migration along the Oregon Trail; and the compelling data compiled by Isaac Stevens all served to focus future railroad ambitions on the Northwest.

During the early 1860s, Josiah Perham, a Portland, Maine, promoter, began campaigning for a northern line after his proposed Missouri River/San Francisco "People's Pacific" railroad bill was pre-empted by the CP/UP. An acquaintance and supporter of Isaac Stevens, Perham had another Stevens on his side—powerful Pennsylvania Senator Thaddeus Stevens, ranking member of the congressional Pacific Railroad Committee. The "Old Commoner" strongly believed in publicly subsidized railroads as a great civilizing agent and had supported the People's Pacific road to California.

Would he lend the same support for a People's Pacific to the Northwest?

Stevens would, but insisted the company be rechartered in Congress to give it broader national support. It should also take the name "Northern Pacific," as that had become the generally accepted designation for the route.[1]

The Northern Pacific Railroad bill was incorporated by an act of Congress on May 23, 1864. On July 2, Abraham Lincoln signed it into law. Chartered to build between Lake Superior and "some point on Puget Sound," with a branch line down the Columbia to Portland, the Northern Pacific acquired a grant of almost 40,000,000 acres, the largest allocation of public land ever given to a private corporation. When considering Asa Whitney's Pacific railroad bills in the 1840s, Congress had been unwilling to give extensive tracts of land to corporations. However, by the 1850s legislators had come to embrace the concept as an essential element of nation building, and large land grants figured prominently in the transcontinental railroad schemes of Thomas Hart Benton and others.

Following the model of the first large land grant given to a railroad—that of the Illinois Central in 1850—the legislation granted alternating, odd-numbered, one-mile-square sections adjacent to the right-of-way in a band forty miles wide in states and eighty miles wide in territories. This checkerboard pattern would, it was hoped, boost adjoining land values and stimulate settlement and development along the right of way. Tracts containing minerals other than coal and iron ore were excluded, in which case the company was allowed to claim "in-lieu" lands in other locations near the right of way. Five years after the completion of the line, all unsold lands were required to be opened to "bona-fide" settlers at a cost not exceeding $2.50 an acre. Construction had to begin within two years of the act's passage, and the government was obliged to "extinguish" the claims of Native Americans to the grant lands.

Northern Pacific stock went on the market at $100 a share when Josiah Perham opened his subscription books in Boston and New York, confident of success. Surely, if men could spend a million dollars a year in New York saloons, they would buy into the great national enterprise!

But, they didn't! As Isaac Stevens had foreseen in 1858: "The great difficulty will be to raise the money, and not to build the road."[2] The subsequent travails of the Northern Pacific would prove him a thousand times right.

In 1865, Perham was tapped out and was forced to sell the Northern Pacific for the sum of his accumulated debts, $102,000, to an eastern syndicate. These twelve well-placed industrialists and financiers—among them engineer/promoter Thomas Canfield, Chicago & North Western Railway president William Butler Ogden, Maine Central president Richard D. Rice, Pennsylvania Railroad president Thomas Scott, and John Gregory Smith, former governor of Vermont and head of the Vermont Central—bought in as "original interests" for $8,500 apiece, and agreed to provide monetary support for the railroad in return for board membership and equal shares in the company.

John Gregory Smith was appointed the Northern Pacific's new president. Among his first acts was to go to Congress and, with the aid of Senator Stevens, get the deadline for beginning construction set back to a more realistic July 1870. To retain the land grant, the railroad was compelled to build at least twenty-five miles in 1871, and forty miles in each of the succeeding two years. Smith also secured a charter amendment permitting the company to issue mortgage bonds covering the costs of track, trains, telegraph lines, and buildings. With this collateral, the Northern Pacific could now attract high-powered investment.

The "original interest" holders then anted up $25,000 for a preliminary survey and hired Edwin F. Johnson as chief engineer. For his assistant, Johnson retained former

Washington Territory chief surveyor General James Tilton, and in the summer of 1867 dispatched him west to make preliminary surveys of the Cascade passes. Three subsidiary parties under W.H. Carlton, J.S. Hurd, and A.J. Treadway reported that the most promising crossings were to be found at Cowlitz Pass (now known as White Pass, south of Mt. Rainier); the divides of the Wenatchee, Skagit, and Skykomish rivers; and at Snoqualmie Pass.[3]

Smith, meanwhile, continued tinkering. By its charter, the Northern Pacific could build a main line over the Cascades to Puget Sound and a branch line down the Columbia to Portland, but it had no franchise to build the "great thoroughfare" Isaac Stevens had envisioned between Puget Sound and Portland. Portland was the commercial center of the Northwest, and omitting this connection would be a major blunder.

Edwin Johnson urged that the latter line be given top priority to save money by avoiding mountain construction, to utilize rivers for hauling construction materials, and "to accommodate the business of that section and facilitate access to and the speedy sale and settlement of the company's lands on each side of the sound, the demand for which will be greatly increased on the completion of the Union and Central Pacific Railroad."[4]

In April 1869, the Puget Sound branch was appended to the NP charter. The Northern Pacific now was a noose poised to close around millions of land-grant acres in Washington Territory. For three years, Smith and Northern Pacific secretary Samuel Wilkeson laid siege to the reigning wizard of Wall Street, Jay Cooke, hoping he would consent to market the railroad's bonds. During the Civil War, Cooke's "popularizing" method of selling government bonds through advertising had made him a financial titan. Some credited him with saving the Union! Railroad building through a wilderness was another story, though, and Cooke informed the NP men that "legitimate banking" should be their only concern.

Still, Smith and Wilkeson refused to give up, and, by 1869, second thoughts began nagging at the great banker.

JOSIAH PERHAM, THE FATHER OF THE NORTHERN PACIFIC RAILROAD.

Minnesota Historical Society

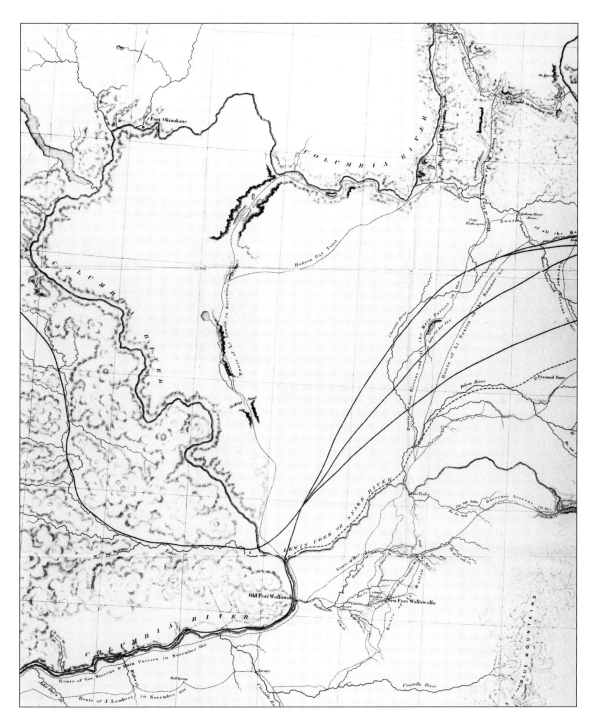

Proposed railway routes in the Columbia Basin.

Isaac I. Stevens, Reports of Explorations and Surveys

19

Cooke had read all the reports from Lewis and Clark, the Hudson's Bay Company, Johnson, and Stevens "as conscientiously as I would study God's holy word."[5]

The enormous potential wealth of the Northwest territories and states in timber, wheat, coal, ore, silver, and gold was staggering, and the Northern Pacific would run right through the middle of it. The eastern cities were getting more crowded, day by day, with the crush of restless humanity—immigrants, busted New England farmers, and footloose young folk. All were merely wanting the opportunity to gain a little land.

Cooke felt his resistance weakening. Still, it was a huge gamble. How much would this railroad cost? Could he sell enough bonds?

Isaac Stevens' survey had only been preliminary; solid figures were needed, so there would have to be an in-depth inspection of the potential land grants—all the peaks, valleys, rivers, forests, farmlands, and minerals. What was it worth as security to investors? What was it worth to potential settlers? Where would the railroad establish its western terminus? On June 1, 1869, two expeditions took to the wilderness to find out: Minnesota governor William Marshall led one party into the Dakotas and eastern Montana, while Thomas Canfield, Samuel Wilkeson, Cooke associate William G. Moorhead, and the Northern Pacific's new chief engineer, William Milnor Roberts, headed for Washington Territory.

After a wearying journey across the continent by rail and stagecoach, the Canfield party arrived in Portland on July 1 and pondered the situation there. It was a mixed review. The Northwest's premier city (in fact, the Northwest's only real city) was born in 1846 at the confluence of the Columbia and Willamette rivers, the region's main avenues of commerce. By 1869, Portland was a prosperous urban center of 20,000 people. No community closer than San Francisco came close in size—not the wheat and gold boomtown of Walla Walla, with 3,000 residents the largest community north of Portland, and certainly not the tiny villages of Olympia or Seattle. But Portland's gateway to the world was the treacherous sand-bar at the mouth of the Columbia—the curse of ship masters and owners the world over. Vessels often were obliged to heave to as long as a week waiting for clearance over the ten-to-twenty-foot shallows. Many didn't make it, and the Columbia's mouth acquired the decidedly inauspicious nickname "Graveyard of the North Pacific." In Portland, too, the river levels along the city waterfront rose and fell drastically, making dockage difficult.

Jefferson Davis had not been kind to the city in his report to Congress: "The unfavorable character of the entrance to the Columbia river, and the great superiority of the ports on Puget Sound, seemed to render it expedient to adopt some one of the latter as the Pacific terminus."[6] But Portland remained a key trading center and the Northern Pacific could ill-afford to ignore her.

Puget Sound beckoned. The party took a steamboat down the Columbia, landed at Monticello (now Longview), and boarded a stagecoach for Olympia. For three days, Canfield, Roberts, and Wilkeson cruised the Sound aboard the side-wheeler *Wilson G. Hunt*, accompanied by a diverse entourage that included Seattle founder Arthur Denny, territorial marshal Philip Ritz, and popular "crank" lecturer George Francis Train. Another sightseer was a veteran agent of the Puget Sound Board of Pilot Commissioners—James G. Swan. He also happened to be the energetic and staunchly partisan mayor of Port Townsend, Puget Sound's port of entry. The "Key City" was a coming place, with a customs office and an excellent harbor. A railway would truly start her on the road to greatness.

Swan planted himself next to Thomas Canfield, and with him watched Whidbey Island and Port Townsend, Bellingham Bay and Fidalgo Island, Port Gardner and Seattle slip by. It was a daunting prospect, Canfield ruminated to his shipmate; Puget Sound had so many promising harbors, any one of which would make a grand railroad terminus. Only one could be chosen. Not to worry, said His Honor: He knew Puget Sound intimately; why not let him look over all the potential terminus sites, and present some recommendations? Canfield, with eastern

Washington, Idaho, and Montana yet to cover, gladly accepted the proposition and swore Swan to secrecy. The mayor of Port Townsend was now a confidential agent of the Northern Pacific Railroad.

The party returned to Portland on July 13, and issued a press release beckoning settlers to the "vast, hundred-armed harbor where the trade of the American Pacific Slope is to be enthroned . . . It is the intention of the Board of Directors of the Northern Pacific Railroad Company to invite the attention of people, and especially eastern capitalists, to Oregon and Washington Territory, and invoke their aid and co-operation in the greatest work of the age . . . as an important auxiliary in populating and developing this section of the Union."

George Francis Train chimed in: Puget Sound was the "Mediterranean of the Northwest," focus of destiny, birthplace of a million fortunes! Where would the railroad terminate? Canfield dared not speculate. Many months of "careful, diligent research" would be expended, "before the terminus of a great national highway is located."[7]

With railroad commission in hand and perhaps a conspiratorial chuckle or two, James Swan worked his way around Puget Sound. He would do his best to be objective. Olympia, founded in 1850, was western Washington's largest settlement (population 1,000), and territorial capital to boot. Budd Inlet was a good harbor, except at low tide, and was in all likelihood the first point where a railroad from the south would strike the Sound. Thus, Olympia deserved "serious consideration," at least as terminus of the Columbia River/Puget Sound line.[8]

Nisqually, immediately to the northeast, had a problem shared by many Puget Sound harbors: It was too deep. There was no anchorage for ships except on the shelf close to the beach, and the nearby broad, swampy Nisqually Delta would require a lot of expensive bridging and filling.

A few miles north, Steilacoom's harbor barely warranted the name, lacked shelter from the wind, and there was little room for railroad yards. Like Nisqually, it had been an outpost and trading center, and like Nisqually,

Steilacoom's day was clearly past. Its prospects as a "great commercial mart," Swan noted, were nil.

Regarding Commencement Bay, where the infant village of Tacoma nestled, Swan was unequivocal: "Notwithstanding all that can be said in favor of this place for a terminus, the great depth of water rendering anchorage inconvenient and almost impracticable will preclude it being considered as a desirable site."

Seattle, a lively little town of about a thousand people, would appear to offer more possibilities. Elliott Bay was capacious and snug, and the place had looked fine to Isaac Stevens.

But not to Swan: "Viewed at low water, and examined by the correct charts of the United States Coast Survey, it will be seen that it is not such an admirable harbor as would at first appear."

Like Commencement Bay, Elliott Bay was too deep. Moreover, Seattle was hemmed in by hills, swamps, and tideflats; solid, level ground was scarce. Lake Washington, just east of town, invited commercial exploitation, but would require a lengthy and expensive canal to link it with salt water. Plentiful coal existed in the nearby hills, but to bring it out efficiently and on any profitable scale would require a substantial investment.

And frankly, there was doubt as to Seattle's staying power: "A large influx of population have been induced to locate there during the past year; drawn thither by the expectation of its being the point of the final terminus and great commercial city. Should such an event occur, there would be much to induce a permanent population, but if the expectation of the citizens are not to be realized there seems to be very little business by which a larger population could be sustained." No, as the future metropolis, Seattle would not do.

Point Elliot, on Gardner Bay, offered the same exposed front as Steilacoom, and was curtly dismissed. On the east side of nearby Whidbey Island, Holmes Harbor and Penn Cove looked inviting. Whidbey was a "garden spot," with the finest farmland in the region and a direct outlet to the sea. Only low, thin strips of land separated both harbors

from the Strait of Juan de Fuca, and canals could be easily cut through. On the other hand, fresh water was scarce.

Far to the north, Bellingham Bay was a grand harbor, and there was abundant coal in the vicinity. Getting into the bay was tricky, however; twisting Rosario Strait was treacherous, lined with hidden rocks and shoals. That, and the wind, tidal rips, and eddies all added up to a captain's nightmare. Fidalgo and Guemes islands had good ocean approaches, but they were far from any of the Cascade passes most likely to be chosen by the railroad. Port Discovery, on the west side of the Quimper Peninsula near Port Townsend, was a large harbor, but exposed to northerlies; wind and tides made it tricky to get into.

In his duties as confidential agent, Swan had performed a most diligent reconnaissance. All the Puget Sound harbors had been carefully considered; all were found wanting.[9]

All, that is, but Port Townsend. Toast of ship captains the world over, Port Townsend Bay was only a day's sail from the Pacific—to Seattle could be as long as three. Tug and pilot fees further up-Sound were bound to be larcenous, and a direct rail link to ocean vessels at Port Townsend would save considerable time and money. Building room and fresh water were present on the Quimper Peninsula in such quantities "as would be requisite for a city the size of New York." High-grade building stone for permanent railroad and commercial facilities (teredoes and sand fleas could devour a stout wooden wharf in three years) was abundant. Isaac Stevens, Captain George Vancouver, various military officers, and Josiah Perham had all attested to the beauty and utility of Port Townsend.[10]

Laying track to Port Townsend from the south would present no problem, assured Swan; the west side of Hood Canal was well-suited for railroad construction. The confidential agent sounded a timely note of warning: The Central Pacific and Union Pacific had already "intimated their intention" of extending to Port Townsend. Others were nosing about, too, notably Oregon railroad and steamboat magnate Ben Holladay, who had surveyed along Hood Canal in 1868. The Northern Pacific had best be on its mettle! At the end of his four-month tour, James Swan informed Canfield that, weighing all factors for a railroad terminus and the next great metropolis of the West, it was Port Townsend by a mile.[11]

Canfield laid out Swan's observations and his own in a confidential report to the railroad directors. At stake was nothing less than locating the future commercial center of the north Pacific, a city which would in all likelihood number one or two million inhabitants by 1900. It was almost too much to grasp; easy ocean access, good anchorage, agreeable location with good drainage and fertile surrounding country, an abundance of fresh water, a defensible location against foreign attack, and a practical approach by railroad ("although in the present state of engineering, almost any place can be reached")—all had to be considered and weighed.

Seattle had "many favorable requisites for a second-class city," Canfield noted. Its 3,000-acre tideflats and the adjoining Duwamish River bottoms could be filled in to serve as a commodious industrial tract. Fresh water was abundant and near at hand in the Cedar River watershed. Elliott Bay was well-protected and easily defensible against invaders.

Tacoma was dismissed with one sentence: "Should not recommend going south of Seattle for a terminus."

The NP would do better to maximize its land grant—2,000,000 acres in every 100 miles—and go further north, Canfield urged, narrowing the field to three places: Port Townsend, Whidbey Island, and Bellingham Bay. In fact, a dual-terminus scheme had great appeal to Canfield, with the branch line from the Columbia running up the west side of the Sound to Port Townsend, and the main line over the Cascades terminating on Whidbey Island, just across Admiralty Inlet from Port Townsend. With its two terminal cities standing sentinel at the entrance to Puget Sound, the Northern Pacific would virtually control the trade of the entire region. To be on the safe side, however, he advised buying land at every prospective site, as "all the lands upon the Sound will be much increased in value" regardless of the final terminus selection.

As a sop to objectivity, Canfield included testimony from knowledgeable (and equally biased) sources advocating a Bellingham terminus. These individuals, with coal mine and real estate investments to promote there, claimed that the increase in grant lands would offset many times over the cost of building additional rail mileage, and that track to Bellingham would promote the "Americanization" of Alaska and perhaps even all of British Columbia.[12]

Canfield and chief engineer Roberts further recommended that the Northern Pacific main line be rerouted down the Columbia River and through Portland, rather than over the Cascades. Portland's population and commerce exceeded that of all Puget Sound cities combined, they noted, and the city was "a point which would furnish much business for our road."[13]

As for the mountain line, it would only be a ruinously expensive 200 miles of track through a sterile region devoid of traffic and population. In fact, they noted, building along the Columbia, a fully developed navigable river, between eastern Washington and Portland also would be a waste of money at this time.

This left the Portland to Puget Sound line, urged by Isaac Stevens and Edwin Johnson; laying track down the Oregon side of the Columbia between Portland and St. Helens, near the mouth of the Cowlitz forty miles to the north, was preferable. This south bank road would benefit by easy connection with Ben Holladay's extensive system of Willamette Valley railroads and steamboats, as well as his promised line to California. Timber, iron, and coal were abundant on the Oregon side, and deepwater vessels commonly anchored near St. Helens, upstream of which rocks made navigation risky. Winter ice-ups seldom if ever extended that far west, and the most feasible sites for a bridge across to Washington were to be found at Martin's Bluff and Deer Island, on the Oregon side across from Coffin Rock and the Kalama River in Washington. Of course, occupation of the south bank would also shut out any rivals from the south and east—i.e., Ben Holladay, or the Central Pacific/Union Pacific.

As Swan had warned, haste was advisable. The Union Pacific already had surveyed a line along the Oregon Trail to the Columbia in 1867, and now even the locals were getting into the act. Two companies, each calling itself the Puget Sound & Columbia River, were incorporated in 1868 to build to the Sound—one spearheaded by Simeon G. Reed and other Portland businessmen, the other sponsored in part by Washington Territory leaders Arthur Denny, Philip Ritz, and Hazard Stevens. Neither scheme panned out, but the menace was clear. So was the potential for profit. "The Puget Sound country has been greatly under-estimated," Canfield concluded, quoting a San Francisco newspaper. "We find this very Territory teeming with varied and inexhaustible resources."[14]

The NP's 1869 explorations confirmed in Jay Cooke's mind the great intrinsic value of the company's land grant and its soundness as a basis of credit. By the sharp-penciled estimations of chief engineer William Milnor Roberts, it was all attainable for the sum of $85,000,000, including rolling stock and bond interest payments. "If judiciously located, honestly constructed, and properly administered," the road would "pay within a few years a fair dividend upon its cost."

The poetic Sam Wilkeson was more to the point: "Jay,

we have the biggest thing on earth. Our enterprise is an inexhaustible gold mine—there is no mistake about it."[15]

Jay Cooke and J. Gregory Smith met in New York on January 1, 1870, and signed the contract that would open the Pacific Northwest. Cooke & Co. agreed to market the Northern Pacific's securities and provide for its cash requirements. On February 15, the first spike of the Northern Pacific Railroad was driven at Thomson's Junction, Minnesota, twenty miles west of Duluth.

In March, Smith and Canfield went to Congress with more resolutions—to redesignate the Columbia River route as the main line and the Cascade route as the branch line; to include the land grant in the Northern Pacific mortgage; and to allow "in-lieu" lands to be substituted for any eligible land grant parcels that might be sold in advance of that particular section being granted, or "patented," to the railroad. With these added enhancements, big investors had no need of reservations about the NP as a paying proposition.

To get things rolling in their new, vast, and largely uninhabited domain (and because the railroad itself was not allowed to purchase land), a coterie of directors formed the Lake Superior & Puget Sound Land Company. They would speculate in land and develop town sites along the right of way, thereby generating cash in advance of revenues from railroad operations and thus help pay for construction. The directors considered this "boomtown" financial scheme to be vital to the survival of the enterprise (though perhaps also anticipating some slight pecuniary advantage to themselves). The president of the Lake Superior & Puget Sound Land Company was Thomas Canfield.

Congress granted the new amendments in May, and Jay Cooke opened his campaign, popularizing the "New Northwest and its Great Thoroughfare." Northern Pacific "7-30" bonds (7% interest per annum, reaching maturity in 30 years) appeared on Wall Street in January 1871. Cooke's publicity machine swung into motion, and NP information agencies were opened throughout western Europe to stimulate immigration to the

railroad's newly acquired lands. Prospective settlers dropped in at these advertising bureaus to fondle crop samples and lose themselves in Wilkesonian imagery— "the mildness of the climate is superabundantly testified to by man and beast . . . limitless materials for the greatest lumber trade the world has ever known . . . the Great Fertile Belt!"[16]

Lovingly etched lithographs enticed immigrants with scenes of waving fields of wheat and the spires of new towns nestled beside shining waters. Tracts of 40, 80, and 160 acres, some with ready-made homes, were platted by the Lake Superior & Puget Sound Land Company and offered at low monthly installments. There may have been some niggling party poopers who poked fun at "Jay Cooke's Banana Belt," but thousands more read Wilkeson's allurements, stroked their whiskers, and packed their carpet bags for the New Northwest.

Puget Sound had a raging case of terminal fever. ∎

AN 1850s VIEW OF STEILACOOM. THIS SMALL COMMERCIAL CENTER ON SOUTHERN PUGET SOUND STOOD ADJACENT TO THE U.S. ARMY'S FORT STEILACOOM, WHICH HAD BEEN ESTABLISHED IN 1849 ON LAND RENTED FROM THE HUDSON'S BAY COMPANY.

Isaac I. Stevens, Reports of Explorations and Surveys

PUGET SOUND AND MT. RAINIER, AS VIEWED FROM WHIDBEY ISLAND. IN 1870, THE NP'S THOMAS CANFIELD RECOMMENDED
WHIDBEY ISLAND AS A TERMINUS, BUT HE LATER CHANGED HIS MIND IN FAVOR OF TACOMA. NOTE THE SEA-GOING INDIAN CANOE
IN THE BAY AND THE SETTLER ON SHORE DRIVING A MULE BACK TO A FARMSTEAD. WELL INTO THE 1860S, BRITISH COLUMBIA
TRIBES SOMETIMES PLUNDERED NORTHERN PUGET SOUND INDIAN VILLAGES AND OCCASIONAL WHITE SETTLERS.

Isaac I. Stevens, Reports of Explorations and Surveys

CHAPTER 3

TERMINAL FEVER

"Thousands of air castles have been built, and paper cities are multiplying in every direction." —Kalama *Beacon*

FROM THE BLUFFS HIGH above the Columbia, the little steamer appeared as nothing more than an insignificant dot on the wide, gray sheet of water. But when it touched shore near the mouth of the Kalama River that day in March 1870, the destiny of the Pacific Northwest was forever altered. For off the boat stepped Northern Pacific officials George Washington Cass, William B. Ogden, Richard D. Rice, and General John W. Sprague, coming to lay claim to Puget Sound. At the confluence of the small river with the greater one, they set a stake. This stake marked the starting point of the NP's Pacific Division, and the beginning of the railroad era in western Washington Territory. Sprague named the spot "Kalama." The railroad men then continued by stagecoach up the rough and wearisome wagon road to Budd Inlet, near Olympia, and set another stake.

Shortly thereafter, Edwin Johnson (now partially retired, but serving as a consulting engineer) sent locating parties into Washington Territory to figure out how the railroad could best reach the Sound. One of these was led by D.C. Linsley, who had orders to explore the mountain passes near the 48th parallel to discover if one might be usable by a railroad, which would make feasible a terminus in the northern part of the Sound. Linsley was also to reconnoiter the east slope of the Cascades along the Stehekin, Twisp, Methow, and Entiat rivers, examine Snoqualmie Pass, and determine the general contour of the Cedar River Valley into Seattle.

With three assistants and six Skagit Indian guides,

Linsley set out in two canoes from Bellingham Bay on May 25, paddling up the Skagit River. Linsley proposed to first tackle the divide at the headwaters of the Suiattle River in hopes of finding a direct route to Lake Chelan and the Columbia Basin. The guides rebelled at the idea, objecting that the route was too rugged. The trail had long before been used by Skagit and Sauk Indians crossing the mountains, they said, but had been abandoned—the route that has since become known as Indian Pass, up the Sauk River, was the only way across. Not to be dissuaded, Linsley offered the guides extra pay and the party made its way along the Suiattle and turned northeast up the little stream called Kaiwhat Creek, known now as Sulphur Creek.

After a grueling struggle, Linsley reached the divide on June 7. At over 6,000 feet, it was obviously too high and steep for a railroad; a tunnel of at least 1 1/2 miles would be required, he noted, through solid granite. Indian Pass was next, and on the 13th, he stood atop the 5,000-foot summit. Not content to stop there, he scaled nearby Indian Head Peak and from there spied another pass just to the north, which later took the name Linsley Pass. Linsley continued eastward down the White and Wenatchee rivers, explored the shores of Lake Chelan, and then made his way south over Swauk Pass, turned west up the Yakima River and crossed Snoqualmie Pass to Seattle.

Linsley's verdict: Feasible routes over the north Cascades did exist and track could be run between the mouth of the Skagit River and Spokane via Linsley Pass for

$13,000,000, or $39,000 per mile—over the steeper Kaiwhat Creek route and along Lake Chelan would cost $16,000,000.[1]

Other groups were similarly occupied that summer and fall. General James Tilton and James Maxwell investigated up the Cedar River and into Snoqualmie Pass; Captain C.S. Kidder reconnoitered southward from Seattle down the White River Valley and across Yelm Prairie; Captain Fife and John Kidder surveyed alternate routes from the Columbia River to Olympia; and Captain Smith platted a line south from Kalama along the east bank of the Columbia. By October, Maxwell had determined upon a good passage through the Snoqualmie divide, with a half-mile tunnel.

"This definitely settles the practicability of the Snoqualmie Pass beyond further cavil," observed the Olympia *Transcript*.[2]

But where would the terminus be? Everyone—reporters, investors, home-seekers, and most particularly the anxious pioneers of Puget Sound—wanted to know. Sphinx-like, the Northern Pacific was silent.

Olympia had taken great encouragement from the surveys and feelings were high that the railroad would, as a matter of course, terminate at the territorial capital and largest settlement west of the Cascades. More thoughtful individuals, though, may have felt the first pangs of doubt, observing that Captain Kidder had set his first stake in Seattle and mapped out a route that swept down the White River and Puyallup valleys and across Yelm Prairie—conspicuously bypassing Olympia.

Agonizing over the railroad's secrecy, the town formed a committee headed by Marshall Blinn and Elisha P. Ferry to assemble land and cash inducements (essentially a bribe) to bring the Northern Pacific into the capital. On December 17, NP representatives Thomas Canfield and Richard D. Rice met with the committee. They were not trying to be secretive, Canfield explained, but no promises could be made as to where the NP would terminate. The railroad had to select the most practicable point to meet the Sound and must consider its best interests. Rice em-

phasized that considerable acreage would be sacrificed from the land grants should the line terminate on the southern Sound. They must wait and see.

With this sobering intelligence, the Olympia committee incorporated the Olympia Branch Railroad Company to treat with the Northern Pacific on terminal inducements, or if necessary build a connection with the NP should it actually bypass the city.

From Elliott Bay came the catcalls of self-confident Seattle: Olympia's harbor was nothing but a mudflat, the town dead on its feet—"Olympia is no rival to Seattle!"

Olympia in turn scorned the "Hog-emites" who were going all-out amassing inducements for a terminus on Nisqually flats. Keep cool, preached a level-headed few: Puget Sound's "hundred-armed harbor" had room enough for a dozen future Baltimores or Bostons! But Olympia's *Washington Standard* seemed to speak for most of those who knew just what railroad terminal status meant: "We will be either a prosperous city . . . or a deserted village."[3]

Early in 1871, Thomas Canfield arrived at Kalama. Pausing long enough to plat a town, he then continued north, locating new stations every dozen or so miles—Olequa, Newaukum, Skookumchuck, Tenino. At Olympia, Tacoma, Steilacoom, Seattle, and Bellingham Bay, Canfield and his agents discretely purchased parcels of land for the Lake Superior & Puget Sound Land Company, while W. Milnor Roberts rode ceaselessly to and fro, pinning down right of way and examining alternative terminus sites. The chief engineer found himself more persuaded than ever by the prospects of Bellingham: It had the best harbor, and he noted that a water-level line could be built along the Sound for minimal cost.

However, he also observed that Seattle looked "better than I had assumed when I was here before."[4]

Kalama became western Washington Territory's first boomtown. In October, the first locomotives in western Washington—little 0-4-0s *Minnetonka* and *Otter Tail*—arrived from San Francisco on the bark *Rival*, and set to work hauling materials. Time was pressing: Congress

ELISHA P. FERRY HELPED DIRECT OLYMPIA'S UNSUCCESSFUL ATTEMPT TO CONVINCE THE NP TO ESTABLISH THE TERMINUS ON BUDD INLET. IN 1872, FERRY WAS APPOINTED TO A TERM AS TERRITORIAL GOVERNOR, AND, IN 1889, HE BECAME WASHINGTON'S FIRST POPULARLY ELECTED GOVERNOR AFTER CONGRESS GRANTED STATEHOOD.

Washington State University Libraries, #85-029

obliged the NP to build at least twenty-five miles in 1871, and forty miles each in 1872 and 1873—a total of 105 miles that would link the Columbia to tidewater. Railroad building in Washington Territory began in earnest in April 1871, as 800 Chinese and white men began grubbing out a right of way north from Kalama, and the official "first spike" was driven there on May 19.

Terminal fever rose in Olympia, where residents held town meetings to pledge land to the Northern Pacific. By the end of April, 4,500 acres and 430 town lots had been amassed. Entirely inadequate, barked railroad committee leader Blinn; dig deeper, or lose the terminus. Olympia dug, but summer brought another round of surveying far beyond the capital, with James Maxwell setting stakes as far north as the upper Skagit Valley. Olympia's worries mounted, as more and more settlers seemed to be gravitating toward Seattle.

Harper's magazine had given the latter town a push in April 1870: "Nine months ago there were not more than 500 people in [Seattle]. Now there are over 1,000 . . . Puget Sound must become one of the centres of world commerce."

Urged to end the suspense, Pacific Division superintendent General John W. Sprague argued that to make a premature declaration about the location of the terminus would inflate land prices beyond even the ability of the company itself to pay and wipe everyone out. Hopeful greenhorns jammed Sound-bound steamers and stagecoaches, and San Francisco lampooned Puget Sound's "terminus saloons and barrooms, terminus hotels, terminus bitters, and terminus cocktails," musing:

"Will this terminus, wherever it may be located, ever become the great city some persons and land speculators are ready to demonstrate? What is to sustain a city upon Puget Sound besides its local resources and its through Asiatic trade, which is always overestimated? Who knows when it will reach the margin of 50,000 population?"[5]

Portland viewed the scuffling among Washington's "clam eaters" with complacent amusement. *Oregonian* editor Clark P. Crandall came to see "terminus disease" for himself in 1871. Already, the race seemed to be fast narrowing to a Seattle/Tacoma contest.

Of Tacoma, he noted wryly, "the founder found it two or three years ago, lying around loose, and as it was the only place not then appointed and ordained for terminus purposes, he went for it, bought it, and had it regularly platted and set down as the place where the job of building the world was commenced . . . and where the job of building the Northern Pacific Railroad—the next greatest work, after creation—is to be finished."[6]

Seattle appeared to offer more substantive prospects. "The only town we visited which presents any notable evidence of present life and business activity, Seattle has more good farming lands to back it than any other town on the Sound . . . At the time of our visit the harbor contained more steamboats, sailing vessels, steam tugs, and small crafts of one sort or another than we saw in all the other harbors. Seattle is, perhaps, the most conveniently situated of all the Sound towns, for commerce with the mills and logging camps, and hence it has and will keep a larger share than any of them, of the local trade. With all its advantages, agricultural, manufacturing, mining, and marine, the town is less dependent than most others upon the event of the location of the railroad terminus, and, hence, it is going ahead somewhat on its own responsibility and merits. It is, however, down on the slate as a candidate for the terminus, and its citizens deem it rank treason to even doubt the eventual ordination of Seattle as the great depot whence the railroad systems of the continent and the commercial navies of the world are to dump their cargoes."[7]

Of course, Seattle had known for some time that she would be "It." Isaac Stevens and *Harper's* magazine said so, and, as early as 1868, the opening of the Western Terminus Hotel and the Railroad Lodging House demonstrated Seattle's boundless self-confidence. Town lots that went for $50 in 1869 commanded $200—even $500!—a year later. It was all part of being the "natural and lawful terminus of the Northern Pacific."

Mayor Swan and Port Townsend hung grimly on. "According to the fixed and unchangeable opinion of its residents," Crandall mused, "it is the only town on the Sound worth mention . . . We did not get a very clear idea whether the railroad is expected to reach Port Townsend by way of the coast range or by tug boat across the Sound."

The local press stoutly continued to maintain that both Ben Holladay and the Union Pacific were heading their way, while Seattle jeered in reply, confident that her own immutable terminus destiny had "hit Port Townsend where she lives, and doubled her up like a superannuated dishrag."[8]

Imaginary cities also got into the act. Promoters William T. "Billy" Ballou, George Barnes, and T.I. McKenny floated rival "Puget City" schemes variously located on Bellingham Bay and the Nisqually Delta. Hucksters hawked shares in bogus terminal sites to the gullible, and even Marshall Blinn, the Olympia railroad committee booster, hedged his bet and did a brisk trade in widely scattered lots, some of them little more than swamp. Landowners, seeking fast sales, printed maps of their property with NP tracks prominently marked— never mind that no locating party had been within miles of their parcels.

"Where is the terminus?" wondered the Kalama *Beacon*. "Thousands of air castles have been built, and paper cities are multiplying in every direction along the bayous of the Sound Country."[9]

On Christmas Eve 1871, the answer seemed to have come. Olympia's repose was shattered at midnight by the clanging of church bells and booming of cannon. A wire had been received at the telegraph office: NP agents General Sprague and John M. Goodwin had accepted quit claims on over 5,000 acres of donated right of way parcels into town. The railroad was coming to Olympia! The company would locate a route into the capital before May 1 of the coming year, and the town's donations would be presented for final ratification at the next NP board meeting.

The hymns were unusually loud in church the next morning. "We do not like to gloat," Olympia smirked, and advised the losers to bear their defeat with "Christian fortitude."[10]

Northward the track gangs slogged. On January 1, 1872, the first twenty-five miles of Pacific Division construction as required by Congress was finished, under the hard-driving command of Thomas Burnside Morris. The first big 4-4-0 road engine to turn a wheel in western Washington was offloaded at Kalama from the bark *Webfoot* in February, and trains began running to Pumphrey's Station at the Cowlitz River crossing.

As if to prepare the terminal grounds, James Tilton made topographic and harbor surveys of Olympia that spring. When the Pacific Division rails reached Tenino in June, the Olympia Branch Railroad committee wrote General Sprague asking what they could next expect from the Northern Pacific. They were rewarded by welcome tidings that the board of directors had ratified the town's donations and would soon pick a depot site in or near the city.

But joy was short-lived. Olympians watched in dismay as the railhead suddenly veered east at Tenino and nosed up Scatter Creek toward Yelm Prairie—and Tacoma. As if shunning a plague zone, the Northern Pacific had bypassed the capital. Consternation grew as Tilton staked the tiny village of Mukilteo, twenty-five miles north of Seattle on Port Gardner Bay as yet another prospective terminal site.

Once more, surveyors ranged through the Cascades: Morris, Tilton, and Hubert Ward retraced Linsley's route as well as Cady Pass further south, and in the process "discovered" Ward's Pass, between the two. L.A. Habersham plotted routes between Seattle and the Canadian border, J. Tilton Sheets worked Snoqualmie Pass and the Snohomish Valley, and D.K. Birnie covered the Puyallup and White River valleys. James McCabe ranged south and east from Kalama along the north bank of the Columbia. However tortuous, however tentative, each survey became a "general route" and went on file at the Department of the Interior. Along each route, an eighty-mile-wide swath of appended grant land was withdrawn from the public domain. From Fort Vancouver to the Canadian border, from the Olympic Mountains to the spine of the Cascades, much of Washington Territory had become the virtual private preserve of the Northern Pacific Railroad.[11]

By mid-summer 1872, however, the railroad was in deep trouble. Cooke's 7-30 bonds (Safe! Profitable! Permanent!) had not sold as well as hoped, and, now, the market was saturated. The annual pre-harvest summer doldrums settled over the economy, as farmers and city folk alike sat on their savings. Public confidence in lending institutions plummeted as word swept across the country that federal gold reserves were being hoarded by European banks— loans were sharply curtailed, speculators grew cautious, builders sat idle, laborers wandered the countryside, and savings disappeared into mattresses to await better times.

Perhaps, too, the jibes at the "Great Fertile Belt" were finally hitting home—drought parched the northern prairies, soil blew away, emigration ground to a halt, and cynics began calling the Northern Pacific "a railroad from nowhere to no place through no man's land."

Nonetheless, scheduled train service between Duluth and Fargo began in March 1872, and track advanced across Dakota at an average pace of two miles a day. Unfortunately, construction and surveying costs were advancing just as fast and outstripping the NP's cash reserve by an ever-widening margin. Expansive, gilt-encrusted J. Gregory Smith went blithely on buying rail and locomotives, erecting gingerbreaded depots, and hiring local "special agents."

Exasperated, Jay Cooke upbraided Smith for spending over $50,000 each month, "for the fun of running a railroad without receipts. You must put on the brakes."[12]

The Northern Pacific construction overdraft reached $5,000,000 and bondholders began cashing in their paper. That fall, Cooke demanded Smith's resignation and installed in his place "original interest" partner General George Washington Cass, who was a well-respected railroad man and a known penny-pincher.

In Seattle, the NP's financial troubles were scarcely noticed in the fall of 1872, in light of the fact that the latest known construction contract extended the right of way eight miles past Tacoma: "Thus virtually settling the point that Seattle, from its commanding position, will be the terminal city, leaving our highly speculative friends with large blocks of ex-terminus property on hand, which will sound large in the hands of their executors or make good assets for a receiver in bankruptcy."

Bemused newcomer Edmund T. Coleman later recalled: "Indeed, it was high treason for anyone to doubt but that Seattle would be the terminus. A friend of mine having ventured to differ with a lady on this point, she put him down in a manner that astonished his weak nerves, and made him repent his temerity."[13]

In October, there materialized in Olympia a resplendent, silk-hatted apparition: President Cass. He was accompanied by Vice-President John C. Ainsworth, Lake Superior & Puget Sound Land Company president Canfield, agents Goodwin and Sprague, former Michigan senator William Howard, land company director William S. King, Division Engineer T.B. Morris, Chief Engineer Roberts, Secretary Wilkeson, and directors Frederick Billings, Benjamin P. Cheney, William Butler Ogden, James Stinson, Charlemagne Tower, William Windom, and Charles B. Wright. These luminous gentlemen boarded the steamer *North Pacific* to see the Sound for themselves and hopefully pin the terminus site down once and for all. Questions of time and money were pressing the issue. If the Northern Pacific did not soon establish itself on Puget Sound and begin earning its keep, the land grants and possibly the company itself were doomed. For four days, Olympia and Steilacoom, Fidalgo and Mukilteo, Port Townsend and Bellingham Bay, Seattle and Tacoma passed in review as the men's toppered heads gravely nodded and shook, mostly . . . at the great expense portending in laying track to Port Townsend, or across Deception Pass to Holmes Harbor, or up to Bellingham.

At Seattle, the directors nodded approvingly upon

GENERAL M.M. McCARVER

seeing Elliott Bay and Lake Washington, and it was evident that the people there had indeed built up a coming city. Just as Swan had said, though, there was little level building room; the place seemed to be all hills, and all the best waterfront land was occupied. The coal, too, was already being mined by locals. It would cost a lot of money to put the Northern Pacific into Seattle: Birnie's survey of the White River Valley that summer revealed that miles of costly filling, bridging, and piling would be required to run track across that sodden plain. Tacoma? The toppers nodded.

Tacoma had had modest beginnings. A Civil War veteran named Job Carr arrived on Puget Sound in 1864 with his wife and an armful of governments maps. He had heard much about the new Northern Pacific Railroad and was determined to be waiting at its western terminus when the cars steamed in. He strode the muddy streets of Seattle and Olympia, sounding out the locals and trying to divine where the railway would go. There was plenty of big talk, and plenty of boosters eager to clap an arm around a stranger and enlist him in their cause. The ex-soldier politely nodded, and followed his nose to Commencement Bay, a broad and beautifully situated harbor that took its name from being the starting place for the U.S. Navy's survey of the Puget Sound coast line in 1841. All Carr's instincts told him there would surely be a city here one day. On Christmas Day, he staked his claim at an inviting spot called by the Puyallup Indians "Shubalip"— Sheltered Place—and built a home. Years earlier, there had been a tiny sawmill at Shubalip, which had been abandoned and the site given back to nature. Carr stayed.

Four damp, lonely years went by before the Carrs were joined by General Morton Matthew McCarver in April 1868. General McCarver (whose title dated from his tenure as commissary-general of the Iowa militia) was the quintessential Victorian promoter with an impressive resume. He had founded, or helped to found Burlington, Iowa; Sacramento, California; and Linnton, Oregon. He had introduced horseradish to the West, and bred the McCarver apple. Like Carr, McCarver was a Civil War

veteran, and like Carr he came to Puget Sound in anticipation of the terminus boom. Unlike Carr, McCarver was not content to wait for trains. At sixty-one, he had grown tired of farming in Linnton, Oregon. Age was creeping up on him and he craved one last adventure before he died. Founding the Great Metropolis of the Northwest would do nicely.

McCarver had left his farm and rode alone to Puget Sound. In his pocket was money supplied by wealthy Portlanders Lewis M. Starr and James Steel, and bonds bearing the florid imprimatur of Ben Holladay's Willamette Valley railroad and steamship companies. McCarver, Starr, and Steel were hopeful of locating a Portland/Puget Sound right of way for either Ben Holladay or one of the Puget Sound & Columbia River Railroad schemes floating about. McCarver delegated himself to scout out a Puget Sound terminus, sell the bonds on the way, and maybe buy up some land for the railroad's use.

A better choice for a trailblazer could hardly have been found. McCarver had long been a vocal exponent of Manifest Destiny, and since the 1840s had been an equally ardent advocate of a Pacific railroad. Narrowing his attentions to Puget Sound, he, like Job Carr, did his homework carefully and realized that a good harbor situated conveniently to the two most promising Cascade passes, Snoqualmie and Naches, stood the best chance of becoming the railroad terminus and next great city of the West.

McCarver stopped at Seattle, looked around, and shook his head. The town was the closest to Snoqualmie Pass, true, but wagons cluttered the streets and advertising signs were everywhere. Seattle was already too crowded— McCarver wanted his own city.

Days later, he gazed upon vast, sheltered Commencement Bay, and that wondrous sensation he had felt at other signal moments in his life—a sensation he hoped to feel once more—boiled up inside. McCarver summoned his family, and, while he awaited their arrival, struck up a friendship with his neighbor, Job Carr. In the summer of 1868, they founded Commencement City, and occupied much of their time exploring the Puyallup Valley and the

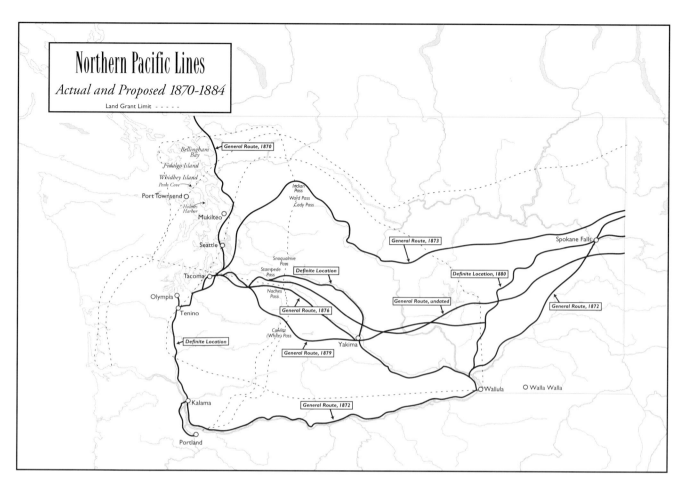

Northern Pacific Lines

Actual and Proposed 1870-1884

Land Grant Limit - - - - -

General Route, 1870

Bellingham Bay

Fidalgo Island

Whidbey Island
Penn Cove

Port Townsend

Holmes Harbor

Mukilteo

Seattle

Indian Pass
Ward Pass
Cady Pass

General Route, 1873

Spokane Falls

Snoqualmie Pass

Stampede Pass

Definite Location

Definite Location, 1880

Tacoma

Naches Pass

General Route, undated

General Route, 1872

Olympia

General Route, 1876

Tenino

Cowlitz (White) Pass

Definite Location

Yakima

General Route, 1879

Walula   Walla Walla

Kalama

General Route, 1872

Portland

Mt. Rainier foothills, looking for something of value beyond the obvious old growth timber—something with which to put their town on the map, something that would secure the undivided attention of the Northern Pacific. They found coal.

"This coal assures our place as the terminus of the great overland railroad," McCarver wrote to his Portland partners in September, and he began buying government land on Commencement Bay.[14]

The two neighbors soon had company. Providentially, these were just the kind of folks McCarver was looking for. One was Philip Ritz, a territorial marshal, Walla Walla landowner, and personal friend of several NP directors.

Ritz had just published a pamphlet describing Seattle as the coming terminal city, but, after riding into Commencement City that fateful summer, he experienced a change of heart. Ritz shook hands with Carr and McCarver, bought some lots, and suggested changing the rather uninspiring name "Commencement City" to the mellifluous one that he had read was the Indian term for Mt. Rainier, the great peak looming forty miles southeast of town. McCarver and his neighbors agreed that "Tacoma" did have a nice ring to it.[15] Soon thereafter, Ritz wrote his Northern Pacific friends Thomas Canfield and Charles Wright that Tacoma was indeed The Place.

McCarver loosed his own barrage of letters—crude,

misspelled, but contagious in their enthusiasm—to all the bankers, businessmen, and editors he had encountered during his peripatetic career, and to the directors of the Northern Pacific. To all, the message was the same: The Great Metropolis of Puget Sound was coming and it would be Tacoma! They would find a paradise here: Coal! Ore! Salmon as big as seals! Clams the size of dinner plates—"Nothing is wanted but industry to make this one of the richest little countries in the world." McCarver puffed so relentlessly he became notorious up and down the Sound as "General Tacoma."[16]

Two years later, another large NP shareholder came looking and cast his lot with Carr, McCarver, and Ritz: wealthy Portland contractor James B. Montgomery. In August 1870, Montgomery took lead-and-line soundings of Commencement Bay, found bottom, and wrote his friend W.G. Moorhead, a junior partner at Cooke & Co., that there could be no better terminus location than Tacoma. Moorhead forwarded the letter to his friend Thomas Scott, an "original interest" partner and president of the Pennsylvania Railroad.

Scott was duly impressed: "His head is level," he declared of Montgomery.

Thomas Canfield, who had so curtly dismissed Tacoma in his 1869 report, was now likewise convinced. With the assistance of McCarver and local NP land agent Edward S. "Skookum" Smith (so-called for his strong physique), he began buying waterfront property in Tacoma. By March 1873, this would amount to 4,000 acres, extending for more than two miles along Commencement Bay and inland up the bluffs. Seattle might have had such friends![17]

Five years after the town's establishment, Tacoma's 150 permanent residents enjoyed the services of a school, stable, general store, post office, the Steele Hotel, Ackerson's sawmill, Anthony Carr's photo gallery, a handful of saloons, and a small coterie of doctors and lawyers. Such was the village that presented itself to the illustrious sightseers aboard the *North Pacific* in October 1872. Tacoma also had something more than land and friendly

natives: she had nothing. She was a virgin, so to speak; there was no landed Establishment, commercial or otherwise, to compete with railroad interests. A "company" town would inevitably flower into the Great Metropolis and the Northern Pacific would reap millions in land boom profits.

Crowded Seattle offered no such fertile ground. Moreover, the northerly harbors and the incipient land grants that Canfield had previously considered were now simply too far a reach for the company's dwindling treasury. By this time, the directors were obliged to dig into their own pockets to keep the track advancing, and the year's forty-mile deadline was fast approaching. It was imperative that the terminus be located soon. Mukilteo was fading to a distant "maybe," even Seattle was looking more and more doubtful. Jay Cooke planned a $2,000,000 seeding investment in the terminal city: Where would those dollars go farthest?

Two top hats rowed serenely over the calm waters of Commencement Bay. Frederick Billings and Charles B. Wright, the NP's two largest shareholders and both members of the executive committee, had liked the look of the place and ordered the *North Pacific*'s paddle wheels stopped. The Puget Sound tour had been exhausting and both men were in declining health, but they re-boarded the steamer in good spirits. Tacoma looked good, indeed! Returning to Olympia, the officials were met at the dock by an anxious town railroad committee. Grave assurances were made: No, nothing had transpired to change arrangements since Sprague and Goodwin had accepted Olympia's gift of 5,000 acres in late 1871 (actually, for some time the two men had been urging the directors to forget Olympia and go to Tacoma). Should the situation change, the town would, of course, be notified.

When considering the matter back in their New York board room, the directors decided—to reserve decision. Two vice-presidents, Judge Richard Rice and Captain John C. Ainsworth, were dispatched to parlay with the men of Seattle and Tacoma, extract the handsomest inducements, and make the final terminus recommendation. Seattle was not amused. The NP's constant speculation, the surveys around and behind the city, and the withdrawal of public land without any corresponding start in construction had taken a toll on Seattle's patience. She was getting worried.

"For two years the people of Puget Sound have been kept in a state of anxiety, enterprise paralyzed, and capital driven to other fields of investment," carped the Seattle *Puget Sound Dispatch*. "The surveys, which have cost the railroad company vast sums of money, all seem to be directed with reference to the land company's possessions rather than to the routes and connections which nature and engineering skill both demonstrate to be the most practicable. The land ring must be served, whoever suffers . . . No competent or experienced engineer or railroad man ever recommended any other terminal points for the road than Superior Bay on the east, and Elliott Bay on the west."[18]

The railroad company took criticism from all sides. A New York newspaper lambasted the NP and its land adjunct as "the monster swindle of the age." The J.P. Morgan-backed Philadelphia *Ledger* spotlighted the company's financial embarrassments and lack of progress. Terrible drought, which was followed that winter by the worst blizzards in living memory, had ravaged the reputation of "Cooke's Banana Belt." Also, the ugly revelations of financial chicanery within the Credit Mobilier, the construction company for the Union Pacific, came to light late in 1872 and shocked the nation, rousing great anti-railroad sentiment. Now, the Northern Pacific and its land company seemed headed down the same, shady path.

Jay Cooke hastened to assure his stockholders: "There is not the slightest probability of there being any cessation in the legitimate demand for lands, unless the world comes to an end . . . The progress of empire is westward."

Privately, Cooke admitted otherwise. In March 1873, the banker called the Northern Pacific directors to his crenellated, suburban Philadelphia mansion, "Ogontz." Crisis was upon them, he intoned. The railroad must begin earning its keep at once, or fail. Large funds on Wall Street awaited investment in the terminal point, wherever and whenever it should be located. There, the Northern Pacific would reap millions in short order. Standing before a large map of Puget Sound, Cooke pointed a violin bow at Commencement Bay. The NP must stop at Tacoma.

What of the land grant further north? Cooke shook his head: There was no money to get to Bellingham, Mukilteo, or even Seattle.

The gentlemen nodded quietly. Billings, Moorhead, and Rice set off at once for the Sound to definitely locate line to Commencement Bay, and 2,000 more Chinese laborers were rushed to the railhead from San Francisco.[19]

There was no time to lose. Portland contractor (and Tacoma supporter) James B. Montgomery was given direction to build 100 miles of roadbed north of Tenino. This would theoretically get the tracks as far as Mukilteo. The northerly sixty miles of the route was optional, but the other forty miles in the contract was binding and would just reach Tacoma. Even so, surveyors again ran a line through Seattle to Mukilteo, and another route east of Lake Washington, avoiding the city altogether and looping well to the north before crossing the Cascades.

Many observers, even railroad officials, remained convinced that the NP would yet go to Bellingham. Despite the secret council at Ogontz, Jay Cooke appeared to be keeping his options open to the last. Advance clearing gangs reached Lakeview, then grubbed on toward the Puyallup Valley, with all apparent intention of bypassing Tacoma and continuing northward.

As Montgomery later affirmed: "The railroad company proposed a little strategy on the cities, towns, and holders of real estate on Puget Sound . . . Everyone from Budd's Inlet to Bellingham Bay thought they had the proper site for the 'terminus.' And it was to put people off the track that the '100 miles contract' was given to me."[20]

Olympia had been clinging to her deal with Sprague and Goodwin as a glimmer of hope, but the May 1, 1872, deadline for locating the right of way into town had long since passed in ominous silence. Another year went by, and, with Montgomery's gangs nearing Tacoma, Olympia's increasingly anxious railroad committee wrote President Cass: We gave you land. Where is the railroad?

Cass' reply came as a shock: Sorry, but the Northern Pacific had no contract with Olympia. Stunned, the capital city barely had time to sputter its apoplexy when locating commissioners Ainsworth and Rice showed up in June. After a bit of red-faced hemming and hawing, they came clean to Marshall Blinn and his angry deputation: Didn't anyone tell you? Your offer was voted down at the board meeting last February! In fact, the board had decided as early as March 1872 that ending the track at Budd Inlet would not do when 150 miles of land grant clear to the Canadian border was to be had.

If NP must enter the capital, the NP board figured it would simply lease the Olympia Branch Railroad, "as this company cannot locate its main line to Olympia without exhausting its right under the charter to locate and construct its road farther north."[21]

Ainsworth and Rice were pleased to make their getaway aboard the little steamer *Alida*, while Olympia, literally left standing on the dock, cursed the railroad "land sharks." The *Alida* paddled swiftly toward Mukilteo.

Port Townsend, Whidbey Island, and Bellingham Bay were by this time also destined to share Olympia's disappointment. Bellingham interests had rallied around Edward Eldridge, a developer and territorial representative, who in 1869 had met Thomas Canfield and lobbied hard for the terminus. The Bellingham Bay Land Association was formed to muster inducements, and, in the summer of 1870, John W. Sprague and Skookum Smith came calling. Evidently, they were impressed: The Northern Pacific promptly filed a general route map with Bellingham Bay as the northern terminus.

The secretary of the interior, however, had a different idea, declaring flatly that the company had no right to "squander the public lands" by paralleling Puget Sound for more than 100 miles before touching water. He refused to approve the route and informed the directors that land could be withdrawn only as far north as Seattle. The railroad had the decision overturned by the Supreme Court, and Bellingham had renewed hope. Unfortunately, the land association failed to come through with the promised inducements, and, by 1873, limited railroad finances rendered the Bellingham option moot anyway.

On May 6, the board passed a resolution to terminate at "Mukilteo, Seattle, or Tacoma, or some place intermediate . . . at whichever point superior advantage shall be found to exist and be offered."[22]

Mukilteo, a slim prospect at best, was quickly disposed of. The village at Point Elliot, founded in 1858 by merchants J.D. Fowler and Morris Frost, was more a bench than a harbor—and too exposed to north winds and strong currents, and too far from the railhead. Ainsworth and Rice shook their heads, and requested that Seattle and Tacoma make their best offers.

On June 24, a sweating Seattle convened in Yesler's Pavilion at Front and Cherry streets to pool its resources. Pledges of land and money were eagerly proffered by 300 townsfolk—among them mill owner Henry Yesler, crusty but generous, who put up $10,000 and a hundred acres, and Arthur Denny, who offered half of all his land outright. By its cigar-smogged conclusion, the congregation had assembled a most substantial package: 450 town lots, 4,800 waterfront acres, clear riparian rights on the vast tideflats, 6,500 additional acres in detached parcels, and some $50,000 in gold bullion, all free and clear should the NP choose Seattle.[23]

Thirty miles south, McCarver's time had come. He and his Tacoma neighbors offered 1,200 waterfront acres at cost, and options on 1,500 more as a bonded donation, plus riparian rights to the town's 600 acres of tideflat. Upland parcels available nearby—flat, broad, and ideal for railroad facilities—totaled some 10,000 acres. All this in addition to what the land company already owned in Tacoma. Nonetheless, McCarver had gotten wind of Seattle's bid and asked the commissioners for more time to raise his ante. Ainsworth and Rice graciously agreed, and, during the breathing spell, the Seattle press took stock.

"The difference in area is in favor of Tacoma, in location

in favor of Seattle," opined the *Puget Sound Dispatch*. "The one is speculative, the other real. Tacoma can offer nothing but a large expanse of wilderness, requiring large expenditures of money to give it any value. Seattle offers a large share of town property in the most thriving and populous town upon Puget Sound."[24]

The note of desperation was clear, and Seattle struggled to outdo herself. At a second town meeting on July 10, attorney James McNaught exhorted citizens to bond their city over to the railroad, to the amount of $200,000 at 7% interest, for the next twenty years: "We must make such donations as will cause them to come here in preference to Tacoma, whether they want to or not!"

White River Valley farmers pitched in, offering prime land. Seattle editors reminded Ainsworth and Rice of the rich coal veins in the nearby foothills, the potential grant lands which stood to be forfeited if the road terminated in Tacoma, and, to further buttress their case, noted the government surveys and official reports that had appeared in the eastern press—"documentary evidence of . . . the utter worthlessness of Tacoma and its bay."

Finally, Seattle appealed to morality and manhood.

"Judge Rice knows too well how the credit of the company has suffered from the public scandal of connection with a land ring no less corrupt than the Credit Mobilier," the *Dispatch* reasoned. "And those who believe that Capt. J.C. Ainsworth would stoop from his high position and bring reproach upon a name heretofore the synonym of manly independence by allowing considerations for the personal interests of partners or associates to cause him to betray the public trust, most foully wrong the man . . . We unhesitatingly affirm, that on the ground of eligibility and fitness solely, no intelligent, disinterested man, no competent engineer acquainted with the subject, has even yet given Tacoma the preference over Seattle for the railroad terminus."[25]

It was a nice try.

McCarver's well was dry, too—Tacoma was clean out of inducements. But he need not have worried. By now, Cooke, Cass, and the board were desperate to make a fi-

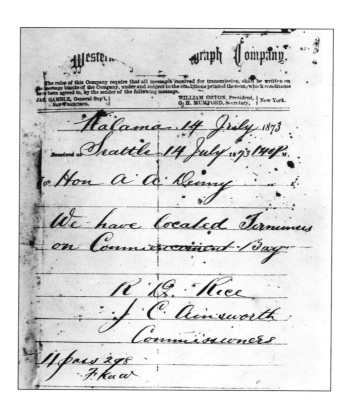

nal decision, and the executive committee—Billings, Wright, Moorhead, and Charlemagne Tower—were unanimously in favor of Tacoma. On June 24, President Cass telegraphed Ainsworth and Rice: "Hold construction in check so as to avoid work beyond terminus when fixed . . . $30,000 and no more will be supplied to carry the line to tidewater."

Thirty thousand dollars would certainly not reach Seattle. After totting up the Seattle and Tacoma inducements, Ainsworth and Rice telegraphed the board: "To carry out plan of a city company on $2,000,000 basis with any prospect of success, as now advised shall unhesitatingly decide in favor of Tacoma."

Around two o'clock on the afternoon of July 14, 1873, Arthur Denny and Morton Matthew McCarver each received a curt wire from Ainsworth and Rice at Kalama: "We have located Terminus on Commencement Bay."[26] ∎

Seattle founder
Arthur A. Denny.

*University of Washington,
Special Collections, #386*

CHAPTER 4

Digging In

"These men entered our territory as a public enemy, intent on plunder."
—Beriah Brown, Seattle *Puget Sound Dispatch*

---

*T*HE NORTHERN PACIFIC telegram signalled a turning point for Seattle, an event that more than any other during the city's first century forged its image of itself, its place in the world, and forced upon it a course of concerted civic action. It marked the end of Seattle's confident, optimistic youth, and the painful beginning of an often-tortured adolescence. The railroad's effrontery in choosing upstart Tacoma over established Seattle was a sharp lesson in the ways of business, and it roused a storm of disappointment and anger which would result in war—sometimes hot, sometimes cold—between the city and the Northern Pacific Railroad for the next seventeen years.

"Land Ring Triumphant!" blustered the *Puget Sound Dispatch*. "This ends the miserable farce played upon the people of Seattle and all the others who confided in the honesty of the Commissioners, under the false pretext that the Northern Pacific Railroad Co. was not owned, controlled and run exclusively in the interest of the land ring—a combination more corrupt and more false to the trust reposed in them for the public benefit, than the Credit Mobilier of infamous notoriety."

The predictable melodrama would be played out: Corrupt manipulators would fleece the country, pocket land grant dollars, and move on, leaving in their wake busted settlers who had staked their all on the railroad. Only a few insiders would prosper.

"Bitter will be the disappointment of many of these over-sanguine individuals," lamented Olympia's *Washington Standard*. "They will realize the fact, that not even a railroad can build a city, and develop the resources of the country at the same time to sustain it."

The warnings went largely unheeded. The stagecoaches from Tenino to Tacoma were filled with "pilgrims to the new Jerusalem," and, in Seattle, signs went up in shop windows: "Gone to the Terminus."[1]

Still, the railroad board had yet to formally ratify their decision. Moreover, certain Tacoma property owners were proving difficult by gouging the company for higher prices. This, Ainsworth and Rice pointedly noted, was in contrast to Seattle's "most liberal donation." Seattle got a thirteenth-hour chance to present McNaught's $200,000 bond proposition. On July 17, Arthur Denny and his "committee of seven" sailed to Steilacoom to meet the railroad agents, and, they hoped, to save their city.

Julius Dickens, editor of the Steilacoom *Express*, looked on in amusement: "The big men from Seattle marched in double-file, arm in arm, to the hotel to meet the locating commissioners, their lofty beavers glistening in the noontime sun like an African's phiz in a field of cane. They came, they saw and—that was all; for the heads of the locating commissioners were too well balanced to lose their equilibrium on meeting this august delegation of great men from the town of sawdust and fleas."[2]

The Seattle delegation elicited little more than bland assurances that their latest offer would be laid before the directors. Certainly, the city was being generous. President Cass was perhaps more favorable to Seattle than the majority of the board, and on the 21st he wrote executive committee chairman Frederick Billings:

"This is bidding up pretty well for Seattle, and if it will cost no more to reach Seattle than Tacoma, we ought not to hesitate about accepting the offer. But the trouble is that Seattle is about a million dollars beyond Tacoma in distance, and this difference in distance is alone equal to the difference in value of the two cities."[3]

Arthur Denny had few illusions as to the eventual outcome. Seattle must not rely on a nearly bankrupt corporation whose intentions were now clear, he lectured his colleagues; they must do for themselves. Returning from the Steilacoom summit, he ate a hasty supper. He then gaveled to order another mass meeting at Yesler's Pavilion, this time to bring down Seattle's curses upon the Northern Pacific and adopt a resolution, which was promptly mailed to the secretary of the interior and the federal land commissioner, demanding immediate forfeiture of all the NP's "general route" land grants north of Pierce County.

All the while, Northern Pacific grubbers and graders hacked their way northward, scraping and leveling roadbed across Yelm Prairie during the long, hot summer days. Pile drivers banged away at the footings for the Nisqually and Deschutes river bridges. Like a tornado, the brown cloud of dust and smoke bore in relentlessly on Tacoma.

But Tacoma herself was now in for a shock. Inexplicably, obstreperous property owners, including McCarver's son-in-law, Clinton P. Ferry, refused to sell a key parcel that would give the railroad unimpeded right of way along the waterfront. The penalty for disregarding the pointed warnings of Ainsworth and Rice quickly became apparent, as the Northern Pacific simply helped itself to Tacoma's name and transferred it to a site two miles to the east: "New Tacoma." Morton Matthew McCarver's dream city was relegated to "Old Town."

There were other advantages to the new site, namely hundreds of acres of cheap, government-owned tidelands and riverfront at the head of the bay, costing far less than the disputed parcels and offering much more room for expansion. By this turn of events, the railroad found itself in possession of 13,000 acres of choice Commencement Bay land, including well over a mile of waterfront—a landed estate on the scale of Chicago, New Orleans, or St. Louis.[4]

For McCarver, this usurpation of his grand vision was a mortifying blow. Bitter at betrayal by the railroad he had fought so hard for, and worn out by the recriminations of former friends and neighbors who blamed him for their losses, the Father of Tacoma soon would die, on April 17, 1875, at the age of 68. "In the march of Empire toward the West," eulogized the *Puget Sound Dispatch* on April 22, 1875, "he was always in the front rank."

With gin mills going full blast, New Tacoma supplanted Kalama as Washington's boomtown. On July 18, General James Tilton's gangs began hewing a railroad terminus out of the Commencement Bay waterfront, the biggest engineering project ever seen on Puget Sound. Laboring men from across the country swarmed in and encamped by the bay, bedding down in the brush after twelve-hour days filled with sweat and sawdust. A minor exodus also fled Seattle: Johnston Brothers' big dry goods store, John Pinnell's "squaw brothel," the city's former two-term mayor H.A. Atkins, and sundry sutlers, grocers, barbers, and barkeeps. In Olympia, Hoffman & Frost's hardware store and the *Tribune* itself pulled up stakes for the terminus. Desperately seeking amusement, Seattle catcalled: "We kindly volunteer the suggestion if it would not have been a more profitable venture to turn the [*Tribune*] establishment into a soap factory—using the editor for one of the ingredients, and his editorials (when not too thin) for the other, with the odor of a virtuous life for flavoring."[5]

Ridiculed or not, Tacoma was the place to be. By summer's end, Old Town was a backwater, while New Tacoma had a post office and claimed 500 "residents"— most of them transient laborers. To take their investment in hand, the NP directors created the Tacoma Land Company on August 23. The land firm then turned over to the Northern Pacific 51% of its stock, and purchased all of the railroad's Tacoma land except a few hundred acres which would be used for shop facilities. The president of the Tacoma Land Company was Charles Barstow Wright. An NP board stalwart since 1871, Wright was a Philadelphia capitalist who had built a huge fortune in Pennsylvania banking, oil, and railroads. Wright would always fondly recall his first glimpse of Commencement Bay:

"As I looked up at the sloping hills and saw how Nature had done everything except build a city, I said to myself, Here is the place! We directors did not dare say a word about what we thought. Speculators would have taken advantage of it, and then, too, it would have given one director a chance to say so and so said so and so—we were watched, and must needs keep our ideas to ourselves. Well, those bluffs and sloping hills reminded me that a city built here could be drained nicely, and so it can."

Wright would become known as the "Abraham Lincoln of Tacoma," and rather less favorably remembered in Seattle.

"Even to this day, I am asked why we did not make the terminus of the road at Seattle," he told reporters in 1887. "We were in Tenino when the panic of '73 struck us. We had to get somewhere. And I'll tell you that, though the charter had fixed this place as the terminus and we had accepted it and all that, we would have struck off to Olympia if we could have found a harbor there. The people [of Tacoma] made us a big offer of land, and by their aid we got here. It was nip and tuck with us, however, and we had no time to spare. We reached here just eight days ahead of our contract and we were awfully glad to get here—we could not have got to Seattle. Forty miles of railway building to a company that has mighty little to go on is an item to be counted, therefore we were only too glad to get safely into Tacoma!"[6]

The genial Wright was pleased to assume the role of civic paterfamilias of the new town, and gave his money and his name to its schools, churches, and parks. In the fall of 1873, Wright retained noted landscape designer Frederick Law Olmsted to plat the city. What he produced was a riot of sweeping avenues and twisting streets laid out in French curves—a startling and visionary departure from the customary frontier grid. Olmsted's sponsors found his plan more confusing than anything else, and it was unceremoniously discarded.

Overshadowing these matters, however, was one plain fact: The Northern Pacific was broke. Jay Cooke and his associates knew that rapid settlement on the land grants was the key to the NP's survival, but far fewer than the 50,000 settlers hoped for in 1873 actually made their way west, and the NP land department's sales were equally disappointing. If that were not enough, a plague of grasshoppers descended on the Dakota and Minnesota farmlands that summer. Other Cooke investments also had sapped his resources, the bond and money markets were both bone-dry, and the erstwhile wizard scuffled from one Wall Street bank to the next begging for credit extensions.

Cooke was forced to sell large blocks of NP stock, then buy them back to keep the roof from caving in. Anxious to save their investments, the directors had no choice but to throw their own funds into construction. As the year's forty-mile deadline loomed nearer, Charles Wright and son-in-law Theodore Hosmer purchased forty miles of rail on personal credit and had them rushed to Tenino. James Montgomery sank over $200,000 of his personal credit into labor and materials before a multitude of creditors caught up with him and put him out of business twelve miles shy of the terminus. To keep track-layers from walking off the job, Mrs. Montgomery herself was compelled to make a four-day ride to Portland to fetch the payroll.[7]

As if this was not enough trouble, on September 11, 1873, the day after the NP board of directors formally declared Tacoma the western terminus, the U.S. warship *Saranac* appeared in Commencement Bay. For two hours, the lumbering side-wheeler attempted to snag bottom with her anchor, then gave up and made for Steilacoom.

Captain Phelps huffed to a reporter: "The grand railroad terminus . . . will never in my opinion be at Tacoma. The place has not one thing to recommend it."

Seattle howled with delight. Fresh anti-Tacoma broadsides were dispatched to the eastern press, and popular local cartoonist Billy Fife produced a sepia lithograph

CHARLES BARSTOW WRIGHT— TACOMA'S FRIEND, SEATTLE'S NEMESIS.
Washington State Historical Society

entitled "No Bottom at Tacoma," which depicted the *Saranac's* boats dangling lead lines as sharks bearing uncanny likenesses of McCarver, Skookum Smith, and General Sprague nipped at the weights. "No Bottom at Tacoma" became a Seattle barroom staple, while Tacomans blustered that it was all a dastardly Seattle fabrication.

The jilted city was further heartened by a Portland *Oregonian* column: "The 'terminus' has affected Seattle less than any other town on the Sound . . . Several of those characters, without which any place is much better, are leaving, but none of the substantial business men are closing up here to open in Tacoma. Certainly trade is not so brisk as if Seattle had been favored with the location; but not securing that great desideratum, they are awakened—not to a sense of helplessness and loss, but to a realization of their own might and strength."[8]

A week after the *Saranac* fiasco, months of rumors finally climaxed in a financial run on Jay Cooke's Wall Street bank. An immediate chain reaction followed, and, within twenty-four hours, no fewer than thirty banks and brokerage houses had failed. With a roaring wail that could be heard a block away, the New York Stock Exchange suspended trading on September 18. The panic of 1873 was on, and the house of Cooke collapsed in bankruptcy, taking the Northern Pacific with it. By the end of the year, thousands of businesses across the country had ceased to exist. Railroad construction ceased, and hundreds of laid-off Northern Pacific employees went "on the bum."

I told you so, sneered Seattle: That Cooke had become too big for himself was evident. In the judgment of the would-be terminal city, his two worst blunders were letting the land sharks run things and shunning the "natural and lawful" terminus. Now see the result! Did it not prove that the judgement of the nation—perhaps even a higher power—was in Seattle's favor?

On October 6, however, the Department of the Interior accepted the NP's latest general route surveys for the branch line from Tacoma to a connection with the main route near Lake Pend d'Oreille in Idaho Territory; Seattle's petition to revoke the land grant north of Tacoma was rejected. This was cause for some concern, inasmuch as the NP's latest general route map showed a rail line arcing from Tacoma up the White River Valley and over the north Cascades to eastern Washington, gulping huge, checkerboard sections of King and Snohomish counties into the Northern Pacific maw—and insolently bypassing Seattle east of Lake Washington.[9]

Still, too, the Northern Pacific had yet to reach Tacoma! Billings, Cass, Wright, and other "original interests" put up $220,000, and Superintendent Sprague hired Skookum Smith to take over Montgomery's contract. By the start of November, Smith had brought the railhead to Lakeview, ten miles south of town, and prepared to run a shortcut straight into Tacoma down a steep grade, instead of the easier but longer alignment originally surveyed via the Puyallup Valley to the east.

Again the money ran out. Smith's company of 400 men, who were owed $73,000 in back wages, laid down their tools, barricaded the end of track (which they dubbed "Skookumville"), and informed Skookum: No pay, no railroad. The laborers petitioned Governor Elisha P. Ferry for redress, serving notice they would occupy the right of way until paid off.

Puget Sound Dispatch editor Beriah Brown embraced the cause of labor with alacrity, and accused Smith and Sprague of lording "it over the unsophisticated people . . . exercising rights of eminent domain by selling privileges to cut timber upon government lands; ordering off settlers or compelling [them] to pay . . . tribute; exacting loyalty and exercising secret surveillance." Sprague and Smith, the "sultan and "grand vizier" of the land ring, were charged with pocketing construction funds: "These men entered our territory as a public enemy, intent on plunder," cried Brown, who went on to say of Skookum Smith: "He is of the material of which pimps are made."

This was the last straw for Skookum, and he let it be known he would hire a "Chinaman" to give Brown a good thrashing. Sub-contractor Henry Failing and the ever-handy Ainsworth stepped in and arranged payment in cash, promissory notes, and tokens redeemable at the Hanson-Ackerson Mill Company store in Tacoma.[10]

Momentarily pacified, Skookum's men hacked their way downgrade into New Tacoma. The little construction engines *Minnetonka*, *Otter Tail*, and—inevitably—*J.C. Ainsworth* and *R.D. Rice* rushed rail and ties forward as fast as their tiny drivers could turn. *Otter Tail* brought the first construction train down the two-percent grade into town, only to turn turtle in the ditch at the bottom. Little but dignity suffered. In late November, the first through train from Kalama pulled unceremoniously onto the terminal wharf bearing Mr. and Mrs. William Blackwell and furnishings for their new terminus hotel, the Bay View House.

The completion of the Pacific Division was observed with appropriate pomp on December 16, 1873. At 3 PM, Skookum Smith, General Sprague, Job Carr, and Morton Matthew McCarver gathered on the NP wharf and took turns trying to outdo each other in florid oratory, then handed the maul around, driving in the last spike. Engine Number 11, the *General Cass*, took the first train out that evening. Aboard were Puyallup Valley pioneer Ezra Meeker, one Harold Cooke, Theodore and Mrs. Hosmer, General Sprague, and 250 pounds of canned salmon. Now all that remained to be laid were 1,500 miles of track between Kalama and Bismarck, Dakota Territory.

George Washington Cass was not satisfied. Fifteen hundred miles was a lot of track. Furthermore, instead of running a railroad like he knew how, he was compelled to spend much precious time refereeing a running feud between the Lake Superior & Puget Sound Land Co. and the NP's own land department. Also, he had to discharge a company policy that was diverting precious construction and operating dollars to land acquisitions and lobbying, which seemed to be making more enemies then friends. Mixing land company and railroad affairs was "very bad policy," Cass complained, and could only further weaken an already dangerously faltering public trust.[11]

On December 6, 1873, Arthur Denny received a wire from President Cass that appeared to offer salvation to

Seattle: "To what extent will your people contribute if the Northern Pacific Railroad is put under contract to Seattle next spring [?]" The press took it as veritable proof that the NP actually would terminate where God and Nature intended.

"Seattle still lives!" rejoiced the *Dispatch*, seeing in the overture "a complete and conclusive acknowledgement of the superior advantages of Seattle for a railroad terminus, and . . . evidence that General Cass and the few honest men associated with him have got out of the control of the

infamous Land Ring . . . nothing is better settled in the public mind than that Seattle will be the main terminus of that road on Puget Sound."

Denny's reply—"If assured of good faith, have no doubt our people would still be liberal on a definite proposition to extend your road to Seattle"—reached Cass promptly.[12] Unfortunately, so did the Seattle newspaper editorials:

"I had . . . reliable information that it would be impossible to obtain from your people sufficient aid to justify further negotiations," a testy Cass wrote after reading the cocksure *Dispatch* and other journals. "This was fully confirmed shortly after by the editors of the newspapers of your city. These editors all assumed that the construction of the Road north of Tacoma was essential to the success of the Northern Pacific . . . and a matter of no great importance to the people of Seattle. Indeed it was stated . . . that the citizens of Seattle had other projects in hand, which would tax their resources to carry through, and which were of more importance to them than the construction of the Northern Pacific Road from Tacoma to Seattle."

The railroad president sternly disabused the city of any notion that the NP would move the terminus. It was only the consideration of including Seattle as a station on the Cascade branch that motivated his inquiry in the first place: "There were reasons existing at that time which made it desirable to commence that work, and which might have commenced if your people had responded as favorably as I anticipated they would, and which I think they ought to have done. But these reasons no longer exist." Case closed.[13]

Scheduled service on the Pacific Division between Kalama and Tacoma began on January 5, 1874. One short freight train a day, with a single coach, sufficed. Hardy riders paid six dollars one way between end points, and a dollar more to and from Portland—a ten-hour journey. There were few sidings, and only Tenino had a depot equipped with an agent and a telegraph. Freight cars were simply left standing on the main line for the next train to shove ahead to the first siding, then cut in behind the locomotive. An engineer had to be of keen memory on foggy Puget Sound nights, lest he find a boxcar in his lap. The men remained alert, and no serious accidents occurred.[14]

Flat on its back that bleak winter of 1874, the bankrupt Northern Pacific was the butt of widows' and orphans' curses and burlesque hall quips, and far from fulfilling its charter as a transcontinental line. Winter traffic on the Eastern Division was so sparse, and bucking snow so costly and difficult, that trains ran no further west than Fargo. The railroad was, however, fortunate in its leadership. General Cass was made receiver, Wright president, and Billings took charge of the reorganization effort. Through a deft combination of belt-tightening, financial legerdemain, and the development of a hardy new strain of winter wheat in the Dakotas, the great enterprise was saved.

Drought, too, was washed away by the first of more than a decade of lush, wet springs. Migration to the "New Northwest" slowly, steadily increased. That spring, the Tacoma Land Company acquired the assets of the Lake Superior & Puget Sound Land Co., and opened its doors to the public. Rock bottom deals were offered Puget Sound merchants removing to the terminus. Remove, people did: during 1872-1874, only 17,000 acres had been bought. In 1875, however, 144,000 were snapped up by eager settlers. Terminal city was on its way, and better things were coming.[15]

"The railroad from Kalama to Tacoma is doing a larger business than ever before," observed the *Oregonian* in May 1875: "On the 14th, sixty passengers were taken on at Kalama, half of whom were left at stations on the way and the other half taken into Tacoma. There were three carloads of merchandise, two of sheep, and three of cattle, and six flat cars were taken along to bring back limestone."[16]

Homesteads sprouted along the line in the Cowlitz, Chehalis, and Puyallup valleys, and in 1875—at the urging of McCarver, Smith, Sprague, and Wilkeson—the Northern Pacific dispatched Pennsylvania geologist Benjamin Fallows into the Cascade foothills east of Tacoma to analyze the veins of bituminous coal that Carr and McCarver had found seven years before. His verdict was highly favorable.

NP vice-president George Stark reported to a pleased President Wright: "The development of the coal mines would stimulate the growth of Tacoma and at once make our large terminal properties productive. Numerous parties on that coast told me that, if this work was commenced, they would at once settle at Tacoma and go into business. The great thing to accomplish . . . is the establishment of business enterprise at our Puget Sound terminus; not only for coal, but also to make available the great advantages of the Sound as against the Columbia River as a shipping outlet . . . To induce enterprise to locate and prosecute business at Tacoma, something must first be done to infuse life into the place. The building of the Puyallup branch for the development of our coal resources seems now to be the wheel which, if started, will put the whole train in motion."[17]

Once more, Wright dug into his purse and purchased thirty miles of British steel rail for the Puyallup branch. A large coal bunker was erected on Commencement Bay just west of the NP wharf, and the town of Wilkeson was platted at the mine head in the autumn of 1876. The following March, Wright's rails arrived in Tacoma, and contractor Ezra Meeker spiked the Puyallup branch into the foothills. Tacoma and the Northern Pacific were in the coal business.

Asserting that the coal line would one day become part of the Cascade branch, Wright staked claim to grant land extending twenty miles north of the new right of way—well into King County. To reinforce his claim, Wright pointed to Cascade branch surveys even then being made in Naches Pass, and promised that proceeds from the coal mines and grant land sales would go toward completing the Pacific Division from Kalama to Portland.

Not so fast, interrupted Seattle, roused to fury by a railroad that would gobble up a lion's share of King County

NP timetable, June 1876.

NORTHERN PACIFIC RAILROAD.

PACIFIC DIVISION.

KALAMA TO TACOMA

— and —

TACOMA TO WILKESON,

(COAL MINES.)

MAIN LINE TRAINS.

DAILY, (EXCEPT SUNDAYS).

LEAVE		ARRIVE
Kalama......11 20 a. m.		Tacoma......3 00 p. m.
Tacoma......7 00 a. m.		Kalama......12 50 p. m

PUYALLUP ROAD TRAINS.

LEAVE		ARRIVE
Tacoma......6.45 a. m.		Wilkeson ....9:00 a. m.
Wilkeson....3:30 p. m.		Tacoma ......5:50 p. m.

CONNECTIONS.

At TACOMA, with Pacific Mail Steamships for Victoria and San Francisco, and with Sound Steamers for Seattle, Steilacoom, Olympia, and all points on Puget Sound.

At Lake View, with Stage for Steilacoom.

At Tenino, with Stages for Olympia.

At Kalama with O. R. N. Co.'s boats for Portland and all points on the Columbia river.

At Portland, on Wednesday and Saturday at 6 a. m. with steamers for Port Townsend, Victoria, Nanaimo, New Westminster and Fraser River.

Through Tickets for sale at Principal Offices of the Company, and at the Office of the O. S. N. Co. in Portland, Oregon, to Victoria and Seattle, and via P. M. S. S. Co.'s Steamships from Tacoma, and O. S. S. Co. and P. C. S. S. Co.'s steamships from Portland, to San Francisco.

Through Tickets to Portland, Oregon, for sale at Victoria, Seattle, Tacoma and Tenino.

S. A. BLACK,
General Superintendent.

W. WAYNE VOGDES,
General Ticket Agent.

W. H. PUMPHREY, Ticket Agent at Seattle, W. T.   oc t 21

NP timetable, June 1876.

without so much as running a locomotive there. The coal line was part of the Cascade branch? Preposterous—Wilkeson was a dead end in a box canyon! It was all just more land ring humbug. Hooting at Wright's delusion of running trains over Naches Pass, where emigrant wagons had only recently been winched down sheer cliffs on raw-hide ropes, the Seattle *Intelligencer* demanded the immediate return of the railroad's King County grant lands to the public domain.

To press Seattle's case, Judge Orange Jacobs was elected territorial delegate to Congress in October 1877. Jacobs let sharp-tongued Seattle lawyer John J. McGilvra do most of the talking at Washington. Standing before the House Committee on Public Lands, McGilvra tore into the Northern Pacific "wolf" licking its chops to devour the King County lamb. Wright's claim that the coal road was part of the Cascade branch was a patent fraud, declared McGilvra, and a ruse to secure the land grants. Naches Pass was totally infeasible for a through line, he continued, and the Northern Pacific had no intention of building the Cascade branch.

The attorney did give the railroad some credit: The proposed King County land grab was not as ravenous as it might have been. It extended only twenty, and not the usual forty, miles north of the right of way, and much of the withdrawn acreage, especially prime farmland in the White River Valley, was already settled or included within the patent of the Kalama-Tacoma Pacific Division. Still, the railroad would "own" much of King County without serving it. This was unconscionable, and Jacobs and McGilvra demanded that the county lands be revoked and set aside instead for the line Seattle was itself building eastward even then—the Seattle & Walla Walla.[18]

The forfeiture fight rumbled to a head in November 1877, as Oregon senator John H. Mitchell sponsored a bill in Congress to give the NP an eight-year construction deadline extension. But only upon meeting strict conditions—that it pay its fair share of taxes on all "earned" grant lands (land through which track had been completed), that it forfeit all "unearned" lands, and that the company make grant lands available for sale to "bonafide" settlers at no more than $2.50 per acre.

Mitchell's bill also called for government oversight of all grant land sales, especially those containing coal and other minerals, and required the company, within nine months of the bill's passage, to begin construction "as far as practicable" along the Oregon side of the Columbia River from Wallula to Kalama. Failure to live up to these conditions would result in 7,000,000 land grant acres reverting to the public domain, and 7,000,000 more going to the Portland Salt Lake & South Pass Railroad (formerly the Portland Dalles & Salt Lake). This "South Pass road" was the particular pet of Mitchell's and Portland Board of Trade president W.W. Chapman, who wanted the line to link Portland with the Union Pacific and thus ensure Portland's continued pre-eminence—before the Northern Pacific could make good on its implicit threat to transfer this distinction to Puget Sound.[19]

Billings and Wright immediately denounced the Mitchell bill as "objectionable and impracticable." Should the legislation pass, they warned Congress, the very existence of the northern transcontinental railroad would be gravely threatened. Who, they asked, would invest in an enterprise subject to such restrictions? Who would buy its securities without the land grant as security?

Wright begged Congress to consider the interests of the railroad "and its ten thousand stockholders . . . The company is not in condition to accept the provision compelling construction to be commenced at Portland and to be thence continued eastwardly along the Columbia River . . . The work requires an expenditure of about thirty thousand dollars per mile . . . Such portion of the road would not pay operating expenses until the road penetrate the tributary country eastward. It is not in the power of the company to perform this requirement, nor can capital be obtained for the purpose. Money can be procured to push the road eastward from the head of navigation on the Columbia River through a fertile country where, in anticipation of the early construction of the road, over a thousand proposed settlers have already filed applications for land."

The land grant was irrevocable, insisted Billings and Wright—although Section 20 of the Land Grant Act in fact declared that "Congress may at any time, having due regard for the rights of said Northern Pacific Railroad Company, add to, alter, amend, or repeal this act."[20]

In February 1878, the Mitchell bill, with McGilvra's Seattle & Walla Walla amendment, emerged from the Senate Public Lands Committee with a "do pass" recommendation. Wright buttonholed Minnesota senator William Windom, a former NP director, who then entered his own bill for a ten-year construction extension unencumbered by any conditions. To demonstrate good faith, Wright dispatched surveyors into the Cascades that spring. The indefatigable W. Milnor Roberts ran a line from New Tacoma to Yakima over Cowlitz Pass (later known as White Pass) immediately south of 14,410-foot Mt. Rainier. He pronounced the 254-mile route "fairly feasible" for railroad use, albeit at a cost of over $6,000,000 and twenty-five miles of snowsheds.

Thanks to the efforts of Billings, Wright, and Windom, the Mitchell bill expired. The railroad accommodated the powerful Portland interests by agreeing to build down the south bank, saying: "This company is desirous of complying with the wishes of the people . . . although by doing so it loses one half the land grant applicable." For its consideration, the NP received tacit congressional assurances that, given reasonable progress, the land grant would remain intact.[21]

The forfeitors were, for the moment, beaten back. That they would not remain quiet forever could be safely presumed, so Billings and Wright hastened to advance the main line westward into Montana. NP directors and bondholders pooled their cash with that raised by a syndicate of eastern friends, and, in January 1879, grading gangs under U.S. Army protection against marauding Sioux began hacking the Missouri Division right of way into the virgin plains west of Bismarck. In October, roadbed for the Pend d'Oreille Division was started east from Wallula Gap toward Spokane Falls. By that time, Seattle had long since been running her own railroad. ∎

Like a primordial beast crawling from the ooze, the *Ant* pauses at one end of the Seattle Coal & Transportation Co. tracks between Elliott Bay and Lake Union. Festive Seattleites gathered for excursions on the city's first steam railway, March 22, 1872.

Museum of History and Industry, #2024

CHAPTER 5

Seattle Spirit and the Seattle & Walla Walla RR

"The railroad is the entering wedge by which only can we open our great oyster, the world of enterprise and prosperity." — Seattle *Intelligencer*

From the time of her founding, there was a locomotive in Seattle's soul. On November 13, 1851, a small band of settlers debarked from the schooner *Exact,* hauled their worldly goods up on the sandy beach at the entrance to a wide harbor, and named the place New York. "New York Alki," teased visiting traders—"New York, by and by" in Chinook jargon.

But the settlers were in dead earnest. Arthur A. Denny and shipmates William Bell, Carson Boren, John Low, and transplanted New York merchant Lee Terry and his brother, Charles, had little interest in farming, fishing, or logging. They were mercantilists and capitalists: budding urbanists.

Arthur Denny soon decided that the exposed sand spit and broad shallows of New York (or Alki, as some of the more modest settlers called it) rendered the place unsuitable for a port city. In early 1852, therefore, he set up his new dry goods store on the lee shore across Elliott Bay. Most of Denny's neighbors followed, and they named their new town "Seattle," after confederated Indian tribal elder Sealth. Henry Yesler arrived shortly thereafter, and fired up Seattle's first sawmill. This became the would-be city's toehold on the future—even the dignified Denny did a stint in the mill when his own business was slack. Providentially, San Francisco provided a ready and voracious market for Puget Sound lumber, given its seemingly annual propensity for burning to the ground.

Indian war broke out on Puget Sound in 1855, heralding a decade of doldrums, but, by the late 1860s, Arthur

Denny's urban dream was slowly but steadily materializing. Fifty or more settlers a year were moving in and Seattle was developing a cosmopolitan economy that belied her size. In 1863, the town got its first newspaper, followed the next year by a brewery, telegraph office, and the first eleven of Asa Mercer's fabled "Mercer Girls," who arrived from New York City to do their bit to swell the population. New York made an even more significant contribution to her erstwhile namesake in 1869, when Manhattan merchants Abraham, Leon, and Sigmud Schwabacher opened a branch of their big dry goods emporium in Seattle. Under managing partner Bailey Gatzert, the firm's Seattle outlet flourished.

Schwabacher's joined the handful of local stores, livery stables, drayage firms, tanneries, territorial university, boarding houses, carpentry and machine shops, banks, small steamboat operators, lawyers, and saloons in serving the town by the end of the 1860s, along with the Railroad Lodging House and Western Terminus Hotel. From 1869 to 1870, the city's population leaped from 550 to 1,107. Surpassing Olympia, Seattle had become the commercial center of western Washington.

Many of Seattle's first citizens got their individual toeholds chopping timber or working in Yesler's mill. Most, like the Dennys, Dr. David S. "Doc" Maynard, and the remarkable Dr. Henry A. Smith, came in anticipation of a railroad terminus. The Reverend David Blaine, Seattle's first minister, bet the city's future on a railroad over Snoqualmie Pass, confident that a "future city here not unlike New York" would arise—"How could the prospects of a future growth at once healthy, permanent and unexampled be brighter?"[1]

On this score, old settlers and newcomers alike were of a common mind. They would not, however, remain content to wait for the first Northern Pacific Palace Cars to heave into view.

After Henry Yesler's mill, coal was the next catalyst for Seattle's growth. Coal was discovered in the Cascade foothills in the 1830s, but thirty years would pass before miners began extracting it from the banks of Squak Creek, near the site of present-day Issaquah. The territorial legislature chartered the Seattle & Squak Railroad in 1864 to haul the product to tidewater, and both Arthur Denny and Henry Yesler endeavored to enlist capital from New York and San Francisco in the service of this new and potentially lucrative Seattle enterprise.

They returned home with empty pockets, and the Seattle & Squak was stillborn. At the end of the decade, the Lake Washington Coal Company opened a mine at a place it optimistically named Newcastle. Its coal was of a high grade, but, again, the firm lacked both operating capital and the means of transporting its product to tidewater. In February 1870, Lake Washington Coal transferred its assets to the newly formed Seattle Coal Company. Peter Bartell, Amos Hurst, and Reuel Robinson created a subsidiary, the Seattle Coal & Transportation Company, to carry the coal to Elliott Bay.

The SC&T, Seattle's first railroad, had primitive beginnings. Mules and horses lugged coal cars from Newcastle along a three-mile wooden tramway to a gravity incline, which lowered the cars to a dock at Murphy's Landing, on the southeast shore of Lake Washington. There, the cars were trundled aboard scows and herded across the lake to Union Bay by the small tugs *Phantom, Fanny, Chehalis, Linnie C. Gray,* and *James Mortie.* Mule power took the loads across the narrow spit of land to Portage Bay, where the coal went aboard another relay of barges for the trip down Lake Union. At the south end of the lake, quadrupeds again took over for the final leg down the mile-long main tramway, plodding along Pike Street to another incline, which lowered the cars on chains to a bunker on Elliott Bay.

Again, San Francisco was Seattle's salvation, eager and willing to pay $7.50 a ton for high-quality Newcastle coal. But the laborious tramway operation restricted the output and ate up the profits. Late in 1871, Seattle Coal's financially exhausted owners sold out to the San Francisco syndicate of Blair, Dinsmore, and Shattuck. General George C. Bode assumed the presidency of the transportation company, and transformed the mule tram into a full-fledged steam railroad. Three-foot narrow gauge track was spiked down, and, on Christmas Day, a sailing ship arrived in Seattle bearing an ungainly little gunmetal black contrivance with *Ant* neatly lettered on its sides—Seattle's first locomotive. A product of San Francisco's Fulton Foundry, *Ant* was a tiny-drivered 0-4-0 resembling nothing so much as a stove on wheels. Eight horses hauled the little engine up to Pike Street, where it was placed gingerly upon the rails, fired up, and given its first trial run before a cheering crowd.

As a wan day broke on March 22, 1872, eager young men buffed the *Ant* to a high gloss. Then they coupled up eight spotless new home-built coal cars temporarily fitted out with benches. The whistle shrilled, folks clambered aboard, and from dawn to dusk Seattleites reveled in "the novelty of a free ride behind the first locomotive that ever whistled and snorted and dashed through the dense forests surrounding the waters of Puget Sound."[2]

The Seattle Brass Band tootled bravely in the chill air. A school special was run for the kids, and those who tired of jolting along behind the *Ant* could cruise Lake Union aboard coal scows. Red-faced with exhilaration, the people of Seattle queued up to immortalize themselves in the Pioneer Association's guest book, then *Ant* settled into the workaday drudgery of hauling coal.

The town was giddy with new self-confidence. "Seattle marches right along," puffed the *Puget Sound Dispatch,* "looking neither to the right or left, increasing in population, building piers, warehouses and buildings just as if there were no such thing as the Northern Pacific Railroad. That's the way to do it."

Others were similarly impressed. "Think of that!" exclaimed Olympia. "The little unpretentious town of Seattle, only a few years old, with less than two thousand inhabitants, boasting her railroad, locomotives, cars, etc. and exporting about 3,000 tons of coal per month, while we, of Olympia, are lying supinely on our backs, shutting our eyes to all such enterprises, and like young birds, holding our mouths wide open expecting the railroad company to drop gold coins into them."[3]

Still, Seattle desperately wanted a real railroad—a main line to the East. And after preening herself for so long, so sure of getting it, the Northern Pacific telegram of July 14, 1873, was a stunning blow. If the Seattle town meeting on July 17, 1873, was a declaration of war on the Northern Pacific, it also marked the birth of a militant new self-awareness in the city. Frustration quickly hardened into boosterism, as the people eagerly embraced the image of their little city battling the "soulless corporation."

"The whole assemblage, representing almost the entire population of the town, seemed actuated by an entire unity of sentiment and the determined purpose to defend and maintain the natural advantages which had given their town the commercial supremacy upon Puget Sound," proclaimed the *Dispatch*.

At the historic gathering, the citizens voted to pledge the more than $700,000 worth of money and land (the original NP inducement package) to a new enterprise "to build a line of railroad via the Snoqualmie Pass to a point on the upper Columbia River opposite or above or below Wallula, with such branches as may be deemed advisable."

A line of Puget Sound steamboats was also included in the charter. Oddly enough, the initial charter of the Seattle & Walla Walla left out Walla Walla, an omission quickly remedied, and the following evening the town gathered again to "perfect the organization." A $10,000,000 capital stock issue was approved, of 10,000

shares at $100 each, and a board of trustees was elected: John Collins, James Colman, Arthur Denny, John J. McGilvra, Angus Mackintosh, James McNaught, Frank Matthias, and Henry Yesler. On July 24, articles of incorporation were filed in Olympia for the Seattle & Walla Walla Railroad and Transportation Company.[4]

It was left to local celebrity Seleucius Garfielde, pioneer coal miner, lawyer, ex-Northern Pacific public relations man, and two-time territorial congressional delegate, to light the fire of action under the citizenry. Garfielde was derided by some as "Seleucius the Babbler" and said to be on the take to the NP. At a town meeting on July 30, though, his oratory set Seattle pulses racing: Build over Snoqualmie Pass! Capture the riches of the Cascades! Steal eastern Washington's wheat out from under the Northern Pacific's nose! Make the railroad a narrow gauge, he emphasized; this would do the job for a fraction of the cost of a standard gauge line. For only about $700,000, Garfielde exhorted, Seattle would have its railroad.[5]

Things started falling into place. The mayor and council passed city ordinance #44 on August 18, granting the Seattle & Walla Walla all the tideflats south of King Street. In October, the territorial legislature approved the grant, subject to the S&WW completing fifteen miles of line within three years. Arthur Denny and his fellow trustees announced that the right of way would be surveyed before the year's end, and construction would commence in the coming spring. In April 1874, NP veterans Thomas Burnside Morris and James Tilton completed a fifteen-mile survey from Seattle to the mouth of the Cedar River. Their cost estimate was somewhat higher than Seleucius Garfielde's hopeful forecast: $14,000 per mile, or in excess of $4,000,000 to connect with Walla Walla by way of the Yakima Valley, slightly less via Priest Rapids. Still, it was expected that abundant Palouse wheat and other freight should enable the Seattle & Walla Walla to pay for itself in three or four years.[6]

Subscription books for the new enterprise were opened in Seattle and Walla Walla. Henry Yesler topped the list with a pledge to underwrite two miles of line. Coal mine

JAMES M. COLMAN, THE S&WW'S SAVIOR IN 1876.
Museum of History and Industry, #88

operator William Renton promised $1,000 cash and "10 Chinamen" for a month's labor. Arthur Denny unsuccessfully probed eastern connections for capital, then joined with his future banking partner, Dexter Horton, in putting up $1,000. Blacksmith C. McDonald offered $16.50 in services, and one J.F. Morrill ended the long list with $5 cash. Chin Gee Hee, a manager of the Wa Chong Company, the Northwest's pre-eminent Chinese labor jobber, threw his weight and the muscle of scores of workers behind the great Seattle enterprise.[7]

The morning of May 1, 1874, found Seattle strangely deserted. Virtually all of its 1,200 citizens were to be found three miles south of town, near a bend of the Duwamish River—Seattle had come to build a railroad. The immediate goal was to construct the right-of-way to the confluence of the Green and Black rivers nine miles south of town, called Mox-la-Push, or "two mouths," by the Duwamish Indians. From there, the line would strike eastward to serve William Renton's coal mine and follow the Cedar River to Snoqualmie Pass.

Roswell Scott, poetic secretary of the Seattle & Walla Walla, posted bills calling the populace forth:

Come all ye adults of mankind
Nor let there be none left behind.

One of the fliers was appended by a smart aleck:

Come each of you and bring your tools
and work away like God-damned fools
Don't beat the devil about the bush
But skoot the road to Mox-la-push.

The male citizens, "many of whom had never used any kind of a pick and shovel except a toothpick and fire shovel," gamely stripped to their shirtsleeves and started grubbing out a right of way while their ladies fried chicken and made cornbread. The little steamer *Comet* brought down a large contingent and an ample supply of stout refreshment, but, after getting hung up on a sandbar for several hours, much of her complement disembarked, "seriously disabled from their over-exertions in attempting to dispose of the commissary stores."[8]

But they all dug in: Dexter Horton, Henry Yesler, Arthur and David Denny, and chief justice Orange Jacobs side by side with C. McDonald and J.F. Morrill. "Never, perhaps, were before seen in any gang of railroad laborers so many soft hands, white shirts, and gold chains," chuckled the press. Noon dinner—ham, chicken, pickles, biscuits, pie, and coffee—was served in an old grist mill at the site of the present-day Lucile St. bridge, followed by an oration by Judge Orange Jacobs, an inveterate story-teller.

Henry Yesler whittled until he had heard his fill, then barked: "Quit your foolin' and get back to work!"

By the sweaty conclusion of the day, the first mile of the Seattle & Walla Walla was cleared, grubbed, graded, and ready for the ties. The toll was frightful, however: "Oh, the wailing for arnica, the lame backs and stiff limbs which followed. Business was practically at a standstill for a week afterwards, while all were recuperating from their unusual exertions."[9]

But something was born that day, something that twenty years later would later be immortalized as "Seattle Spirit."

Railroad building was daunting work for amateurs, however determined, and the second railroad picnic on May 15 saw noticeably fewer white shirts in attendance. Nevertheless, a determined group kept at it through the summer. Out of the thick Duwamish Valley underbrush, a roadbed steadily took shape, and, by the end of October, some twelve miles between the city and Renton had been graded. The bond subscription drive seemed to be going well, too.

Sadly, the Chinese help was not fully appreciated. "No Mongolians," argued the editor of the *Dispatch*, favoring white labor whose wages would be kept in the community and "not be hoarded away and finally shipped off to Hong Kong."[10] In August, Asian laborers, many of whom had been "loaned" to the railroad by white employers such as

William Renton, were run off the grade by whites. The sheriff stepped in to protect the Chinese, and work continued, but it was an unhappy portent.

Seattle's spike-driving enterprise put the city in the national spotlight and drew new settlers, while the press delighted in reporting that the stumps on Tacoma's pretentiously named Pacific Avenue still outnumbered the houses. Then there was the story of Andrew Keller, who decided he had had enough of waiting for big things to happen at Tacoma, set his house down on a log raft, and floated it—wife, children, chicken coop, and all—back to Seattle.[11] However militant she may have been, though, Seattle remained a small and isolated community, vulnerable to the vagaries of a roller coaster Victorian economy still becalmed by the panic of 1873.

During the chill, rainy winter of 1874-1875, Newcastle coal moved, but nothing much else did. Logging, construction, and all other trade were at a near-standstill, with hard cash and jobs scarce. May Day enthusiasm quickly faded, and Seattle & Walla Walla pledges went unremitted. Only a thousand or so of Seattle & Walla Walla's 100,000 shares had been sold, mostly in exchange for land, for which buyers were few. Laborers drifted away in search of better luck, and for rails, locomotives, and rolling stock, there was no money at all.

Early in 1875, Arthur Denny made the grueling journey to Washington, D.C., to ask Congress for a subsidy. In the growing anti-railroad climate, he was peremptorily refused, and at the Seattle & Walla Walla's eastern terminus, at Dayton and Waitsburg, and at Seattle, the most earnest entreaties of Denny and McGilvra could not coax coins out of the hard-pressed citizens. Then, too, many eastern Washington business leaders and editors spurned "Seattle's railroad," and pledged their allegiance to Dr. Dorsey S. Baker's Walla Walla & Columbia River Railroad.

The Seattle & Walla Walla did have an ally in Palouse farmers. Along the Snake River, sentiment was rising in favor of the Seattle road as a means to break the monopoly Ben Holladay's Oregon Steam Navigation Company enjoyed on the Columbia. Riverboat tariffs were high, padded by surcharges for portaging around the numerous rapids. Wheat growers held mass meetings to demand railroad rate regulation and local subsidies for the Seattle & Walla Walla, and succeeded in getting these items included in the planks of both the territorial Republican and Democratic parties that fall.

Fortunately for Seattle, San Francisco's appetite for coal was insatiable. In September 1874, the *Ant* was joined on the Seattle coal road by aptly named engine Number 2, the *Alki*, which replaced the horses on the Newcastle-Lake Washington segment. Elegant Baldwin 0-6-0 Number 3, the *Geo. C. Bode*, arrived in June of the following year and replaced *Ant* on the Seattle leg. The three little kettles were soon hauling over 100 tons of coal a day to the Pike Street bunker. Big-time shipping came to Seattle in March 1875, when the Goodall, Nelson & Perkins Steamship Company began the first regular steamer service between Elliott Bay and San Francisco with the sidewheelers *Dakota* and *City of Panama*. The Pacific Mail Steamship line entered the scene in September, offering every-ten-day service.

Things seemed to brighten steadily during 1875. The first Polk City Directory was published that year, and reason for optimism was readily apparent in its listings: 272 diverse business establishments including a cigar maker, several steam laundries, dentists, druggists, jewelers, numerous hotels and chop houses, a grist mill, candy and nut shops, boot and shoemakers, a brewery, tanneries, machine shops, furniture makers, sixteen wholesale houses, a sash and door factory, and two shipyards.

Seattle was taking on a "pretentious, city-like appearance," the *Dispatch* noted approvingly, and despite economic doldrums, the population—3,100 white men and women, some 250 Chinese, 50 to 100 Indians, and an average transient population of 300—managed to double that of the previous year. A visit in July by Central Pacific Railroad president Collis P. Huntington, and the signing of a contract for 6,000 tons of Newcastle coal per month for his locomotives, stirred expectations

THE SEATTLE & WALLA WALLA RAILROAD'S FIRST TIMETABLE, SUMMER 1877.

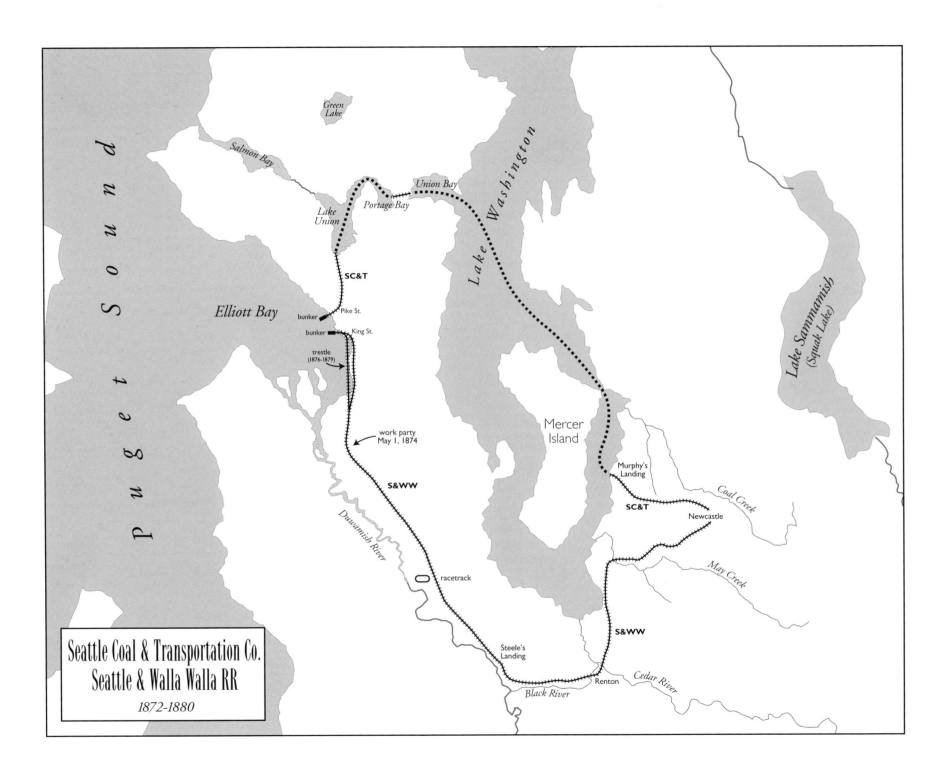

Green Lake

Salmon Bay

P u g e t   S o u n d

Union Bay

Portage Bay

Lake Union

Lake Washington

SC&T

Elliott Bay

bunker   Pike St.

bunker   King St.

trestle
(1876-1879)

Lake Sammamish
(Squak Lake)

work party
May 1, 1874

S&WW

Duwamish River

Mercer
Island

Murphy's
Landing

Coal Creek

SC&T

Newcastle

May Creek

racetrack

S&WW

Steele's
Landing

Renton

Cedar River

Black River

Seattle Coal & Transportation Co.
Seattle & Walla Walla RR
1872-1880

that "many heavy capitalists" were about to take the city in hand.[12]

They did not. The Seattle & Walla Walla languished, and its founders puzzled over what to do. They held Washington Territory's first grand lottery to raise money; Henry Yesler put up first prize—his sawmill, valued at $100,000—and a thousand tickets were sold before district court judge Joseph Lewis declared the lottery illegal.

Seattle Spirit was flagging, and the exasperated press conducted an all-out war on the "selfish greed and personal jealousy of many who became seized with the idea that the road would be built any way, and that they could hold onto their possessions and reap all the advantages of the enterprise and labor of others without making any sacrifices themselves."

It was no use looking to outside agencies for salvation: "Capital is sensitive and suspicious . . . The people of Seattle must themselves show their faith by their works before they can induce outsiders to invest." Large property owners, those who complained about high taxes, and those who stubbornly refused to buy Seattle & Walla Walla bonds were especially fair game: "Individual rights are sacred, but the rule which governs communities is the higher law of necessity. Where the common interests or the common defense is concerned, those who will not volunteer must be drafted . . . the property holder who refuses to bear his share of a project so manifestly for his own as well as for the public interests, lacks both public spirit and common honesty. He should be treated as a public enemy."

Still, nothing happened.[13]

In February 1876, the Seattle & Walla Walla trustees convened to ponder their situation. Smoke rings curled toward the ceiling. Amateur railroad building was going nowhere; a solid business footing was essential.

But how . . . and who?

Someone sighed, then spoke: "I'll take the elephant off your hands." To Seattle's eternal salvation, that someone was James M. Colman.

A native of Dunfermline, Scotland, Colman had come to Puget Sound in 1861. A highly talented mechanical engineer with a Clydebank-hardened head for business, he opened the Port Madison Mill, made it the dominant lumber producer on the Sound, then in 1872 leased Henry Yesler's old mill, long eclipsed by larger mills at Port Gamble and Blakeley. On behalf of the San Francisco firm of Preston & McKennon, he modernized Yesler's sawmill and brought it back to profitability.

To complete the first twenty-mile segment of the Seattle & Walla Walla and furnish it with rolling stock, Colman proposed a $125,000 issue of Seattle & Walla Walla mortgage bonds, with the railroad itself as collateral. He himself pledged $10,000 in cash, if others would follow suit for at least $60,000. Leading wholesaler Bailey Gatzert put up $3,000, and the Dennys, Angus Mackintosh, and others of the tiny Seattle Establishment raided their modest savings. It was not enough; by April, only $20,000 had been pledged. The Scotsman grimaced and dug deeper, staking a lordly $20,000. This did the trick. Next month, two years after the May Day work party, picks and shovels

The *A.A. Denny* after being rebuilt in Seattle from an 0-4-4 to an 0-6-4, in 1878.
University of Washington, Special Collections, #5476

month came locomotives: an 0-4-0 from San Francisco, leased to haul construction trains, and an elegant little twenty-one-ton 0-4-4T, a product of the William Mason Locomotive Works of Taunton, Massachusetts. This machine was shipped west in kit form, assembled at the Puget Foundry, and given a name all agreed was most appropriate: *A.A. Denny.*

The first Seattle & Walla Walla passenger trains began rattling over the trestle in December. These were weekend specials to the new racetrack on the Duwamish River, five miles south of town. Overseeing everything as superintendent, master mechanic, construction supervisor, locomotive engineer, even spike driver—"last man in bed at night, and the first one up in the morning"—was James Colman. By the end of February 1877, the Seattle & Walla Walla was complete and ready to run. On March 7, Colman cracked the throttle of the *A.A. Denny* and inaugurated full service between Seattle and Renton. Guests aboard the trim, home-built passenger coach and four unsoiled new coal cars were delighted by the smooth ride, and, after four merry hours, the excursion was back in Seattle.

Thereafter ("barring occasional interruptions from lazy cattle that lie down to sleep on the track"), strings of heavily laden coal jennies racketed ceaselessly over the Seattle tideflats. A new *Alki* arrived on the *Courser* in May 1977. A little 4-4-0, the *Alki* joined the *A.A. Denny*, and by summer, the rolling stock fleet numbered an impressive forty-five coal cars, twelve flat cars, three boxcars, three cattle cars, and a passenger coach, baggage car, and caboose. Even more impressive, most of this assemblage, including the wheels and frame castings, was built in Seattle. The Seattle & Walla Walla was a boon to local industry, particularly machining, and Foster's Boiler Shop, the Puget Foundry, and Stetson & Post all took fierce pride in outdoing each other in the quality and precision of their work.

Colman beamed like a proud papa over the gleaming little *A.A. Denny,* and boasted: "There is not a single piece of machinery about this engine that cannot be duplicated

were flying again. Colman was hailed as the man "doing more for the permanent prosperity of the town than any other who ever resided in it."[14]

A rejuvenated work force moved as if possessed. William H. "Joe" Surber's men threw a two-mile-long pile trestle across the lower Elliott Bay tideflats, Eaton and Webster erected bridges and piling for the six miles from the city limit to Steele's Landing (later Foster) on the east bank of the Duwamish River, and Henry Yesler saw to the regrading of the overgrown 1874 right of way. A new coal wharf, bunker, and shop building rose at the foot of King Street, and in September the square-rigger *Harvest Home* arrived with the first two miles of Seattle & Walla Walla rail in its hold. Chinese and white spike-drivers quickly laid track over the ten miles into Renton. Next here and done as well as anywhere."[15] Through the long, steamy summer, the air was brown with cedar smog and brash with the clanging of steam hammers, the rip of band saws, and the puffing of trains.

On June 11, the Seattle Coal Company's Pike Street bunker collapsed in a cloud of coal dust, victim of six years of munching pile worms. It was a fitting and timely end to an era in the city's history. Next day, the SC&T contracted with the Seattle & Walla Walla to provide all-rail service from Newcastle. The indispensable Colman coughed up $20,000 more, and in January 1878 finished the tortuous extension from Renton, complete with two dizzying matchstick trestles over May Creek. Engine Number 4, the *Georgina*, a new Baldwin 0-6-0, joined the S&WW roster that month, along with the locomotives of the pioneering Seattle Coal & Transportation Co. On February 5, trains began running between Newcastle and Seattle—a steady conveyor delivering 500 tons of coal to the King Street bunker each day. The Newcastle mine was the richest on the West Coast, and, by the end of the decade, Seattle the coast's busiest coal port. At a total cost of $350,000, the city's little railroad was a roaring success.[16]

But menaces lurked along the scenic S&WW route. It was a tricky piece of railroad replete with twenty-three trestles, innumerable blind curves, steep grades, slide-susceptible earthen cuts, and flood-prone flats. Running trains on this route called for brassbound Victorian grit, and eyes in the back of an engineman's head. Popular young engineer Daniel McMaston was crushed to death beneath the *Alki* in May 1878 while attempting to adjust a spring, and the *Georgina* and *Geo. C. Bode* crashed head-on near Black River in July, owing to "misapprehension" of a schedule change.

The *Geo. C. Bode* was patched up just in time to meet a stray rail placed on the track by miscreants. Such aimless vandalism was not uncommon during hard times, and no doubt added to the dry native humor which is the lot of railroad crews everywhere. More predictably, banks slid onto the tracks during the sodden winters, track was washed out by the frequently overflowing Black and Duwamish rivers, and derailments were frequent. General Manager Colman became accustomed to dragging himself out of bed, donning oilskins, and joining the cleanup crews.

Shifting the coal cars at the King Street wharf was perhaps the most dangerous work of all. Brakes and couplings were worked manually, and maimings, crushings, severings, even death were all too common. Getting out the coal and running the trains was bitter, unrelenting work, but it contributed to Seattle's prosperity with immediate and tangible results.

Other dark forces conspired against the Seattle enterprise. The *Intelligencer* accused Tacoma *Herald* editor Francis Cook of fomenting "anti-Seattle & Walla Walla" sentiment east of the mountains and holding rallies against the project.

"I have no faith in the S&WW railroad," declared one Yakima speaker: "No one outside of Seattle has any confidence in it. There is no substance, no money, no foundation to it. Its object is to enhance the value of Seattle property. We will be old and gray before we get that road . . . The Northern Pacific Company is the one in which our hopes now center, and to it we will give our support."[17]

More than any other factor, though, the major obstacle to the Seattle road's ultimate completion seemed to be Seattle itself. The city appears to have entirely expended its resources getting the Seattle & Walla Walla only as far as Newcastle, and that thanks more to J.M. Colman's largesse than anything else.

"A railroad across the Cascade mountains is actually the one condition accorded by fate, on which this town is permitted to exist and flourish as a town," reminded the *Intelligencer*, calling for a universal 20% tax on all city property to achieve the fateful objective.

Another suggestion was scrip, which "receivable at par from hand to hand here at home, through a sort of common consent and public *esprit du corps*, would effectually relieve the distress attendant on the present monetary stringency, and achieve the construction of the road at the same time."[18]

Esprit was slow to materialize, however, and editors once again zeroed in on "a portion of our property holders, controlled by a greed that devours its own substance [who] hope to share in the profit without contributing of the substance . . . The time has come when this niggardly spirit cannot, and ought not, to be tolerated in this community."

But times continued lean and public auctions of household effects were not an infrequent spectacle. Not just a niggardly spirit, but bickering and backbiting also cast an ugly pall over the community. Those of wealth or accomplishment were especially vulnerable. Colman, who had almost single-handedly given Seattle twenty miles of railroad, had stepped on sensitive toes in the process, and found himself "the object of more personal detraction and abuse, probably, than any other man in this town."

Hometown spite-mongering had nearly wrecked the Seattle Coal & Transportation Co., scolded the *Dispatch*, and the same danger awaited the Seattle & Walla Walla. "The practice of assailing the characters of our representative men prevails in this community to an extent greatly to be deprecated, and it has damaged our common interests to an extent beyond computation, in prejudicing strangers and capitalists against settlement or investment."[19]

Seattle & Walla Walla trustees John Leary, Bailey Gatzert, and Angus Mackintosh took matters in hand in June 1878 and proposed a new issue of $200,000 in King County and $50,000 in Yakima County mortgage bonds, to come due only upon completion of 100 miles of line between Renton and Thorp in the Kittitas Valley by October 1, 1880. The ink on the new subscription blanks was scarcely dry, though, when rumors spread that, in return for their labor, "Chinamen" would take over control of the line.

The *Dispatch* scorned the rumor as just another canard of Seattle's enemies and slapped down those who objected to hiring Chinese labor. "Well, who will be injured by that? If white men cannot or will not do it, it would be the most stupid folly to forego all the advantages to be derived from it rather than allow Chinamen to do it."

Backbiting and nay-saying aside, enough Seattleites wanted the railroad that they subscribed to almost $100,000 worth of bonds and, in August, crews began grading east from Renton up the Cedar River toward Snoqualmie Pass.

Newspapers kept up the pressure: "The community is scanning the list and sifting out the friends of the town from those who are only parasites upon it."

Seattle's pockets were only so deep, though, and by summer's end the bond drive fizzled out. After six miles had been cleared, work stopped.[20]

Nevertheless, the coal and the racetrack specials kept rolling. During the summer of 1878, the *A.A. Denny* went into the King Street shops for surgery. It had proven top-heavy and of insufficient power, so the four large drivers were exchanged for six smaller ones. The pride of the Seattle & Walla Walla emerged as an 0-6-4T. The new wheels were cast in the Puget Foundry along with a new set of enlarged cylinders, the first such castings made in the territory. These improvements gave the *Denny* more pull for the heavy coal trains. It returned to render the line stalwart service for the next nineteen years.

Joe Surber's trestle across the Elliott Bay tideflats was destined to serve a far shorter term. After only two years, teredos had so thoroughly gnawed at the long structure that Colman decided to abandon it and run the line along the beach at the foot of Beacon Hill. This stretch—a portion of which is still in use today—was completed in December 1879.

Though it fell far short of its eastern terminus, the Seattle & Walla Walla Railroad proved itself eminently useful as a vehicle of local growth and, to a greater or lesser extent, of local pride. Mining, logging, manufacturing, machining, and a multitude of service industries all benefited directly from the railroad. The tempo of settlement increased as a result.

Still, the Seattle & Walla Walla was a dead end road. ■

SEATTLE & WALLA WALLA-COLUMBIA & PUGET SOUND ENGINE ROSTER; NARROW GAUGE.

No.	Type	Builder	Dates/notes
1	0-4-4	Mason	1875—*A.A. Denny*. Built as Stockton & Ione No. 2, *Amador*. Returned to factory, sold to S&WW, 10/1876. Rebuilt to O-6-4T, 1878. Retired 11/1895, possibly used as stationary boiler in Seattle shops.
2	4-4-0	Porter Bell	1877—*Alki*. Retired 1897.
3 (1st)	2-6-2T	Baldwin	1874—*Geo. C. Bode*. Built as 0-6-0T for Seattle Coal & Trans. Co., to S&WW, 2/1878, rebuilt as 2-6-2T. Destroyed in Seattle fire, June 1889.
3 (2nd)	2-6-0	Brooks	1881—Ex-Union Pacific, former Utah & Northern, to C&PS, 11/1889. To White Pass & Yukon, 1897; on display in Whitehorse, YT, as WP&Y No. 52.
4 (1st)	0-6-0T	Baldwin	4/1875—*Georgina*. Built as SC&T No. 3, to S&WW, 2/1878, C&PS, 11/1880. Retired by 1890.
4 (2nd)	2-6-0	Brooks	1881—Ex-Union Pacific, former Utah & Northern, to C&PS, 1890. To WP&Y No. 2, 1897, renumbered 52, scrapped 1923.
5 (1st)	0-4-0T	Fulton	9/1871—*Ant*. Built as Seattle Coal Co. No. 1, to SC&T, to S&WW 1877, renumbered 5, 1878. To C&PS No. 5, 11/1880. To Ordway & Weidler, 5/1883, to Mosquito & Coal Creek, 10/1883, to Long-Bell Corp., 1923. Scrapped by mistake after being set aside for preservation, ca. 1940.
5 (2nd)	0-6-0	Baldwin	8/1875—Ex-Pacific Coast No. 1, to C&PS, 12/1883, rebuilt from 2-4-2T to 0-6-0. To Puget Sound Sawmill & Shingle, 7/1896.
6	2-6-0	Porter-Bell	2/1878—*Rainier*. Ex-Walla Walla & Columbia River No. 6, *J. W. Ladd*, to C&PS, 7/1881. Possibly sold to M. Earles, 1898.
7	0-4-0T	Porter-Bell	2/1872—*Hyak*. Ex-Walla Walla & Columbia River No. 1, *Walla Walla*. Off roster 12/1897.
8	2-8-0	Baldwin	5/1885—To WP&Y No. 5, 1897. Later Klondike Mines No. 2; on display in Dawson City, YT.
9	2-8-0	Grant	8/1882—Bought secondhand from Grant, built as Toledo Cincinnati & St. Louis No. 63. To WP&Y No. 3, 1897. Scrapped as No. 53, 1918.
10	4-4-0	Baldwin	3/1878—Ex-Olympia & Chehalis Valley No. 1, *E.N. Ouimette*. To C&PS 5/1891. To WP&Y No. 4, 1897, to Tanana Valley No. 50, 1907, to Alaska RR No. 50. Scrapped 1930.

An NP construction train in Washington, ca. 1884. Four pile-driving gangs of this type were at work during peak construction on the Seattle branch.

University of Washington, Special Collections, #11201

CHAPTER 6

THE VILLARD BOOM

"You have opened to us the doors of new life, and new liberty!"
—Dr. Thomas T. Minor

SEATTLE IN 1877 was a gangly adolescent, a child outgrowing his first toy train. It had its sawmills, its small machine shops, its furniture factory and barrel factory, and its little railroad to Newcastle. The Seattle & Walla Walla was fine as far as it went, which was twenty miles. The odds of it going farther were, most realized, slim at best, and wisdom prevailed that it would take somebody bigger than James Colman to make the city's dream of having a national connection a reality. Thus even before the Seattle & Walla Walla's festive inaugural run in March 1877, Seattle hopes were stirred by rumors that the pioneer transcontinental line, the Union Pacific, was on the verge of building a northwestern extension.

The notorious "robber baron" Jay Gould was the Union Pacific's chairman, and, early in 1877, Seattle was intrigued by reports that he was rebelling at the overlordship of Collis P. Huntington, the all-powerful leader of UP's transcontinental partner, the Central Pacific. Rumor had it that Gould was anxious to secure a western terminus of his own in the far Northwest, independent of the CP.

"Jay Gould is the controlling spirit of the Union Pacific road, and has had cause more than once to complain of the 'dog in the manger' policy of the Central Pacific magnates," noted the *Puget Sound Dispatch*.[1]

Gould was poised to defy Huntington and strike out for Puget Sound, enthused the press, and word spread that he was discussing a partnership with the rising star of Pacific Northwest transportation—Henry Villard.

The German-born Ferdinand Heinrich Gustav Hilgard came to America in 1853, adopted the name of a former schoolmate (which he pronounced "Viller"), and achieved modest success as a Civil War correspondent and later as an agent for German investors in American railroad securities. Berlin and Frankfurt banks had bought heavily into the Oregon railroad and steamboat interests of Ben Holladay, an expansive and colorful individual who had built up one of the West's largest stagecoach lines, and then began crafting a transportation empire in the Willamette Valley of western Oregon.

During the early 1870s, Holladay had parlayed the Germans' money into a network comprising the Oregon Steamboat Co., Willamette Valley Navigation Co., Oregon & California Railroad, and Oregon Central Railroad. This constituted the Northwest's reigning transportation monopoly, all tributary to the regional trading center, Portland. There, from his riverboat gothic mansion, Holladay (whom Mark Twain dubbed "King Hurry") held sway over railroads, steamers, newspapers, wharves, warehouses, judges, the state legislature—even, some said, Oregon senator John H. Mitchell. Trouble was, Holladay had taken the Germans' money and kept it.

Early in 1874, the German bankers approached Villard, on vacation in Heidelberg. He knew America, they implored; he knew the ways of such as Holladay. Would he go to Oregon and find out what had become of their investment? That April, Villard sailed west.

Henry Villard had been none too impressed with the smooth-talking but transparently fraudulent Holladay,

who was the very archetype of checker-vested, foghorn-voiced Wild West shysterdom. But Villard's eyes widened as he scanned the panorama from the Portland hills, and the figures turned over and multiplied in his mind as he watched sternwheelers paddle by heavily-laden with wheat from the Palouse country. Trade was growing fast.

On the Columbia River, the Oregon Steam Navigation Company, controlled by Portland businessmen, was swamped with business. Ben Holladay was, despite all his pretensions, almost broke; his reputation and credit were shot, and his railroads only unfinished stubs unable to pay their expenses. Villard absorbed it all, and with mounting excitement hurried home to convince the stolid Berlin bankers that they held in their hands the key to a great fortune. His powers of persuasion were considerable, and, by June 1879, Villard found himself at the head of the combined Holladay and Oregon Steam Navigation systems.

Henry Villard brought to the schemer-infested West a welcomed Teutonic uprightness. Grateful to be rid of the corrupt, rate-gouging Holladay, farmers and the Portland Establishment alike welcomed the newcomer with enthusiasm. They cheered as he promised to extend the Willamette Valley railroads, provide good service at fair rates, and not try to pocket the state legislature. Senator Mitchell and Portland Board of Trade president W.W. Chapman wasted little time in urging the new transportation king to marshal his Wall Street and Berlin connections and bring Portland a railroad from the East.

With a natural bent for "broad gauge" enterprise, Villard needed no convincing. That June, he merged the pieces of the old Holladay and the Oregon Steam Navigation companies into a new enterprise, the Oregon Railway & Navigation Company. By this time, Villard—a natural-born networker long before the term was conceived—was well-ingratiated with the Union Pacific's Jay Gould. With Mitchell and Chapman prodding him along, Villard offered the Wall Street legend half-interest in his new company and proposed that they split equally the costs of building between Salt Lake City and Portland. With eyes on an independent western terminus, Gould and Union Pacific president Sidney Dillon agreed, and promised a million dollars to get construction started.

Villard began laying track along the south bank of the Columbia that fall—then the Union Pacific backed out. Huntington had put his foot down. There would be no Union Pacific defection to Oregon, he informed Gould and Dillon. Should they persist in their errant expansionism, he would simply pull his traffic off the UP and route it over his new Southern Pacific line then advancing through Texas and Arizona. Gould and Dillon caved in, and Henry Villard was on his own. Not that he minded. His confidence growing by the day, Villard confided to his engineering assistant Hans Thielsen: "My preference was all along to proceed on an independent basis."[2]

Villard barely had time to compose himself after this turn of events, however, when he found himself cowcatcher-to-cowcatcher with a major threat—a revived

Northern Pacific. Through his 1875 reorganization program, President Frederick Billings had succeeded in bringing the moribund northern transcontinental back from death's door. Four years later, just as Villard was pulling things together along the Columbia, Billings secured financing from Drexel, Morgan & Co. and other Wall Street banks to push the main line west from Dakota Territory. In October, grading gangs began working eastward from Wallula Gap. In November, Henry Villard returned from a European vacation to find his new empire in mortal danger.

It was Billings' unalterable intention to lay rail across the Cascades to Tacoma. "On the Sound I believe commerce in time will do its chief work instead of on the Columbia River," Billings had told his board.

The Northern Pacific was charter-bound to complete its Cascade branch, and the directors were anxious to prove on their heavy investment in the Tacoma terminus. Agitation for land grant forfeiture remained strong, and the government railroad auditor had informed Billings that retention of much of the land grant in Washington Territory hung on the prompt construction of the Cascade Division.

For Villard's OR&N, this portended a devastating loss of traffic. "The mere threat [of the Cascade branch] would greatly affect the market value of . . . [the] companies' securities," Villard noted in his memoirs.

Billings also reserved the option of building the NP main line down the Columbia. In this event, Villard would be finished.[3]

There was little Villard could do against the Cascade branch, but he could keep Billings out of the Columbia Gorge. To ensure "absolute control of the Columbia Valley and approaches thereto," he quickly began fortifying his perimeter. Oregon Railway & Navigation Company vice-president Thomas Oakes was instructed to secure "all the obtainable land at all points where such ownership will enable us to throw difficulties in the way of the construction of another road."

The level ground at Wallula Gap, strategic gateway between the Columbia Gorge and the eastern Washington interior, was promptly occupied, and Villard threw further difficulty in Billings' way by backing the Mitchell bill forfeiting the Northern Pacific's Columbia River land grant.

Billings protested: "I do not complain that you seek to develop and strengthen your enterprise. But you have a large field for development in the roads you have planned. You will have plenty of business to do in your own field. Why, virtually, put a pistol to the breast of the Northern Pacific at Ainsworth or Wallula, and say thus far and no further?"[4]

The Northern Pacific savior had prevailed against the forfeiture fanatics, and was not about to be sandbagged by a schemer who would dead-end his railroad in the eastern Washington desert. In March 1880, he clenched his teeth and agreed to divide the "Inland Empire" with Villard. Northern Pacific would stay north of the Snake River, and the Oregon Railway & Navigation Co. south. Billings would forego building along the Columbia, and accept trackage rights over the OR&N. This meant renouncing the land grant along the river, but a saving of millions of dollars in construction costs. In October the agreement was signed. Billings and Villard each believed he had outfoxed the other.

Billings remained wary and went after money to complete the main line east of Wallula. The land grant was intact, he explained to Wall Street bankers; its traffic was picking up, public confidence in the company was growing, and the Northern Pacific was regaining its stature on the Stock Exchange. President Rutherford Hayes, General William T. Sherman, and other important persons wired Billings their congratulations for saving the great national enterprise. Suitably impressed, the houses of Drexel, Morgan & Co., Winslow, Lanier & Co., and August Belmont & Co. floated a new $40,000,000 mortgage bond issue in December 1880. Frederick Billings' portrait was printed on the certificates.

But where Billings moved, Villard walked in his shadow. Certain that, traffic agreement or no, Billings

BEN HOLLADAY.
Oregon Historical Society, #049501

would in time "resort to aggressive construction against us" along the Columbia, Villard ingratiated himself with the NP's bankers, and proceeded to draw their allegiance away from Billings. Surely, Morgan and company must know what risks Billings was about to take with their investment, Villard lectured: The Cascade branch would ruin them! There was no business there—Billings and Wright wanted it only to boom their company town, Tacoma![5]

Billings got wind of what was going on. "Villard has said that matters could be arranged all satisfactorily if we agree not to build over the Cascade Range," he complained to General Sprague. "I tell him frankly that it is our business to go to tidewater on the Pacific coast, and it seems to me—especially as he is now building down the river—that the Company should go over the Cascade Range . . . It is mortifying to find that this great company is to be subordinate to the OR&N."[6]

Sprague in turn complained to Billings that Villard was overstating his earnings and watering his stock, a view many on and off Wall Street would come to share. But the wizard was not to be denied. That fall, Villard began buying NP stock, a bloc large enough to enable him to dictate that there would be no construction west of Wallula Gap until the mainline from the East was finished.

Thus far, it had not been Villard's ambition to take over the Northern Pacific. He wished only to effect a truce under which his OR&N could prosper. He also wanted two seats on the NP board of directors. This, Billings refused. Stung by the rebuff, Villard realized that complete control was his only real option, and in February 1881 launched his bold main thrust against the Northern Pacific.

He spent twenty million buying up more stock, bubbling to William Endicott, Jr.: "I feel more confident than ever, now, of our ability to swallow the Northern Pacific, however large a bite to digest it may seem . . . I am still absolutely convinced that I have never done a more prudent thing than to embark in this bold venture, and that it will result more profitably and gloriously than anything I have yet undertaken."

When the money was gone, Villard turned to that favorite Wall Street device, the syndicate, to raise more. Fifty-five friends and acquaintances were invited to buy into a venture, the purpose of which would remain a secret for the short term.

"The very novelty and mystery of the proposition proved to be an irresistible attraction," Villard gloated, and on the 11th, excited investors mobbed his Mills Building offices begging for shares.[7]

Before the end of his list of names was reached, the syndicate—which the press promptly dubbed the "Blind Pool"—had amassed $16,000,000. Villard himself put up $900,000, and car builder George M. Pullman, eager for his business, half a million. By the end of the month, Henry Villard held 60% of NP's outstanding common stock.

Billings did his best to freeze the raider out, barring the door to his boardroom and throwing a large bloc of reserve stock into the hands of those friendly to his management. Villard accused Billings of fraud, and offered to buy him out for nine million. Billings loved the Northern Pacific; it was the culmination of his life's work, and he fervently wished to see it through to Puget Sound. Nevertheless, the ceaseless struggles with Villard, his bankers, and Congress had worn him out. Enough was enough; the ever-useful J.C. Ainsworth brokered a face-saving deal, and in May, Billings surrendered.[8] Though he remained on the board of directors, the man many considered the savior of the Northern Pacific took the money and a well-earned vacation. At the annual stockholders' meeting in St. Paul on September 15, Henry Villard took the president's seat. He promised that he would have the railroad completed between St. Paul and Tacoma in two years.

The rise of Henry Villard electrified Seattle. Well it should have—he was already well-entrenched there. In anticipation of a Northern Pacific terminus, Philo Remington, founder and owner of the Remington Arms Company, had (with partner and NP original interest holder William S. King) bought land in Seattle in 1870.

The terminus went south, and six years later, Remington sold the property to his son in law, Watson Carvoso Squire, a Remington executive who was smitten with the West and who had no intention of spending the rest of his days in Ilion, New York. Landing at Elliott Bay in 1879, Squire liked what he saw and set up law practice in Seattle. Squire joined the Seattle & Walla Walla board of trustees, and journeyed to Wall Street in hopes of floating a bond issue to extend the coal road over the Cascades.

At this he failed, but he did pick up something even more valuable: The acquaintance of Henry Villard. Squire at once pitched the Seattle & Walla Walla bonds to Villard, who expressed his interest, not merely in buying bonds but the whole operation. He told Squire he had given the matter some thought, and dispatched OR&N superintendent Brandt to go to Seattle and have a look at the property.

An excited Squire wrote Arthur Denny: "His well-known financial ability and enterprise leave no doubt that the sale of the road to him will greatly benefit at once the minority stock remaining in the hands of others, but also your town generally."

With Villard at the helm, Squire concluded, Seattle's long-awaited rail link with the nation was all but assured. Brandt's verdict on the coal road soon came in positive, and Villard heard more glowing accounts of the region from his local agent William Belvin, himself a Seattle resident. Another verdict, however, came to Villard from his friend Joseph Norton Dolph, an influential Portland lawyer who would go on to become a United States senator. Dolph, Villard informed Squire, had been less than impressed by the Seattle & Walla Walla, and felt the company was in a "dreadfully complicated condition." Villard had no alternative but to go see for himself, so at the beginning of April, he set out for Puget Sound.[9]

A week later, Henry Villard was enjoying the view of Mt. Baker from a steamer deck, in company with Squire, Boston banker William Endicott, Jr., retail giant Marshall Field, and George M. Pullman. The salt air was invigorating and Villard was in an expansive mood. Dolph's

gloomy assessment to the contrary, Squire ventured, Seattle's coal mine and railroad were doing a handsome business; after all, they enjoyed a virtual monopoly. Villard nodded; the prospect was tempting, but a large capital infusion would be required to improve and expand the operation in accordance with Villard's already well-known "broad gauge" proclivities. This called for more data, so he sent his geologist cousin, Eugene Woldemar Hilgard, and civil engineer Thomas R. Tannatt into the Cascade foothills.

Their reports were favorable: Newcastle coal was of high quality, more plentiful and more easily mined than that at Wilkeson, and the Seattle & Walla Walla Railroad was earning a tidy profit. More ominously, the citizens of Seattle continued to entertain ambitions of running that railroad into eastern Washington, and San Francisco coal baron C.B. Shattuck was considering buying the property himself.[10] Most alarmingly of all, the Northern Pacific was rumored to be eyeing the Cedar River lignite beds. This would never do.

Villard passed the summer in deliberation with Squire, Tannatt, Arthur Denny, and his bankers, and by October he was ready to move.

"For reasons of policy in connection with N. P. and in order to get in position to control coal trade of eastern Washington territory," Villard wired Thomas Oakes, "I have decided to purchase Seattle road."

All summer, rumors of the Villard negotiations titillated Seattle, and hopes were high.

"The Oregon Railway and Navigation Company has been an undoubted benefactor wherever it has operated," enthused the Seattle *Intelligencer* when the deal was done, "and is gratefully looked upon by all the people whose interests are affected by it. In having it identified with them, the citizens and property owners of Seattle and King county are to be congratulated."[11]

By this time, Villard was thinking big indeed. On October 21, he formed a corporation to harvest the natural resources of his fast-expanding fiefdom—the Oregon Improvement Company. Empowered to build and operate railroads, steamboats, ferries, warehouses, wharves, locks, mines, and flumes from Alaska to California, Oregon Improvement was dedicated to reaping the Northwest's bounty—and keeping out rivals.

Oregon Improvement immediately tendered $350,000 for the purchase of the Seattle & Walla Walla. Villard assured the line's directors, those same Seattle elders who still had their hearts set on rails over Snoqualmie Pass, that in excess of $5,000,000 was at hand to complete their railroad to eastern Washington. Not only that, there would be a web of Cascade branch lines, and a connection with the Northern Pacific. Through trains would come to Seattle from Portland, California, and points east, perhaps even bypassing Tacoma. Seattle would be a terminus!

Villard followed up with an offer of $400,000 to the Seattle Coal & Transportation Co., owned since the late-1870s by Philo Remington and Frank Osgood, for its Newcastle mine, sailing colliers, and all other properties. On November 26, the Seattle trustees—James M. Colman, Arthur Denny, Bailey Gatzert, and Angus Mackintosh—journeyed to Olympia and conveyed the coal company and the Seattle & Walla Walla to the Oregon Improvement Company. A new railroad company was created to carry on the work of the Seattle & Walla Walla, and given a name well-calculated to appease Seattle's railroad aspirations: the Columbia & Puget Sound.

At long last, Seattle's dream of salvation by eastern capital had come true. "Seattle's Future Assured!" trumpeted the press.

The Oregon Improvement Company lost little time in fortifying its Seattle beachhead. All through early 1881, the reassuring sounds of hammer, saw, and pile driver clattered over the tideflats, as an enlarged, bi-level coal bunker, six-stall engine house, and two-story depot rose on King Street, along with a big new wharf at the foot of Main. To promote development along the city's extensive inland waterways, Villard engaged noted civil engineer Henry Gorringe to make preliminary surveys for a ship canal between Lake Washington and Puget Sound, a thing dreamed of since the city's infancy.[12]

Henry Villard's Puget Sound dealings had thus far been conducted largely behind the scenes. In October 1881, Seattle, Tacoma, and Olympia met him face-to-face. What they saw was a tall man of reassuring bulk and dignified carriage. A slight Germanic accent may have startled some, but the shock soon dissipated. If anything, the inflection was professorial, and the demeanor both sober and supremely self-confident.

Tacoma was the first stop, and the capitalist anticipated a cool reception. The terminal city had not been pleased to see its old friends Billings and Wright sidetracked by this upstart Seattle bedfellow. Randolph Radebaugh's *Ledger* had been downright hostile, and General Sprague and many others wary at best. Would Villard move the terminus? It was standing room only at Alpha Hall on October 4, and Villard quickly got down to business.

HENRY VILLARD (HOLDING HAT) POSES WITH A GROUP OF ASSOCIATES AND AIDES. ON HIS IMMEDIATE LEFT SITS T.F. OAKES.

Author's collection

Brandishing a sheaf of critical press clippings, he declared: "Efforts have been made in this town to abuse, slander, and vilify me to an extent that pained and surprised me . . . neither the slander nor the abuse that has formerly been heaped upon me here have affected me any more than the wind which blows across your bay; neither will the compliments that have been bestowed upon me on this occasion influence me in the least in doing my duties as president of the Northern Pacific Railroad Company. That duty, I consider to a great extent identical with the interests of your town."[13]

Henry Villard had come a long way. As a young journalist he had won the confidence of Abraham Lincoln, had smoothed the ruffled feathers of General William Tecumseh Sherman, had scooped rival reporters on the Battle of Fredericksburg, and had gone on to finesse the likes of Ben Holladay and the German financial establishment. He had come to America with neither money nor English language. Now, he had both; he would deal with Tacoma as he had with all the others. A pleased murmur rustled through the audience as Villard wove his spell.

Tacoma's future, he continued, lay in Palouse wheat: "It is claimed that it is far less expensive to bring sea-going vessels to Tacoma than to Portland. If that is a fact . . . the Oregon Improvement Company shall build a large warehouse here, to make a beginning towards making Tacoma a shipping point."

The departure of the first grain ship from Tacoma the day before lent further weight to Villard's prognostications.

As for that chronic Puget Sound hunger—large capital—the canny financier raised pulses: "There must be a money power here to control the movement of wheat from interior points. It may be that the Improvement Company will afford it."

And no, he would not take the terminus away. Silk hats nodded, and the saloons of Pacific Avenue were jolly that night.[14]

Seattle greeted its new benefactor with a rousing cheer as he promised "within twelve months of today, an unbroken railroad from St. Paul to Tacoma and Seattle. We expect to put in an extension of the Washington Territory branch from some point south of Tacoma to Seattle."

Puget Sound clearly bested Portland as a shipping point—"that I do not dispute." But as cheap rail transport was the best thing he could offer the Sound, he explained, it would come most easily and cheaply, at $5 a ton, via the water-level Columbia River route through Portland. Puget Sound communities that would be part of this bold new vision must naturally do their part in providing the proper facilities. In Seattle, Villard declared, this meant a grain warehouse and a railroad right of way to his recently acquired properties at both ends of the downtown waterfront. These, Seattle would be only too pleased to provide, and Villard wrapped up his speech praising the energy and thrift of the city and the good prospects they boded for his "large landed interests" there. He capped his visit with a $2,000 endowment to the territorial university. As night fell on Elliott Bay, Arthur Denny and his neighbors retired, too excited to sleep.[15]

A hushed legislature attended the great man in Olympia on October 8. The New Northwest, Villard declared, was the greatest, best-endowed country on earth, and he always made it a point to promote the territory when meeting with his European financial friends. Great, untapped capital was eyeing the region, making plans—plans that promised untold prosperity.

True, his enterprise was a monopoly. But it was a "benevolent" one. He was doing all he could, and more than anyone else, Villard declared, to advance the welfare of the region. Seattle, Tacoma, Olympia, Portland—all would get good railroad service, at equal rates. Such benevolence, he noted pointedly, would of course render superfluous any restrictive railroad legislation. The lawmakers agreed. As if in anticipation of his visit, they had only the day before expunged an 1875 rate statute from the books.[16]

A new era had dawned in Washington. Only one small cloud hung over these otherwise festive proceedings: Villard stopped short of promising immediate construction of the Cascade branch.

A roundabout "main line" through Portland was hardly the stuff of Puget Sound dreams, but Villard made it plain the mountain line would have to wait: "My personality has been identified very largely in the public mind here with the question of the construction of the Cascade branch. You may remember that upon my first appearance in the board of directors of the Northern Pacific, I telegraphed out here that the Cascade branch should be built under any and all circumstances. I intend to keep that promise. But I am not able to tell you at this moment when it will be built, nor am I able to tell you now from which direction it will be built . . . surveying parties are in the field, but have not reported final results."[17]

Under Villard's predecessors, all the likely (and unlikely) passes had been extensively surveyed and resurveyed. Early in 1880, Watson Squire had urged Frederick Billings to hasten the Cascade branch, and build it over Snoqualmie Pass. Billings was inclined to go along. Snoqualmie did indeed look like the easiest route, he wrote John Ainsworth, and if this was confirmed by W. Milnor Roberts (in the field at that very moment) then the NP should go there, "no matter how it affects Tacoma."

Roberts confirmed Snoqualmie's advantages, but Billings nonetheless sent engineers Isaac Smith and Virgil Bogue back into the hills early the following year to study the alternatives. A promising pass was located at the head of the Green River, in the next watershed south of Snoqualmie Pass and of scarcely greater elevation. Then Villard intervened.[18]

Seattle and Tacoma sat in silence as he lectured: "Considering the scantiness of the population, considering the slow development, so far, of the country between here and Walla Walla, we could not carry wheat over the Cascade range at anything like the rate we carry it down the Columbia River today . . . I do not believe that the country between here and Walla Walla can possibly be developed, even under the stimulus of railroad construction within the next five or eight years, to make this road a paying one. The Cascade branch will be an enormously difficult and expensive line. It cannot possibly be built in one sea-

son, and unless you wish your present comparative isolation to continue for a long period, you must gladly accept this connection with Portland we are ready to offer you, and that I hope will be effected next year."[19]

With an 1880 population in excess of 20,000, versus Seattle's 3,500 and New Tacoma's 1,250, Portland remained the Northwest's leading city. The natural handicaps debated since the days of Jefferson Davis and Thomas Canfield continued to bedevil the city, however, most notably the treacherous sandbar across the mouth of the Columbia. "Hogbacks" and rocks lurked in the channel between Astoria and Portland, and ships' masters saved their saltiest epithets for the Columbia, its larcenous pilot and tug charges, dockage fees that ran as much as ten times those on the Sound, and the long waits for clearance over the ten-to-twenty-foot shallows at the bar.

Portland paid heed. "Just as certain as fate," prophesied the *Oregonian*, "Tacoma or Seattle will become the shipping point of the Northwest, if the Columbia bar is not improved and the channel not deepened."[20]

Then, too, there was Puget Sound's sudden emergence as a coal mining and shipping center for the Oregon Improvement Company, an irony that could not have escaped the Oregonians—a name of "Washington Improvement Company" would certainly have been more to the point. Cursing the "mossbacks" in her midst, Portland began rousing herself from complacency.

Villard and his lieutenant, Thomas Oakes, had themselves become increasingly vexed at the lack of enthusiasm toward their efforts in the first city of the Northwest.

"There has been a lamentable lack of enterprise here," Oakes complained to his boss. "A large number of persons have made a great deal of money and live in fine houses but they have shown so little public spirit, it is not difficult to guess their money has been made almost exclusively in trade without competition."[21]

Villard agreed, and when he came to town, he spoke bluntly. Portland would soon be the focal point of 2,000 miles of railroad, and would always remain the commercial center of the Northwest. But she must "take possession of the grain trade of Puget Sound," dredge the Columbia, and get to work! The city must not succumb to narrow jealousy of Seattle or Tacoma, Villard admonished; all would share equally in the coming prosperity. Henry Villard offered a radical new vision of multiple centers united by steel into a harmonious whole, a regionalism grown beyond old local aspirations.

"Our great object," he declared, "must be . . . to open as many channels of transportation as we can create, and to let commerce flow through them as freely as possible." [22]

Villard was ahead of his time, and only the passing of decades would soften the rivalries between Portland and Puget Sound, and Seattle and Tacoma.

On June 24, Henry Villard convened the Blind Pool at his office and revealed that their money had purchased not only the controlling interest in the Northern Pacific, but proportionate shares in a new "financiering company," one that would dwarf all his previous works and unite the interests of the Northern Pacific and Oregon Railway & Navigation Co.—the Oregon & Transcontinental Company.

Among the first of a new breed of American holding companies, Oregon & Transcontinental was even more far-reaching than Oregon Improvement in its mission to dominate the transportation picture on the West Coast. The holding company would retain controlling stock ownership in, and provide financing for, both the NP and OR&N. And, as the Northern Pacific had no charter franchise to do so, it would build branches to feed the main line.

Oregon & Transcontinental quickly filed articles of incorporation for a multitude of branch lines in Minnesota, Dakota, Montana, Oregon, and Washington, enveloping the entire northern tier and slamming the iron door against all would-be intruders. In Washington, these included a line from Wallula Gap to Puget Sound over "Snoqualmie or other available pass," a branch from Renton into the Cedar River coal beds, and rail running from Portland to Seattle and the Canadian border. Through the device of sinking funds, these branch rail-

roads were to be built and owned by the Transcontinental Company, then turned over to the Northern Pacific once their bonded debts had been retired.

The Portland *Oregonian* hailed Oregon & Transcontinental as "the most stupendous scheme yet undertaken on the American continent," and looked forward eagerly to "The enormous development of the country which . . . will produce changes of a most wonderful kind." [23]

In November, the Pacific Coast Steamship Company, biggest on the West Coast, was brought under Oregon Improvement Co. control. The man who had come to the United States as a penniless immigrant now stood at the head of the nation's greatest transportation network.

In January 1882, Villard put into motion his promise to put Seattle on the main line. Northern Pacific's western counsel, Seattle attorney James McNaught, opened negotiations with the city council and landowners for right of way through the city. Mass meetings were convened to ascertain the sense of the community in deeding over waterfront and tidelands. What emerged was a resolution dedicating a double-track, standard gauge right of way, to be used by any and all lines into the city, for the purpose of distributing freight to the wharves and businesses along the waterfront: "Appreciating fully the great benefits already conferred upon us by the roads of Mr. Villard, we are willing and anxious to afford to him and his companies all necessary facilities for the purposes of aiding shipments at our city front." The council wired Villard, inquiring what agency would operate their new railroad.

He replied on February 22: "It being doubtful whether the Northern Pacific Railroad Company can build the line under the terms of its charter . . . we propose to connect your town with Tacoma by a standard gauge line to be owned by the Transcontinental Company, but operated by the Northern Pacific."

On March 14, city ordinance 259 was signed into law, giving the Oregon & Transcontinental and the Oregon Improvement companies a mile-long, thirty-foot-wide right of way from King Street to Clay Street, on the north waterfront. The council required that the right of way be held in trust for joint use by any other line that might come to Seattle, and that O&T "construct and operate a standard gauge railroad from Seattle to a point on the North Pacific [sic] Railroad Company's constructed line, so as to connect the City of Seattle with Eastern Washington, either by way of Portland . . . or the Cascade mountains within two (2) years, and on failure to do so this right herein granted shall be void."[24]

South of Tacoma at Lakeview, a mountain of stockpiled new steel rails rose, gratifying evidence that Villard meant business. "Tacoma will be effectively sidetracked, and will only be known as a way station and as the great terminus of a small coal road," chortled the Seattle *Chronicle*.

Certain Seattle waterfront property owners, though, were proving difficult. "There has developed a degree of opposition to our companies . . . that was unexpected and, we think, without reason," complained Oregon Improvement's general manager, San Francisco attorney John L. Howard. "The people here are perhaps not aware of the fact that the present, and to a great degree future, welfare of Seattle depends upon the action of the Northern Pacific. Mr. Villard, by concentrating his efforts at another point on the Sound, could crush for a long time the aspirations of this place."

The property owners wanted the railroad, to be sure, but were of contrary opinion as to where it should run. Some wanted the track in front of their places of business, others wanted it in back. In the end, Howard and McNaught were compelled to thread their right of way through the parcels, pillar-to-post, along the meander line of Elliott Bay. This twisting path of compromise would later become notorious as the "ram's horn."[25]

Meanwhile, Tacoma seethed. Seattle would be the end of the line, and what was the end of the line, but the terminus?

"Seattle, it appears, is to have a broad-gauge railroad branch," sniffed the *Ledger*, "and great excitement in consequence of the expectation is reported from that town including unusual activity of spirits and prosperity to the gin mills . . . It is not a little astounding that the denizens of Yeslerville should, instead of promptly seizing their grip-sacks and hieing with speed to the site of the future great city, continue in fancied security and idleness to nurse the fond hope for the supremacy of Yeslerville."[26]

Brave words hid growing worries. Editor Randolph Radebaugh had never trusted Villard—the man was a windbag and a stock-waterer to boot! Radebaugh had warned everybody, and the *Ledger* had never relaxed its guard. Now Tacoma would catch it!

Seattle only laughed. "It is almost painfully amusing to observe the efforts made by our contemporaries of Tacoma to suppress the connection of the Northern Pacific Co. with the railroad now building into Seattle," snickered the *Post-Intelligencer*. "As the rose smells the same no matter what you call it, so it will be with the thirty mile section of railroad now building in this country. It will be Northern Pacific to all intents and purposes, and will make this city the extreme Northwest terminal city of the vast railroad system of the United States."[27]

But not everyone in Seattle had been mesmerized by "Prince Henry." As the winter of 1882 passed without visible sign of survey or construction, grumblings began to be heard in the barrooms of Commercial Street: Villard was gobbling up the country; he would skim off the coal and go back to New York; he would have his way with Seattle and cruelly cast her aside—he would NEVER build the Cascade branch! "Benevolent monopoly" was still monopoly! Villard had promised $5,000,000 to finish the Seattle & Walla Walla. Well, how about it?

"We have been promised a road over the Cascades," complained the *Chronicle*, "and so far as we are aware, we are expected to live and grow wealthy on promises."[28]

At the beginning of April, Seattle's impatient railroad men took action. H.B. Bagley, Judge Thomas Burke, George Harris, John Leary, Judge J.R. Lewis, William Renton, Mayor Henry Struve, and Henry Yesler incorporated the Seattle Walla Walla & Baker City Railroad, to cross Snoqualmie Pass and meet the Union Pacific in central Oregon. Yesler was named president of this Seattle & Walla Walla reincarnation. That time-honored Seattle device, the subscription book, was opened and the citizens signed up for $150,000 in bonds. Establishment leaders advanced $4,000 cash to survey a line along the east shore of Lake Washington and up the Cedar River to the summit of the pass, where several of their number, notably Arthur Denny, owned iron mines.

The prospects of the Seattle Walla Walla & Baker City brightened considerably when Bagley, Leary, and Yesler made a gentlemen's agreement with San Francisco coal barons Pierre B. Cornwall and Darius Ogden Mills to run the railroad to their new mines at Black Diamond, forty miles southeast of Seattle. The Seattle company would build the roadbed, and the San Franciscans would equip it with narrow gauge rails and rolling stock; requisite noises were made about extending the line over Snoqualmie Pass to eastern Washington. Again, the subscription books were turned open, this time netting a $100,000 in pledges.

Timid souls feared the consequences of antagonizing Henry Villard. Judge Thomas Burke, the most aggressive of Seattle's railroad activists, was not among them.

"Those who are taking an active interest in the new enterprise are in no sense unfriendly to the Villard companies," Burke explained. "But is this any reason why we should fold our arms and wait for Mr. Villard to do everything for us? We think not . . . No one will question the great importance to the territory of a railroad through the Cascade Mountains . . . By showing a sturdy, manly disposition to take hold of the matter and help themselves, instead of offending Mr. Villard, the people will cause him to respect them all the more."[29]

Mr. Villard did not quite see it that way, and when Arthur Denny wrote him asking that he begin to put his promises into motion, as the people were becoming restive, he scribbled on the back of Denny's letter: "Simply nothing in all this. It would be suicidal for the Seattle people to build a foot of railroad in opposition to our interests. No."[30]

Villard went back to busying himself with the myriad details of railroad building, high finance, and picking out artwork for the sumptuous new townhouse he was erecting on New York's Madison Avenue.

Seattle complaints persisted, though, and an exasperated Villard had his friend John Leary lay down the law. Seattle must understand, Leary declared, that Villard was carrying out as rapidly as possible all he had promised the people. The city did not seem to realize the magnitude of these undertakings, or the vast sums of money expended in Oregon and Washington within the past three years— over $31,000,000!

Puget Sound owed its present prosperity to that vast expenditure, the Seattle lawyer continued, and by September 1, the Northern Pacific would be in Seattle. What more could one ask? Leary then exposed the Cornwall-Mills deal as a sham: They had for some time been secretly treating with the Oregon Improvement Company to haul their coal, and had no intention of building any new railroad with Seattle. Cornwall was, in Leary's opinion, an "unprincipled scoundrel" who had taken the city for a ride. Villard had spoken. Seattle's home-grown railroad dream retreated back into hibernation.[31]

In any case, the real work had already begun. Northern Pacific chief engineer R.M. Armstrong and his men were busily surveying the White River Valley during the summer of 1882, as McNaught secured easements from farmers. On August 19, articles of incorporation were filed at Olympia for a railroad between Seattle and the Green River, to connect there with the Northern Pacific. Henry Villard was chairman of this new Oregon & Transcontinental branch, and fellow directors included Armstrong, Senator Joseph Norton Dolph of Oregon (a staunch Villard ally), Seattle wholesaler Bailey Gatzert, and Oregon Railway & Navigation Co. general manager Charles H. Prescott. Though all but the northernmost two miles of the new line would run well inland, it was named the Puget Sound Shore Railroad.

During its 1870 surveys, the Northern Pacific had run a line from Lakeview to Seattle, in easy curves and long tangents up the Puyallup and White River valleys. Fourteen years later, though, and despite both Villard's earlier announcements and the stockpiled rail, there would be no Tacoma bypass. Instead, Armstrong laid out the Seattle branch in two segments: A Northern Pacific spur off the Wilkeson coal line just east of Puyallup, which would run seven miles north up the White River Valley; and the Puget Sound Shore Railroad, running the remaining twenty-three miles into Seattle. The two companies would meet at the Stuck River about two miles south of present-day Auburn.

Though he had given lip service to the Wilkeson coal branch being part of the future Cascade Division, by 1882 Villard had decided that the cross-Cascades line should strike eastward from a point in the White River Valley, the better to access the Green River and Cedar River coal fields as well as either Snoqualmie or Green River passes, the most likely Cascade crossings. Until such time as it could be incorporated into the Cascade Division, the seven-mile Northern Pacific spur from Puyallup to the meeting point at Stuck Junction would be built and operated without charter—a railroad orphan. A Lushootseed Indian word, "Stuck" is interpreted variously as "small stream," "plowed through," or "log jam." Before long, "Stuck" would take on new meaning.[32]

By mid-October, the right of way between Puyallup and the Black River was surveyed and ready for grading. On November 1, the Northern Pacific awarded the contract for construction of the Seattle extension from Puyallup to the Black River to the Joseph F. Nounan Company of San Francisco, and partner J.R. Myers of Portland. Thomas Alvord was engaged to move material to the railroad "front" by scow and river steamer up the Duwamish.

By the 25th, Nounan's force of fifty whites and over two hundred Chinese was hard at work: "The white men clear the way, and the Chinamen do the grading . . . We expect to have our contract completed on or before the first of June, next. High water is the only thing that will prevent."

White laborers got $2 a day, "Chinamen," $1. Native Americans were also put to work: "They are good choppers and care nothing for the mud." Nounan confidently expected the line to be finished by June 1, 1883.[33]

As things turned out, however, high water prevented this. As happened every winter, the White and Stuck riv-

ers overflowed, putting large areas of the valley under water. The ground was permanently marshy in many places, and, as surveyor Birnie had revealed ten years earlier, extensive piling was necessary to anchor the roadbed along much of its length. Progress was slow and slogging, but by the end of March the first sections of fifty-six-pound rail were spiked down.

The press gazed in wonder at the transformation being wrought. "In three years' time Mr. Villard has revolutionized the trade and agriculture of the northwestern portion of the United States," observed the *Post-Intelligencer*. "The people of this region can move freely in every direction, in winter and in summer; can market their crops when they please; and can get to market as cheaply as their brothers in Ohio."

Railroad grubbers dug drainage ditches in the White River Valley, opening thousands of acres of prime bottom land to cultivation. Land values rose, as did the market value of valley livestock, hay, lettuce, and potatoes. Puyallup Valley pioneer Ezra Meeker had enjoyed great success with his hop fields, and, with the coming of rail transport, western Washington hops took command of the world market. Another 200 men were at work along on the Columbia & Puget Sound's Cedar River extension east of Renton, and traffic on the NP's Pacific Division between Kalama and Tacoma was booming. Each day, another one or two hundred settlers arrived on Puget Sound.

"People and capital will pour in upon our western slope without limit," exulted the Olympia *Transcript*, "and the whole condition of our wild and unsettled state will change to one of busy thrift and prosperity."[34]

In April 1883, Henry Villard stepped aboard a special train in Chicago for his annual spring tour of the West. He made a record-breaking run to San Francisco, then turned north, anxious to view the progress on the rapidly advancing Northern Pacific main line. By any standard, it was a marvel. Leaping the Rockies and Bitterroots, blasting into the Clark Fork Valley, and sweeping over Marent's Gulch west of Missoula, the northern transcontinental was being pushed across some of the wildest country on earth with astonishing speed. Twenty-five thousand men labored at Villard's command on one of the greatest engineering projects of all time, making real the vision of Edwin Johnson and Isaac Stevens. Villard savored the thought, even as a multitude of other matters demanded his attention: A new terminal company in Portland; finalizing the lease of the Oregon & California to the Transcontinental Company; and keeping the peace in Seattle.

On April 20, Villard stood in the Odd Fellows Hall before an audience of two hundred. Judge Thomas Burke had, in his eight years of residence in Seattle, made himself chief custodian of his adoptive city's railroad dream. He had little use for the Northern Pacific, C.B. Wright, or any others who would threaten Seattle's well-being. Now, Villard had some explaining to do.

Burke rose briskly and fired three questions at him: When would the Northern Pacific be completed to Puget Sound? Would Villard honor his promise to build more railroads in King County and connect Seattle directly with the Northern Pacific? Why had the Cascade branch not been started?

The Villard antennae were, as usual, well tuned. He opened with a jocular introduction that may have also concealed a slight nervousness: "I was told last evening that I was to attend a conference of businessmen here this morning. This certainly does not look like a business conference, but rather like a town meeting."

He praised the "astounding vitality and growth" of the city, then turned to his pet theme: "I took occasion during my last visit to the Pacific coast to say that, part seriously and part humorously, we were a benevolent monopoly. I mean by that, simply, that whatever financial power we commanded through this monopoly should not be exercised for the exclusive benefit of our corporations, but for the benefit of the community from which we derive our prosperity as well."

A faint defensive note crept in as he intoned: "I think what has been done here by us during the last three years bears witness uniformly of that fact . . . but for the fact that we have represented strong concentrated financial power, the great enormous and rapid development that has been going on in the last three years you would not have seen in the next twenty years."[35]

Villard stood up vigorously for the land grant. Forfeiture was a threat not just to the railroad, but to the entire Northwest and the prosperity everyone wanted. In 1881, President Chester Arthur had halted government inspection and acceptance of Northern Pacific construction, subject to the disposition of the land grant forfeiture bills then pending in Congress. Hundreds of miles of main line were held in limbo, bonds could not be converted into cash, and grant lands could not be sold until the Department of the Interior approved completed sections of line. All the while, construction expenses ran upwards of $2,000,000 a month.

Like Billings before him, Villard had appeared before the House Judiciary Committee in June 1882, and testified that the company was having serious trouble selling its bonds and guaranteeing future construction, thanks to those reckless elements who demanded forfeiture. National heroes—ex-President Rutherford Hayes, General Nelson A. Miles, General William T. Sherman—defended the Northern Pacific as essential to the national welfare. Two months later, President Arthur lifted the freeze.

Villard cautioned Seattle on its close shave: "Those attacks, while they have had no practical effect as far as our claim to the land grant was concerned, yet tended to and did affect the credit of the company on the money market . . . there was mortal danger of another collapse and absolute suspension of work on the main line. It would have kept you back here from five to ten years."

As for the Cascade branch, Villard remained unwilling to commit himself to a timetable. Eight million dollars would be required to build it, he patiently explained. That money, and the manpower and supplies, could not be diverted from the task of finishing the Northern Pacific mainline by fall. "My paramount duty is to give this isolated coast communication direct by rail to the rest of the United States."[36]

The effectiveness of Henry Villard's diplomatic skills may be judged from the fact that he not only pacified Seattle, he extracted from its citizens the pledge of a $150,000 subsidy. This money, he explained, would enable him to honor his commitment to push the Columbia & Puget Sound up the Cedar River, convert it to standard gauge, and extend it into the foothills to a "common point" with the NP Cascade Division, all by May 1, 1884. Villard promised that all the coal traffic from new Cedar River mines would be exclusively contributory to Seattle, and that the Northern Pacific would sell to the Oregon Improvement Company all its holdings in the Cedar River fields—removing the danger that King County coal might have to pass through Tacoma.

Judge Thomas Burke had drawn up the subsidy resolution the night before, and at the conclusion of the Odd Fellows meeting, Chief Justice R.S. Greene asked all those in favor to stand. No one remained seated.

Villard assured the gathering that all his promises would be kept, and bowed out with a masterful flourish: "I think I will contrive to ride into Seattle in the first week of September in my private car, directly from New York!"

Like a swooning teenager, the *Post-Intelligencer* was all but swept off its feet: "He evidently thinks well of Seattle . . . it is very plain that no other place in the territory stands higher in his estimation."[37]

Rats! said Tacoma. "The people of Yeslerville will have to sell their mills, their waterfront, and exhaust the funds in all their purses and banking houses to raise $150,000," sniped the *Ledger*.

Now, now, Villard assured a Tacoma audience at Cogswell's Hall; no one was going to take anything away from them, "despite unfounded newspaper statements to the contrary." Too much money had been invested there for that to happen.

Villard again turned on the charm. "You know, the future of your town is really in the hands of the Tacoma Land Company, not of the Northern Pacific Railroad. It is presided over by your best friend, Mr. Charles B. Wright, who does more for your town than anyone else I know of. It is Tacoma all the time with him!"

Laughter and applause followed, and Villard kept the mood jolly with a sly dig at the big city to the south: "I am obliged, I am sorry to say, to take the building of a hotel in Portland, for with all the wealth there is in that city, there is not enough enterprise among the citizens to provide a hotel for visitors." And he praised Tacoma's astounding vitality and growth.[38]

The railroad king then sprang a nice surprise on the Tacomans. "After floundering among the uncertainties of the proper route . . . for years and years," Villard announced, the Northern Pacific had finally chosen its Cascade crossing—Stampede Pass.

In March 1881, Virgil G. Bogue had planted his stake atop a 3,600-foot summit forty miles northeast of Tacoma, at the head of the Green River. On his maps, he labeled it simply Pass No. 1. Other nearby routes, including Yakima Pass, were duly noted as Passes 2 and 3. The trail cutters made camp beside a lake near the summit of Pass 1, only to desert in revolt against their unpopular foreman. Young Johnny Bradley stayed behind, and nailed a crudely-penciled name board to a tree: "Stampede Camp." The lake took the name "Stampede," and the pass soon thereafter. Bogue's assistants Adna Anderson and Henry Thielsen suggested he name the pass after himself, but Stampede had already caught on, so Bogue made it official.

This he came to regret, "because the pass was discovered by me after a most difficult expedition."

The railroad briefly tried "Garfield Pass," after the recently martyred U.S. president, but to no avail. Whatever the name, Tacoma and Seattle had a pass they could both live with.[39]

Up the White River Valley the grading gangs slogged. Progress on the Puget Sound Shore right of way continued slow in the spring of 1883, as Myers' and Nounan's men fought through the marshes and heavy underbrush. Extensive piling was required, even on firm ground, due to the frequent floods. Track gangs were often short-handed—

liquor was a constant distraction, and in summer men drifted off to cut timber or go salmon-fishing. Men were also scarce on the lagging Portland-Kalama section, which had been put under contract to James B. Montgomery the year before.

Engineer Hans Thielsen announced that he had received orders to begin construction of the Cascade Division from Stuck Junction to Stampede Pass,[40] but the labor shortage precluded this. By late summer, however, six crews were hard at work on the Puyallup-Seattle line, and, at a half-mile a day, track crept up the valley. East of the mountains, more graders began working westward up the Yakima River from Pasco.

In Seattle, pile drivers were transforming the landscape. Early on, it had been determined that the Puget Sound Shore and Columbia & Puget Sound would share the nine miles of line from Black River Junction into the city. In exchange for widening and improving the right of way, the Puget Sound Shore would be allowed to lay a third rail outside the narrow gauge track; the two companies would share maintenance responsibilities. Upon reaching the Seattle tideflats, the standard gauge line would diverge from the Columbia & Puget Sound and enter the city on a 2,000-foot-long pile trestle, terminating in its own yard immediately southwest of the Columbia & Puget Sound depot and roundhouse at Second and King. Actually two parallel trestles (one for the mainline and one for a side track), the structure would form an enclosure 110 feet wide, creating ample space for warehouses and yard tracks. Terminal amenities would at first be modest. In the absence of turning facilities, Shore road trains would halt at the north end of the trestle, unload passengers and freight in the open, and back up to Tacoma. As it thrust boldly across the flats during the summer of 1883, the trestle was a striking new addition to the city—a symbol of a bright future.

Seattle's pulse quickened when on August 23, the *Post-Intelligencer* announced that, at 3 PM the preceding day, the east and west ends of the Northern Pacific had come together fifty miles west of Helena, Montana.

The streets buzzed with excitement: "The town was full of people last night, sure enough. The streets are crowded at 7 or 8 o'clock as they are seen in few cities of less than 50,000 inhabitants."

Civil War hero General William Tecumseh Sherman paid a call and added to the glamour: "I have visited Puget Sound on several occasions and have always believed that on its shores a great commercial city would spring to rival San Francisco . . . I see no reason why that city should not be Seattle. True, you have as rivals Victoria and Port Townsend . . . and Tacoma and Olympia . . . but Seattle has a long start in the race, and in her citizens I see men who will take care that she keeps in the lead of all competition."[41]

Henry Villard's finest hour came on September 8, 1883, as he presided over the driving of the last spike of the Northern Pacific at Gold Creek, Montana. Four long trains, bearing such eminencies as August Belmont, Marshall Field, Joseph Pulitzer, the inevitable George M. Pullman, U.S. senators and diplomats, and the cream of European finance, industry, science, and letters, descended from the East upon the lonely spot fifty-five miles west of Helena. Another section steamed in from Portland bearing Charles B. Wright, Senator J.N. Dolph, and Seattleites Arthur Denny, Bailey Gatzert, and Mayor Henry Struve.

Villard made the keynote speech, paying tribute to Lewis and Clark, his Northern Pacific predecessors, the stockholders, and "the honest toilers who earned their bread in the sweat of their brows for our benefit."

Then, as dusk fell, he took his turn swinging the maul with Frederick Billings, Ulysses S. Grant, and Crow Indian chief Iron Bull. The Fort Keogh army band played "Yankee Doodle" and "Die Wacht am Rhein," and the locomotives of the eastern and western sections touched cowcatchers. As night fell, Henry Villard and two trainloads of VIPs departed west.[42]

At five o'clock on the sunny afternoon of September 13, Villard's six-car special arrived in Tacoma. Towering grandly in the southeast, the "Mountain of Tacoma" ("called only in the Seattlese tongue Rainier") displayed its rosy crown to the delight of the awe-struck easterners. Villard and retinue stepped down from the cars and marched up Pacific Avenue. Charles Wright had gone east, and did not attend the great celebrations, but it was his idea that Villard walk through town, and Villard made sure he got a laugh out of it: "This is Mr. Wright's programme, and I am going to obey orders!"

They passed beneath a grand triumphal arch bearing the legend, "West, United, East," then Villard gripped his lapels and spoke:

"In the last week of April, last, I promised the citizens of the terminal city of Tacoma that I would appear here early in September with the first through cars from New York city. I stand here now to say that I have redeemed that pledge, for, behold, there are two cars straight from New York City! . . . I am pleased to see the prosperity you have been having since my last visit here a few months ago. The gentlemen may have noticed an unusual number of tree stumps in this town. I hope that their number has not given them an unfavorable impression of the city. You ought to remember that New York City, as well as Philadelphia and Boston, rose out of tree stumps. And I have no doubt that in a very short time all the stumps will have disappeared, and that a great and glorious city will have taken their place!"[43]

Brass bands, triumphal arch, and arteriosclerotic Gilded Age catering were not sufficient to keep the kinetic Mr. Villard in the terminal city. Ending his remarks, he bid Tacomans a hasty "Adieu," and ushered his party aboard the steamer *Queen of the Pacific*. That evening, they steamed up to Victoria, British Columbia, and the following morning, the *Queen* turned its prow toward Seattle.

The *Post-Intelligencer* had primly lectured the populace not to importune Mr. Villard for money, however worthy the cause, and not to be otherwise obnoxious. "Don't brag. Don't attempt to hide such disadvantages as may and do exist in any growing city. Don't overstate products, resources, or climatic advantages, nor indulge in undue boasting. Above all, do not attempt to exalt our city by disparaging comparisons with others."[44]

Possibly, this counsel was neglected amid a cornucopia never before seen on Elliott Bay. Hundreds of clams simmered in a titanic chowder, and a herd of beeves, sheep, and porkers was readied for the spit. Ladies' auxiliaries prepared vats of coffee and sandwiches, and the menfolk had, by mid-afternoon, already made considerable inroads into untold gallons of spiritous substances. "Rice in China style" was in the offing from the Chinese community, and Duwamish Indians readied a huge pit for a salmon bake on the university campus. The decorations committee had erected two huge four-sided arches over Commercial Street and garnished them with pine boughs, mountain ash, and glowering carven eagles. Japanese lanterns swung quaintly overhead.

All Seattle lined the waterfront on the afternoon of the 14th. At four o'clock, a rustle of excitement burst forth as the *Queen of the Pacific* rounded West Point and entered the harbor. A grand flotilla of steamers, sailboats, and canoes fell in behind and, like ducklings, followed the big liner to the Main Street wharf. The venerable sidewheeler *Eliza Anderson* shepherded the polyglot fleet, her calliope shrieking a serenade. Henry Villard appeared on the gangplank, disembarked to a thirty-eight-gun salute, and at the direction of civic dignitaries took up a purposeful stride uptown to the university campus. In his wake trailed mounted police, Civil War veterans, the Carbonado and Queen City bands, Sing Verein glee club, civic dignitaries, and the fire department. Railroad laborers and loggers stumped stolidly along behind, followed at last by the cheering townsfolk.

At the temporary university pavilion (flying a banner emblazoned, "Alki"), Villard praised the astounding vitality and growth of the city. "I told my guests on board the steamer that they would soon view the most enterprising town on Puget Sound! As I saw the immense crowd upon the docks, I said to myself, 'Is it possible this is the population of Seattle?' Certainly it must have multiplied since I was last here!"

He got his biggest laugh poking good-natured fun at civil engineer Hans Thielsen, who had been unable to lay rail into town in time for Villard's private car. "I have brought the culprit with me, and you may try him by a jury of twelve good, honest, and wise men, and punish him as you like!"[45]

Then Dr. Thomas T. Minor intoned from the city's deepest soul: "Sir, we have waited long for this day—for years we have waited! Isolation is the severest of prison discipline, and isolation in a community active and industrious, enterprising and aspiring, is as it is in solitary confinement, the severest punishment it can undergo . . . we have suffered under it and longed for relief from it, and rejoice now without measure in at last feeling that we have union, and that the doorway is opened between us and the civilized world . . . Why, if you had seen the folks for weeks here at Puget Sound, you could see every time they set their feet to the ground, it was as though they had a new life and new pride, new power and strength . . . You have opened to us the doors of new life, and new liberty!"

Nellie Powell, daughter of the university president, then made a florid address thanking Villard for the "broad highway from New York, the empress of the East, to Seattle, the Queen City of the Northwest Sea," after which Secretary of the Interior Carl Schurz exhorted Puget Sounders to guard their natural resources and prevent forest fires.[46]

Villard's brother-in-law, Frank Garrison, was impressed by the Seattle celebrations. "We were amazed to see such a thriving, wide-awake town, which showed such indications of energy and enterprise at every turn." Comely Nellie Powell's orations left Henry Villard and his guests "quite swept from their moorings," but Garrison was less moved: "No one but myself seemed to find her production a trifle sophomoric."

Still, the fete had been impressive: "Harry [Villard] responded in a manner which I am sure strengthened the admiration for, and faith in him, which the people of Seattle have felt ever since he gave the town its first forward impulse."[47]

The great university reception had been scheduled for eight in the evening, after which Villard and his party were expected to adjourn to hotels for the night. Shortly, however, he took his leave of Seattle. "We deeply regret our inability to stay longer with you!" he shouted in a voice by now well-frayed by last-spike oratory.

"We will always bear in grateful memory this day. New York and Seattle are comparatively much nearer than they were, and hereafter, we will undoubtedly see each other much oftener. Good night!"

To thunderous cheering, Henry Villard re-boarded the steamer for Tacoma and the train east. Seattle would have the clambake and barbecue all to herself.[48]

The spike was driven, but much to Tacoma's consternation, there still seemed to be confusion over just where the terminus was.

"The crowning fact is accomplished, the last spike has been driven home and the Northern Pacific Railroad is practically completed," cheered the Portland *Oregonian*. "It is no qualification of this statement to say that it is only completed to Portland, for this is the end of the line."

The *Ledger* sneered: "Is the end in the middle or is it sticking out over the edge?"

Portland had a point. Construction on the thirty-six miles of track from the city to Hunters Landing, across the Columbia from Kalama, had been bogged down by shortage of labor and materials. This did not prevent eager contractor James Montgomery from wiring Villard at Gold Creek that the last spike on the Pacific Division was driven: "You now have all rail between St. Paul and Tacoma."[49]

Steel had been hastily slapped down, and in fact the line was unballasted and far from ready for service. En route to Tacoma, Villard and guests sailed from Portland to Kalama on the steamers *S.G. Reed* and *R.R. Thompson*, while their Pullmans were deadheaded gingerly up to Hunters and ferried across by barge.

The most serious affront to terminus dignity came, predictably, from the city on Elliott Bay. On September 8, acting Seattle mayor Unit M. Rasin wired: "To the Mayor of St. Paul, Minn.: The Western Terminus of the N.P.R.R. greets the Eastern Terminus."

A brass band stands ready to rend the air for the Villard reception beneath one of a pair of evergreen arches on Seattle's Commercial Street.

Washington State Historical Society

The University of Washington building on Denny knoll is decorated for Henry Villard's triumphal entry into Seattle, September 14, 1883.

University of Washington, Special Collections

Tacoma erupted in apoplexy: "The asylum for the insane is the only fit abode for the sender of that telegram."

The identity crisis only worsened when the following four sections of the last-spike specials, bearing 200 Villard guests and eastern journalists, descended upon Tacoma on September 14. It became readily—awfully!—apparent that scurrilous editors and shadowy hucksters had successfully insinuated into the visitors' minds "stale lies invented in the Sawdust City," most heinous being that Seattle was the terminus!

The perfidy was quickly exposed. "As each section of Mr. Villard's guests reached Tacoma," declared the *Ledger*, "it quickly became apparent to them that they had reached the end of the track. They saw the insane folly of Mr. Acting Mayor Rasin's telegram . . . the whopping lie that no coal is shipped from Tacoma . . . they gave expression to feelings of hot, honest indignation against the mendacity of the Seattle boomers. The refutation of this Seattle lie took place in the presence of about one-half of the whole visiting party. Henceforth and forever, the wholesale lying of the Seattle boomers will have been shorn of its power for evil among the business and newspaper men of the East. The days of successful mendacity in the interest of the Sawdust City are numbered."[50]

Like a stubborn child, however, Seattle was slow in taking her medicine. The *Post-Intelligencer* crowed happily that Tacoma was soon to be relegated to "a place where the locomotives running from Seattle to Portland will stop to water and oil up. That's the milk in the cocoanut which has soured the stomach of our neighbor. It isn't pleasant to be a way station close to a live metropolis like Seattle."[51]

Regular St. Paul-Portland service began September 12, on a ninety-six hour schedule (seven additional hours were required to reach Tacoma). A first class ticket cost its bearer a lordly $95, while an emigrant berth could be had for $65, still no mean sum at the time.

Villard had fortunate timing. When he began his empire-building, the government had returned to the gold standard, stimulating the money market and unleashing a great tide of investment. One of many who rode to wealth on this great wave of Gilded Age prosperity, Villard grabbed his main chance and, with a few lightning financial coups, dazzled the likes of J.P. Morgan and a succession of U.S. presidents. He rallied the popular imagination to him with charisma wedded to unbounded optimism. It was a boom time for America that, Villard later recalled, "was never witnessed before and is not likely to be witnessed again," and the meteoric rise in his own holdings' stock values filled him with a sense of invincibility.[52]

Villard was criticized by some as an extravagant visionary, but he also worked hard to put solid footing under his edifice. Throughout 1882-1883, his Northern Pacific immigration agencies lured thousands of German, Scandinavian, and British settlers onto the land grant. California and the Southwest were eclipsed, and even cocky San Francisco bemoaned the "strange fondness of immigrants for the wet slopes of the Cascade Mountains and the solitary banks of the great Columbia."

Sam Wilkeson, the *New York Times*, and Eugene V. Smalley's *The Northwest* magazine all ballyhooed the latest developments along the "Great Steam Highway." Not about to haul new customers on yesterday's trains, Villard and Oakes gorged the railroad on the choicest morsels of the Pullman Car Company, greatly elevating the general tone of American railroad service. Sumptuous new Palace Cars, comfortable emigrant sleepers, and the first dining cars in the West enticed plutocrat and settler alike to take "The Dining Car Line to the Pacific." By July 1882, Villard claimed 300 settlers a day were riding Northern Pacific cars west.[53]

But the railroad baron had had good reason to hasten his Puget Sound celebrations—he was in deep trouble. As he stepped onto the dock at Seattle, he had been handed a sheaf of telegrams all bearing the same grim tidings: The stocks of all Villard's companies—NP, OR&N, OIC, O&T—were tumbling on Wall Street.

A reporter watched as the great capitalist blanched: "It seemed to me that he was turned into a marble statue. I shall never forget the terrible look of agony on his face."

It had been an anxious summer. Villard poured over $3,000,000 of his own funds into construction, but in June, chief engineer General Adna Anderson, R.M. Armstrong's successor, informed him that, despite earlier predictions, costs were now running $14,000,000 ahead of estimates.[54]

It all began piling up around him: The bills for tunneling under Bozeman and Mullan passes; bridging the Missouri, Snake, and Clark Fork; cutting back the crumbling bluffs along the Yellowstone; the recklessness of the forfeiture fanatics; the stubborn refusal of President Arthur to allow land patents; the communication breakdown with the engineering department; and, now, the almost obscene perversity of the short-sellers who, for selfish gain, were ganging up hyena-like to drive the great enterprise—the hope and dream of millions—to the ground.

Even as the last spike specials chugged west, the bear raid was on in earnest. Rumor spread that many of the old Blind Pool were selling out and had even been observed jumping off the special trains at way stations to wire liquidation orders to their brokers. The extravagant last spike celebrations drew fire from stockholders, bankers, and the old "Billings crowd" on the NP board. The *New York Times* hinted that Oregon & Transcontinental's safe was empty, and the stampede accelerated.[55]

At the annual stockholders' meeting on September 20, Vice-President Oakes revealed the grim truth. The Northern Pacific was $8,000,000 in the red, and needed $12,000,000 more to be considered operable by even minimal standards. The following month, and under growing pressure from his bankers, Villard relinquished control of the Oregon Railway & Navigation and Oregon & Transcontinental companies. In December, auditors found Villard's books a hopeless tangle and with both the NP and O&T approaching bankruptcy. As Villard withdrew to his gloomy new townhouse, the hard-nosed Oakes took charge and reined in the overcharged juggernaut with layoffs and stop-work orders; even the gas in the Portland general offices was shut off.

As the momentous year drew to a close, Villard was near financial and physical collapse, the press predicting his imminent resignation.

My "fate was certainly tragic," Villard would later recall, and my "brief career was everywhere used to point a moral."[56]

As Villard slumped, Seattle had reason to be distressed. Under the "Moses of the Northwest," the town had prospered and grown to maturity as a city of over 6,000 people. Outside capital had followed Villard's lead in investing in Seattle; hundreds of new homes appeared, and in the heart of downtown at Yesler's Corner, a three-tiered Victorian wedding cake—the new Yesler-Leary Building—was stunning proof that Seattle had arrived.

With considerable satisfaction, the *Post-Intelligencer* took stock. "Seattle is getting her 'long-felt wants' supplied with gratifying rapidity. During the past year the telephone and electric lights have been introduced, an immense progress has been made in the development of a school system, and a vast deal done in the way of street improvements . . . More money has been put in fine residences and grand business houses than in any previous three years. For the first time something like real and permanent waterworks have been attempted. An opera house is beginning."[57] What now?

On December 23, the paper published a letter from Charles Wright to a Tacoma businessman. Its contents were far from reassuring:

"I am quite positive that the Northern Pacific has no landed interests at Seattle. The NP RR Co. has no interest in the line to Seattle further than Stuck Junction, 16 miles from Tacoma. I can say that the NP Co. has no intention of spending any money at Seattle on account of railroad or any other facilities. I think you will find the trains between Tacoma and Seattle treated as local trains. There is already a syndicate forming to make a proposition to build the Cascade division, and they favor the Natchess [sic] Pass . . . The feeling among the Northern Pacific stockholders is quite strong against the companies that are so closely allied with the Northern Pacific Railroad, and I expect to see the latter company separated from them at no distant day."

Like the classic, mustachio-twirling melodrama villain, Wright gloated over the inevitable demise of Seattle's friend. "Well, Mr. Villard has not been a success. We need successful men at the head of railroads . . . Anyway, we won't be troubled with Mr. Villard but little longer."

So much for the man who had finished the railroad and saved the land grant. Wright took his place in Seattle's demonology as the man who would crush the city out of existence.

The *Post-Intelligencer* warned the city to expect the worst. "Mr. Wright evidently is bitterly hostile to Seattle, and all that he can do against this place will unquestioningly be done."

Apparently, he wasted little time. On the "New and correct map of the lines of the Northern Pacific," the Seattle branch mysteriously disappeared, much to the consternation of the *Post- Intelligencer*.[59]

The Queen City of Puget Sound now found itself a tiny, disconnected dot. The accursed land ring was back! The paper found a wan ray of hope in the belief that the headlights of other railroads' locomotives were even then casting their rays toward Puget Sound, and would be in Seattle before too many more years passed. But those headlights were still far below the horizon.

The other shoe dropped on January 4, 1884, when Villard relinquished the presidencies of the Northern Pacific and the Oregon Improvement Company, and went into seclusion at Dobbs Ferry, New York.

Seattle eulogized the man who had ended its isolation. "Henry Villard has done more for the people of the Northwest than any other man . . . To us he has been a friend, not partial, but just; not a narrow-minded, selfish advocate, but a broad-spirited officer and honorable man."

The man who took over Villard's board seat—Charles Wright—had other ideas: "Instead of carrying out the policy of the former board of managers as set forth in the former resolutions of the Northern Pacific board of directors, and as promised by him when he assumed con-

trol . . . to permit the head of Puget Sound, where the company has the largest interests, to have the benefit of the terminus, inducements were made to another locality, 40 miles distant by rail, and where the Northern Pacific has no interest whatever, solely to benefit Mr. Villard's Oregon Improvement Company, a rival corporation to the Northern Pacific."[60]

Though Tacoma had prospered under the Villard boom, Seattle's rival was pleased to say I told you so. Randolph Radebaugh, the acerbic editor of the Tacoma *Ledger*, had distrusted Villard from the time he took over the NP; now that he was in disgrace, the editor pulled out all the stops. Villard had been a traitor to the Northern Pacific and its stockholders, Radebaugh harped, and his evil pact with Seattle had contributed to his downfall.

"We have been blamed for having treated him with civility while he was president, knowing as we did that his rule meant harm to Tacoma. To have called public attention to his crookedness would only have served to provoke him to retaliation; a word of his would have done Tacoma great harm in the esteem of outsiders. He was small enough to have spoken that word in anger."[61]

Tacoma—thanks in no small part to "traitor" Villard—could at last feel she was shaking off her stumptown swaddling clothes. In January 1884, New Tacoma, now a respectable city of 4,000, gobbled up Old Town, and shortly thereafter congressional delegate Thomas N. Brents, a Walla Walla Republican, co-sponsored a bill proposing that, when the territory finally became a state, it should be named "Tacoma."

Not all were impressed by terminus boosting. Banker Noah B. Coffman came to Tacoma early in 1883, lured from Nebraska by the promise of a "great terminal and commercial city" in the offing on Puget Sound. Stopping over in San Francisco, Coffman found a great division of opinion among influential men on just where that "future great city" would be: Portland, Tacoma, Seattle? "At present no one knows—not even Villard," declared a prominent publisher, "and the answer is at present the search of speculators, investors, and capitalists."

Most of the businessmen Coffman interviewed seemed to feel that Portland would remain dominant and at least hold her own when river improvements, now being started by the government, were completed. Nevertheless, Puget Sound had room for any number of "important cities" and certainly would become Portland's strong rival.[62]

Coffman found strong views on his adopted Tacoma. The "future Sound city," the San Francisco publisher asserted, would definitely "*not* be New Tacoma. True the Northern Pacific owns more land there than at any other point, but it takes men, united capital, and influence, independent in action, in a town to build it up. Tacoma lacks this. Should it lose its railway prospects tomorrow, the existence of the town would almost disappear at once. It is a mushroom town, and like the mushroom, shut off the subsistence of its hope and it will shrink to nothing in a day. Its land location is very unfavorable. One railroad has an entrance through its bluffs, but a system of radiating roads would have a sorry time getting into it."

Most of the influential men Coffman interviewed gave Seattle the nod as the "first-ranking Sound city."[63]

Sobering intelligence, this, but Coffman nevertheless stuck to his plan, and, even as the Villard bubble burst, gamely opened his new bank at the terminus. Much of the 150-man workforce at the Northern Pacific shops was laid off, land sales and bank deposits dwindled, and men drifted away. Weeds grew in the bare foundation of the Portland Hotel, which became known as the "Villard ruin."

Hard times settled over Puget Sound. ■

SEATTLE, WASHINGTON TERRITORY.

OREGON IMPROVEMENT COMPANY'S COAL DOCKS, SEATTLE, W.T.

Top: In this lithograph, Seattle is poised for rapid expansion in the 1880s. Bottom: The local passenger steamer *North Pacific* and the Pacific Coast Steamship Co.'s *Umatilla* are tethered to the quay.

Washington State Historical Society

CHAPTER 7

ORPHAN ROAD

"All we want is fair play." —Thomas Burke

HENRY VILLARD'S HOUSE of cards was wobbling in the autumn of 1883, but it was hard to tell that out in the White River Valley, where the railroad gap between Seattle and Tacoma was fast being closed. Fourteen hundred Chinese workers hastened to finish the last miles.

"Laborers swarm through the fields like bees," marveled the *Post-Intelligencer*, "and the grading and leveling . . . give one the impression that the whole face of nature is being torn up."

Hundreds more pushed the Cedar River extension east from Renton. As a Columbia & Puget Sound construction train left Seattle for the "front" one morning, a reporter noted its makeup for posterity: two flat cars of ties, two flats with a pile driver, two carrying squared timbers, one with flooring, one with old wheelbarrows, one with new wheelbarrows and carts, one with scrapers and picks, one bearing Chinese laborers, one boxcar filled with miscellaneous merchandise, one passenger car, and one caboose filled with people and their belongings—"railroad building in good style and in a big hurry."[1]

The Puget Sound Shore's trestle across lower Elliott Bay was finished in September and became known as the "broad gauge strip." By year's end only three miles between Titusville (later Kent) and Black River Junction remained to link Seattle and Tacoma. Funds evaporated from the Villard coffers, though, and winter floods once more inundated the valley. In January, construction ceased; Seattle would spend another wet winter in isolation.

Things looked grim. The Cedar River extension was also stalled, and the Oregon Improvement Company had spent almost $150,000, the amount of Seattle's promised subsidy, while falling far short of its goal. General Manager John Howard begged the city council for an extension of the deadline from May 1 to August 1. He sweetened his appeal with some good news: Oregon Improvement would assume the Oregon & Transcontinental Company's obligation to complete and operate the Puget Sound Shore. No time was wasted, and by the end of June the Seattle-Tacoma line was spiked to completion.

Things livened up on Elliott Bay, as a crew began driving pilings for the waterfront right of way. Still, the relations between the Villard companies and the Northern Pacific remained confused and, now, antagonistic. Seattle had a brand-new railroad, all shiny and ready to run. But who would run the trains? What would be the rates? Who would be in charge?

No one seemed to know. So nothing happened. Cows roamed the right of way, and the press found a nickname for the unused track: "Orphan Road."

The management of the Northern Pacific had more pressing matters to worry about. Robert Harris, the well-regarded former chief executive of the Chicago Burlington & Quincy and a Northern Pacific director since 1880, took over the presidency. Well-seasoned in both railroad operations and railroad politics, the practical Harris started the depleted firm on another long and laborious climb to solvency, and set about untangling the books of his and the Villard companies. Among his first acts was to declare that construction of the Cascade branch would begin as soon as financing could be secured.

Despite this fortuitous announcement, however, the Northern Pacific came under assault from diverse quarters. Settlers complained that the railroad was reneging on its promised selling price of $2.60 per acre for land, and demanding as much as $20; eastern Washington farmers complained about back-haul freight rate "arbitraries" that favored the coastal terminal points, Portland and Tacoma; and in Seattle, the non-operation of the Orphan Road provided the land grant forfeiture militants with fresh ammunition. Charging that the NP's iron grip on the land was "retarding the growth of the country," these forces joined in an all-out offensive against the corporation in the spring of 1884. The Northern Pacific land grant united the ordinarily disparate interests of eastern and western Washington, and swept aside statehood, women's suffrage, and prohibition to become the year's hot issue—in fact, the best political show the territory had seen in quite a while.

President Harris was quick to parry the new attacks. Appearing before Congress, he assured the lawmakers that the Cascade Division would soon be fully underway, reminded them that the Northern Pacific had made good on all its past promises and deadlines, and declared emphatically that the land grant was irrevocable. Thousands of settlers were streaming into the Northwest, he noted pointedly, and their myriad hopes would be dashed to bits should the financing of the Cascade Division be scared away by the extremists.

Harris then journeyed to Tacoma, and reiterated Charles Wright's claim that the Wilkeson coal branch was part of the Cascade Division; not only that, but he dangled the possibility that Naches Pass might supplant Stampede.

Seattle howled in anguish. The chamber of commerce had only lately been seduced by Northern Pacific land agent Paul Schulze into signing, by a slim majority, a resolution denouncing land grant forfeiture. Quickly thinking better of its action, the civic organization reversed itself. It

didn't hurt, either, that civic leaders Judge Thomas Burke, Arthur Denny, and John Leary were anxious to win clear patents on their mineral claims in Snoqualmie Pass.

Seattle joined other Washington communities—Yakima, Colfax, Dayton, Olympia, Goldendale—in denouncing the "hideous incubus" of the Northern Pacific, and demanded revocation of the entire King County land grant. The chamber of commerce printed up a map of Washington entitled "Under a Black Cloud," a frightening vision of a territory all but consumed by the Northern Pacific, and mailed it to newspapers across the country.

The *Post-Intelligencer* declared all-out war on the railroad and rallied the citizens in a series of town meetings, crying: "The call to action is now imperative. It is plain that the Northern Pacific Company means to discriminate against Seattle in every way possible, and to try to dwarf her industries and crush her commerce."[2]

A carnival atmosphere prevailed on Saturday evening, March 22, as a brass band beckoned Seattleites inside Yesler's Pavilion. The old barn was packed with folks ready to give the NP its comeuppance, and as they waited for the speeches to begin, many in attendance grimly recalled the days more than a decade earlier, when they had first arrayed themselves against the giant corporation. Lawyer William H. White, popularly known as "Warhorse Bill," got things rolling briskly by condemning railroad "hokus pokus" in switching its main line to the Columbia and hoodwinking Washington Territory out of land tax revenues. Two great and good men—Governor Stevens and Captain McClellan—had had a vision, a vision of a railroad over Snoqualmie Pass. Other great men followed and began to build a railroad. For what?

"For the benefit of C.B. Wright? No! For the benefit of the people!"[3]

Dr. Thomas T. Minor urged his "Fellow citizens of Yeslerville and future State of Tacoma" to demand revocation of the land grant, and likewise condemned the new Simon Legree of Seattle: "We have seen the broad, fair-minded Villard displaced by the narrow and bigoted

Wright, and today we read that this great commonwealth is to be named after one of his hobbies—Tacoma!"

The idea that the NP honestly intended to build the Cascade Division was "all bosh," yelled attorney John J. McGilvra. As proof, he displayed a letter purportedly in Wright's handwriting, which proposed to abandon the Cascade line altogether once the railroad's patent to the land grant along the Wilkeson coal branch had been secured.

Chief Justice J.R. Lewis raised a hearty laugh in his counseling. "We had better take our bearings and our latitude, provided the parallels have not been stolen," and he recited a bit of doggerel: "Railroad, railroad, ichry am, Northern Pacific Railroad, you we dam!" Lewis urged the gathering to appoint a delegate to go to Congress and demand forfeiture: "I'll be one of twenty, or one of fifty, to put up the money!"

This, and another resolution overturning the earlier chamber of commerce resolution opposing forfeiture, were speedily adopted and the hat was passed to pay the delegate's expenses—Judge Lewis leading off with $50.[4]

The crowd filed out of the hall, humming with reborn militancy. All, that is, but attorney James McNaught. Both a kingpin of the Seattle Establishment and western counsel for the Northern Pacific, the alarmed McNaught rushed to his office and dispatched an urgent wire to President Harris apprising him of the ugly mood in Seattle.

Well-seasoned in frontier politics (and, as one of the first authentic "dandies" in the Territory, well used to jibes), McNaught was not afraid to buck the current. At the second meeting on the 27th, he got his licks in:

"This is my love feast. The one on last Saturday evening was yours. For 17 years I have been in Seattle, and have attended every railroad meeting . . . and have always contributed of my means to help along the enterprises that have been started here, and by so doing I have helped build up the town, as well as benefited my own pocket. I don't think the people have had sufficient cause for all this demonstration against the railroad company . . . The statement that the Northern Pacific Railroad is retarding the growth of the Territory is not true, and the road across the mountains will be the means of bringing happiness, wealth, and prosperity to many homes."

To back this up, he read aloud Robert Harris' reply to his urgent telegram: "You may inform the people of Seattle that it is the policy and intention of this company to push the Cascade Division to completion as speedily as practicable. The company will adopt the pass that is best for crossing the Cascade range without regard to the interests of any special point, and it will be the aim of the company to serve the business of Seattle and all other points on the Sound with complete fairness."

Harris was an honorable man, continued McNaught; from a humble laborer he had worked his way to the top. He had no intention of abandoning Villard's policy of making Seattle a "common point" with Tacoma and Portland, and he most assuredly would complete the Cascade Division, via Stampede Pass.[5]

Unimpressed, the militants hissed at McNaught and scoffed at Harris' "pleasantly-sounding rubbish."

There was a moral principle involved, and John Kinnear, also a leading Seattle attorney and a representative to the state legislature, laid it out neatly: "A laborer does not demand pay for services he does not perform, and why should a railroad demand land from the Government that it has not earned?"

The "soulless corporation" was no different from any individual, Kinnear insisted; it must honor its contracts, pay its taxes, or pay the penalty. This new articulation that individuals and corporations should be treated alike under the law, coupled with land grant forfeiture, quickly became known—proudly to supporters, and derisively to detractors—as the "Seattle Idea."[6]

Chief Justice Lewis was next on his feet, brandishing a "Black Cloud" map and raising hoots of angry laughter by suggesting the territory simply be renamed "Northernia Pacifica Railroadia."

He elaborated: "The Northern Pacific Railroad Company . . . have attempted to steal the name of our grand old mountain, and are trying to steal the name of our state; they are trying to gobble up all our land without having earned an acre, and I would not be surprised to find them attempting to steal the air we breathe!"

Judge Thomas Burke cleared his throat and jerked to his feet. Seattle's railroad battle was just the kind of excitement the little barrister had been looking for when he came to town nine years earlier, and his natural bent for civic loyalty and a good fight guaranteed that he would elbow his way into the middle of the fracas.

"If we make this fight," he barked, "we must remember that we are facing a corporation of great wealth, which is vastly unscrupulous and selfish."

Harris and Wright were not to be trusted—they spoke with forked tongues! There was but one way to deal with them: "Stand as one man and build a road of your own. There is money and brains enough to build a road to Ellensburg within the next eighteen months!"

Burke's voice rose another notch as he thundered: "The Northern Pacific Railroad Company despises the people of Washington Territory, and much talking and hard words will not frighten them a bit . . . If we make a strike, let us strike with effect!"

To show just how the NP was strangling Washington, Burke told a story of a recent encounter with an acquaintance of Union Pacific's Sidney Dillon. "We have had an eye on Puget Sound for a long time," the Union Pacific president had confided, "and would now have had our road well on toward those waters had it not been for the land grant held by the Northern Pacific . . . which makes an unequal fight for us." It was an outrage![7]

The muttering grew warmer, and the judge with it. Swept away by the moment, Burke made a startling revelation, one that would open a new chapter in Seattle's history:

"This very week, a corporation has been formed by citizens of Washington Territory to build a railroad across the mountains from Seattle via Snoqualmie Pass, and every one of you will within the next ten days have an opportunity to prove your faith by your works . . . if we show ourselves worthy, there will be representatives of eastern capital here within thirty days who will furnish what additional monies are needed to complete the road."

If everyone put their shoulders to the wheel, the judge concluded, Seattle would show the world what she was made of![8]

Following Burke's defiant threnody, "Warhorse Bill" White was nominated to take the Seattle Idea to Congress. The hat was passed, and with $729 in his pocket (for which the Tacoma *Ledger* derisively dubbed him "729 White"), the forfeiture fighter embarked for the terminus on April 4. From the gangplank he exhorted:

"Comrades! You are now raising your voices against a greater evil than that which threatened the country when the war trumpet of '61 called you from your peaceful homes! The fear is now entertained by many of our best men that the national and state legislatures of the Union, in creating these vast corporations, have evoked a spirit

C&PS No. 7, *Hyak*. Note "cat's head" at the base of the smokestack.

Museum of History and Industry, #6507

which may escape and defy their control . . . this power has escaped in this territory and it threatens to make vassals of us all!"[9]

The Tacoma *Ledger* heaped scorn on the Seattle "cranks." Burke in particular made the perfect target: "What a spectacle this Lilliputian judge, with arms stretched heavenward, must have presented with this grand eloquence rolling off his tongue like rain water out of a tin spout!"

The Northwest magazine blasted: "Some foolish people, excited by the foolish newspapers of [Seattle], have joined in this clamour until it has swollen to the dimensions of a local craze. The town hoped to be the western terminus of the Northern Pacific Railroad, although another place was designated as such terminus many years ago . . . Their antagonism will soon cool off, however, and will accomplish nothing. The Cascade Branch, in which they themselves have a vital interest, will be built and Washington Territory will get its much needed east and west trunk line railroad in spite of the racket at Seattle."[10]

General Sprague, NP stalwart and first mayor of unified Tacoma, rallied his forces at Alpha Opera House against: "The enemies of the Northern Pacific Railroad Company and of Tacoma."

It was pure spite that was motivating the Seattle crowd, declared the general. "They put themselves on record as saying 'If you cannot build the road so as to enhance the value of my corner lot, then we don't want any of it. When the Cascade Division shall be built . . . whether it terminates at Seattle or at some other place, every square mile and every acre of the entire territory will be benefited."

Others defended the land grant, the railroad, and "Mount Tacoma" itself. "The enmity, jealousy, and hatred of Seattle would try to wipe out the great mountain that bears the name of this place," griped Mr. Elwood Evans. "They don't like the idea . . . that the Queen City, or the King City, or their city of all other kinds shall be overshadowed!"[11]

A resolution condemning forfeiture as an injustice to the railroad and an injury to the people was drafted for presentation in Congress by delegate Brents. Tacoma found strong allies in Spokane Falls, Vancouver, and, logically enough, Sprague, Washington. The *Ledger* also had on its side the Portland *Oregonian*. The Northwest's most influential daily, the *Oregonian* opposed the forfeiture movement as nothing less than regional suicide, and—as long as it promised to run along the Columbia—strongly supported the Northern Pacific both as a vehicle of regional development and a counterweight to California-Central Pacific "monopoly power" on the West Coast.[12]

Seattle's militants were fighting a losing battle. Billings, Villard, and Harris had done their work well, and in Washington, D.C., "729" White quickly discovered just how many legislators held Northern Pacific stock. And with the likes of Ulysses S. Grant, Rutherford Hayes, William Tecumseh Sherman, and other powerful friends on the railroad's side, the NP and its land grant were virtually impregnable. In June, a chastened Warhorse slunk quietly home.

Robert Harris faced other nuisances. After Villard's collapse, Elijah Smith, a crusty Bostonian and large NP stockholder, had taken charge of the Oregon companies. As had Villard in 1880, Smith recognized the threat the Cascade Division posed to the OR&N, and began a campaign to neutralize it. First, to gain a policy-making voice and counter the dominant Tacoma faction, he ran for election to the Northern Pacific board. He was rejected. He then tried another tactic—canceling the 1880 NP/OR&N traffic agreement and proposing that NP lease the OR&N, in hopes of unifying the interests of the two companies together in OR&N territory. As the talks dragged on, the voluble "Lijer" enlivened stockholders' meetings with speeches and petitions demanding a halt to the Cascade Division, which he charged was being built in advance of need and against the stockholders' interest. Much to Smith's disgust, though, Harris was more determined even than Frederick Billings to see the Cascade Division through.

"He believes he is the man born for the occasion, that it is the effort of his life," Smith griped to William Endicott,

Jr. "He winds himself up in such a frame of mind that you can do nothing but let him spin out. With the Tacoma land interest in the saddle they will ride as they apparently can do with the view of their own interests."[13]

Smith was outgunned, but he could provide a few annoyances.

The standoff at Stuck Junction was one of them. Rumors of the imminent opening of the Orphan Road came and went, and the *Post-Intelligencer* sighed: "So many lies have been told about this piece of road that the people won't take stock in these reports until the whistle of the locomotive is heard."

Elijah Smith's local representative was John Muir (no relation to the naturalist), a Villard protege who had served as western traffic manager for the Northern Pacific before being named both general manager of the Oregon Improvement Co. and president of the Columbia & Puget Sound. While at NP, Muir had the previous year issued a promotional pamphlet featuring Seattle as the "Queen City of the Sound."[14]

Now, however, he was less than enthusiastic about the prospects of the Seattle branch. For starters, it was just a bare skeleton of a railroad. The line had not been ballasted, nor was there so much as a sidetrack at Seattle; trains could not switch cars or turn around, and the track did not extend to the docks. Five hundred dollars would pay for a sidetrack, but at least $24,000 in other improvements—culverts, sidings, turntable, water tank, freight house, depots, and ballast work—were required to make the road operable by minimal standards. The Puget Sound Shore's owner, Oregon & Transcontinental, had no money to spend on such improvements, and neither (ironically enough) did the Oregon Improvement Company, overdrawn in its accounts and struggling to stay afloat. There seemed to be few on-line traffic prospects, and Muir was doubtful the Orphan Road would even earn its expenses.

If Seattle wanted the railroad, Muir wrote his boss, the least it could do was pay for a sidetrack: "As there is not very much money to be earned on this route and as the people of Seattle are very anxious to have it opened, I told [Superintendent] Weymouth that if their anxiety would lead them to put up $500, we would open the road at once."[15]

The Northern Pacific had even less reason to cooperate. Under the Villard arrangement making Portland, Tacoma, and Seattle "common points" with equal freight rates, the NP was faced with the dubious prospect of hauling loads the extra distance from its terminus to Stuck Junction for nothing, unless it could bite into the Improvement Company's share of the through rate—a favor Smith and Muir were ill-disposed to grant.

Nevertheless, a flurry of memos passed between OIC and NP and officials trying to find some way to run the Orphan Road. Robert Harris agreed to lease the Puget Sound Shore a locomotive and cars, and let it have eighty-five percent of local receipts. Still there was the problem of Seattle's wholly inadequate facilities, a problem Elijah Smith refused to rectify.

Seattle hardware dealer George Dearborn called on Smith in New York to demand train service, and was promptly hit up for the $500 for the sidetrack. Dearborn seemed agreeable, June 15 was set as the opening date, and timetables were printed up. But the 15th passed without sign of a locomotive, as the NP refused to accede to Muir's demand for a seventy-five-cent "arbitrary" per hundred pounds of freight to cover wharfage and drayage costs in Seattle. Smith and Harris stood firm; anyone or anything going to Seattle could take the boat from Tacoma.[16]

The terminal city gloated. "Each day drives another nail in the coffin of Villard's wild scheme of operating a railroad over forty miles of rough and swampy country," lectured the *Ledger*: "The Seattle papers are deceiving themselves in predicting the opening of the road to traffic. There is no business for it."

The upper White River Valley was only in the infancy of cultivation, the paper noted, and the steamboats made quicker time between Tacoma and Seattle, at a fraction of the cost of rail operation.

Still, the line might as well be run by somebody: "It is to be hoped that the matter will soon be straightened out so that an occasional train may be run to Seattle, just to accustom the people there to the sight of a locomotive. The opening of this road would be a convenience to both Seattle and Tacoma, and a great benefit to many people along the line."

A note of anxiety over terminus enterprise crept into Radebaugh's otherwise jocular musings, and he sounded a warning note: "It therefore behooves the merchants of Tacoma to be up and doing if they would get a share of the White River trade . . . Hitherto all the White river trade, which is three times as large as that of Puyallup valley, has gone to Seattle."[17]

On the morning of June 17, James McNaught received a wire at his Seattle law office from Vice-President Oakes in Kalama: He was on his way to Seattle with a small party and would arrive, by train, that afternoon. The excited lawyer hustled around town spreading the word.

McNaught had a flair for the dramatic, so he also rounded up flags, bunting, and a small cannon left over from the 1856 Indian war. Town cynics promptly made book on the odds of the train actually showing up.

But show up it did.

The first standard gauge passenger train into Seattle arrived at 2:45 PM: Northern Pacific 4-4-0 locomotive Number 306 and coach 118, bearing Oakes, Pacific Division superintendent Buckley, and John C. Bullitt, a Philadelphia lawyer and friend of Charles Wright. McNaught gleefully rallied his friends around the artillery piece, and, as the little train clanked down the broad gauge strip, the cannon roared twenty-one times in salute, proclaiming the dawn of a new era in Seattle.

As engineer P.R. Church and fireman Ben Holgate brought the engine and coach to a stop amid a thousand cheering Seattleites, Oakes stepped onto the planking and was immediately asked why regular trains were not running yet.

Ask the Oregon Improvement Company, he shot back, it was their railroad; the Northern Pacific owned no line into Seattle.[18]

PUGET SOUND
Shore Line.
Time Table.

Local train leaves Seattle for Kent, Stuck Junction, etc., at 2:55 p. m.

Returning, leaves Stuck Junction at 8:10 a. m. and arrives at Seattle at 10:05 a. m.

Through train leaves Seattle at 6:40 for Tacoma and intermediate stations.

Returning leaves Tacoma at 4 p. m., and arrives at Seattle at 6:15 p. m.

T. J. MILNER,
Superintendent.

W. R. THORNELL, Gen. Ft. & Pass. Agt.

RAILROAD AVENUE, CA. 1887, WITH SEATTLE LAKE SHORE & EASTERN TRACK ON LEFT, AND VILLARD "RAM'S HORN" RIGHT OF WAY ON RIGHT, LOOKING NORTH FROM MADISON STREET.

University of Washington, Special Collections, Peiser #116

SCHEDULE, SUMMER 1886.

The officials conferred briefly at the McNaught law office, did a little sightseeing, then returned to Tacoma on the steamer *North Pacific*, leaving the special train to deadhead backwards to the terminus. The *Post-Intelligencer* took a jaded view of the "great train with three men on it":

"Mr. McNaught is the only loser by the visit, as he will have a powder bill of $15 or $20 to foot, but he don't care, he's rich, and then, it was necessary to raise a crowd to witness the arrival of the 'first train.' In a month or so there will be another batch of railroad officials out from the East, and perhaps they'll conclude to ride into Seattle on the 'second train.' In case they do, the cannon will be brought out again, and we'll have a regular old 'parrot and monkey time.'"

The cynics appeared to have won the day; no more trains followed, and cows reclaimed the track. Seattle, predictably, blamed the Northern Pacific, while the Northern Pacific blamed the Oregon Improvement Company.

The NP was prepared to begin service "at a moment's notice," Oakes told a *Ledger* reporter: "We should be only too glad to do that, or anything else to please the people of Seattle, within reason." It was the Oregon Improvement Company that was holding everything up.[19]

And then, suddenly, there it was. On Sunday, July 5, Northern Pacific engine 315, a baggage car, and coach steamed miraculously into town after a three-hour and twenty-five minute dash from Tacoma.

According to an incredulous *Post-Intelligencer:* "The trains were started so suddenly that people could not fully realize the road had been opened to traffic, and in Tacoma, where the idea was entertained that we would be disconnected from rail communication by taking up the track, they could not believe it."

The first timetable appeared July 10: Train 23 departed Tacoma at 10:15 PM, arriving in Seattle at 1:38 AM; Number 24 left for the south the following afternoon at 1:50, tail-first.

A week later, a distinguished visitor rode up the Orphan Road. Robert Harris intended to run the Northern Pacific in an impartial, businesslike manner. "It is highly objectionable for the company to agree to anything as to one point that it will not equally extend to any point," he confided to Vice-President Oakes.

Seattle, and every other point, would get a fair shake. But the equable executive was ill-prepared for the reception tendered him in Seattle on July 17. The town railroad militants—Thomas Burke, Arthur Denny, John Leary, Judge J.R. Lewis, John McGilvra, and Henry Yesler—met Harris at the chamber of commerce office.

Confronted with this stone-visaged phalanx, Harris opened with a wan attempt at humor: "I have been warned by the Post Intelligencer that there are a great many things that I do not know. That I am pretty well aware of!"[20]

Throats were cleared. Grimly, Thomas Burke rose and presented Harris with the full plate of Seattle grievances: Northern Pacific refused to connect at Tacoma with either the Puget Sound steamers or the new Seattle trains; folks going either way were stuck overnight in Tacoma; consignments were broken up at the terminus, delayed without explanation, and charged discriminatory rates; NP ticket agents played deaf and dumb when asked for passage to Seattle; and the "consarned" train did not get into town until two o'clock in the morning!

Like the well-intentioned neighbor blundering into a domestic spat, the courtly Harris tried to smooth things over: "I regret the confusion in the mind of the community caused by our agents. It was only that the interests were managed by the same head, by Mr. Villard, that this difficulty has occurred."

As for the local train service: "That is a question between the Oregon Improvement Company and the Northern Pacific. To get all those things working smoothly takes some little time, and the officials who have managed the business did not understand their business properly. The matter of the arrival of the trains we cannot change any. We leave Portland as soon as our [transcontinental] train gets there . . . we are running very carefully on some parts of our road, and are liable to slides in some places. I will try to see to it that there is not discrimination, nor shall you have any just grounds for complaint . . . I suggest that every question between the Northern Pacific Company and the Improvement Company will be satisfactorily adjusted."

The Villard plan for connection between the Columbia & Puget Sound and the NP at the "common point" in the Cascade foothills would come to pass if Harris had anything to say about it: "The door will be wide open at the junction point. We want open doors for what business may come along from China and the islands."[21]

Harris cheerily reminded his listeners that the Cascade Division was coming right along, and would be a boon to all of Puget Sound. Moreover, he assured them, Naches Pass was out; the latest map of definite location, now en route to New York for board approval, took the line from South Prairie, near the junction with the Wilkeson spur, to the Green River:

"The location of the line from Green River and the location up the Yakima to a point involves the necessity of going through the Stampede Pass or some pass further north. We certainly could not retract and go down to Naches, but we could go up the Snoqualmie. The Stampede Pass is the one that General Anderson recommended . . . for the obvious reason that it is eight hundred feet lower than the Naches."[22]

If the mood was temporarily lightened by this intelligence, Harris brought things back to earth by condemning the forfeiture fanatics. Seattle, he suggested, would do well to desist:

"We will make all the land a great deal more valuable, I will say five times. I could say ten, and we will sell for $2.50 an acre land that is worth $10 or $20 . . . by reason of the building of the road. If you want the road to be built sooner than it can any other way, you had better let the Northern Pacific go ahead and do it. There is not a congressman and there is not a gentleman anywhere who will not look into this thing and see it correctly and say that it would be wise for Congress to resume the lands, unless they want to stop the building of the Cascade Division altogether. Of course I understand that some gentle-

men in Seattle think that if the Northern Pacific was out of the way somebody else would build it quicker."

They would find themselves in for a long wait, Harris ventured. "I know there is some little difference between planning railroads and building them."[23]

James McNaught then took the floor and attempted to soft-pedal Seattle's militancy: "Until the past fall and winter, the people of Seattle were heart and hand with the Northern Pacific, and were in favor of retaining the land grant. But in a very few weeks a change came over the spirit of their dreams. The populace and people were in favor of forfeiture." But, McNaught temporized, "The businessmen of Seattle have never been, and are not now, in favor of forfeiting the land grant of the railroad, if it will construct the road across the mountains."[24]

Thomas Burke would have none of it. Leaping to his feet, he proceeded to serve Harris his full dose of the Seattle Idea:

"We have built our towns and cities, and developed the country. We are building our own railroads, and after all this is done, in comes the Northern Pacific Railroad and demands to give them more than half the country. For what? Broken promises? For retarding the growth of the country by holding it in bondage? The people of Seattle have never received any favors from the company, and they have never expected any. All we want is fair play. As a simple illustration of the childish hostility shown by the company to Seattle, I will refer you to the course of the company when, about a year ago, an edition of the Northern Pacific folder was published in which Seattle was spoken of as the 'Queen City of Puget Sound.' With the change of administration, the great corporation was stirred to its lowest depths, and promptly the whole edition was suppressed! Today your trains are run so as to cause this city and the travelling public coming here as much inconvenience as possible."[25]

"Well," Harris swallowed, "the main thing is to place a tunnel of two miles in the Stampede Pass, and to put you in full communication with the east. And then you can go down to Tacoma as often as you want, and catch a train."

Red-faced Judge Burke had the last word: "We will never want to go there!"

Harris made his escape, and Tacoma chuckled at his hot reception in "Yeslerville."

"The seat of President Harris must have been exceedingly warm," scolded the *Ledger*. "Pretty much every official of the Northern Pacific . . . has received the same treatment at the hands of Seattle as that meted out to President Harris . . . The attempts of the company thus far to placate unreasonable enemies has only resulted in puffing them up with an inordinate idea of their own importance, and the company should now try the plan of leaving them severely alone."

Radebaugh taxed the Seattle fanatics with scaring investors away from railroad securities, scaring farmers who had in good faith purchased railroad land, and drying up the money market: "The action of the demagogues . . . in proposing a forfeiture of the land grant has thrown a cloud upon the title of these farms which results in a money stringency from St. Paul to Tacoma."[26]

Radebaugh was not alone in his concerns. Cooler heads in Seattle were also beginning to wonder if things had not gone too far.

"The door was thrown wide open and our skeleton exposed, and to what purpose?" mused the *Herald*. "Simply to allow the Tacoma Ledger an opportunity to arraign Robert Harris severely, and destroy the chances of his fulfilling the promises he made while here . . . Our leading citizens had better consider this matter seriously and carefully, and determine if this open war between the Northern Pacific and Seattle cannot be brought to a close. There is nothing in it but business stagnation for us."[27]

At the moment, however, things were picking up nicely. The first Seattle trains consisted of a single coach and baggage car, but, as more and more carloads of hay, hops, potatoes, mail, and merchandise rolled through the White River Valley, train size grew.

"The slow time made over the road has been against it," the *Post-Intelligencer* reported, "as well as the lack of a trainman with gumption enough to tell passengers arriving from Portland they could continue on to Seattle for a dollar . . . The other day two passenger coaches came and went full, and yesterday three."

The trains were locals only; the Northern Pacific was declining both to assign an agent at Seattle and forward freight beyond Tacoma except by steamers of the OR&N, with which it had an interchange agreement. Through passengers were also obliged to change trains. Nevertheless, one could board the cars on Elliott Bay and ride to the Hudson River. Seattle's motto, "New York Alki," had come true.[28]

Then the trains stopped. On August 21, Puget Sound Shore Railroad superintendent Thomas J. Milner received a telegram curtly informing him that the Northern Pacific was terminating its end of the service and recalling its equipment. There was no further explanation. Had Robert Harris, his seat still warm, decided to leave Seattle "severely alone"? Many believed as much.

It was a lingering disagreement, actually, between the Northern Pacific and the Oregon Improvement Company over dollars and terms that embargoed the Orphan Road. General Manager Muir considered the Puget Sound Shore's earnings "rather poor picking" that barely paid operating costs. The primitive conditions at Seattle remained problematic. "As you have no facilities for delivering freight to the boats at Seattle, except by paying drayage and additional dockage," NP's Jule H. Hannaford wrote Elijah Smith, "I do not see how we can consistently turn over through business to your company."

The situation was soon addressed. Under Oregon Improvement control, the Pacific Coast Steamship Company had grown to a substantial fleet of more than a dozen modern steamers—including the *Queen of the Pacific*, *City of Puebla*, and *Umatilla*—serving the West Coast from Victoria to San Diego. Without railroad connections at Seattle, however, this fleet was living on half a loaf, and Smith had little choice but spend the money on an extension from the broad gauge strip onto the south side of the OIC's City Dock at the foot of Main Street. That August, Seattle entered the intermodal age.[29]

Then there was the question of hops. Since the 1860s, hops had been a prime crop of the Puyallup and White river valleys, and, by reciprocal contract signed in June, the Puget Sound Shore was obliged to ship this potentially lucrative produce via the Northern Pacific and Tacoma, at 55¢ per ton, instead of via OR&N-OIC steamers from Seattle—at $20 a ton.

Understandably, Muir tried to wriggle around the deal. "It is our object to see business go via the ocean," he wrote Smith on August 21. "As far as we can we will quietly let the business go via Seattle."

Apparently, they were not quiet enough. Hannaford got wind of the subterfuge and wired Muir sternly: "It has been reported to me that you are offering rates and are endeavoring to divert hops from us . . . Will you quote rates over our line only."

Muir reported to his boss that the Northern Pacific's "fear of losing the hops business" was the real reason for the embargo.[30]

There were other problems. NP division superintendent James Buckley complained that running backward from Seattle to Tacoma was courting disaster. Neither side could agree on how to pay the train crews. Until this matter was settled to the NP's satisfaction, Oakes informed Muir, no trains would run. It was hopeless, Muir sighed: The Puget Sound Shore really had no reason to exist—it was "simply a terminating link for the Northern Pacific," he told Smith, and before long would doubtless be absorbed by the transcontinental. Until then, though, the small road must not be bullied. Elijah Smith's verdict was succinct: "If it don't pay . . . we should shut it up."[31]

Robert Harris agreed that his company should take over the short line. At Tacoma on August 23, he and local NP officials incorporated the Northern Pacific & Puget Sound Shore Railroad. This entity would take full legal control of the unchartered Puyallup-Stuck Junction branch, and acquire the Puget Sound Shore. It would also build a railroad and telegraph lines between Seattle, Bellingham, and Fidalgo bays. Concurrently, the Northern Pacific & Cascade Railroad was organized to build additional branch lines in the Carbonado coal fields. All these lines were "intended to be feeders of and to be operated in connection with the Northern Pacific Railroad."[32]

Other factors prompted the creation of this new hybrid, most notably increasing railroad activity further north. Summer 1883 saw the birth of two Bellingham Bay railroads by local and outside capital intent on reaping the coal and timber resources of the northern Sound—the Bellingham Bay & British Columbia Railroad, created by San Franciscans Pierre B. Cornwall and Darius Ogden Mills, and the Bellingham Bay Railway & Navigation Co., spearheaded by Senator Eugene Canfield, cousin of Thomas Canfield. These ventures appeared to have real money behind them, and boded a definite threat to the Northern Pacific's Puget Sound monopoly, especially if they should extend into Canada or southward to Seattle. Cornwall and Canfield both made a big show of surveying and initial construction, a show that properly alarmed Robert Harris when he paid his visit the following July.[33]

The Northern Pacific & Puget Sound Shore was a first step toward realizing the Villard plan of absorbing the independently chartered branch lines into the NP, a necessary step in giving legal standing to the unchartered Puyallup-Stuck Junction "orphan," and a strategic move to expand the NP's scope and pre-empt competition in a region of fast-growing importance. The scheme would hang fire for several years, however. Finishing the Cascade Division was the immediate priority, and the substantial improvements needed on the Puget Sound Shore, along with its continuing floating debt, further weighed against timely consummation. Beyond any of these factors, the scheme's implications for Tacoma, and the dominant board faction that had invested heavily at the terminus, were profound.

Its railroad to the outside world idled after only one month, Seattle's sense of outrage, always acute, was freshly ignited. To chamber of commerce complaints, Robert Harris insisted that the Northern Pacific was ready to resume service "on a fair basis,"[34] but was being stonewalled by the Oregon Improvement Company. He proposed to reopen the Seattle branch, splitting local receipts fifty-fifty, and generously offered the use of Northern Pacific rolling stock. Less generously, he remained firm in his insistence that the right to set through rates be reserved to the NP alone; the Puget Sound Shore could take its pickings and like it.

"This would not do at all," Muir complained to Smith. What's more, Muir charged, Harris was playing a cute "game of freeze out" in a shrewd calculation intended to depress the Shore road's earnings so he could pick it up it at a bargain basement price. Muir informed the Seattle Chamber of Commerce that Harris' "fair basis" would force the Puget Sound Shore out of business.

Perhaps the chamber would be interested in knowing, too, that in a meeting with Elijah Smith, Harris had bluntly stated that "nothing could be done in an agreement between the two companies ignoring Tacoma as the terminus . . . and the distributing point for the Sound."

Muir pushed the right button. For Seattle, the Northern Pacific remained the goat. Still, rapidly increasing settlement and agricultural development in the White River Valley could not be overlooked, and, in March

1885, Harris and Muir met in New York and agreed that the Orphan Road should run on "almost any terms" the Northern Pacific desired, provided they not mean an outright money loss to the Oregon Improvement Company. Harris submitted the proposition to the NP executive committee, but that Charles Wright-dominated body refused even to consider the matter. Cows would rule the Orphan Road for another six months.[35]

Tacoma gloated over the demise of "the back-down-from Seattle bobtailed train," and Seattle looked desperately around for other connections—the Canadian Pacific, pushing steadily west toward Burrard Inlet, and the Union Pacific, reaching from Salt Lake City toward a junction with the OR&N at Huntington, Oregon. Perhaps they could be coaxed further. The city also took up the matter of John Howard's Cedar River subsidy. Moreover, Pierre B. Cornwall and Darius Ogden Mills once more entered the picture and promised the Columbia & Puget Sound a $50,000 loan to extend to their Black Diamond coal mine. With this backing, the city council gave Howard the nod in September; subscription books were reopened, and in short order $77, 825 was pledged. Roadbed advanced up the Cedar.

With King County deprived of train service and the farmers of the Palouse still groaning under discriminatory rates, the land grant forfeiture movement reached its climax in the autumn of 1884. Thomas Burke wrote a pro-forfeiture Democratic Party plank, and on October 4 opened the territorial Democratic convention in Walla Walla with a bitter broadside at the "monstrous, grasping corporation":

"We denounce, as fraught with peril to our rights and liberties, the high handed attempt of the Northern Pacific Railroad Company to control the legislation and politics of this territory . . . Here the pioneers came long before railroads, and hewed out homes in the forests, and built up prosperous towns and cities, and after these pioneers are gray and bowed with age, this railroad company comes along to relieve them of their property."[36]

Charles S. Voorhees of Colfax was nominated the party's congressional candidate and contributed his own fiery anti-NP orations. The territorial Republican Party platform also called for forfeiture of unearned lands along the Columbia and managed to garner a near-majority. Thomas Brents, the incumbent Republican delegate, had co-sponsored a bill forfeiting the Columbia River land grant, the sacrificial lamb accepted by the railroad and forfeitors alike, but he and his successor, J.M. Armstrong of Spokane Falls, were dismissed as "tools of the monopoly" by the militants. Monopoly or not, the Republicans still commanded majority support in much of the territory and it was only the large King County vote that narrowly tipped the vote to Voorhees. (In November, Democrat Grover Cleveland would be elected U.S. President on a national platform that also included forfeiture.)

Robert Harris remained philosophical. "Voorhees elected will by no means be so violent and extreme as Voorhees the candidate," he confided to Thomas Oakes. "We may rely upon the people of Washington eventually to acknowledge what makes for their own interest."[37]

During the summer, powerful Oregon senator Joseph Norton Dolph, an ex-NP attorney and a co-incorporator of the Puget Sound Shore Railroad, stepped into the forfeiture fray and put up his own version of the sacrificial lamb bill as a "firebreak" around the forfeiture movement. With the Oregon Railway & Navigation Co. already entrenched on the Oregon side of the Columbia, the Northern Pacific about to build the Cascade branch, and the river country rapidly filling with settlers (constituents) anxious to secure title to land, Dolph was on firm ground. Like the Mitchell and Brents bills, his would foreclose NP's Wallula-Portland grant in exchange for a time extension on construction of the Cascade Division.

Land contiguous to the Cascade Division was another story. "The citizens of Washington Territory were among the earliest and most intelligent friends of the Northern Pacific railroad," Dolph declaimed before Congress on July 3. "They believe that they are entitled to direct railroad communication with the eastern portion of the territory, and with the main line of the Northern Pacific

railroad by way of the Cascade branch. I believe they are so entitled . . . I have no doubt that the effect of the forfeiture will be the necessary suspension of the work of construction upon this branch as well as upon the mainline."

Dolph's bill was one of three aimed at the NP land grant in 1884.

Nevertheless, Robert Harris felt fully justified that September in reporting to the board and stockholders: "Such firm reliance is placed in the good faith of the people and the Congress . . . and in the justice and legal impregnability of the company's position," that forfeiture was a virtual impossibility. Events proved him right.[38]

While the Orphan Road rusted, things elsewhere were moving. In June, an astonishing cargo arrived in Portland aboard the bark *Tillie Starbuck* from the Wilmington, Delaware, shipyard of Harlan & Hollingsworth: 579 crates bearing the 57, 515 pieces of the Northern Pacific's Columbia River car ferry. Assembled during the summer in a Portland shipyard, the 360-foot craft was the second largest of its kind in the world (after Southern Pacific's 370-foot *Solano*), capable of carrying twelve passenger cars or twenty-seven freight cars on its three parallel tracks. "*Kalama*" had been lettered on the transfer boat's name board, but during his summer inspection tour Robert Harris decided the name was homely and too easily mispronounced, and had it changed to "*Tacoma.*"

It was not until October that the west-bank Portland-Hunters line was at last ready to run. Beginning a quarter-century of faithful service, the Northern Pacific flagship began ferrying trains which presented a startling contrast to the little mixed affairs of 1873. Long strings of ten or more coaches and, since April including Pullman sleepers, rushed settlers to the terminus behind hooting 4-4-0s newly converted to burn Wilkeson coal. Passengers sat down to cutlets and squab in Villard's new dining cars, first in the Northwest. If all went well, the Portland-Tacoma journey consumed seven hours.

Aboard the swaying coaches, toppered and bonneted gentlefolk rubbed elbows with a more earthy crowd.

"The cars are crowded and the passengers are steadfastly engaged in occupying more space than the rules allow, but the trainmen permit," observed a Montana visitor. "On our right sit a couple of Portland 'dudes,' who find no end of material for shallow comment, criticism, and boisterous laughter. They are giddy youths, endeavoring to create the inference that they are worldwide travelers. They call to the train boy at the car's length . . . expostulate loudly, and in vigorous tones condemn the Puget Sound country as one of high prices and inferior accommodations."[39]

Soot blew in through the windows in summer, quids of tobacco besmirched the aisles, and the cars were ripe with ambiguous odors; reclining seats, steam heat, and air conditioning were unknown.

Freight, freight, and more freight was coming up the line. A *Ledger* reporter visited the Tacoma wharf one day in November and jotted down the consist of a typical arriving train: three cars of merchandise, one car of sheep, one car of cement, one car of merchandise, one car of sugar, and one of whiskey, all bound for Tacoma, Port Townsend, Victoria, and "way stations." Despite lingering dull times, settlement and business development were growing steadily. Between 1873 and 1884, Seattle's population increased from 1,400 to almost 10,000; barking at her heels, Tacoma was pushing 6,000. Men laid off early in the year were re-hired by summer, and at the Tacoma car shops hundreds were kept busy turning out a seemingly endless stream of freight cars.[40]

The race for Puget Sound supremacy was heating to a boil, and the Seattle-Tacoma feud with it. Seattle editors missed no opportunity to tweak the terminal city, the railroad, and its "little suckling," the Tacoma Land Company.

"The [railroad] company dictates every movement, social, business, political, and municipal," observed the *Post-Intelligencer*. "The population basks in the company's smiles and cringes at its frowns. Little attempts at rebellion are promptly put down. The company . . . tells the people who shall preside at their public meetings, who shall lead off in society, who shall be their officials, and

STANDARD AND NARROW GAUGE RAILS MEET AT THE SOUTH END OF THE BROAD GAUGE STRIP, CA. 1888. ON THE LEFT IS PUGET SOUND SHORE NO. 1 LEADING A THREE-CAR TRAIN, WHILE STANDING AT RIGHT IS COLUMBIA & PUGET SOUND 2-8-0 NO. 8 LEADING A STRING OF C&PS ENGINES. NO. 8 WAS THE LARGEST OF THE SLIM-GAUGE C&PS LOCOMOTIVES, AND LATER WAS SOLD TO THE WHITE PASS & YUKON RR. TODAY, IT IS PRESERVED AND ON DISPLAY AT DAWSON CITY, YUKON TERRITORY. THE ENGINES ARE GAILY DECORATED, PERHAPS IN OBSERVANCE OF THE FOURTH OF JULY.

Mendenhall collection

who shall be placed under the ban of popular disapproval . . . If one wants to live and prosper there, he soon finds it necessary to fawn upon the powers that be . . . Independence of the railroad element means social ostracism and business destruction. This is recognized all through town."[41]

Banker Noah B. Coffman, who the year before had come so hopefully to Tacoma, found himself among the disillusioned. "The Tacoma Land Company had assumed an air of perfect confidence that in the titanic struggle with Seattle, Tacoma was a sure winner. The tense atmosphere of speculation and uncertainty made me restless. The overlordship of the Company's managers was distasteful to me. It reached into public business, social relationships, and private transactions. Values seemed to me to be unstable."

Disillusioned, Coffman pulled up stakes for the "more wholesome environment" of a Chehalis Valley farm.[42]

Other Tacomans grumbled at railroad overlordship as well, particularly its hogging the waterfront and its failure to improve its facilities, symbolized by the meager little frame station at 17th and Pacific, built in September 1883 and sarcastically dubbed "Villard Depot" by rueful residents. Malcontents rallied around John E. Burns, who derided General Sprague as the "autocrat of Tacoma" and led the fight against railroad bullying. In a bid to recapture the Tacoma waterfront, Burns and his coterie began making "improvements" of their own on the tideflats in the spring of 1884—driving piles and planting oyster beds.

Sprague took vigorous umbrage to Burns' accusations. "I have felt a deep interest in the welfare and prosperity of this city on the question of public policy, and I have usually exercised a citizen's privilege and have expressed my views as my best judgement dictates . . . If it is true, as charged, that I have controlled the affairs of this city for the last five years, I have done a grand, good work, for its growth and prosperity have been almost without parallel in the United States."

Meanwhile, NP engineer Isaac Anderson bought up every pile-driver on the Sound and out-piled the insurgents.

The waterfront remained in railroad hands, but a residue of bitterness would linger for many years.[43]

Self-important Seattle remained the favorite target of Tacoma editors. The Queen City had no railroad, Randolph Radebaugh chuckled—why not try balloons? "It is a fact that Seattle, having failed to succeed in operating the few miles of railroad now under her control, by reason of a lack of money to purchase locomotive fuel, will be able to keep up the operating expenses of balloons at little or no outlay of cash. There is a surplus of gaseous matter floating about the city which might be economically applied to inflating the aerial machines. Balloons are certainly the hope of our subscription paper neighbor."[44]

But not all of Seattle was of one mind, either. The Herald sensed danger in "stuffing a deluded constituency with anti-railroad taffy . . . Our best policy is to make the most of the railroad mess which Villard left to the N.P.R.R. Complete the Cedar River road to the 'common point' at once, and extend every facility to the Northern Pacific to build its Cascade branch. Do anything, in heaven's name, that will enable a long suffering people to have through railroad connections with eastern Washington . . . We are tired of this child's play, and so is the public."

As for perennial hopes that the Union Pacific or Canadian Pacific would soon be at the city's doorstep, these were ephemeral at best: "Some will swear the vapor noticed 'round the base of [Mt.] Rainier is steam issuing from one of Jay Gould's locomotives. Yes, we think we can see one now, in our mind only . . . No, we have no faith in the energy of the boy who was trapping rats. When asked how many he had, he replied, 'After I catch this one and two more I will have three.' Give us a side grip on rat No. 1, there is plenty of time to wait for number two or three."[45]

Rat number two came within reach in November 1884, as the first Union Pacific trains from Salt Lake City steamed into Portland over the OR&N from Huntington, Oregon. For the next twenty years, Seattle would court the UP and find it a handy "club" against the Northern Pacific. In December, the Seattle Chamber of Commerce gave Robert Harris an ultimatum: Open the Orphan Road at once, or Seattle merchants would boycott the NP and give all their business to the Central Pacific and Union Pacific. Harris ignored the threat, and the boycott drew only half-hearted participation.

January saw the Columbia & Puget Sound's Cedar River extension reach the new coal towns of Black Diamond and Franklin; only a few miles now separated the narrow gauge from the common point. And at four o'clock on the afternoon of January 23, the little flag-bedecked *A.A. Denny* crept down the Seattle waterfront, its clanging bell announcing the completion of track to Columbia Street. Hundreds watched as photographer J.C. Haines crouched under his black hood and committed the event to posterity.

Despite signs of optimism, times remained hard for many during the long, gradual recovery from the Villard bust. A prime target for frustration became the Northwest's hard-working railroad builders—the Chinese. Seattle's Chinese community had its beginnings in 1868 when Chin Chun Hock founded the Wa Chong Company. At its Mill Street office, Wa Chong manufactured cigars, sold tea, and offered a tailoring service. Chin Gee Hee arrived in 1875, became Hock's partner, and began importing Chinese laborers to help grade city streets and build the Seattle & Walla Walla Railroad. Thousands more crossed the Pacific or were "imported" from San Francisco to meet the huge labor demands of the Northern Pacific. During the height of the Villard boom, more than 15,000 Chinese were at work on the main and branch lines of the Northern Pacific.[46]

Chinese workers proved to be tireless, efficient, and uncomplaining. Without their contribution, the Pacific Northwest would have had a much longer wait for both railroads and ultimate prosperity. When times were good and the territory was eager for railroads, the Chinese were welcomed, as long as they kept to themselves. Lean times were another matter, and the habits of many "Celestials"—sending money home to China rather than spending it in the territory, live hog butchering, wearing pigtails—struck idle, brooding whites as alien and unwholesome.

In the doldrums of 1885, unemployed Caucasian laborers forgot their previous grudging admiration for "good old John Chinaman." Tempers flared when word got around that the Northern Pacific had replaced white laborers by coolies, at half-pay. Children threw rocks at Chinese, and their parents took up the cry of "The Chinese Must Go!" Here was one thing Seattle and Tacoma could agree on, and Chinese workers who had so recently brought rails to both cities were attacked, burned out of their houses, and run out of town.

While the more sober and affluent condemned lawlessness (if, for no other reason, than for fear eastern capital would be scared away), most concurred that the Chinese were a "disturbing element in the community." Thomas Burke, who had served many Chinese clients in his law practice, begged his neighbors not to succumb to lawlessness, and David Denny praised the Chinese for their sobriety and industriousness. For these considerations, such moderates were scorned as "White Chinese" and hooted down at town meetings.

At the height of the hysteria, merchants were visited by Chinese exclusion committees. A refusal to sign their petitions was under pain of a boycott or broken shop windows. In Tacoma, the Chinese residents were marched out of town in a body and put aboard trains for Portland. The *Ledger* primly recommended the "Tacoma Method" as the ideal solution to the Chinese "menace."

Under orders of Governor Watson Squire, federal troops bivouacked on the streets of Seattle and Tacoma to protect Chinese life and property. After climaxing in scattered skirmishes and a few fatalities, the movement ran out of steam in the improving economy of 1886. Anti-Chinese sentiment and discrimination continued strong, however. Ironically, it was at this time, and at the home of the "Tacoma method," that tea shipments from China began arriving, presaging a coming era of Far East trade on Puget Sound.[47]

Meanwhile, the Orphan Road rusted. Robert Harris paid a call at Seattle in July 1885, and again tried to make peace with the chamber of commerce. Dry goods leader

Bailey Gatzert informed Harris: "Had the road between Tacoma and Seattle been operated since its construction in a proper manner, there is no doubt a city of 30,000 people would already be here established, looking for transportation to your company."

Business was business, Harris nodded, and promised to continue talks with Elijah Smith until satisfactory results could be obtained. "It will be no fault of mine if that road is not soon in operation!"[48]

It wasn't, and exasperation grew. As John Muir had hoped, prevailing Seattle opinion blamed the NP and took pity on the little Oregon Improvement Co. as just another hapless victim of the monstrous, grasping corporation. Especially irked were valley farmers, who had signed over liberal rights of way for a railroad that did not run, and whose produce now had to slog to market in wagons over poor or non-existent roads. One of them, Erastus "Foghorn" Green (whose basso-profundo orations were well-known in the valley) decided enough was enough, and called a mass meeting in the little White River Valley community known locally as both Kent and Titusville, to try to get their railroad back. On September 26, several hundred cigar smoking, tobacco chewing farmers, businessmen, lawyers, and other citizens filed into Templars Hall.

Judge J.R. Lewis opened the proceedings with the declaration that it was the Seattle Idea that had taken the land grant forfeiture movement clear to the White House. Quoting at length from several law books, Lewis declared that the sole object of a railroad's existence was to serve the public good. If it refused, the "aggrieved parties"—in this instance farmers and anyone else who had deeded rights of way to the Puget Sound Shore—were entitled by eminent domain to file suit for the line's operation, or to repossess its franchise and turn it over to someone who *would* operate it. An anxious murmuring filled the hall. Then Lewis blamed the whole mess on Charles Wright, who was said to spend his waking moments in fear that the Orphan Road would boom Seattle and "thereby rob the legal terminus of a portion of its glory."[48]

The ever-vigilant James McNaught sprang to his feet and objected to forcing the operation of a railroad "without money, without motive power or rolling stock, and which under the circumstances, would only involve a money loss to its owners."

Yes, it was unfortunate that the Northern Pacific and Oregon Improvement Company could not come to terms, but the ongoing negotiations between Robert Harris and Elijah Smith were evidence of good faith. McNaught lambasted the Seattle Idea: Such foolishness had "forfeited for the town of Seattle the favorable consideration of the Northern Pacific railroad." Loss of business establishments in Seattle and King County, sacrifice of millions of dollars in tax assessments, and scores of "tenantless houses" in a depressed Seattle, were all the result of antagonizing the corporation.[49]

"I regret that the assembly has not been served with more substantial pabulum from Mr. McNaught," grumbled Judge Cornelius Hanford. He seconded Judge Lewis in demanding that railroads uphold their charter obligations; the railroad should serve the purposes of its creation and be available for the public use and benefit. If the corporation differences could not be harmonized on account of a dog-in-the-manger policy on the part of any one of the companies, "the dog should then be lifted out and the willing ox be permitted to eat."

Oregon Improvement Co.'s John Howard explained that the Puget Sound Shore was owned by Oregon & Transcontinental, and that, while his company had no interest in it, Elijah Smith had assumed a caretaker role toward the property. Smith would much prefer to operate the Orphan Road, Howard affirmed, but, as neither he nor his stockholders believed it would pay, and the NP refused to compromise and the Oregon & Transcontinental could not afford to, it sat idle.[50]

Judge Orange Jacobs lightened the mood with an amusing anecdote involving a philosopher, a cow, and a knothole.

Just then, John Howard shouted for recognition, waving a telegram. It was from Elijah Smith (it had been received at McNaught's law office in Seattle, rushed to Black River Junction by train, and relayed on horseback to Titusville by McNaught law partner John Mitchell). Howard read the wire to a hushed crowd: "Negotiations referred to yesterday resulted in arrangement that will enable us to open road about October 1st." Applause erupted, chairs scraped, fresh cigars were lit, and the great Titusville railroad meeting adjourned with high hopes.[51]

Thomas Oakes arrived in town on October 15, inspected the Orphan Road, and promised that trains would be running by the end of the month: "We shall furnish such trains as the trade demands and run to the joint interests of the people and the road. You should remember that the Northern Pacific owns no line into Seattle, though it naturally should be the possessor of the track owned by the other two connecting companies. It was no doubt part of Villard's program to merge the lines into the Northern Pacific system, and who knows what may be the ultimate outcome? The opening of traffic now is about all that the people should expect. Things must have a beginning and this one seems to me to be a promising one."[52]

The line had never been ballasted and had suffered several washouts during its year of dormancy, so laborers promptly set things right. A turntable was installed at the north end of the broad gauge strip—no more backing down to Tacoma. Thomas J. Milner was named joint general manager for both the Puget Sound Shore and Columbia & Puget Sound, and Troilus H. Tyndale—Henry Villard's cousin,

THE GREAT SEATTLE FIRE OF JUNE 6, 1889, LEFT THE WATERFRONT COMMERCIAL FACILITIES IN CHARRED DEVASTATION. IN THIS VIEW LOOKING NORTH FROM YESLER AVENUE, THE TWISTED RAILS OF THE SEATTLE LAKE SHORE & EASTERN ARE ON THE LEFT AND THE THREE-RAIL RAM'S HORN TRACK IS TO THE RIGHT.

Museum of History and Industry, #1340

Blind Pool accountant, and OR&N assistant secretary—became the Puget Sound Shore's new president.

On October 26, the cows were permanently banished from the Orphan Road and twice-daily service began. The "through" train left Seattle at 2:25 AM, to connect at Tacoma with the Portland train; this delivered eastbound travelers to the Oregon Railway & Navigation Co., which after the cancellation of the traffic agreement connected with NP trains at Wallula Junction. The northbound through schedule departed Tacoma at 8:10 PM, to reach Seattle at 10:35. A local was scheduled out of Seattle at 3:10 PM, to run only as far as Stuck Junction, where engine and crew would lay over for the night and return to Seattle next morning. Northern Pacific engines and crews would now stick to home rails and turn at Stuck Junction, so Milner leased 4-4-0 Number 3 and a passenger coach from the OR&N. The fare to any point on the line was $1.

Seattle was pacified, but just barely. Complaints of delays and other imperfections were quick to arise, prompting the *Ledger* to note:

"The Seattle Post-Intelligencer must have a sour stomach . . . after clamoring for many weary months for the operation of the 'Orphan' road, the *P.I.* began to grumble within two days after the trains commenced to run. Nothing will please our dyspeptic contemporary except the operation of the entire Northern Pacific railroad system in the interest of Seattle."[53]

Division Superintendent Buckley and freight agent W.B. Curtis vehemently denied any anti-Seattle subterfuge. The only grievances either gentleman had ever heard of were those mysteriously appearing in the columns of the Portland and Seattle papers.

Seattle dyspepsia became apoplexy on March 16, 1886, when the departure of the early morning Tacoma train was set ahead four hours, from 2:25 to 6:40 AM, causing it to miss the southbound Portland connection by two hours. Travelers going south or east were now faced with a 15 to 22-hour layover at the terminus, and the press took it as an escalation of war: "The malignity,

the bitter spirit of hatred, with which the blow was aimed is too clear and too plain for the warmest admirer of the Northern Pacific Railroad to longer deny that the corporation is the bitter and unrelenting enemy of the city."[54]

"Bosh!" snorted Oakes, wiring his explanation to President Harris. "I made change recently localizing train so that people residing midway between Seattle and Tacoma could arrive in Tacoma in the morning . . . and leave in evening on return trip."

The Seattle run was losing at least $500 a month on its former schedule, he added. If Seattle wanted the trains run to its liking, Oakes suggested, it could jolly well fork over the $500 every month. If the NP was going to do business on the Orphan Road, he wrote later, that business should benefit Tacoma: "Running our trains as we did before, all local business went to Seattle." If Seattle paid her way, fine, but "some assurance must be given that they will discontinue their hostility to this company."

As usual, Harris replied diplomatically. "There can be no doubt that we should run the trains in the manner that is best from a business standpoint. Public opinion will support us in this just as surely as it will condemn us if we undertake to run them to the disaccommodations of business . . . We will stand better with the Territory by trying to do what is fair and reasonable with every part of it than by unnecessarily antagonizing any section."[55]

However equable he may have been, Robert Harris was not above a little backroom arm-twisting. In October, Seattle lawyer John J. McGilvra met with him in New York.

Put the trains back on their old schedules, requested McGilvra.

"Call off your dogs," replied Harris; the schedule would hold unless Seattle held her tongue. Also, an offensive forfeiture resolution put up by the "carpetbagger" Voorhees must be withdrawn.[56]

McGilvra reddened, took his leave, and when he got home composed his response: "Your attitude, your words, and your acts combined constituted the best possible illustration of the old fable of the wolf and the lamb, so far as the disposition of your company to act the role of the wolf is concerned; but in this case, the lamb is a stalwart young city by the sea, disposed to stand his ground; and besides, Mr. Wolf, the shepherd is at hand, and the dogs will not be called off."

The Seattle Idea would remain steadfast, McGilvra declared, as long as the railroad persisted in its "plain, palpable, and deliberate attempt . . . to destroy a pioneer city of twelve thousand people . . . You, as an intelligent man, must know that Seattle is the proper terminus for your road."

Harris stood his ground, and Seattle and looked north for salvation. The Canadian Pacific Railway was completed from Montreal to Port Moody, British Columbia, in November 1885. With the start of regular service early the next year, the CPR began an aggressive bid for the Seattle trade, touting a superior route and service while declaring in cunning sales pitches that Seattle had not been given due deference by certain other railroad companies.

"Seattle is now independent of the townsite-booming, rule-or-ruin policy of the Northern Pacific Railroad!" cheered the *Post-Intelligencer*, observing that many shippers were routing their trade via the CPR.[57]

Closer to home, Judge Burke had finally made good on his March 1884 pledge of a new railroad backed by "representatives of eastern capital." In April 1885, he and other railroad militants formed the Seattle Lake Shore & Eastern to cross Snoqualmie Pass to an eastern Washington junction with an unspecified major line. With big money in the offing, this boded well for Seattle.

In January 1886, the Northern Pacific announced that the final seventy-five mile gap in the Cascade Division between Green River and Ellensburg would be closed as soon as possible. After considering a temporary cog railroad, Oakes announced that a switchback would carry trains over the 3,664-foot summit until the two-mile tunnel, 1,100 feet lower, could be finished.

On July 27, the Northern Pacific & Puget Sound Shore bestirred itself and purchased the uncharted Puyallup-Stuck Junction line from the NP for the cost of construction, $275,000, payable in equal amounts of the new corporation's capital stock and first mortgage bonds. The seven-mile orphan at last had a legal guardian. That September, the inadequacies of the Puget Sound Shore's equipment and service became glaringly apparent when the road's lone passenger coach was sent up for repairs at the Columbia & Puget Sound shops; hapless passengers were hauled in a boxcar.

East of the mountains, the sheriffs in Ellensburg and Cle Elum despaired of keeping the peace in their railroad boomtowns, and the NP attempted to enforce liquor bans at the "fronts." Still, the railheads advanced inexorably towards union on Stampede summit. Seattle rubbed her hands and vowed not be deprived of her rightful share of the avalanche of traffic, especially Palouse wheat, expected to flow toward Puget Sound over the completed Cascade Division. At the end of 1886, the chamber of commerce wired Robert Harris and Elijah Smith, asking each whether or not the city could expect rate parity with Tacoma and Portland. Seattle stood ready to build grain warehouses, the chamber declared, in the event of a positive answer.

Smith's answer was prompt and tart. As the Puget Sound Shore was a virtual hostage of the NP: "This question might be more readily answered by the Northern Pacific Railroad Co."

With the Cascade Division about to become a reality, Seattle also felt renewed interest in a connection at the common point—the projected junction of the Columbia & Puget Sound and the NP eight miles east of Franklin. Smith made it clear there would be no such extension "until we have some assurance that freight and passengers delivered by our line to the N.P.R.R. would receive the proper attention and be forwarded with the same dispatch that their own passengers and freight receive."

James McNaught confidently asserted that the connection would soon be built and Tacoma sidetracked, while the *Ledger* guffawed: "If Seattle is determined to

Puget Sound Shore engine roster

No.	Type	Builder	Dates/notes
1	4-4-0	Pittsburgh	4/1888—To NP 367, 1890. Later NP 804.
2	4-4-0	Hinkley	?—Leased from OR&N, 1887, returned 3/1888.
3	4-4-0	?	?—Leased from OR&N, 1887, returned 3/1888.
366	4-4-0	Baldwin	3/1890—Ordered by PSS, but delivered as NP 366, renumbered 740.

have the eight miles of road, we suggest that the money raised two years ago on the famous $150,000 subscription be appropriated for that purpose . . . It is quite doubtful if there is any other place in the world where so many railroads and things are subscribed and so few railroads and things are built as in Seattle."[58]

The common point would twist in the wind for two more years. Columbia & Puget Sound superintendent Thomas Milner declared in March 1887: "It would cost $150,000 to build a road from a point near Franklin to the common point, and lay a third rail and put a standard gauge rolling stock on the Cedar River extension . . . and we have been unable to demonstrate to Mr. [Elijah] Smith how we could make such a road pay. To be sure, it would be a great accommodation, but we can perform all the service almost as well by the [Puget Sound Shore] short line, and you must remember that every dollar earned by the common point line would be a dollar taken from the Shore line."

In December, John Howard resubmitted his subsidy request to the Seattle City Council, to run the C&PS to the common point and convert it to standard gauge.

The council turned him down curtly: "The time for subsidized railroads in Seattle has passed."

After further prevarication, Milner announced in December 1888 that rail to close the gap was on the way, aboard the sailing ship *Henry Villard*. The rail wound up elsewhere, though, and no more was heard of the common point extension.[59]

In answer to the chamber of commerce query, Robert Harris reaffirmed: "It is the policy of the N.P.R.R. to secure the business of Seattle and all other points on the Sound to the furthest extent practicable, and discriminate against none."

He remained adamant, however, that the forfeiture cranks be silenced. During the year, Nebraska senator Van Wyck had entered an amendment to the Dolph bill, hanging Congressional fire since July 1884, to forfeit all "unearned" NP grant lands including those contiguous to the Cascade Division. On June 9, the amended bill cleared the Senate and was referred to the House.

Thomas Oakes wired NP land department head Paul Schulze: "You can say to the people of Washington Territory that if bill number eighteen hundred and twelve, the Dolph bill (amended by Van Wyck) becomes a law, the Northern Pacific company will be obliged to stop work on the Cascade division."[60]

Oakes' pronouncement seemed to have the desired effect. Even the Seattle press sensed it was time to cool things off.

"The time has certainly arrived when the 'Seattle idea' should pass from the politics of the territory," declared the *Times*. "Further agitation by the people . . . can have no influence upon the forfeiture issue . . . Seattle cannot do without the Northern Pacific, and the Northern Pacific cannot do without Seattle."[61]

Nor could Congress unite on the issue: The House called for revocation of all NP land from Bismarck west, while the Senate demanded only the Columbia River and Cascade Division tracts. In August, the Dolph-Van Wyck bill was tabled, never to rise again.

Before 1887 was several months old, it was readily

apparent that Seattle was becoming the focus of Puget Sound railroad activity. The Seattle Lake Shore & Eastern began laying rail eastward amid reports of heavy Wall Street backing. The St. Paul Minneapolis & Manitoba had already reached western Montana and President James Jerome Hill was casting his one good eye on the Sound. And the Canadian Pacific was garnering a substantial share of the city's trade. To the astute Robert Harris, it was only too clear that if the Northern Pacific could not accommodate the Queen City, and soon, others would.

It may have been more than mere coincidence that, on May 23, Assistant General Manager Buckley announced: "From this time on, the Northern Pacific Railroad will be run on strictly business principles, and all side-issues will be dropped."

James McNaught, too, perceived a "more liberal spirit" in the NP management toward Seattle, for good reason: "It is a fact that one car of freight is brought to stay at Tacoma, where ten cars go to Seattle."

Behind the scenes, the Northern Pacific board passed a resolution to furnish "reasonable connection" for Seattle, and instructed local personnel to cooperate with the Oregon Improvement Company in seeing that the city's wants were satisfied.[62]

Liberal spirit did not extend to Puget Sound editors. "The approaches to Tacoma on all sides are infested by the enemies of Tacoma who industriously ply their avocation of lying and slandering in the effort to fill the minds of travelers with prejudice against the fairest city of all the northwest," warned the *Ledger*.

PUGET SOUND SHORE LOCOMOTIVE NO. 1, BUILT BY PITTSBURGH LOCOMOTIVE WORKS AND DELIVERED IN THE SPRING OF 1888. THIS 4-4-0 WAS REDESIGNATED NORTHERN PACIFIC NO. 367 IN 1890, AND NP NO. 804 IN 1897.

James M. Fredrickson collection

The Seattle *Times* sneered back at its rival: "It perches up on the bold bluff at Tacoma with a restless eye upon all the surroundings, and never fails to screech at any movement of society, capital, or commerce which has not for its Mecca the boom town at the base of Mount Rainier."

And from Portland, the *Oregonian*—which until the advent of the Cascade Division had considered the Northern Pacific a friend—sounded its alarum of a huge Puget Sound conspiracy to drain the Willamette Valley of settlement. "Persons who have traveled over the Northern Pacific tell us that on every train . . . there are 'rounders' whose sole business it seems to be to talk about the 'terrible dangers of the Columbia River,' to disparage Portland and to assure all who will listen that the Northern Pacific will take the whole business of the Northwest away from this dangerous channel and doomed city."[63]

Most, however, looked forward to a new boom era approaching with the completion of the Cascade Division. The previous year, *The Northwest* magazine had predicted 100,000 settlers would move west during the ensuing twelve months, and offered encouragement:

"There are no hardships to endure worth mentioning. Farming settlement rarely goes more than twenty five miles from a railroad and the railroad brings all the usual comforts and luxuries of civilized life . . . To people who do not spend their leisure time in whisky shops, or flourish revolvers as an evidence of courage, life is about as quiet and orderly in Montana as in Ohio; indeed, it is much safer than in some of the East Side wards of New York City."[64]

Opening of the Cascade Division in July 1887 (and all-rail service to California over the Oregon & California railroad) did indeed spark a five-year period of unprecedented growth and prosperity on Puget Sound. Carloadings on the Orphan Road shot up from an average of six tons of freight a day to twenty or more. A Puget Sound Shore train arrived at Seattle on August 12 with one passenger coach, two cars of lumber, two cars of shingles, six cars of produce, two cars of cattle, two cars

of hogs, and five cars of general freight—grain, hides, condiments, coal oil, hay, wool, lime, corn, machinery, flour, and hops. The broad gauge strip and Oregon Improvement Company wharves were piled high with goods, and Seattle and Tacoma both puffed up happily with gingerbreaded new homes, brick office blocks, thickets of telephone poles, and horsecar lines.

Even more electrifying news came in September: Henry Villard was back!

The unlikely bedfellows of Elijah Smith, Robert Harris, and Charles Wright turned to Villard to mediate a dangerously escalating railroad rivalry east of the Cascades. Unless the NP, OR&N, and UP could come to terms, redundant line construction and rate wars portended to ruin them all. At Wright's behest, Villard, the great harmonizer, resumed his old NP board seat, but declined an offer of the presidency in deference to his old friend, Thomas Oakes.

While Villard made plans to bring about a truce by means of a joint NP/UP lease of the OR&N, Seattle celebrated with "jollifications" that almost eclipsed 1883's. A great bonfire blazed on Front Street, skyrockets whooshed into the night, revolvers were emptied with abandon, and a long Victorian conga line snaked uptown to the *Post-Intelligencer* office.

Dr. Thomas T. Minor wired Villard congratulations: "Our confidence and faith in you has never faltered, and tonight, with illuminations, cannon, and universal rejoicing, we are celebrating your returning to the directorate of the Northern Pacific."[65]

Minor also submitted Seattle's latest list of demands: End pro-Tacoma rate discrimination; abolish delays at the terminus; build to the common point; improve service on the Orphan Road; and restore Seattle to its rightful place in Northern Pacific brochures and maps. If that were not possible, Minor suggested, perhaps the NP could let the Union Pacific have trackage rights into the city and give it the service it deserved.

"Have faith and be patient," Villard replied. "Your just claims will be recognized." On November 2, 1887, the

Northern Pacific executive committee entered a resolution "to . . . see if an arrangement cannot be made by which this company shall acquire control of the Puget Sound Shore line."[66]

Up on Stampede Pass, Nelson and Sidney Bennett were driving their men hard in the two-mile summit tunnel. Tacoma excursionists journeyed to the east portal boomtown of Tunnel City, and cheered as the drillers picked up the tempo—ten, twelve, thirteen feet a day. Boring operations were state-of-the-art; a steam plant drove air compressors powering the latest drills, and the tube was bathed in electric light. Still, it was arduous work at best, and Sidney Bennett complained to his brother that he had three full crews on the job—"one coming, one drilling, and one quitting."

Confident Stampede Tunnel would be ready for traffic by the contract deadline of June 1, 1888, the Bennett brothers promised the first man through the hole a thousand dollar bonus, and the winning side a steak dinner with all the whiskey they could drink. The tunnel would knock a good four hours off the present time over the awkward and dangerous switchbacks; more than one engine lost brakes and took off into the ether. Thankfully, fatalities were few.

On May 3, specially picked "wrigglers" bumped heads in Stampede Tunnel. Their teammates shoved mightily on them until the west side man popped through victorious. On his heels was Sidney Bennett's wife, who, legend has it, stripped to her corset, slathered herself with lard, squeezed through the aperture, and emerged bruised but grinning to announce: "The drinks, gentlemen, are on my husband." Trains followed on the 27th.[67]

Things were busier than ever on the Orphan Road in 1888. Business was double 1887's, and hops accounted for much of the increase. With the fields of Britain and Europe decimated by disease and parasites, Puyallup and White River hops now commanded the world market, and long hops specials became a common sight. The Puget Sound Shore was compelled to lease two coaches from the Northern Pacific to handle the crowds, and in April purchased its first new locomotive, 45-ton 4-4-0 Number 1, a product of the Pittsburgh Locomotive Works. A used Hinkley engine, 35-ton Number 2, was acquired from the OR&N at the same time.

The mixed-train era ended in November, as "express" service was inaugurated—real passenger trains. Freight and passengers would now travel separately, though freights would "carry a caboose for the accommodation of passengers for whom it may be convenient." Times were indeed changing, and in April, "Seattle, The Beautiful and Prosperous Queen City of Puget Sound" was featured in *The Northwest* magazine.[68] If Charles Wright objected, no one was listening.

Though his urban dream was swiftly materializing, Arthur Denny was not entirely pleased with the new dispensation. The Seattle founder published his *Pioneer Days on Puget Sound* that year, and with stern pioneer rectitude excoriated the newcomers who seemed to want something for nothing—"degenerate scrubs too cowardly to face the same dangers that our pioneer men and women did, and too lazy to perform an honest day's work."

But progress was not to be denied. Relieving Robert Harris that March, President Oakes declared that "Seattle is one of the great cities of the Northwest. Many plans are afoot by the NP, and insure unprecedented progress for the booming place."[69]

Others resisted change. Cows were loath to give up their accustomed sunning spots on the Orphan Road, and stock claims rose along with traffic levels. Shore road president Tyndale complained of persistent gouging by avaricious ranchers, adding: "Whenever a cow is killed, we require engineers to fill out a blank form for such cases. I remember that one of the questions is, 'Was the animal badly hurt?' Once, an engineer who had run over a cow answered, 'Pretty badly hurt. She had her head and her two hind legs cut off.' Another question is, 'What was the disposition of the carcass?' An Irish engineer replied, 'Mild and gentle.' Still another is, 'Where was the animal struck?', and the reply was, 'Forty feet in the air'."

Tyndale praised a recent court judgement that held railroad companies harmless for stock killed on their rights of way. But he observed that the decision, while praiseworthy, would "work a hardship on engineers, for it will remove about the only opportunity they have for working off their surplus wit."[70]

More serious were pedestrian casualties along the line, which people found a convenient walking path. Engineers had standing orders to whistle at curves and other sight impairments, but still bumped or ran over individuals who failed to "look out for the cars."

Train-wagon collisions at crossings were frequent, and one engineer in particular became notorious for his altercations: "If this gentleman keeps on at the same rapid pace, he will soon have a record which will rival that of Jesse James or the Younger Brothers," complained the press, agitating for crossing guards and lights at the "death traps."[71] The poor yard track and primitive rolling stock caused frequent derailments in the Seattle yards, and collisions and runaways off the coal ramp were not uncommon; severe injury and death stalked the trainmen.

Such was the state of railroad affairs when, on the afternoon of June 6, 1889, the great Seattle fire erupted from an overturned glue pot. Conflagration engulfed the dense wooden blocks of the lower business district and waterfront, and by evening the entire southern half of downtown, including the landmark Yesler-Leary Building, was no more. Most of the railroad complex—the Columbia & Puget Sound shops, depot, wharves, numerous rolling stock, the old faithful coal-hauler *Geo. C. Bode*, and waterfront right of way—was destroyed. The broad gauge strip, adjoining freighthouse, and coal bunker all sustained damage.

Chaos reigned only temporarily. The following day, many businesses, "burned out but still on deck," reopened in tents, and, by June 10, large crews were busy rebuilding the rail facilities. Freight trains were held on sidings outside town for the few days it took to restore order, and a temporary depot was established at the south end of the broad gauge strip. Despite their feud with Seattle, both the Northern Pacific and Tacoma came through handsomely with special relief trains manned by volunteer crews and filled with donated food, clothing, tenting, and other necessities.

The *Ledger* noted approvingly that anyone now passing unkind words about Tacoma on the charred plank sidewalks of Seattle would be soundly thrashed. Henry Villard wired Arthur Denny: "Fullest sympathy for all the sufferers." A few days later, he and Oakes slipped quietly into town, viewed the blackened remains, and just as quietly slipped away. The leading businessmen quickly made plans to rebuild in fireproof materials, and scores of boxcars began descending upon Seattle, loaded with brick and Wilkeson sandstone.

Wood sufficed for the Puget Sound Shore's new depot, which opened in August at Third and South Weller on the west side of the broad gauge strip. The yellow, green, and brown frame structure looked "just like the 'Yaller Gal' at the corn huskin,'" mused the press, but was hardly the grand union depot of Seattle's dreams. The Northern Pacific had trimmed a full twelve hours off its present four-day St. Paul-Seattle time the previous April, and put on a second daily, summer-only transcontinental, a "limited express" complete with new vestibuled Pullmans and chair cars. Still, none of these deluxe carriages would enter the Queen City. Despite vague promises, Seattle passengers were still confined to day coaches on the connecting "stub" to and from Puyallup. The lucky ones got seats; frock-coated personages were often to be seen standing grimly in the aisles, even the baggage car.

But the Orphan Road was not long for this world. Rumors of imminent Northern Pacific acquisition intensified, and, in July 1889, the Puget Sound Shore filed supplementary articles of incorporation allowing it to sell its railroad and right of way—a clear indication of what was to come.

At the end of October, the Northern Pacific & Puget Sound Shore announced it would purchase the Puget Sound Shore at the beginning of the new year. ■

In ca. 1887-1888, one of a pair of the PSS's leased OR&N locomotives pauses in Seattle.

Paul Dorpat collection

CHAPTER 8

City of Destiny

"Seattle! Seattle! Death Rattle! Death Rattle!
Tacoma! Tacoma! Aurora! Aurora!" — George Francis Train

In the summer of 1884, there materialized atop the bluff overlooking Commencement Bay an apparition the likes of which had never been seen on Puget Sound: The Tacoma Land Company's grand new Tacoma Hotel. The onetime stumptown had become a city of almost 6,000 souls and The Tacoma became the symbol of the brave, brash new terminal city. Wealthy guests at Charles Wright's proud hostelry enjoyed sitting on the broad verandah, sniffing the mill smoke, and surveying the growing number of ships riding at anchor on the bay. For most residents of the Pacific Northwest, however, times were lean, and the staff of the Tacoma—including Jack, the inn's pet bear—often greatly outnumbered the guests.

"I have been a close observer of financial matters for the last thirty years," exclaimed Frederick Billings in July 1885, "but at no time within that period has business depression been so perplexing as it is now, or so general."[1]

People held grimly on, and hoped for better days to come with the opening of the Cascade Division.

The following February, Charles Wright wrote his friend John Adams Paddock, bishop of the Olympia Diocese: "I congratulate Tacoma on the prospects of the completion of the Cascade division . . . I now have many inquiries from capitalists who are investing in western Washington."

But Wright was obliged to temporize. "Really, the future for Tacoma looks very well on account of the railroad improvements, but her business people should be more self-reliant. What Tacoma wants is manufactories."

Randolph Radebaugh, the tirelessly boosting editor of the *Ledger*, agreed. "There should be a prompt and energetic reaching out for the trade all round us . . . We have great promise—we want push. The Cascade branch is coming, but the city meantime is here and should do business."[2]

Push was something Seattle seemed to have plenty of; why not Tacoma? Enter George Francis Train.

The aptly named Train, who styled himself many things—"The Original Pacific Railway King," "peripatetic humbug," "Livest Man in Two Hemispheres," and just plain "Citizen Train"—had been a major Gilded Age celebrity. Nephew of Boston shipping magnate Enoch Train, George Francis became an early apostle of the "Young America" movement, and amassed a modest fortune as a shipping agent and business promoter. Restless and obsessed with the need to make himself heard in a strident epoch, he fashioned himself into a "crank" and embarked on the lecture circuit. Railroads, personal hygiene, and Manifest Destiny were all grist for his mill, and Train enjoyed widespread celebrity during the 1860s. He also was party to the creation of the Union Pacific and its infamous construction company, the Credit Mobilier, and a prime mover in the development of Omaha, Nebraska.

In 1869, the great crank was invited by his old friends Captain John C. Ainsworth and Ben Holladay to make a July Fourth oration in Portland. Train's visit to the Northwest neatly coincided with that of the Northern Pacific Canfield-Roberts-Wilkeson reconnaissance party, and

TRACKLAYING ON THE EAST SIDE OF STAMPEDE PASS, 1887.
Eastern Washington State Historical Society

Captain Ainsworth graciously asked the celebrity along on their Puget Sound cruise aboard the *Wilson G. Hunt*. From the sidewheeler's deck, Train was enthralled enough by the beauties of the Sound to name it the "Mediterranean of the Northwest." His glowing imprimatur sufficed, along with the florid descriptions of Sam Wilkeson, to lure many a settler to the inland sea.[3]

After enjoying his spell of fame, Citizen Train faded into obscurity, whiling away much of his time feeding the pigeons in New York's Madison Square, reading to children, and storing up resentment at the society that was passing him by. Then one day late in 1885, he spied a copy of the Tacoma *Ledger* in the lobby of his residence, the Ashland House. Tacoma! What fond memories that name stirred! The white-haired curmudgeon hustled up to his tiny room, and with his customary red and blue crayons scrawled off a ream of copy to Radebaugh. The editor had to have his wife decipher Train's scribbling, but what emerged bowled him over. Here was just the Tacoma boomer he was looking for!

The page blared, "Great are the Psychos and George Francis Train is their prophet!" In January 1886, "Train's Vander-Billion Psychos, New History of the Vanderbilts," made its *Ledger* debut. "Psychos" was a stew of pent-up hucksterism, anger over a lifetime of perceived slights, and wonder at human folly, symbolized by the era's greatest symbol of wealth, the Vanderbilt family. It was goofy, it was surreal, it was barely coherent—and it got folks' attention:

Tacoma (as Worlds New Tea Port
"Young Giant of the Wilderness")
Now *Ledgerizes* type-Report
To Radebaugh Printers Success!
Big Thing (By George) Cosmos around
When all Mankind can Type and Talk
On any subject in New York
(And Boston) yet in Puget Sound
My Publisher is *Ledger* found!
All right for you! Now Psycho-Town
To "Vander-Billion" Shylock Down!

Although mistake about Chinese
The Town that don't go back on Train
Will go ahead (as Giant Trees)[4]

Radebaugh had found his miracle weapon, and it was not long before he gleefully "trained" it on his rival editors to the north.

The Seattle *Call* dismissed Train's column as "slush," and the *Chronicle* ridiculed the "blatherings of that pyramidical idiot, George Francis Train."

This was better yet! The editor and the crank could not have been happier:

"O.K. Tacoma says to all 'Psychos' don't mind Call and Chronicle! They are very jealous pack over there at Seattle? Trouble with them is 'Psychos' do not boom Seattle? But when they write such 'bilious comments' they advertise 'Ledger Psychos' good! Give them 'Psycho-Blast' and Puget Sound will hold high Carnival!"[5]

Readers shook their heads and giggled. Sure, he was crazy (Train was said to shun the company of adults and avoid shaking hands so as not to be robbed of electrodynamic energy). But he sold papers, he sold Tacoma, and he hit Seattle where she lived:

Seattle! Seattle! Death Rattle! Death Rattle!
Tacoma! Tacoma! Aurora! Aurora!
Your "Pyramid" is feeble when
You come abreast Tacoma Men
With your "Seattle-Blatherings"!
Keep up Type Boom of howl in Tomb
Your "Cultus" (Idiotic) shows
How dismal is "Town Catacomb"[6]

McCarver would have smiled.

For Tacoma, there was plenty to smile about. Even as the first Psychos took Puget Sound by storm, the final contract for the Cascade Division was let. Thousands of Chinese began shoveling thick, gooey snow off the grade up from the Yakima Valley, and timber-cutters began denuding the forest of the thousands of firs needed for

GEORGE FRANCIS TRAIN PEERS TOWARD DESTINY.
Washington State Historical Society

cribbing and trestlework. Thomas Oakes announced that vast grain facilities, able to handle 150,000 tons a year, would be built at Tacoma in anticipation of the opening of the Cascade Division. The population reached 8,000, closing in steadily on Seattle's 11,000, and Radebaugh proclaimed the "New Era Dawning":

"The outlook for Tacoma is decidedly promising and will cheer us on in the endeavor to make this place what it should be—the empire city of the northwest."

It took Citizen Train to hit upon the perfect nickname for the boomtown. Steilacoom *Express* editor Julius Dickens had used the term "City of Destiny" a decade earlier, but the Tacoma boomer now made it common currency, and it did not mean Seattle:

CITY-of-DESTINY! How Seattle howls with Hydrophobia! (Laughter) Look at this mad yelp of Dying Wolf! (Oh!).[7]

Amid the gaiety, however, were rumblings of discontent. The railroad took pride in the Tacoma Hotel—but little else, it seemed. The Northern Pacific had won its "pile-driver war" with John Burns, and the tideflats and waterfront had been staked in and fenced off for warehouses, shops, and yards that never seemed to materialize. The railroad did not even have a proper office building at its terminus, but like some fly-by-night outfit leased cubicles upstairs in the old Blackwell Hotel on the wharf.

Leading businessmen and many others who had invested

PORTRAIT OF A BUDDING METROPOLIS, TACOMA IN CA. 1880 WITH THE NORTHERN PACIFIC'S WILKESON COAL BRANCH CROSSING THE TIDEFLATS AT UPPER RIGHT.

University of Washington, Special Collections, #5378

A NORTHERN PACIFIC COAL TRAIN STOPS IN PUYALLUP, CA. 1880s.

Washington State Historical Society

their all in Tacoma were losing patience, and, at chamber of commerce meetings presided over by Mayor Sprague and NP superintendent Buckley, they vented their frustrations.

"The company has been promising and promising, but they do nothing, and we are sick of it," blasted iron works owner David Lister.

Realtor W.J. Fife complained: "I have been dying by inches for the past twelve years here under this steady growth process. Steady growth in a new town means three generations before it comes to anything worth plotting on a map . . . and if we ever expect to do anything, we must make a spurt—in short, we must boom!"

General Sprague scowled as the talk veered toward sedition.

"The Northern Pacific Railroad Company's attitude toward the town has always been one of repression instead of the opposite!" barked loan broker T.J. Nixon.[8]

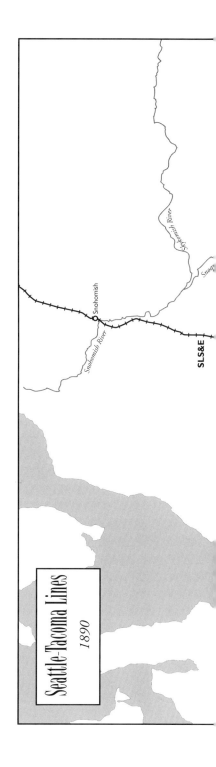

Seattle-Tacoma Lines
1890

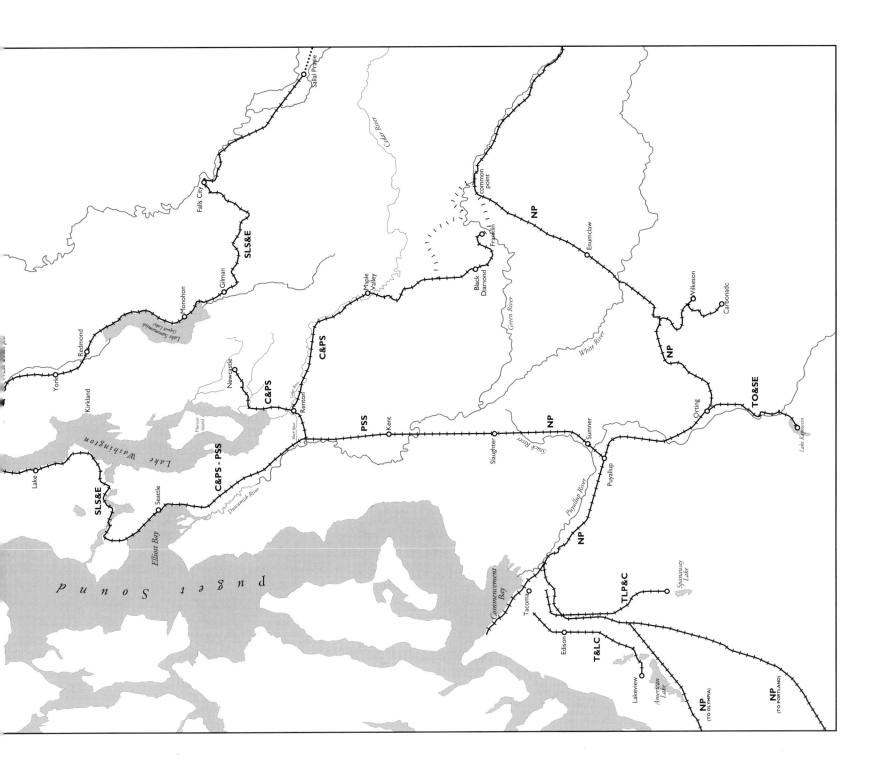

Puget Sound

Lake Washington

Elliott Bay

Commencement Bay

American Lake

Spanaway Lake

Lake Sammamish

Lake Kapowsin

Mercer Island

Cedar River

Green River

White River

Stuck River

Puyallup River

Duwamish River

Black River

Cedar River

Sallal Prairie

Falls City

Gilman

Monohon

Redmond

York

Kirkland

Lake

Seattle

Newcastle

Renton

Kent

Slaughter

Maple Valley

Black Diamond

Franklin

common point

Enumclaw

Wilkeson

Carbonado

Orting

Sumner

Puyallup

Tacoma

Edison

Lakeview

SLS&E

C&PS

C&PS

C&PS

C&PS - PSS

PSS

SLS&E

NP

NP

NP

NP

NP

TO&SE

TLP&C

T&LC

NP
(TO OLYMPIA)

NP
(TO PORTLAND)

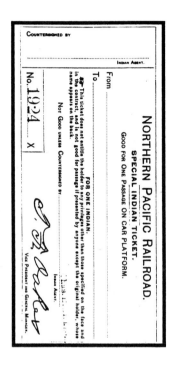

When the city council demanded that the railroad declare its intentions once and for all, Charles Wright himself came west and did his best to mollify the insurgents.

"There is no [ill] feeling whatever between the chamber of commerce and the railroad company," he assured the press, "none whatever. They wanted us to do certain things, but they knew we were straining every muscle to complete the Cascade Division."

The godfather of Tacoma promised that a fine new office building would soon appear on the bluff overlooking the bay. That, and the arrival of the first train direct to the terminus over the Cascade Division in the coming year, should put an end to the quibbling.

In the meantime, the chamber of commerce offered the railroad free office space in its own meeting rooms for a year, much to the amusement of the *Post-Intelligencer*, which sarcastically noted that the "improvement" should "add three people to the population and ought to set up the value of its property 25 percent or more!"

Even the *Ledger* sounded a peevish note. "Any attack on Seattle will not lessen the humiliation of Tacoma at the city's failure to grow with the completion of the Northern Pacific."[9]

High atop Stampede Pass, the final clang of a maul on June 1, 1887, silenced most of the whining. "Like a great dark snake coiling out of the hills," the first Northern Pacific through train over the Cascade Division steamed into the City of Destiny at 7:15 PM on July 3, 1887—two gasping 4-4-0s lugging thirteen coaches of six hundred happy people.

As guests cheered from the verandah of the Tacoma Hotel, the train squealed to a halt on the wharf, and a beaming Charles Wright exclaimed: "This is the happiest day of my life!" Tacoma hailed the "genuine last spike," and all but outdid her 1883 lavishness with miles of evergreen garlands and scenic dioramas of Mt. Tacoma. Giant portraits of Wright and George Francis Train looked down approvingly from high atop the Gross Brothers' San Francisco Store.

The following day's merry-making was opened by a cannon salute from the visiting HMS *Caroline*, the ship which had provided the inspiration for Gilbert and Sullivan's "HMS Pinafore." Orations droned out over the field above the bay, and a veteran Civil War drummer rendered a percussive imitation of "an engine pulling an excursion train over the switchback of the Northern Pacific railroad to Tacoma," to the delight of Wright and Oakes.

Ex-governor Elisha Ferry (a Seattle resident) evoked good-natured laughter as he proclaimed: "Let me express the feeling that the union and harmony which now exists between the two cities may continue! Rivalry will exist in the future the same as to-day, but let us see who will do the most for ourselves and our territory!"

Eager to oblige the former governor, the fire departments, baseball teams, and gun clubs of Seattle and Tacoma engaged their counterparts in spirited competition. Citizen Train declared: "There are busy times ahead for everybody on Puget! 'Psycho mustard seed' is growing apace! Within short time the west will be obliterated, the west will be the center!"[10]

Not even the return of "Seattle's pal" Henry Villard in September dampened Tacoma's enthusiasm. Indeed, a "grand congratulatory" rally was held at the Alpha Opera House, and Villard was praised as a doer and a builder. Even Randolph Radebaugh would let bygones be bygones:

"It is true that the notoriety given to Mr. Villard's apparent favoritism for Seattle became a potent factor in advancing the interests of that town and in limiting the speed of Tacoma's growth. Such appears to have been Mr. Villard's interest against us, but . . . matters have greatly changed. We have no reason to fear his re-election . . . Being a man of brain and most admirable pluck, there is no reason why we should not give him courteous welcome."

From Madison Square, George Francis Train gave his: "Post Seattle wiregrams, cannon, bombs, fireworks, procession. Celebrating Villard's election. Death rattle."[11]

Tacoma's glory years were upon her. Settlers and money poured in, land sold sight unseen at wildly inflated prices, and substantial homes, brick business blocks, and "$100,000 corporations" sprouted overnight. The press gushed over the mighty names of railroading, finance, shipping, and lumber—Wright, Oakes, Billings, Ainsworth, Montgomery, Benjamin P. Cheney, Charlemagne Tower—who had invested in Tacoma property. Promoters had a field day, and no scheme was too outrageous; local Northern Pacific official A.L. Horner proposed building an ice chute from Mt. Rainier to Tacoma. When it was pointed out that friction from the rushing ice blocks would set the flume afire, he patiently explained that water from the melting ice would put the fires out.[12]

A more substantive development took place in June 1888, when the St. Paul & Tacoma Lumber Co. was organized by a syndicate including Henry Hewitt and Alexander Griggs to begin the large-scale marketing of timber in the East and Midwest. To feed the lumber company and the Northern Pacific, that same month Thomas Oakes incorporated the Tacoma Orting & Southeastern Railroad, one of the nation's first standard gauge logging railroads. The 7.64-mile TO&S was completed by the NP from Orting to a point near Lake Kapowsin a year later. On the Tacoma tideflats rose the St. Paul's two giant sawmills, symbols of boomtown virility. The face of the terminal city was further transformed as dredging of the Puyallup River and waterfront commenced, to create landfill and deep-water moorage for more than a mile of new grain warehouses and wharves.

Uptown, where finishing touches were being put on the turreted Northern Pacific headquarters building, school children sang L.F. Cooke's "Tacoma, The City of Destiny," and chanted, "Seattle Seattle! Death rattle death rattle!"

During an 1890 visit, Charles Wright provided a fitting epitaph to his fondest dreams. "What I have seen . . . is far beyond my expectation. I did not picture such widespread and substantial growth. Indeed, it is all very gratifying. I saw Chicago grow up from a village to a great city . . . Well sir, this city is growing just as Chicago grew."[13]

Tacoma had fulfilled her destiny. ■

Workmen of the Northern Pacific shops at Tacoma about the year of 1889 & 1890 where the Union Station now stands.

EMPLOYEES PROUDLY POSE AT THE NORTHERN PACIFIC SHOPS.
Washington State Historical Society

Happy days on the Seattle Lake Shore & Eastern, an inspection train headed by the *H.L. Yesler* pauses at the end of track on the north shore of Lake Washington, September 8, 1887. Not all can be identified, but intermingled among the Seattle luminaries present on the occasion were Col. A.B. Rogers, J.R. Lewis, Thomas Burke (short man in light bowler), Col. Charles Sheafe, Leigh S.J. Hunt, T.T. Minor, Frank Osgood, and John Leary. The man to Burke's right possibly is Daniel Gilman.

Washington State Historical Society

CHAPTER 9

Burke, Gilman, and the Seattle Lake Shore & Eastern RR

"How is the fishing on Wall Street . . . any bites?" —Thomas Burke

THOMAS BURKE STOOD on the dock, watching Warhorse White sail into the sunset. The rally had been exciting —Seattle would fix the Northern Pacific! But he had gone out on a long limb. At the town meeting that March day in 1884, he had told everybody there was big money—eastern capital!—ready and waiting to build a Seattle railroad.

"This very week," he had thundered, "a corporation has been formed by citizens of Washington Territory to build a railroad across the mountains from Seattle via Snoqualmie Pass . . . We must put our shoulder to the wheel and demonstrate to the world that we want this road, and that it will pay, and that we have faith enough to put our money and our lands into it, and the completion of the road is an accomplished fact!"[1]

Perhaps the blasted Tacoma *Ledger* was right; maybe he did love the sound of his own voice too much! Now, he had to make good. The judge gnawed his lip, and stumped uptown.

Ten years earlier, Burke had been city attorney in Marshall, Michigan. To the young barrister, the Upper Midwest was proving dull. Marshall had lost its railroad headquarters to a neighboring community and was dying slowly on the vine. An acquaintance suggested he try his luck out West; he had spent some time in Seattle, on Puget Sound, he told Burke—things were jumping there! The young attorney needed little encouragement; he wrapped up his affairs, and headed west.

In May, he landed on Elliott Bay with scarcely ten dollars in his pocket, and settled in to build a frontier law practice. Within two years, he had become probate judge, bought a little land, and by the end of the 1870s had established himself as one of Seattle's solid citizens. The judge pitched enthusiastically into the land grant war and other skirmishes with the Northern Pacific Railroad, and acquitted himself admirably. Now, having promised the city a new railroad all its own, the real test of Thomas Burke's mettle began.

Providentially, Burke had the help of a better talker than even himself. Daniel H. Gilman had arrived on the Sound from New York in 1883, eyes open for the main chance. Born in Levant, Maine, Gilman had won something of a name for himself by valorous conduct during the Civil War, and had gone on to a modestly lucrative law practice in New York. He was restless, though, and like so many looked westward in search of greater success. The 38-year-old Gilman quickly familiarized himself with Seattle's commercial possibilities, and focused his attention on promising coal deposits south of Squak Lake (now Lake Sammamish). He also met Thomas Burke. Fired by the same ambitions for their adoptive city, the two became fast friends.

Gilman had little money, but he did have certain valuable eastern connections. One of these was a man Gilman had met during his tenure in New York: Franklin M. Jones, a partner in the Wall Street investment banking house of Jameson, Smith & Cotting.

Early in December, Gilman wrote Jones proposing they join forces in "a scheme I have for making a few millions":

A coal and transportation business "under peculiarly favorable circumstances and surroundings . . . to rival and I think fully equal the Oregon Improvement Company."[2]

Specifically, he conceived of developing a large coal mining operation at the Squak veins, along with a system of barges running from the mines down Squak Lake and Squak Slough, Lake Washington, and through a canal to a bunker on Puget Sound. "There's millions in it," he assured Jones, urging him to come and see for himself. As added inducement, Gilman offered a Puget Sound cruise aboard Charles Wright's steam yacht.

While awaiting word from Jones, Burke and Gilman spent long evenings plotting the future with Arthur and David Denny and John Leary. Inevitably, the barge scheme quickly evolved into a railroad to eastern Washington. This, the railroad Seattle had always dreamed of, would tap Arthur Denny's iron deposits in Snoqualmie Pass, make the city a grain shipping port, and at last give the Northern Pacific a well-earned trouncing. Never mind that Snoqualmie Pass fell within the NP land grant; the numerous forfeiture bills pending in Congress would doubtless take care of that!

In January, Jones wrote Gilman expressing mild interest in his scheme. No specific commitment was offered, but Burke and Gilman were nonetheless beside themselves with excitement. At the *Post-Intelligencer*-sponsored anti-Northern Pacific town meeting on March 29, Burke broke the news that "eastern capital" was in the offing, and Gilman redoubled his assault on Jones.

A railroad over the mountains "is not difficult of construction," he promised, and would open a region rich in freight—coal, iron, marble, timber, cattle. Political factors were also auspicious: "The temper of the territory is such that very large aid can be obtained for a railroad across the mountains to that magnificent empire, the great bend country, and the great basin of the Columbia."[3] They couldn't lose!

After his one expression of interest, Jones fell mum, and Burke and Gilman decided that if Wall Street would not come to Seattle, Seattle would go to Wall Street. The hat

was passed among the Seattle elite, and $500 was produced to buy Gilman a trip east. Again, Thomas Burke stood on the dock, his fingers crossed. Gilman got as far east as St. Paul, where he managed to elicit a few encouraging words and little else from local capitalists, and in June he returned, empty-handed but not daunted. The partners remained buoyant and confidant that, with just a touch more groundwork, eastern capital would embrace their great and worthy vision.

Judge Burke drew up a suitably impressive prospectus and articles of incorporation for Seattle's new railroad enterprise, while Gilman again went to work on Jones. He labored to change the New Yorker's bleak eastern view of Pacific Northwest weather, and portrayed himself as a younger, more resourceful Henry Villard. Oregon Improvement was a dead duck, he scrawled—it was poorly managed, its stocks were tumbling, and its mines were on fire. Where Villard had failed, Gilman would triumph.

More weeks passed without an answer, and Gilman began to sound desperate: "There is no better or safer place for the investment of money on bond."[4]

Wall Street remained mum, but this failed to turn the Seattleites from their grand plan. On April 15, 1885, Burke and Gilman incorporated the Seattle Lake Shore & Eastern Railway Company in association with William Cochrane, J.W. Currie, Griffith Davies, David Denny, George M. Haller, George Kinnear, John Leary, J.R. McDonald, Angus Mackintosh, T.T. Minor, and Frank H. Osgood, to "build to Spokane and Walla Walla by the Snoqualmie or other available pass . . . and connect with some eastern trunk line," most likely Seattle's favorite Northern Pacific antidote, the Union Pacific. McDonald, partner with Burke and Gilman in the Seattle Lumber Company, was named president, Gilman general manager, and the board quickly pooled money enough to pay chief engineer Frederick H. Whitworth for a preliminary survey.[5]

Three years earlier, King County auditor M.S. Booth had proposed a route for the stillborn Seattle Walla Walla & Baker City, but this had been rejected as it did not tap the Cedar River coal fields. Now, with the Columbia &

Puget Sound's Cedar River extension to Franklin in operation, Booth's more northerly route was eyed favorably. He had enumerated the many selling points this Seattle road would offer potential investors—extensive coal and gypsum deposits near Squak Lake and east of the mountains; coal, iron, and precious metals in Snoqualmie Pass; abundant timber, grazing, and wheat lands on both sides of the Cascades; and lucrative hops fields in the Snoqualmie Valley. He had also predicted the eventual popularity of Snoqualmie Falls as "a place for summer resort and pleasure."

Booth's route looped north to Lake Union and Union Bay, down the west shore of Lake Washington to Renton, and then eastward up May and Coal creeks toward the mountains. At Gilman's suggestion, and to give the Seattle Lake Shore & Eastern "a country of its own…and a business free from the competition of the Columbia & Puget Sound or any other transportation lines," the route was altered to follow the north shores of Lake Union, Union Bay, and Lake Washington, and the east shore of Squak Lake. It would traverse Snoqualmie Pass, cross the Columbia at Priest Rapids, then proceed south to Wallula Gap before turning east into the Palouse wheat country.[6]

None of this would happen without money, however, and the silence from New York was maddening. Gilman kept turning the screws. The Columbia & Puget Sound's Cedar River extension was "proving to be a bonanza," he wrote Jones in August; so would the Lake Shore, "as you would readily see if you came here and saw how I have got the pins set up."

Jones did not come, and by October Gilman was pleading: "Your people could have made millions twice over, by taking us up and building this road we have laid out." Along with all the other advantages, they would occupy Snoqualmie Pass and be a railroad force to be reckoned with; one of the "stronger companies" would undoubtedly want that all-important gateway to the Sound, and then he, Jones, and all the others savvy enough to get in on the ground floor could name their price. Gilman namedropped shamelessly, hinting of inside connections with Robert Harris, Thomas Oakes, and the Union Pacific's Sidney Dillon, and beat relentlessly the refrain of great fortunes lying around waiting to be scooped up—anything, to prod inert eastern capital into motion.[7]

At last, there was nothing left but to journey once more to New York. Late in 1885, Gilman set forth, finely printed prospectus and Seattle's hopes in hand. For a year, he paid his dues in the back alleys of Wall Street. Burke mailed pin money from time to time, prodding anxiously: "How is the fishing on Wall Street . . . any bites?"

Gilman thought he had one in a man named Gaston, who spoke of his own connections and a sure thing just waiting to be plucked from the silver lodes of Colorado. Gilman strung along with Gaston for several months before it became obvious that he had been led down a blind alley, and that Gaston was simply a kindred schemer with no more money nor connections than himself.

There were no other bites, and, predictably, the Tacoma *Ledger* sneered: "The Seattle Lake Shore & Eastern Railway Company, like so many of the grand schemes which have gained for Seattle a reputation for enterprise, is all on paper."[8]

Finally, in November 1886, Jones bit. The Lake Shore prospectus had at last reached the inner sanctums of Jameson, Smith, and Cotting, and the partners were impressed. Gilman had caught a big one; James D. Smith was president of the New York Stock Exchange during 1885 and 1886, and commodore of the New York Yacht Club. More big names—Chace and Butts of Providence, Rhode Island; C.E. Curry of Boston; Thomas Logan, a man with substantial interests in eastern railroads; and Chicagoan Henry Crawford—were also ready to get involved.

Gilman was especially smitten with Crawford who promised to pump at least $200,000 into the venture, Gilman informed Burke, and was "a very bright railroad man and lawyer, and in conjunction with J.S., & C., has ambitious views regarding our scheme." Crawford also had a private railroad car, which impressed Gilman to no end.

Best of all, Burke and Gilman would remain in charge: "We are still our own masters!"[9]

Perhaps, but the easterners were quick to impose some major changes. With transcontinental aspirations, they moved the Lake Shore's prospective eastern terminus from Walla Walla to the unpropitious-sounding town of Deadwood, Dakota Territory. In addition to the main line, there would be two additions: An Eastern Division extending westward from Spokane Falls and meeting the main line near the Columbia; and a Northern Division to run inland from Seattle to the Canadian border and connect there with the Canadian Pacific, and develop the rich timber and farm land along the west slope of the Cascades—a route that had been suggested to Burke in the spring of 1886 by one Major Jones of the U.S. Army Corps of Engineers.

The easterners inflated the original $5,000,000 Lake Shore stock issue to $15,000,000, and incorporated the Puget Sound Construction Company to finance and build the railroad. This "in-house" construction company was given the first forty-mile contract, from Seattle to Snoqualmie Falls, at an estimated cost of $200,000. Five- and ten-mile sections would be sub-contracted to local firms.

This was a conservative plan to build in small portions and allow revenues from completed line to pay for following sections. For each mile finished, the construction company (actually a general contractor) was to be paid $20,000 in mortgage bonds and $10,000 in railroad stock. Glowing accounts of the new railroad's resources, doubtless emanating from Gilman, were placed in the railroad and financial press, spurring investors from both coasts to quickly sign up for Puget Sound Construction's $500,000 stock issue.[10]

Burke went to New York to assist in closing the deal. Ushered into the Jameson, Smith & Cotting offices one morning, he was greeted by Amos Cotting. The firm was pleased to take up the Seattle proposition, the financier murmured. There was, however, one small condition: As a show of faith, the judge would have to put $10,000 of his own into the construction company.

"Good heavens, man!" the judge yelped—"I haven't $10,000 cash, and never had!"[11]

The firm insisted, not unreasonably, that Seattle men contribute something to a Seattle enterprise, so Burke borrowed the money from banker Angus Mackintosh, and Gilman, forever short, ventured $25,000, which he cadged from everyone else. No matter; at last, the Seattle Lake Shore & Eastern was rolling. In December, Lake Shore chief engineer John G. Scurry and City Engineer Reginald H. Thomson began surveying lines between Seattle, Squak Lake, and Sallal Prairie, five miles east of Snoqualmie Falls.

The Lake Shore soon had company. Up to this point, the Oregon Improvement Company had been content to sit placidly back and imagine it would one day claim the Snoqualmie Valley and the western slope of the Cascades at its leisure. Now, however, the advent of the Seattle Lake Shore & Eastern threw the OIC into a panic. General Manager John Howard blustered to reporters that the Columbia & Puget Sound would extend to the Canadian border and have trains running into the Snoqualmie Valley within the year, then scrambled aboard a train to New York to light a fire under President Elijah Smith. They must act at once, he warned, or be forever cut off by the Northern Pacific to the south and the Seattle Lake Shore & Eastern to the north. Smith concurred, and at the beginning of January 1887, Howard rushed surveying crews into the field to stake their claim.

Their first objective was to occupy the strategic Snoqualmie Falls narrows at the foot of the valley. The Seattle road's Scurry and Thomson got there first, planting their stakes only one day ahead of the Improvement Company gang.

Howard's boys arrived at the falls only to find Lake Shore right of way already hastily hacked out of the brush and cursed: "Scurry and his dudes have been here ahead of us!"[12]

Disgusted, they combed the approaches to the Squak and Snoqualmie valleys for alternate routes—in vain. Oregon Improvement was shut out, and first sod on the Seattle Lake Shore & Eastern was turned the following month.

The Northern Pacific also tried to outflank the Lake Shore. NP land department chief Paul Schulze declared that Snoqualmie Pass fell within the land grant and that, under this circumstance, it was unlikely another railroad would ever cross the pass. The Northern Pacific made its Snoqualmie Valley move in April 1887. "We have been slashing the right of way for a short branch of fourteen miles, shooting off at Green River and extending into the Snoqualmie iron mines," declared Second Vice-President Adna Anderson.[13]

However, the NP had other, more pressing matters to tend to. After making its initial feint, the Snoqualmie campaign was allowed to run out of steam, and the branch line (subsequently formalized as the Green River & Northern) petered out a few miles north of the Green River. The Seattle road had the field to itself.

Daniel Gilman continued his assault on big money. Even as he reeled in Jameson, Smith & Cotting, he set his sights on more exotic game, namely Peter Kirk, the owner of Moss Bay Iron and Steel Co. Ltd., in Workington, England. At the suggestion of Henry Crawford, Burke and Gilman had first contacted Kirk in September 1886 to inquire about furnishing rail. Gilman sniffed capital ripe for the plucking and forwarded the ironmonger an ore analysis from Arthur Denny's Snoqualmie Pass iron mine. Kirk was suitably impressed, visited Seattle that fall, and began making plans to mine the Snoqualmie ore and build a steel mill in the vicinity.

Of course, such an installation would be an enormous boon to the Seattle area and the Seattle Lake Shore & Eastern. While Gilman worked his wiles in New York, Burke stroked Kirk and endeavored to secure his signature on a contract linking a Denny iron mine lease to exclusive haulage on the SLS&E.

The Englishman was no easy mark. Burke quickly found out that he had his hands full just keeping Kirk out of the clutches of rival suitors. To the judge's vexation, Kirk considered Tacoma and Sallal Prairie for mill sites, dickered privately with Arthur Denny over a non-conditional lease of his Snoqualmie Pass iron mine, and even had the gall to treat with the Northern Pacific and the Oregon Improvement Company.

Paul Schulze took Kirk by the arm and warned him away from Snoqualmie Pass, pointing instead to the superiority of the coking coal at the NP's new mines in Roslyn and Cle Elum.

Arthur Denny dismissed Schulze's claims as "nothing but bluster . . . We expended a large amount of money in opening roads and developing [the mine] even before the Northern Pacific Railroad had filed a map by any route across the mountains. This is well known and recognized by everybody except Mr. Schulze and the land ring."[14]

The OIC's John Howard also buttonholed Kirk and offered to extend the Columbia & Puget Sound to whatever place he might locate his mill.

Kirk bridled at Burke's none-too-transparent efforts to make him toe the Lake Shore line, and tension rose.

Lacking his partner's *sang-froid*, the judge sweated and implored Gilman to bring the New Yorkers west and bludgeon the Englishman into signing by force of numbers: "Hurry up. Foreign relations damnably strained in Bulgaria."

Not to worry, replied Gilman: "Evidences multiply that Kirk is simply bluffing."

The "evidences" were Kirk's ostensibly confidential telegrams to his associates in England; Kirk and Franklin Jones used the same stockbroker and the man obligingly let Jones read the coded cables. Gilman breezily assured the judge that as far as the steel mill scheme went, there were other fish in the sea: Henry Crawford himself was a major party in the Joliet, Illinois, steel works and could readily fill the Englishman's shoes. "If Kirk won't play fair with us, we won't play with him at all, and we won't need to."[15]

Nonetheless, it was time for a show of strength, and Gilman promised the judge that he and the easterners would soon be on hand and set things right. As advance guard, Colonel Charles Sheafe, the Lake Shore's newly appointed general manager, was dispatched to Seattle to help Burke "pacify Kirk and the Denny people until the whole circus arrives."

Gilman cautioned Sheafe to "talk to no one except Burke and Kirk, keep as shady as you can, don't know any more than the law allows."

Sheafe's relocation to Seattle also would neatly finesse a potentially troublesome circumstance. One outgrowth of the forfeiture fight against the Northern Pacific was a territorial statute prohibiting absentee corporations from owning more than 5,000 acres of land (excluding railroad right of way). Burke saw to it that Sheafe established residency in Seattle, making a majority of the Lake Shore board of trustees "locals" and thus satisfying the legal requirement.[16]

The whole circus showed up (in Crawford's private car) on the 22nd of December. The easterners made a two-day tour of their investment and left town promising that Lake Shore trains would be running between Seattle and Spokane within two years.

Judge Burke rubbed his hands happily. "Their impressions were all favorable," he bubbled. "They expressed themselves as agreeably surprised at the size of the place and the thrift, energy, and enterprise of its citizens . . . I am assured that work will commence on the road within thirty days after the completion of this matter."[17]

Burke and Gilman quickly began pulling things together, obtaining from Henry Yesler a key section of waterfront property for the southern terminus, securing easements from rural property owners, and taking options on 700 acres of Dr. Henry Smith's pioneer donation claim at Smith Cove, on the north waterfront. The Smith Cove Land Company was then formed to handle the development of coal bunkers and wharves at the main terminal site. To mine the coal at Squak Creek, the Seattle Coal and Iron Company was incorporated, with Gilman president.

A milestone in Seattle's development came on January 25, 1887, when Mayor Henry Struve and the city council signed into law City Ordinance 804, the Railroad Avenue ordinance. Created by Thomas Burke and Judge Cornelius Hanford to secure for the Seattle Lake Shore & Eastern a clear, unimpeded thoroughfare through the city, Railroad Avenue promised a straight, 125-feet-wide "grand highway for railways and general traffic," built well to seaward of existing buildings and the 1882 Villard right of way.[18]

To retain this franchise, the SLS&E was required to begin construction by the coming March and complete forty miles by July 1, 1888. Connection in eastern Washington with a major trunk line must be effected by December 1, 1891, and at least two trains a day were to be run each way. By "common user" clause, any other railroad entering Seattle would receive equal privileges; tenant lines would be required to maintain the planking of the avenue in good condition, and engines and cars were not to "stand on the tracks longer than necessary."

There were two small problems with the Railroad Avenue arrangement. One was that it was technically illegal; neither local nor territorial legislatures had any right to assign title to tidelands. These were held in trust by the federal government and title could be granted only when a territory entered statehood. Burke knew it, but kept his worries to himself, and took the added precaution of obtaining deeds from individual shoreline property owners. Once the Seattle Lake Shore & Eastern was safely established on Railroad Avenue, he figured, there was little chance it or any other line would be pried loose. Firm precedent already existed in the 1873 grant to the Seattle & Walla Walla/Oregon Improvement Co. In any case, tideland litigation would take years; might as well build a railroad in the meantime.

Another potential hangup was the 1882 Villard waterfront right of way. Snaking along the Elliott Bay government meander line, this franchise had been granted to the Columbia & Puget Sound and Puget Sound Shore companies, to run one mile from King Street to Clay Street. The intent had been to serve the terminal facilities Henry Villard and others had promised to build on the north waterfront. These never materialized, nor had the Columbia & Puget Sound upheld the other terms of the franchise—converting to standard-gauge and extending to the "common point" in the Cascade foothills. The Columbia & Puget Sound provided freight service over the single

track as far north as Pike Street, but the Puget Sound Shore did not. By 1887, this dead-end line had become little more than a nuisance.

Passage of the Railroad Avenue ordinance was intended to excise this blot from the waterfront and give the Seattle Lake Shore & Eastern thirty feet on the east side of the thoroughfare, the prime inner margin next to the business houses. Everybody else would get leftovers on the water side or, even worse, in the middle. Any road wanting to do business with the landside warehouses would have to pay the Lake Shore tribute for access, and just how this new scheme would go over with the original franchise-holders was not difficult to imagine.

Burke, who had originally opposed granting the Villard franchise, nonetheless expressed confidence that "we shall be able to bring powerful pressure to bear to make them behave themselves."

They didn't. Within days of the ordinance's passage, an Oregon Improvement crew was hastily laying track north of Pike Street and installing a third rail for standard gauge use.

"The matter has been kept very quiet for some reason," noted the press, "but the work is being pushed with vigor just the same, rain or shine."[19]

There were other annoyances. Eugene Canfield had, like his cousin, Thomas, come to Puget Sound in the early 1870s with railroads on his mind. Unlike his cousin, he decided Bellingham Bay would be the future great city. He bought 5,000 acres there, then retired to Illinois to bide his time. In 1883, Canfield decided the time had

A WAGGISH ENGINEMAN HAS PLACED A FERN IN THE FLAG HOLDER OF SEATTLE LAKE SHORE & EASTERN LOCOMOTIVE NO. 4, *Thomas Burke*. NO. 4 BECAME NORTHERN PACIFIC NO. 1148 IN 1901, AND WAS SCRAPPED AT SOUTH TACOMA IN 1920.

Paul Dorpat collection

come. That July, he formed the Bellingham Bay Railway & Navigation Company, to run track from Bellingham Bay to the Canadian border, and began developing new coal mines, sawmills, and wharves at the bayside communities of Whatcom and Sehome.

The following year, he obtained a charter from Congress to cross navigable water between Whatcom and Seattle, and to extend his railroad to that city and connect with the Puget Sound Shore. Late in 1886, ex-NP engineer James Sheets ran a survey from the Canadian border to Seattle, and, the following spring, Canfield promised the Seattle City Council a completed railroad within two years. A thirty-foot slice of Railroad Avenue was his.

Alerted to the incursion by a distressed Burke, Henry Crawford attempted to buy Canfield out. The price was too high, so in February 1887 he, Burke, and Gilman incorporated the Seattle & West Coast Railroad Co. to head off the impudent Canfield and link up with the Canadian Pacific at the border. The first leg would run north fifteen miles from a junction with the Lake Shore at West Coast Junction (later Woodinville) to Snohomish. Simultaneously, hundreds of men took to the nearby forest to begin cutting the 26,000 piles for the Railroad Avenue trestle. The first five-mile grading contract between Smith Cove and Union Bay was awarded to the Kerns Brothers. The cost of the forty miles from Seattle to Snoqualmie Falls was estimated at $577,000, or $14,425 a mile.[20] The $800,000 Lake Shore bond issue, $400,000 stock flotation, and the eventual revenues to be derived from operations through such bounteous country ("There's millions in it") all appeared to offer more than adequate security.

Turning of the first sod and driving of the first piles for the Seattle Lake Shore & Eastern began in April 1887. All through the spring showers, Chief Engineer Scurry pushed the roadbed speedily along Lake Union and Lake Washington, as scows ferried men and material to the advancing front. Picks and shovels were flying, too, at the Squak mine, and there were gratifying signs of activity at Smith Cove. At the end of June, the Seattle Lake Shore & Eastern's first new locomotive arrived from the Rhode

Island Locomotive works—a trim, forty-five-ton, 4-4-0 American Standard type: the *D.H. Gilman*. The *Gilman* was soon joined by the *Thomas Burke*, *F.M. Jones*, and *H.L. Yesler*, along with passenger cars sporting a glossy deep ochre varnish.

The British bark *Persian* arrived in Elliott Bay on August 11, bearing in her hold over 1,000 tons of sixty-pound rail fresh from the Workington, England, plant of Peter Kirk's Moss Bay Iron & Steel Co. The first sections were swung onto the wharf at Smith Cove. A small but festive party cheered as Thomas Burke gripped a maul and hammered home the first spike, after which they adjourned to "jollification" in the *Persian's* saloon.

Work continued its breathtakingly swift pace, and by October the Railroad Avenue trestle was finished, track laid to the north end of Lake Washington, and grading completed to West Coast Junction. On the Eastern Division, crews grubbed out right of way west from Spokane Falls. On the 25th, the first revenue train left Columbia Street for Union Bay; the *D.H. Gilman* headed up a coach, baggage car, boxcar, and several flats of construction materials.

Thereafter, cash receipts from the haulage of lumber, shingles, cattle, and passengers began flowing into the company coffers. Thanksgiving witnessed the first public excursion to the end of track, near present-day Bothell, followed by regular service to Union Bay. Until ballast work was finished, the little steamers *Edith E.* and *Squak* forwarded passengers and freight to points on Lake Washington, Squak Slough, and Squak Lake.

In 1888 came more heartening progress. Two sturdy 2-8-0s were purchased for freight service, along with more coal cars, boxcars, and coaches. In March, the Railroad Avenue depot at the foot of Columbia Street opened its doors and the Seattle & West Coast steadily approached the Snohomish River, and on April 15 rails reached Gilman at the south end of Squak Lake. Lumber traffic in particular was brisk, and the daily mixed train generally consisted of six or more freight cars and two passenger coaches. Forney engine Number 6, an 0-4-4T named

J.R. McDonald, arrived in May, and, on August 28, suburban passenger service began between Columbia Street and Gilman's Addition, north of Smith Cove.

But Seattle's railroad was in trouble. Though logging camps and shingle mills were springing up along the line and offering a fast-growing trade, revenues still lagged well behind expenses. Costs were huge—for the terminal property at Smith Cove, Belltown, and on the waterfront; the two-mile Railroad Avenue trestle; extensive bridging and filling along the lakes; office rent in Seattle and New York; locomotives and cars; and Gilman's numerous trips to Wall Street. The early $14,425 per mile construction estimates fell far short of reality. Even the relatively flat and easy Eastern Division out of Spokane was running $15,000 per mile, and along the heavily wooded shores of Squak Lake it was closer to $20,000.

Most of the cash for these transactions came from the Puget Sound Construction Company. When this ran out in the fall of 1887, the company folded. A new one, the Seattle & Eastern, was formed in November. A $1,000,000 bond issue was floated and the railroad's obligation to its new construction company was increased by $3,000 per mile. Like the Oregon Improvement Company, the Seattle & Eastern had high hopes of operating not only railroads but also canals, wharves, telegraph lines, wagon roads, and steamships, as well as developing townsites.

Burke happily looked forward to doubling his money. His $10,000 "show of faith" in the Puget Sound Construction Company had netted him more than $20,000 in Lake Shore stocks and bonds. But he was fooling himself. Stock certificates, however finely engraved, were no substitute for cash, and, of that, there was simply not enough. The stack of unpaid bills from local contractors mounted.

Next to go was the Seattle & West Coast. Henry Crawford's till ran dry in the spring of 1888, leaving the Lake Shore little choice but to absorb its sister road. With a heavy debt load of its own, this quickly proved to be a financial ball and chain. Further impairing the Seattle road's income, the Gilman coal mine and its bunkers at Smith Cove were not yet up and running, thanks, Gilman said, to "enemies" in New York. Infuriatingly, Peter Kirk continued to dither on where to locate his mill, seriously dimming the prospects of a lucrative traffic source. NP's Schulze bragged to reporters that Kirk was on the verge of building his steel mill at Cle Elum, while ugly rumors of shady financial chicanery within the railroad and its construction company began making the downtown rounds.

These constituted an embarrassment the Seattle road could ill-afford. Lake Shore stock had done poorly on the open market, and now stopped selling altogether. Burke and Gilman found themselves skating on a thinning crust of short funds, disappearing credit, watered paper, and fast-evaporating public confidence. The judge may well have recalled ruefully Robert Harris' admonition that there was indeed some little difference between planning railroads and building them.[21]

The territorial legislature was beginning to cause even more problems. Since the Credit Mobilier exposé of 1872, popular feeling toward railroads had turned ever-darker, and by the late-1880s a long list of grievances had been compiled—for high and discriminatory freight rates, monopoly, influence-peddling, stock-watering, land grant hoggishness, not to mention poor service, rude employees, and downright dangerous conditions while traveling on trains. The legislature joined in this growing disillusionment and in December 1887 began talking about a crackdown—a new railroad tax code, rate ceilings, and a territorial railroad commission.

Burke shuddered. The bill would "do tremendous evil, particularly to King County," he warned an associate. "If these bills become laws, we will not be able to raise another dollar for the Seattle Lake Shore & Eastern!"[22] Though such restrictions could not have been welcomed by its management, the judge smelled a Northern Pacific rat and warned that the big road favored the legislation "for the purpose of killing off the Seattle Lake Shore & Eastern."

The New Yorkers did indeed convey their alarm and Burke lobbied vigorously against the legislation. His

S., L. S. & EASTERN RAILWAY
TIME TABLE.

DAILY, EXCEPT SUNDAY.

	LEAVE	ARRIVE.
For Snoqualmie and way points............	8:40 a. m	4:15 p m
For Gilman and way points.........	8:40 a m / 12:40 p m	11:30 a m / 4:15 p m
For Snohomish and way points.........	8:40 a m / 4:25 p m	8:30 a m / 4:15 p m
*For Lake Washing-Ravenna Park & suburban points.	8:40 a m / 1:45 p m	8:30 a m / 3:30 p m
For Edgewater, Fremont and suburban points......	6:00 a m / 10:15 a m / 1:45 p m / 6:25 p m	6:50 a m / 11:30 a m / 3:30 p m / 7:15 p m

SUNDAY TRAINS.

	LEAVE.	ARRIVE.
For Snoqualmie & way points, giving 5 h'rs at the Falls	8:40 a m	7:05 p m
For Snohomish and way points............	4:25 p m	10:05 a m
*For Lake Washington, Ravena Park & suburban p'nts	10:15 a m / 1:45 p m	11:30 a m / 3:10 p m
For Edgewater, Fremont and suburban points	6:25 p m	7:15 p m

*Connect with steamer at Union Bay or Yesler for Hougthon and Kirkland.
Special rates for excursion, picnic and fishing parties furnished on application.
E. W. RUFF, Gen. Pass. Agt., Boston Block.
F. W. D. HOLBROOK, Manager.

SEATTLE, LAKE SHORE & EASTERN SCHEDULE, SEPTEMBER 1889.

concerns about the dampening effect of new laws on outside investment were shared by many others, and, with the aid of Don Carlos Corbett, Burke's man in Olympia, the bills were quashed.

Burke could not smother the rumors of the Lake Shore's troubles. The press sniffed blood, and began predicting that it was only a matter of time before Seattle's railroad was swallowed by a big company—maybe even the Northern Pacific!

Disgusted at the very idea, the judge vowed that "the Lake Shore will not swerve from its original plan of becoming a transcontinental line."

Publicly, Burke kept the faith in the Seattle road. "Within two years," he told the *Post-Intelligencer* in March 1888, "the Seattle Lake Shore & Eastern will be handling the bulk of traffic to Puget Sound."

Privately, his optimism was fading. "We have two tables and but one table cloth, and a short one at that," he confided to Gilman.[23]

Burke and Gilman looked eastward for salvation. Burke had been in correspondence with eastern Washington investors regarding possible new funding for the Eastern Division (which reached Davenport, forty miles west of Spokane, in April) as a counter to NP/OR&N monopoly. These negotiations were helped along by Paul Mohr, who replaced Charles Sheafe as chief engineer in early 1888. Mohr was a Spokane resident and had elicited encouraging responses from local financial and business interests.

In May, Burke, McDonald, and John Leary went to Spokane and in a town meeting made a personal appeal for a cash subsidy, to enable the road to "join hands with Seattle at the Columbia." They succeeded in raising pledges of $175,000. For the moment, hope was restored.

Sniffing a good prospect, the New York construction firm of Ryan & McDonald called on Mohr and bid on the job of finishing the main line. They got it, and in May the "greatest railroad contract ever let at one time in Washington" was signed, to close the 225-mile gap from Gilman to Davenport.[24]

More good news came that month—Peter Kirk finally caved in. Under relentless pressure from *Post-Intelligencer* owner Leigh S.J. Hunt, the Englishman at last agreed to build his new integrated steel mill on the eastern shore of Lake Washington. The mill site received the fitting name of Kirkland, and in August, Kirk, Arthur Denny, Leigh Hunt, and others incorporated the Moss Bay Iron & Steel Company of America. A forty-five-year lease was taken on the Denny iron mine to provide ore. The Seattle Lake Shore & Eastern would build a branch to the mill site.

Burke and Gilman enjoyed a spurt of renewed hope; if they could just hold out a little longer!

But crisis kept following crisis. A rift with the New Yorkers developed in June when James Smith and Amos Cotting showed up in Seattle and discovered that Gilman had not troubled to clue them in on the Spokane and Ryan & McDonald deals. They were understandably furious at being kept in the dark. Gilman had already fallen under a cloud at the New York office, in the wake of a tantrum he had thrown over the partners' unwillingness to okay immediate construction of the Eastern Division. Burke begged his impetuous friend to watch his "devil of a temper," and pleaded the necessity for maintaining harmony in the ranks.[25] Gilman was put on a short leash, but the damage had been done, and the ranks began to break.

The Bellingham interloper, Eugene Canfield, provided yet another nuisance. Canfield considered his Bellingham Bay Railway & Navigation Co. franchise to cross navigable water north of Seattle to be exclusive. Thus, when Lake Shore crews reached the Snohomish River in June 1888, and had the effrontery to begin sinking bridge footings, he applied to the district court in Seattle for an injunction.

The following morning, Canfield's process-server took his seat on the Snohomish train. Minutes before departure from Columbia Street, Judge Burke was apprised of the man's intentions. He hustled down to the depot, clambered aboard the locomotive, and ordered the surprised crew to hightail it to Snohomish—without their train. After a headlong dash, Burke convinced County Sheriff Billy Whitfield that "desperadoes" in distant parts needed his urgent attention. As the engine backed down to Seattle for train and writ-server, the judge set the bridge builders hammering double-quick. Canfield's man duly arrived, but in the sheriff's absence was unable to serve his paper. Presently, the Seattle Lake Shore & Eastern was across the Snohomish River. Burke and Gilman gave Canfield the slip until his injunction could be quashed.[26]

This little victory aside, everything seemed to be unraveling. Ironically, traffic was growing, but the company did not have enough rolling stock to handle it all and Burke had to ride herd on local shops to step up car production. The judge took it from all sides—from Northern Division laborers threatening to burn bridges if they were not paid; from father-in-law Judge John J. McGilvra, lecturing Burke sternly that, "the people would not feel as proud of the Seattle Lake Shore & Eastern as they do at present," if its defaulting on its creditors were to become common knowledge; from Lake Shore trustee and co-counsel George M. Haller, harshly critical of the Credit Mobilier-like relations of railroad and construction companies; and from sub-contractor Thomas Earle & Co., who confiscated a load of new rails in lieu of payment, then threatened to institute receivership proceedings, which Burke turned aside only with difficulty and more bad feeling.[27]

Burke bore up gamely and refused to admit defeat, at least publicly. He continued to assure reporters that all was well, and appealed to Jones' sense of pride in his investment as reason enough to see it through, promising him profits such "as to astonish your partners and give us a genuine triumph."[28]

Reality was another story, however. In July, Jones placed the Lake Shore bonds on Wall Street; they flopped, in a market where Northern Pacific and Oregon Improvement were selling briskly. Smith, Cotting, and Crawford decided enough was enough and withdrew from active support, leaving Jones, Thomas Logan, Henry and Philip Armour, and Burke and Gilman to salvage the situation as best they could.

Ryan and McDonald were next to bow out, and by August 1, 1888, construction on both divisions was at a standstill—the Northern Division stalled six miles north of Snohomish and the main line just east of Gilman. Adding insult to injury, the Seattle Coal & Iron mine at Gilman had only recently opened and begun shipping coal, when the miners walked out on the first of several sporadic strikes. In the absence of demonstrable progress, Seattle and Spokane bond subscribers welshed on their pledges.[29] Things looked grim that fall and winter of 1888-1889, and along Front Street sporting men made book on when the woebegone Seattle Lake Shore & Eastern would tumble into the hands of a receiver.

Burke, his lesson in railroad-building fully and painfully absorbed, was despondent. "The company's credit is utterly gone," he wailed to Gilman. "Nobody would trust it for five cents now."

The great Spokane hope had gone up in smoke, "and what to do I don't know. It is evident that we need a little strengthening medicine all around."[30]

That medicine seemed to come within reach in the following spring when Jones and the remaining partners proposed raising the capitalization of the Seattle & Eastern Construction Company from one to three million dollars. The only catch was that Seattle would have to put up $250,000. Despite the clouds hanging over the whole enterprise, Burke's standing was such that Seattle's quarter-million share was subscribed to in short order. The easterners suffered the embarrassment of coming up short, and the judge refused to release the Seattle pledges until the construction company resumed work on the Northern Division.

"It is idle to expect the people of Seattle in their present straightened circumstances to pay the assessments . . . unless work is progressing rapidly," he informed Jones.[31]

At Burke's insistence, they were obliged to raise the balance within their bond syndicate to get things moving again. At the same time, Burke objected to a Seattle & Eastern dividend lately released by a minority of the trustees, and he threatened to recall the payment. Tension between the Seattle and New York offices grew.

The only real hope seemed to be inclusion, as Gilman had foreseen, in a major railroad. In the spring of 1888, he began putting out feelers. Frustrated with the easterners' conservative building policy, he wrote Canadian Pacific president William Cornelius Van Horne that March, suggesting a partnership and cash advance to finish the Seattle road to the border. With a Seattle connection, he prodded, this would be good business for the CPR.

Van Horne was not buying, and Gilman next sounded out Oregon Improvement's Elijah Smith. John Leary fielded expressions of interest from Villard and Oakes at the Northern Pacific, and *Post-Intelligencer* publisher Leigh Hunt broached the subject with the St. Paul Minneapolis & Manitoba's James J. Hill.

Burke was wary: "I distrust Villard—I fear Greeks bearing gifts. I have no doubt Villard is friendly to Seattle, but still, it is hard to serve two masters. As for Mr. Smith, if given the chance, he would sell us out bag and baggage!"[32]

Never afraid of wearing out his welcome, Gilman made another foray to Wall Street in December. He apparently smoothed things over with the easterners, for he returned boasting of cash in hand to finish the railroad.

Gilman blasted the "certain cliques and quarters" who were spreading scurrilous rumors of insolvency. The Lake Shore would remain independent, and fulfill its stated mission: "We are perfectly satisfied with our property . . . We are strong enough and rich enough to completely equip and operate our lines as now proposed."[33]

There would, however, be one slight change: Snoqualmie Pass was out. The main line was to be rerouted over Cady Pass, at the headwaters of the Wallace and Wenatchee rivers, to allow a more direct route between Spokane and Seattle. This would also remove the Lake Shore from the shadow of paralleling the Northern Pacific and its land grant. "Seattle's own" Snoqualmie Pass would see only a spur to the Denny iron mine west of the summit. At the confluence of the Wenatchee and Columbia rivers, where Chief Engineer Mohr planned his big bridge, Burke, Gilman, and George Haller took options on land in anticipation of a town that subsequently materialized as Wenatchee. It would be one of their more successful ventures.

The Seattle Lake Shore & Eastern struggled gamely on. Separate freight and passenger trains were running to and from Snohomish by October 1888, while mixed consists of coal, lumber, merchandise, and a passenger car or two rattled down the main line. Suburban service was extended to Ballard in February 1889, as Seattle gave a convulsive heave and pushed its city limits two miles north of Green Lake, to the east shore of Mercer Island, as far south as Allentown, and into the middle of Puget Sound.

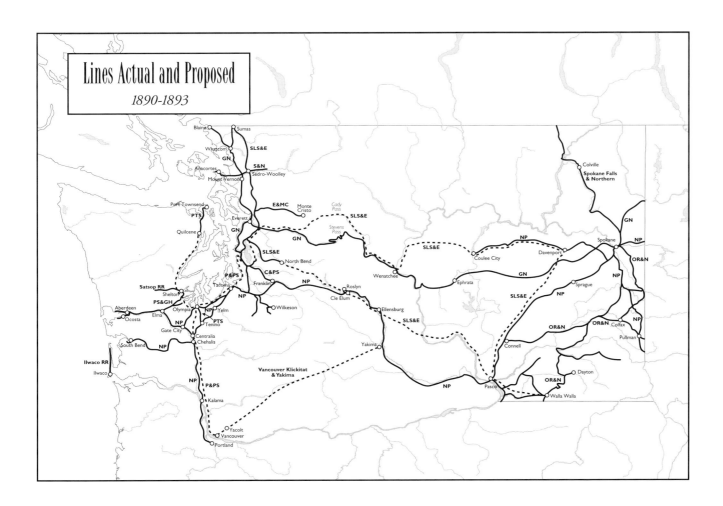

Lines Actual and Proposed
1890-1893

Revenues increased steadily, giving Burke and Gilman new cause for hope.

Tiny drivers churning, the three little Forney tank engines shuttled two-car "push-pull" suburban trains between Columbia Street and the embryonic new suburban townships whose creation had been stimulated by the railroad. Boulevard, later called Interbay, was established in 1888 by Gilman on his addition north of Smith Cove. Across Salmon Bay to the north, Ballard had been founded in 1882 by William Ballard, but had remained a somnambulant fishing village until the advent of the Seattle Lake Shore & Eastern. Prompted by the coming of

the railroad, sawmills, shipyards, and factories sprouted on Salmon Bay. William Ballard, John Leary, and B.J. Tallman formed the West Coast Improvement Company to develop industry at Smith Cove, Gilman Park, and Salmon Bay. Canal locks and a railroad making a "grand circuit" of the north Seattle suburbs were envisioned, and the company got so far as to survey line around Green Lake and build a trestle across the bay, which was appropriated by the Seattle Lake Shore & Eastern.

Two years later, Burke, Gilman, and John Leary resuscitated the scheme in the Salmon Bay Railway & Development Company, an even grander plan involving steel mills

and a railroad from Salmon Bay to the head of Lake Washington, and into Snoqualmie Pass to the Denny iron mine. With visions of vast mills and car foundries, Gilman attempted to rope James J. Hill into the venture, without success. Like so many of their undertakings, the SBR&D ended up as little more than a modestly fruitful real estate speculation.[34]

Where virgin timber had recently stood, the suburban townsites flourished with the advent of the Seattle Lake Shore & Eastern. On the south shore of the bay, developer John Ross sited the township of Ross, destined to quickly fade. Fremont, one mile east of Ross and across the stream connecting Lake Union and Salmon Bay, was platted in 1888 by Carrie and Edward Blewett and named for their hometown of Fremont, Nebraska. Next stop was Edgewater, established in 1890 by William Ainsworth and Corliss P. Stone and optimistically named after Chicago's Edgewater Park. Latona, one mile east, was founded by developer James A. Moore and named after James M. Colman's steam launch (itself named after the Greco-Roman goddess, mother of Apollo and Diana). Brooklyn, later to become University, was founded in 1891 by Moore and James W. Clise. Heading north along Union Bay, track arrived at the sylvan retreat of Ravenna, which had been sited and named in 1887 by W.W. Beck and named after Ravenna, Italy. Nearby Ravenna Park, Seattle's first, offered an alluring wilderness getaway for city residents who flocked to purchase $1.50 roundtrip tickets on the Burke-Gilman line. Track took a sharp bend to the southeast, and next found Yesler Junction, end of the suburban district. There, a spur took off to serve a big new sawmill built by Henry Yesler at the tip of what would later become Laurelhurst. The mill burned down in 1895.

Fremont and Edgewater boasted 600 residents by the summer of 1889, along with schools, steam laundries, carpentry shops, tanneries, sawmills, a broom factory, hardware store, meat markets, restaurants, and lodging houses. Rails reached Snoqualmie Falls that June, and, on July 4, the first of many Sunday excursions to the scenic landmark rattled merrily down the line. Even at the stiff fare of $2 a head, these became all the rage, and helped boost receipts.[35]

Yet another blow descended on June 6, 1889, as the great Seattle fire destroyed the Railroad Avenue area and the Columbia Street depot. Lake Shore trains temporarily terminated on the north waterfront, as rebuilding proceeded swiftly. On the morning of July 11, came good news as trustee Angus Mackintosh announced that financing had been secured to finish track to the Canadian border. To avoid charges of being another "Credit Mobilier" that had dogged the Lake Shore and its allied construction companies, Mackintosh emphasized that bids would be open, and the lowest bidder would get the job.

"As a result of this news," he beamed, "the outlay of a million dollars in railroad work will stimulate business of all kinds, and aid Seattle in regaining all and more that she has lost by our recent disaster . . . This renewed activity and immediate connection with the great Continental route, and the rebuilding of the city on a greatly enlarged and substantial foundation, will give Seattle an impetus not enjoyed by any other city in the Northwest!"[36] All along rebuilding Front Street, the mood was upbeat.

Northern Division construction resumed in September, and through the autumn the ring of axes and the boom of blasting powder echoed along the north Cascade foothills as 800 men grubbed out roadbed between Sumas, Lake Whatcom, Arlington, and Snohomish. Wages were high—$2.25 a day for beginning laborers—but even so, men were scarce. Seattle-Arlington service began in June 1890, and Sedro was added in November. The Canadian Pacific's Seattle agent promised that his trains would be ready and waiting at the border when the first Lake Shore train steamed in.

Still, the ink ran red. General Manager William Thornell reported to the board that net income for April 1888 to May 1889—$97,866.99—was higher than he had anticipated. But so were expenses: "The type of locomotive in use by this company, the wear and tear upon cars in the logging traffic . . . the expense incident to a safe maintenance of the three miles of waterfront trestle" all kept the overhead high.[37]

Much early construction work had to be redone, and extensive cribbing and shoring up of water-saturated right of way was required on the marshy lakeside sections. In submitting his resignation, Thornell charged that the construction companies had "hung up" the railroad's cash and dragged it down.

More financial cribbing, too, was required of the remaining easterners. Gilman made another trip to New York in October 1889, and returned with his customary sanguine pronouncements: "The company is in sound financial condition, and the greater part of the money necessary for the completion of the northern branch is subscribed and put up." Rails and more rolling stock were on the way.

This would prove to be Gilman's last mission on behalf of the Seattle Lake Shore & Eastern. Soon thereafter, he withdrew from active participation in the scheme he fathered. Burke, too, was at the end of his tether. Seriously cash-strapped, he begged Jones to sell out his Lake Shore stock (which by year's end would sink to ten on the exchange) at ninety cents on the dollar.[38]

In November, President J.R. McDonald announced that the Lake Shore was actively seeking inclusion in a big road. *Post-Intelligencer* publisher Hunt stepped up his negotiations with St. Paul Minneapolis & Manitoba president James J. Hill, vouching for Burke and the Lake Shore's traffic prospects in glowing terms, and emphasizing that the line offered to Hill's "Manitoba road" a ready-made entrance to Seattle. The following February, Manitoba (by this time GN) vice-president Colonel William P. Clough came to town, looked things over, and retired without comment. Burke started his long and anxious love match with the Great Northern, and dangled the Lake Shore as handy bait.

It was, he wrote Clough, "almost a business necessity for you to absorb the Seattle Lake Shore & Eastern . . . You could practically gain absolute control of the valuable territory."

Sorry, answered Clough. It was "impracticable to fit that property into our . . . system."[39]

The judge also courted the Union Pacific. "If this system could be owned and developed in connection with the Union Pacific system, its value to the latter company would be very great," he wrote a UP official in April 1890. "Whether we regard the Seattle Lake Shore & Eastern Railway system as an independent or as an auxiliary to the Union Pacific, it is without doubt one of the most valuable roads in the country."[40]

The Seattle road did not fit the Union Pacific's plan, either. Apparently, however, it did fit others. On February 18, state senator Byron C. Van Houten, representing himself as the holder of $41,000 worth of SLS&E stock, brought suit in Spokane against the railroad, charging fraud and collusion. The company, he said, was being fleeced for the benefit of the Seattle & Eastern Construction Company and inside speculators. Furthermore, Van Houten asserted that, as there had been no further construction on the Eastern Division, it was now in default of its bonds. Motion was made to place the line in receivership.

The suit had its backers. "What the bondholders want is to divorce the railway company from the construction company, in order that the road may be built through to Seattle, which will never be done so long as the construction company has control," declared a Van Houten supporter. "Three companies, the Northern Pacific, Union Pacific, and Manitoba, stand ready to bid for the privilege of completing the road the moment the divorce is granted . . . The road is tottering now, and its only salvation lies in the successful issue of the suit."

Tacoma also got its digs in. "The Seattle Lake Shore & Eastern railroad is in exceedingly bad shape, and about to die a painful death," gloated the *Ledger*. "It had nothing but Seattle wind behind it, and the wind has given out. The history of the corporation proves that a flimsy boom could not build a railroad, and at last Seattle people have been forced to confess that their town can never be but a large way station."[41]

Typically, Burke smelled a Northern Pacific rat, and charged that the suit was nothing more than "an infamous conspiracy against the people of the entire state and especially against Seattle and Spokane"—a transparent NP plot to discredit the Lake Shore and depress its stock, so it could gobble it up, kill the competition, and keep other lines out of the state (Washington had become a state the previous November, 1889).[42]

The NP had in fact been hounding the Lake Shore in the Spokane area by filing injunctions against crossings, attempting to capture control of the Eastern Division right of way, and, failing that, building a branch line parallel to it. None of these ploys succeeded.

"Both the Seattle Lake Shore & Eastern Railway Co. and the Seattle and Eastern Construction Co. are in excellent financial condition," Burke added, and the Northern Pacific resorted to this mendacity "because it must crush out the Seattle Lake Shore & Eastern Railway Company and its threatened competition now or never."

Burke hurried to Spokane, got a change of venue to Seattle, and quickly made hash of the suit. Van Houten had declared a personal net worth of $10,000 in a recent divorce hearing, Burke noted—how could he suddenly and mysteriously have acquired a $41,000 stock portfolio?

"Most of the bonds Van Houten claims to own were purchased during the last few weeks in New York," declared the *Post-Intelligencer*, "and were evidently obtained for the purpose of this suit. If all the facts were to come out, Van Houten would probably be shown up in a very bad light."

So too, it was suggested, would the Northern Pacific. District court judge Cornelius Hanford evidently agreed, and on March 9 threw the suit out.

A triumphant Burke led local stockholders in a last, rousing cry of defiance. "The Lake Shore road has never been stronger!" he blustered. "We will stand as before, and maintain our independence!"

To Franklin Jones, he crowed: "It was a scheme worthy of the days of Fisk and Gould, but the weapons employed were old and rusty and did but blundering work."[43]

The Northern Pacific would not be denied. In June, James Smith warned Gilman of "swift and mysterious movements on Wall Street"—NP was buying Lake Shore stock.[44] President Thomas Oakes and Chairman Henry Villard had been watching developments in the Puget Sound region—the impending invasion of Jim Hill's Great Northern in particular—with growing concern. Acquisition of the SLS&E Northern Division would checkmate Hill, in one stroke throwing the NP right across the GN's path, and tapping the rich farmlands of the upper Sound country and securing a Canadian connection. Nor could the Lake Shore's dividend-hungry shareholders turn down the acquisition by the large and prosperous transcontinental. The Armours, Edward Christian, Thomas Logan, and James Smith pooled their stock and sold it to the Northern Pacific. The wolf was at the door.

As a prelude to the takeover, Oakes wrote John Bryant, the Lake Shore's latest general manager, on March 11, proposing they join in running a "belt line" around Lake Washington: "As I am confident your company is not committed to an agreement with [the SLS&E], a close alliance between our interests can be brought about. The construction of the belt line at Seattle will be the first step in that direction."[45]

On July 21, Oakes announced in New York that the Northern Pacific had purchased a majority interest in the capital stock of the Seattle Lake Shore & Eastern. The NP would rent the Lake Shore for $80,000 a year, assume interest payments on outstanding SLS&E bonds, and complete the line from Arlington to the international boundary.

James McNaught, co-signer of the agreement, clarified that Villard's Oregon & Transcontinental Company was behind the deal: "For a certain consideration to be paid by the Oregon Transcontinental Co., the Northern Pacific guarantees the bonds of the road . . . The Northern Pacific has not secured any lease, and it will be some time yet, I imagine, before anything is done by the Northern Pacific looking to the operation of the Seattle Lake Shore & Eastern." The Seattle road would retain nominal independence.[46]

Either way, Thomas Burke was less than elated. "The city council should now be on their guard," he warned. "The Northern Pacific is going to make a last desperate effort to obstruct the Great Northern along the city front . . . and the city council to a man should stand like sentinels on guard to prevent the Northern Pacific from carrying out its purposes."

Though it had failed to make money, and failed even to cross Snoqualmie Pass, the Seattle Lake Shore & Eastern had nonetheless succeeded in realizing Burke's dream of making Seattle a force to be reckoned with.

The *Post-Intelligencer* observed: "It is worth noting the wonderful change there has been in the railroad situa-

tion since the Seattle Lake Shore & Eastern entered the field . . . The Northern Pacific has treated the little road with contempt, heaping ridicule upon it, sneered at it as a 'paper road' and a line 'built of wind,' and after all, it has become the pivotal point in railroading on Puget Sound. The NP seeks to control it, realizing its power."

And, as the new year began, the same newspaper presented this eulogy: "The Seattle Lake Shore & Eastern was the balm that assuaged the grievous hurts inflicted upon Seattle by the Northern Pacific. It was the stimulant that aroused the people from despair and defeat. It was the child that was long regarded with jealous and fostering care by all people of Seattle. In so far as it served to stir up the energies and enterprise of the people, it has fulfilled its purpose."[47]

Best of all, business was improving. The extension of track during 1890 invited substantial development near the line. Shingle mills and logging camps sprouted every few miles along the right of way—Arlington, Edgecomb, Springfield, Machias, Wickersham—pushing the young Washington lumber industry into the north Cascades. Each mill sent out from six to twenty carloads a day, and, by summer, three daily freight and passenger trains were needed to handle local traffic alone. The outlook improved even more dramatically when, on April 13, 1891, track was finished to the border at Sumas. The Canadian Pacific arrived the following month, opening a long and fruitful era of international trade through the Sumas gateway.

Less successful was the great steel-making venture of Peter Kirk. Despite substantial financial support, his Moss Bay Iron & Steel Co. ran out of money late in 1889. Moss Bay was reorganized early the following year as the Great Western Iron & Steel, and Kirk succeeded in buying machinery and erecting buildings at the new east Lake Washington town site he christened Kirkland. Kirk and Leigh Hunt attracted additional eastern backers, including John D. Rockefeller, and a rail spur was laid from Kirkland Junction, two miles south of Woodinville, to the mill site. Just as things seemed to be coming together, Black Friday intervened—April 5, 1893, when the nation's booming late '80s economic engine ran out of steam and fell into a sinkhole of depleted gold reserves, over-capitalization, and loss of public confidence.[48]

Kirk's machinery and partially completed structures rusted where they sat. Another casualty of the early 1890s was the Lake Shore's suburban service. By 1892, electric street railways had reached Ballard, Fremont, and Latona, and the trolleys drew off much of the steam road's patronage. Chief among these was the West Street & North End Electric Railway, whose board, ironically enough, included Burke and Gilman.

Cursed by overextended credit, heavily watered stock, miles of expensive track through undeveloped territory, and beholden to absentee capital, the fragile Seattle Lake Shore & Eastern was a prime example of the precariousness of western enterprise and railroad building. For years, the Seattle press agitated for more local manufacturing and basic industries, such as the steel mill, but it took more than newsprint to make these things a reality. In the meantime, neither increasing revenues, the Sumas gateway, Northern Pacific ownership, nor eastern capital could save the Seattle road from the panic of '93. By June, the Seattle Lake Shore & Eastern was broke.

Thomas Brown was appointed receiver, and on the 30th, Seattle district court judge Cornelius Hanford declared null and void the Northern Pacific/O&T lease. The Lake Shore's bonds were sold to the Union Trust Bank of New York. The Northern Pacific could do nothing for its fledgling; by August, it too was bankrupt.

The Lake Shore offered "hard times" rates, but could not reverse the sharp drop in passenger and freight business. Brown reported a paltry $3,263 net income at the end of August, down from $31,852 for 1892. By the third quarter, 1895, net income was a pathetic $623.17. Wages and staff were slashed, and trains cut to one a day, leaving Seattle for Sallal Prairie at 8:25 AM and connecting at Woodinville for Sumas. Over angry objections from mill owners, the railroad was forced to require advance payment from shippers just to keep trains running.

Litigation settled in upon the Seattle road and would drag on for years. The Northern Pacific sued the Lake Shore trustees for $2,250,000, the cost of supplies and rolling stock it claimed to have furnished the Seattle road between 1890 and 1893. The trustees countersued, charging that the NP had failed to live up to its agreement to guarantee the SLS&E bonds, and that during the lease period it had squandered Lake Shore resources. The NP denied all charges and countered that it had rescued a worthless property with worthless stock, and was making it into a paying one. Other actions followed: A suit against the NP's Lake Shore bond guarantee by a Minneapolis stockholder, and an 1895 stockholder action charging fraud and mismanagement.[49]

The Seattle Lake Shore & Eastern was also a pawn in a game of railroad tug of war. Angling for his own track into Seattle, Canadian Pacific president Van Horne asked the trustees to give his company a 99-year lease.

Great Northern's Hill was also rumored to be plotting with Burke to buy the SLS&E. "He and the Canadian Pacific will doubtlessly arrange such a course as will completely shut out the Northern Pacific from through freight," said the *Times*.

In all of these contests, the Northern Pacific emerged the winner. Judge Hanford upheld its suit against the trustees in July 1895, and, three years later, NP beat Van Horne back to his side of the border once and for all. By this time, Hill (who never really had any interest in the trouble-plagued SLS&E) had his own line between Seattle and Canada, and was well on his way toward capturing control of the Northern Pacific itself.[50]

The Seattle Lake Shore & Eastern died on May 16, 1896. Foreclosure proceedings were instituted against the road by its bondholders, who purchased the property and on June 30 conveyed it to the Union Trust Co. for $1,000,000. The company was reorganized as the Seattle & International Railroad. The Spokane-Davenport Eastern Division, all forty-seven miles of it, was granted independent existence as the Spokane & Seattle Railway. Fearing foreclosure on its $5,000,000 bond guarantee, the

Seattle Lake Shore & Eastern engine roster

No.	Type	Builder	Dates/notes
1	4-4-0	Rhode Island	6/1887—*H.L. Yesler.* To Seattle & International No. 1, 7/1896, NP No. 1145, 4/1901. Scrapped 5/1919.
2	4-4-0	Rhode Island	6/1887—*D.H. Gilman.* To S&I No. 2, 7/1896, NP No. 1146, 4/1901. Scrapped 5/1919.
3	4-4-0	Rhode Island	8/1888—*F.M. Jones.* Ordered for Midland Rwy., sold to SLS&E. To S&I No. 3, 7/1896, NP No. 1147, 4/1901. Scrapped 1/1924.
4	4-4-0	Rhode Island	2/1888—*Thomas Burke.* Ordered for Midland Rwy., sold to SLS&E. To S&I No. 4, 7/1896, NP No. 1148, 4/1901. Scrapped 11/1920.
5	0-4-0	Rhode Island	1/1867(?)—Possibly ex-Providence & Worcester No.12, *Jack Quint.* Bought by SLS&E 4/1888. To S&I No. 5, 7/1896. Sold 10/1900.
6	0-4-4T	Rhode Island	6/1888—*J.R. McDonald.* Built as Forney 0-4-4T, rebuilt to 2-4-4T. To Stone & Webster No. 6, Larson Box No. 21, 1925.
7	2-8-0	Rhode Island	6/1887—*S.V. White.* To S&I No. 7, 7/1896, NP No. 48, 1/1901. Scrapped 7/1912.
8 (1st)	0-4-0	Smith & Porter	1870—Ex-NP *Otter Tail.* Bought by SLS&E 4/1888, sold 5/1892.
8 (2nd)	2-8-0	Richmond	1895—To S&I No. 8, 7/1896, NP No. 47, 1/1901. Scrapped 1927.
9	2-8-0	Rhode Island	6/1887—*James D. Smith.* Ordered as Minneapolis & Pacific No. 22, to SLS&E 2/1888, S&I No. 9, 7/1896, NP No. 49, 1/1901. Scrapped 9/1910.
10 (1st)	0-4-4T	Rhode Island	7/1888—To Tacoma Lake Park & Columbia No. 10, 5/1892. Scrapped 1940.
10 (2nd)	2-8-0	New York	7/1889—Ex-Montana Union No. 158, to S&I No. 10, 3/1899, NP No. 84, 4/1901. Renumbered 132. Scrapped 11/1933.
11 (1st)	4-4-0	Rhode Island	8/1888—*A.M. Cannon.* To S&I No. 11, 7/1896, renumbered 101, to NP No. 1149, 4/1901. Scrapped 1926.
11 (2nd)	2-8-0	Schenectady	4/1900—To NP No. 45, 4/1901, rebuilt to 0-8-0, 1912. Scrapped 1926.
12 (1st)	4-4-0	Rhode Island	8/1888—*P.F. Mohr.* To S&I No. 12, 7/1896, renumbered 102. To NP No. 1150, 4/1901. Scrapped 11/1920.
12 (2nd)	2-8-0	Schenectady	5/1900—To NP No. 46, 4/1901. Rebuilt to 0-8-0, 1912. To Washburn Lignite, 9/1925.
13	0-4-4T	Rhode Island	6/1889—To Seattle Terminal No. 1, 7/1890, possibly to NP 1071, 8/1902. Off roster 3/1907.
14	4-6-0	?	?—Ex-Satsop RR No. 3, *Dottie.* Bought by SLS&E 11/1889, sold 5/1892.
15	4-6-0	Rhode Island	2/1890—To S&I No. 15, 7/1896, NP No. 299, 4/1901. Renumbered 365. To Columbia Cowlitz & Cascade No. 2, 2/1921. Scrapped ca. 1930.
16	4-6-0	Rhode Island	8/1890—Built for SLS&E, but delivered to NP. Carried numbers 430, 16, 310, 328, 388. To Inland Paper No. 388, 1/1923. Scrapped 7/1948.
17	4-6-0	Rhode Island	8/1890—Built for SLS&E, but delivered to NP. Carried numbers 431, 311, 329, 389. Scrapped 2/1925.

Northern Pacific tried to block the deal. In this, it was unsuccessful, but Lake Shore bonds remained in circulation and legal squabbles with the NP continued.

Depression faded and times gradually improved on the Seattle road, stimulated by the Klondike gold rush of 1897, the Sumas gateway, and steadily increasing regional growth. Demand for local passenger service grew to such an extent that a second daily train between Wooley and Seattle was added in April 1899 to allow farmers to make a day's flier into Seattle, much to the consternation of rural merchants. And, with more railroads eyeing Seattle—the Chicago Burlington & Quincy, Chicago Milwaukee & St. Paul, Chicago & North Western—periodic rumors surfaced that the Seattle & International would yet build over Snoqualmie Pass to meet them. It was not to be.

The inevitable came on April 1, 1901, as the Seattle & International ended independent existence and became the Seattle Division of the Northern Pacific. The exuberant years of home-grown Seattle railroading were over, and Thomas Burke and Daniel Gilman could look proudly upon an achievement that had contributed much to their city's growth.

For the Seattle Lake Shore & Eastern, Thomas Burke provided a fitting epitaph: "The city of Seattle should always retain a warm place in its municipal heart for the little railway that came to its relief in the darkest hour of its history."[51] (Today, the Burke-Gilman recreational trail for joggers, walkers, and bikers remains on much of the old SLS&E route, to Seattle's lasting delight.)

Thomas Burke and Daniel Gilman are Seattle's Mutt and Jeff, an unlikely duo that provided much-needed energy and ambition at a critical time in the city's development. Thomas Burke's biographer, Robert Nesbit, labeled Gilman a "shoestring operator with a talent for keeping up appearances among moneyed people," a schemer who talked big while Burke acted.[52]

Those appearances were important, no less in 1885 than a century later. Burke's prognostications of "practically limitless" eastern capital, coupled with Gilman's abundant talent for hinting at great forces aligning in Seattle's favor,

helped stimulate growth in a time of desperate optimism. Burke was always the first to credit his friend's "indomitable perseverance" for the successful creation of the Seattle Lake Shore & Eastern, and it was Gilman, after all, who successfully lured the large Wall Street backing Seattle had long dreamed of catching. The judge provided solidity, sobriety, and legal acumen, and it seems fair to say that one could not have done without the other. Perhaps, too, some of Gilman's glibness would have stood the dour Arthur Denny and Henry Yesler in good stead during their searches for outside capital twenty years earlier. ■

Seattle, Lake Shore & Eastern Railway

Thos. R. Brown and John H. Bryant, Receivers

Trains leave and arrive foot Columbia street

TIME CARD
In effect September 15, 1895:

No. 3 †	No. 1.*		No. 2.*	No. 4 †
4:50pm	9:00am	lv..Seattle..ar	5:25pm	10:40 am
6:04pm	10:15am	Woodinv'leJc	4:19pm	9:20 am
	11:04am	.. Issaquah ...	3:25pm	
	12:04pm	.Snoqualmie.	2:31pm	
	12:15pm	.North Bend.	2:20pm	
6:47pm	10:53am	. Snohomish .	3:41pm	8:33 am
8:45pm	12:51pm	... Wooley ...	1:53pm	6:30 am
	4:00pm	..Anacortes..	9:00am	
	....	..Hamilton ..	12:50pm	
	1:24pm	.Wickersham.	1:25pm	
	2:55pm	....Sumas....	11:55am	
	5:50pm	ar Vanc'rBC lv	9:00am	

*Daily   †Daily except Sunday

SHORT AND DIRECT LINE TO ALL
POINTS IN BRITISH COLUMBIA

Through the Principal Lumber Districts of
Western Washington

General Office, Colman Block, Seattle

A. D. SCROGGY,
Gen. Fr't & Pass' Ag't

Light rail 1880s-style, SLS&E engine No. 10 and a suburban coach pose about 1889. With cessation of suburban service, diminutive Rhode Island-built No. 10 was sold to the Tacoma Lake Park & Columbia short line in May 1892, and was scrapped in 1940.

University of Washington, Special Collections, #17761

SLS&E schedule, December 1895.

CHAPTER 10

Pax Northernia Pacifica

"Seattle was determined to conquer, and she has triumphed most gloriously!"
—Judge Orange Jacobs

THE 1890s PROMISED exciting things for Seattle, not the least being the final reckoning with its ancient enemy, the Northern Pacific. The great corporation had extended the olive branch in the form of equal grain rates with Tacoma and improved service.

The *Post-Intelligencer*, on New Year's Day 1890, celebrated this change: "For seventeen years, Seattle has been engaged in a civil conflict unparalleled in commercial history . . . the Northern Pacific Railroad has probably now abandoned forever that policy of discrimination against Seattle which must have driven it back into the obscurity of a mushroom city but for the sublime courage and energy of her people. Finally, with laggard steps, the corporation gave way. The company expunged the remaining exception from the adjusted schedule, better accommodations were afforded, little by little the inequalities were leveled, and with the last hour of 1889 disappears the final vestige of the once-broad line of demarcation between favored Tacoma and ostracized Seattle."[1]

On January 10, the board of directors ratified the purchase of the Puget Sound Shore Railroad by the Northern Pacific & Puget Sound Shore Co., for $1,000,000. Thirty-six years after Isaac Stevens had mapped it out, the Northern Pacific was a through line to Seattle, and the Orphan Road passed into folklore.

Puget Sound Shore president Troilus Tyndale reminisced on the history of the controversial stretch of track: "[Ira A.] Nadeau and I were the whole railroad. I was president and treasurer . . . and Nadeau was all the other officers. Mr. Villard let us run the road for more than a year without a word of interference, and Nadeau brought up the earnings so successfully that Mr. Villard was enabled to sell the twenty-three mile road to the Northern Pacific for $1 million."

Eugene Smalley's *The Northwest* magazine put it thus: "Seattle is at last a Northern Pacific town . . . Seattle used to fight the N.P. with all the energy and business acuteness for which she is remarkable and once made a big effort at Washington to have the land grant of the road forfeited by Congress. Now she will no doubt become a fast friend of the gigantic corporation . . . Times change and the interests of men and towns change too."[2]

A key item of business was grain. To qualify for NP's rate parity with Portland and Tacoma, Seattle was required to provide storage space for at least half a million bushels. In February, therefore, the Seattle Grain Elevator & Warehouse Company was organized and formally incorporated on March 25 as the Seattle Terminal Railway & Elevator Company. Leading Seattle men—William Ballard, Thomas Burke, Jacob Furth, Bailey Gatzert, Leigh Hunt, and Senator Watson Squire—made up the terminal company board, and G.F. Austin was sent to San Francisco to inspect facilities there and plan the erection of Seattle's first grain elevator.

There was little space for an elevator on the downtown waterfront, so a site across Elliott Bay in West Seattle was purchased from the West Seattle Land & Improvement Company. To link the facility to the "mainland," Seattle

BY THE END OF THE 19TH CENTURY, SEATTLE'S FRONTIER ERA RAILROAD FACILITIES WERE CONGESTED TO THE BURSTING POINT. A TURN-OF-THE-CENTURY VIEW LOOKING NORTHWEST FROM BEACON HILL SHOWS THE BROAD GAUGE STRIP CRAMMED WITH FREIGHT. THE LARGE BUILDING IS THE SEATTLE TRANSFER CO. WAREHOUSE; THE OLD PSS/NP DEPOT IS TO THE LEFT OF THE SMOKE PLUME. THE COLUMBIA & PUGET SOUND RR CURVES ALONG THE OLD SHORELINE TO THE RIGHT. THE BLOCK-LONG GN FREIGHT HOUSE IS VISIBLE IMMEDIATELY LEFT OF THE TALL SMOKESTACK. BY 1906, THE AREA WOULD BE RADICALLY TRANSFORMED, AND THE GN AND NP AT HOME IN NEW KING STREET STATION.

Museum of History and Industry, #83.10.6049.3

Terminal contracted with the San Francisco Bridge Company at the beginning of April to build a three-mile-long pile trestle across the bay. A single-track line was speedily located—running west from the broad gauge strip at South Weller Street, dipping to the south, then turning to the southwest at so-called Railroad Avenue Y. There it would extend on the trestle (Railroad Avenue West) across the tideflats to the grain terminal, then continue past the facility to the Seattle ferry dock just southeast of Duwamish Head.

Time was short. The terminal company had contracted with eastern Washington grain merchants to load three ships by August 15. On the 10th, the trestle was finished, and the track hastily spiked down. For passenger service, Seattle Terminal leased from the Seattle Lake Shore & Eastern a locomotive, coach, and combination car, and for freight operations bought two large Baldwin 0-6-0s from the American Construction Company. On August 13, the Seattle Establishment boarded a four-car special at the NP depot and rode across the bay to open the new grain terminal.

Judge Orange Jacobs proclaimed: "Seattle was determined to conquer, and she has triumphed most gloriously! The opening of a wheat elevator in Seattle means the culmination of a great victory by endurance over the opposition of corporations!"[3]

On October 22, the square rigger *Mary I. Burrell* weighed anchor with 40,000 sacks of Seattle's first grain shipment in her hold.

On March 15, the Northern Pacific & Puget Sound Shore asked for a franchise on Railroad Avenue, the main thoroughfare along the waterfront created by Thomas Burke to—in theory—accommodate all lines into town. This came hard on the heels of the rival Great Northern's demand for a four-track right of way covering sixty feet of the avenue, a franchise Burke had swiftly shepherded through the city council to approval. Shortly thereafter, Northern Pacific president Oakes showed up, and promised that complete terminal facilities would be built in the city. Moreover, the Northern Pacific & Puget Sound

Shore would act on its 1884 charter and run a "belt line" from Black River Junction along both east and west shores of Lake Washington, and north to Bellingham Bay, Fidalgo Island, and the Canadian border. Surveys would begin immediately.

"We had been striving for a long time to get control of the Puget Sound Shore road, but were not able until Mr. Villard again came into power," Oakes said.[4] Now, the NP was anxious to meet all of Seattle's needs.

Certain things had to be fixed however: first was granting the Northern Pacific its requisite portion of Railroad Avenue, where a nasty squabble was developing among the NP, the Seattle Lake Shore & Eastern, the Seattle & Montana (Great Northern's local proxy), and the Columbia & Puget Sound; second was coming to acceptable terms over the disposition of the old 1882 Villard right of way along the meander line, held by the Northern Pacific and the Columbia & Puget Sound and something the city now wished to remove. Oakes made it clear that his company would relinquish its share of this so-called "ram's horn" franchise, inherited from the Puget Sound Shore, only in exchange for equivalent room on Railroad Avenue. The trouble was, after the Seattle & Montana and Seattle Lake Shore & Eastern had taken their shares, there were only twenty-two feet left. And Oakes wanted thirty-seven.

Do not let one company (the Seattle & Montana), "whose only capital is gall and wind," monopolize the waterfront, he warned the city council. "We do not promise to come here with a transcontinental line. We are here with a completed line and are transacting business . . . Thirty-seven feet is enough for us, with all our business— it ought to be enough for the Seattle & Montana."[5]

Councilman Niesz interjected: "The reason we gave the Seattle & Montana so many feet was because they said they would require as much, having 8,000 cars to handle here, this being their terminus. These are railroad problems and can probably be better solved by railroad companies than by ranchmen or councilmen."

Mayor Robert Moran piped up: How about a Pullman sleeper for Seattle? The city had been promised one for some time (if one believed the newspapers), but Seattle passengers were still forced to change cars in the wee hours, and ride daycoaches "foul from tobacco smoke and spittle."

"The Pullman Company are very anxious to get a car on here," Niesz broke in.

"No one is anxious," grumped Oakes. "We cannot put a through car on because there is not the business for it. If the people want a through sleeper, they should give us more patronage."

Niesz grumbled, "I don't think other cities are required to do that."

Oakes deftly changed the subject, and dangled the bait of a big new $300,000 passenger station. "We are here knocking at your doors and ask you to let us in Railroad Avenue, of which we ask a small amount. We are here to stay, we intend to do half the business wherever we go, and will continue to do it if we have to do it for nothing, and don't you forget it!" Oakes thumped the tabletop, sat down, and then slapped his knee to make sure everyone got the point.[6]

They did. The NP held its own on the waterfront, and by dint of skillful lobbying, dogged litigation, and covert acquisition managed to steadily enlarge its presence there, despite the determined opposition of James J. Hill and Judge Burke. In April, its crews began driving piles across the tideflats for a new mainline into town and a trestle paralleling the Seattle Terminal line to West Seattle. The company also bought thirty acres of tidelands near Railroad Avenue Y for the development of new yard facilities, and late in the year made the first of what would eventually be extensive purchases on the waterfront—Henry Yesler's wharf.

As if to show faith, Oakes smartened up his Seattle passenger service. On March 1, a new Tacoma, Olympia, and Chehalis Express went into service, along with additional Tacoma and Portland trains, and, for the first time, twice-daily summer transcontinentals. These would continue to terminate in Portland and bypass Seattle, but offer direct connections at Tacoma. Best of all, Seattle got its sleeping car; tourist sleepers began running into the city June 15

and, after more city council prodding, first-class through Pullmans to Portland and the East entered Seattle for the first time on August 22. Business boomed, and the finely varnished new sleepers were filled as quickly as they could be rushed into service.

The service was not quite perfected, however, and even the normally loyal Tacoma *News* was roused to complain after a conductor brandished brass knuckles aboard the Pacific Express: "There is one thing that may retard immigration into this state, and that is the unpopularity of the Northern Pacific railway with the traveling public . . . There are but few passengers who come to Washington over that line but have a grievance, and generally a good one . . . If some of the officials were made to serve as section hands, and gentlemen and businessmen substituted in the official positions, the road might appear to better advantage."

Reversion to a once-a-day transcontinental schedule in the fall spurred a fresh round of complaints. Trains were often standing room only, and Seattle agent Nadeau defended the company:

"We are running a full train of twelve cars each, and as soon as the travel warrants will break the train into two sections. The road wishes to run one train a day and keep it on time. The plan worked very satisfactorily last year. Every other transcontinental road had a tie-up of from one to ten days, but we did not miss a single train. Our time is good, too, for a transcontinental train that is only an hour late in winter is doing pretty well . . . It is cheaper to run two sections of the same train through than to run two separate trains. The two sections keep so close together that one set of station and switch hands can look after it . . . Thirty five miles an hour is very rapid running between here and St. Paul, when the grades are considered . . . The fares are very low. You can go to St. Paul second class for $35, and that is less than two cents a mile. The great mass of people travel second class; indeed we sell fifteen second class to one first class ticket. So the majority of people ought not to complain that traveling is expensive."

PUGET SOUND SHORE R. R.
TIME TABLE.
TAKING EFFECT SUNDAY, OCT. 5, 1889.

Trains leave Seattle as follows:
Atlantic express.........................5:05 a.m.
Tacoma express.........................10:30 a.m.
Portland express.........................7:00 p.m.
Through Freight ....5:30 a.m.
Local Freight.............................11:15 a.m.
Trains arrive at Seattle as follows:
Eastern and Southern express.......9:55 a.m.
Tacoma express.........................4:15 p.m.
Portland express.........................9:55 p.m.
Local Freight.............................9:15 a.m.
Through Freight.........................5:15 p.m.
All the above trains run daily.
Southern and Eastern Mail carries Pullman sleepers.
Depot and Ticket office Depot street corner of Weller and Second streets,
Tickets on sale to all points in the United States, Canada and Europe.
I. A. NADEAU, Manager.
E. TONKIN, Ticket Agent.

FINAL PUGET SOUND SHORE SCHEDULE, OCTOBER 1889.

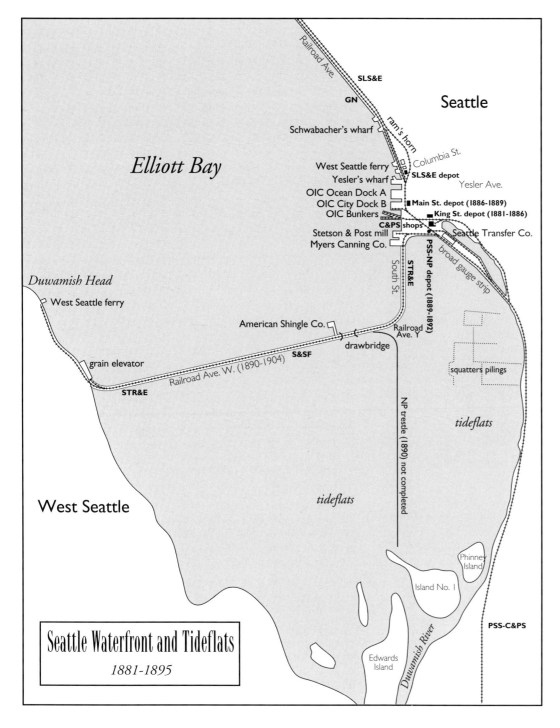

Railroad Ave.

SLS&E

GN

Seattle

Schwabacher's wharf

Elliott Bay

ram's horn

Columbia St.

West Seattle ferry

■ SLS&E depot

Yesler's wharf

Yesler Ave.

OIC Ocean Dock A

OIC City Dock B

■ Main St. depot (1886-1889)

OIC Bunkers

■ King St. depot (1881-1886)

C&PS shops

Stetson & Post mill

Seattle Transfer Co.

Myers Canning Co.

PSS-NP depot (1889-1892)

Duwamish Head

South St.

broad gauge strip

West Seattle ferry

STR&E

American Shingle Co.

Railroad Ave. Y

drawbridge

grain elevator

S&SF

Railroad Ave. W. (1890-1904)

squatters pilings

STR&E

NP trestle (1890) not completed

tideflats

West Seattle

tideflats

Phinney Island

Island No. 1

PSS-C&PS

Edwards Island

Duwamish River

Seattle Waterfront and Tideflats
1881-1895

Still, complain they did, aggravated further by the dingy, shack-like Weller Street depot and its swarms of pushy hotel runners and hack drivers, who fell shouting upon detraining passengers, grabbing valises and elbows.[7]

Overall, though, the mood was bright, as Puget Sound enjoyed an unparalleled boom. Seattle's population attained 43,467 in 1890, an astonishing spurt from the 9,786 residents of a decade before, and coming within 3,000 of Portland's. Tacoma zoomed from 6,000 to 36,006, and its grain shipments, by 1890, almost matched Portland's. Other traffic through the terminus—lumber, coal, hops, produce—kept pace. Foreign trade increased tenfold over 1880's $360,000.

Senator Watson Squire, who had invited Henry Villard to invest in Puget Sound's future, summed up the mood of the time: "Our resources are unlimited. In fact, we have only begun to discover them. More than that, we have a progressive, hustling population. Our businessmen, our farmers, our mechanics—in fact all our citizens are essentially Western men. They recognize what the future has in store for them, and almost without exception they are making the best of their opportunities. Scores of fortunes have been made in the new state within a few years past, and others are now in the course of manufacture that will some day astonish the East."[8]

Riding the crest of the boom, the Northern Pacific began a major expansion campaign in western Washington. First target was the lush valley of the Chehalis River extending to the Pacific coast, a timber-rich region hitherto neglected by railroads. Eastern Washington railroad promoter George W. Hunt was already grading roadbed towards Grays Harbor, and in March President Oakes warned board chairman Villard that the Union Pacific was also on the verge of moving in: "In view of all the schemes afloat in the interest of other companies, I think the time has arrived for prompt action in taking possession of the country west of our Pacific Division."

Villard agreed, and, on May 7, NP incorporated a local road, the Tacoma Olympia & Grays Harbor Railroad, to take it to the Pacific. Hunt's road, already under construction west of Centralia, was absorbed, and would link up with the TO&GH at Gate City, twenty miles south of the capital. An additional line, from Chehalis to South Bend, on Willapa Bay, was commenced, and Oakes briefly considered laying track between Yakima and South Bend. To manage and ultimately absorb these local roads, the Northern Pacific formed an umbrella company, United Railroads of Washington, on August 2. In the customary Villard manner, United Railroads would take out mortgages on the small lines, issue consolidated bonds, complete construction, and turn the properties over to the parent corporation.[9]

In its TO&GH guise, the NP roadbed speared west from Lakeview across the Nisqually Valley. The railroad promised Olympians that trains would be running into their city by January 1, 1891—in exchange for a $50,000 subsidy, a proposition that doubtless galled older citizens with bleak recollections of earlier dealings with the corporation. Their sense of *deja vu* must have been complete when, at 4 PM on New Year's Day, church bells again tolled for the NP. This time, track actually made it to the city limits. A tunnel was bored to carry trains beneath the capital; this opened in May, and regular service between Tacoma and Olympia began in July. Rails pushed toward surf, and, by July 1892, the Northern Pacific was advertising weekend seashore excursions to its new western outpost at Ocosta, just ten miles from the Pacific.

Closer to Seattle, the railroad considered its strategy. After announcing a Lake Washington belt line during his March 1890 visit, Oakes looked over the preliminary surveys and changed his mind. "It is not practicable to locate and build a line on either side of Lake Washington that would be acceptable to the Northern Pacific Company's high standard of construction," he told reporters. "So we have just now decided to abandon the building of the line by either of those routes."

However, too many hopes were riding on Peter Kirk's steel mill on the eastern shore of the lake for this decision to stand. Machinery was on order, the infant townsite of Kirkland was humming with activity, and the English ironmaster remained anxious for a rail connection. With the Seattle Lake Shore & Eastern financially unable to pay for any more construction, Kirk and *Post-Intelligencer* publisher Leigh Hunt asked attorney James McNaught if he could not use his influence with the Northern Pacific management to get a spur run to the mill site.

McNaught came through, and on May 19 the executive committee passed a resolution agreeing to a partnership between the Northern Pacific & Puget Sound Shore and the Seattle Lake Shore & Eastern in a twenty-year contract to build and operate the Lake Washington belt line. This was soon broadened to include shared rights on Railroad Avenue and the Seattle docks, and Northern Pacific & Puget Sound Shore completion of the Lake Shore's Northern Division to Sumas.[10]

On July 3, James M. Colman, A.S. Dunham, Jacob Furth, Leigh Hunt, and James McNaught incorporated the Lake Washington Belt Line Company. The new enterprise would promote industrial development on the lake, and back it up with railroad connection and tidewater access via a Lake Washington-Puget Sound ship canal.

"The company has already acquired several thousand acres of land on the shores of Lake Washington on which it proposes to locate various manufacturing companies," McNaught elaborated. "In fact, it is our purpose to centralize manufacturing on Lake Washington as far as possible."

The trustees had high hopes of obtaining "sufficient money to carry on all business at a very low rate and comparatively little expense," and successfully competing with eastern industry. The usual portents of vast capital waiting in the wings were trumpeted by Hunt's *Post-Intelligencer*, apparently justified when John D. Rockefeller took a heavy subscription in the Belt Line Co.'s $2,000,000 stock issue. The Belt Line's rosy prospectus promised completion of railway to the Denny Iron mine and over Snoqualmie Pass within two years, and blithely represented the entire projected map of the line along the east side of Lake Washington as "now completed."

The Northern Pacific agreed to build the Kirkland branch—with a catch. The original mill site on the shore of Lake Washington would not do; the railroad insisted on running along the top of Rose Hill, a mile east, making for a much easier grade but making water access—a prime selling point of the whole Kirkland promotion—problematic. Leigh Hunt reluctantly gave in, and the mill was duly relocated to the NP's satisfaction. The Kirkland spur was completed between Kirkland Junction, south of Woodinville, and Rose Hill in August 1891, and thousands of tons of machinery, equipment, and building materials made their way to the mill site; integrated steel making in Washington was on its way. Roadbed snaked north from Black River, through Renton, and up the east shore of Lake Washington to Mercer Slough, followed by rails, which reached Renton in December 1891.[11]

The year 1890 witnessed the beginning of the long and painful Northern Pacific digestion of the Seattle Lake Shore & Eastern. On July 21, Oakes announced that the NP had assumed controlling interest in the Seattle road, and would guarantee its bond interest payments. The Seattle Lake Shore & Eastern kept its name and nominal independence, and the Northern Pacific got track to the border, holding the line against newcomer Great Northern.

In August, NP made an agreement with Elijah Smith to assume operation of the Oregon Improvement Company-controlled Seattle & Northern; this brought the Northern Pacific into Anacortes, where it and the OIC began plotting to develop a new port city. That fall, the S&N was finished to Hamilton, fifty miles to the east, at the base of the north Cascades. Thousands of Northern Pacific tracklayers swarmed over much of western Washington, earning a payroll in excess of $200,000; during 1890-91, a fair portion of Puget Sound prosperity could be credited to the once-reviled corporation.

As the Northern Pacific spread its tentacles, its old nemesis, the land grant forfeiture movement, withered away. In October 1890, President Benjamin Harrison signed into law a bill which confirmed the Northern Pacific's right to all grant land coterminous with completed line. Forfeit, however, would be the section along the north bank of the Columbia River. Thomas Oakes had no regrets:

"This bill takes out of the jurisdiction of Congress forty-eight million acres of land, and absolutely secures them to the company—worth in the opinions of experts, fully one billion dollars. The forfeiture is of advantage to our company, as it never expected to acquire those lands. On the contrary, it will inure to its benefit, as it will throw open to occupancy a large body of land in Washington and Oregon heretofore reserved."[12]

In September 1891, the man who had bankrolled the Northern Pacific and started it on its long trek west visited Puget Sound. Jay Cooke made his first trip over the line, stopped in Tacoma, and marveled at developments since the dark days of 1873: "It is impossible, my dear friends, to express the astonishment which we all feel in regard to the progress here."

In Seattle, the venerable capitalist urged the rival towns to "lay aside their petty spites . . . In after years, the people of both cities will look back with contempt upon the quarrelsome days, and wish that these disputes had not tarnished the record of their cities."

Hard on Cooke's heels came Henry Villard. On October 29, he received a warm Tacoma reception, praised the growth and vitality of the city, and rode the first excursion train to Aberdeen Junction over the newly completed Tacoma Olympia & Grays Harbor Railroad. In Seattle, the city's old friend urged construction of the long-debated ship canal linking Lake Washington and Puget Sound. The Oregon Improvement Company had made initial surveys for a canal as early as 1881, and, a decade later, Villard was candid in explaining that the Northern Pacific needed the canal's saltwater egress to ensure the viability of the Lake Washington Belt Line Company.

James McNaught followed up in November, proposing in a chamber of commerce meeting that the city memorialize their new state senators, Squire and Allen, for canal bill support. The railroad lawyer assured the city council that the Northern Pacific would join with them in applying pressure for congressional action.[13]

Growing money worries doomed the Belt Line, however. Right of way disputes in Renton also prevented forward progress, and it soon became evident that much of the roadbed along the swampy lakeside would have to be resurveyed. More critical to the steel enterprise, there would be no extension of the former Seattle Lake Shore & Eastern to the Denny iron mine at Snoqualmie Pass, let alone into eastern Washington. Peter Kirk's mill was destined to become a statistic on the long list of casualties of the coming panic of 1893, and the vaunted Lake Washington Belt Line Company would follow it into bankruptcy in June 1896.

Jay Cooke's admonitions to cease municipal feuding fell on deaf ears. Seattle and Tacoma went happily about their accustomed business of inflating each others' crime and suicide rates, and deflating each others' census and trade figures. As always, Seattle complained that train schedules favored Tacoma.

"Now, if there were any great works of art to be seen in Tacoma, if there were any objects of interest to attract and instruct the inquiring mind, the stop would not be so heart-breakingly dreary," carped the Seattle *Press-Times*. "But Allen C. Mason's mummy cannot be seen at all hours, and the box of monkeys . . . which that always enterprising citizen has promised the Point Defiance Park, has not arrived yet."

A Northern Pacific official dismissed the complaints: "You can't run a railroad to suit everybody, and the most of these persons who aspire to become 'kickers' have never completed their education in the art of traveling. Some of them, if they started from anywhere to any other place, would not make as good time as a barrel of salt shipped by freight."[14]

Tacoma had in fact been feeling more and more slighted of late, and the spectacle of a Northern Pacific president waxing enthusiastic over Seattle's glowing prospects was too much to bear. "We timidly suggest," the Tacoma *Ledger* lamented, "that the Northern Pacific is in danger of violating its pledges to the people of Tacoma by permitting its officials and employees to engage in the building of rival towns, and in directing and attracting away from this city eastern and foreign capital."

Seattle offered a pointed response: "Tacoma is becoming weaned away from its idol. Its school teachers still fondly cling to Mount Tacoma, and the News still yearns for the Democratic national convention, but the patron saint of the City of Destiny has been proved a delusion and a snare . . . It will be fortunate in the long run for the people of Tacoma to learn that they must fight their own battles. The Northern Pacific will squeeze Tacoma just as it has every other town."[15]

Oblivious to jibes, though, Tacoma forged ahead. The "placid bosom" of Commencement Bay bristled with sail and steam tonnage lined up at berths to load grain, lumber, and other freight from masses of boxcars. "Tacoma again leads the shipping of Puget Sound by a large margin," boasted the *News* in September 1892. "The great advantage of Tacoma is its quick dispatch in lumber and coal . . . As to the exportation of wheat, comparisons cannot be made, as she is the only city on the Sound whose handling of wheat is worth noticing."[16]

Dredging and filling of the tideflats, begun in 1887, continued steadily, and a solid line of huge warehouses crept along the waterfront, ultimately reaching a continuous length of almost two miles. Throughout the early 1890s, Tacoma would with considerable justice declare itself Puget Sound's leading seaport.

Far from squeezing its terminal city, the Northern Pacific poured millions into new facilities. The scene of 1884's pile-driver war on the flats blossomed into a huge new freight yard and a twenty-two stall brick roundhouse at the head of the bay, and early in 1891 the long-lamented "Villard depot" gave way to a larger Pacific Avenue station cobbled out of the old repair shops. Uptown, the Tacoma Land Company began planning a stupendous French chateau on the bluff: The Tourist Hotel, a confection of turrets and towers that would eclipse The Tacoma itself. Noteworthy, too, was the new Northern Pacific Beneficial Association's Employee Hospital on Wright Avenue. Perhaps the most significant of

paid me their silver dollars for lectures, but there where we found shanty of old Carr, at the old sawmill keeping company with a grizzly bald-headed eagle and a polecat, I planted the future."

The Seattle press sarcastically proposed sending Chief Sealth's wizened old daughter, "Princess" Angeline, along to keep Train company, but the dignified elder would have none of it. She said: "Chief Seattle was my father. He is dead, and if I should start off with George Francis Train, my father's spirit would be very angry. Angeline does not want any truck with George Francis Train, or any other fools."[17]

For the great crank ("Lunatic by law through six courts"), this would be the last boom out of his Tacoma cannon. After his circumnavigation, Train retired to a South Tacoma cottage, where he passed the time entertaining flocks of local children. Summer passed, the kids scattered, celebrity faded, and Citizen Train grew morose. On a rainy October evening, he told a friend that there was nothing left for him but to "return to silence," and quietly boarded a train for the East. A year later, however, he again circled the globe, this time on behalf of the Bellingham Bay communities of New Whatcom and Fairhaven. Train's parting words to the Pacific Northwest echoed Jay Cooke's: "Puget Sound towns must stop battling Puget Sound! They must hang together, or hang separately."[18] Train faded into obscurity, and on January 18, 1904, the strange and luminous spirit of the 19th century passed peacefully into the Beyond.

George Francis Train's colorful copy from Nagasaki and Shanghai stimulated an already growing American interest in the Asiatic trade. As early as 1884, the Northern Pacific dispatched an agent to China and Japan to investigate the possibilities, prodded by announcements that the Canadian Pacific Railway would put on steamers between British Columbia and the Orient upon completion of its trans-Canada mainline. The reports were encouraging: Increasing freights were crossing the ocean between Shanghai, Yokohama, and San Francisco, and Chinese firms had already chartered sailing ships and were offering rates as low as $9 a ton to Portland.

these improvements materialized late in 1890 at the south Tacoma suburb of Edison; an eighty-acre, one million-dollar shop complex, among the largest railroad maintenance facilities on the West Coast.

The year 1890 was also a good time for George Francis Train to stage a comeback. After two years of relative quietude, he sallied forth on March 18, with the backing of the *Ledger*, on a round-the-world dash to beat Nelly Bly's seventy-two-day record and draw new attention to the City of Destiny.

The three-time globe-girdler reminisced fondly: "Twenty-one years ago, on the OR&N steamer Willson [sic] G. Hunt, supplied me by Captain Ainsworth, I launched this magic town of nation's great inland sea . . . Olympia and Seattle made big bid for historical point and

"Feel positive no difficulty would be experienced in getting up a line which would be a subsidiary and a valuable ally to the Northern Pacific," agent H.M. Kersey wrote Thomas Oakes, who in turn confided to Oregon Improvement Co. general manager John Muir that movements were afoot in London banks to finance a Tacoma-Yokohama Northern Pacific steamship line—"in fact, the arrangement is practically consummated."[19] Still, the time was not quite ripe, and the deal fell through. Negotiations in 1890 and 1891 with the Pacific Mail Steamship and Fairfield Shipbuilding companies were no more successful.

Instead, the Northern Pacific first got its feet wet in Alaskan waters. In August 1889, it acquired control of the Washington Steamboat & Transportation Co., renaming it the Puget Sound & Alaska Steamship Company. This move was made, in the words of NP official Theodore Hosmer, "to extend the interests of the Northern Pacific . . . The Northern Pacific spends hundreds of thousands of dollars each year in advertising the Alaska tourist business. It brings the tourist to Tacoma over its line, and then a rival company's steamers takes them to Alaska."

Under president Walter Oakes, son of Thomas Oakes, and general manager Henry F. Jackson, the PS&A bought the screw steamers *City of Kingston, City of Seattle, Sehome,* and *State of Washington,* and placed them in service between Tacoma and Victoria, Whatcom, Port Townsend, and Alaska. Walter Oakes brought in seasoned men to help run the new enterprise, most notably Captain Charles Peabody, who would go on to become a major figure in Puget Sound maritime annals. Profitability eluded this railroad gone to sea, however. In a field already dominated by the fleets of the Pacific Navigation Co. and the Oregon Railway & Navigation Co., the Puget Sound & Alaska was one line too many.

"If we loaded our boats full of freight and carried no passengers," complained Henry Jackson, "we should be behind at the end of the year . . . The passenger business just enables us to make some money, but we are not making enough to repay our losses in past years."[20]

The Klondike gold rush brought boom times to north-ern waters, but in 1899, new Northern Pacific president Charles Mellen turned the operation of the Puget Sound & Alaska over to Dodwell & Carlill's Washington & Alaska Steamship Co. Walter Oakes and Captain Peabody struck off on their own and formed the Alaska Steamship Company. (Late in 1901, after James J. Hill had gained control of the NP, he ordered the sale of the W&A to the Pacific Coast Steamship Co., owned by the Pacific Coast Co., which he had controlled since 1889. Hill's lines became the dominant power on Puget Sound and Alaskan waters, and—mirroring the coordination of the NP and GN within his Northern Securities Company—the Alaska Steamship and Pacific Coast Steamship companies worked cooperatively, avoiding the rate wars and excessive competition that ruined many a small shipping line.)[21]

As the 1890s dawned, the growing Asian market, and the CPR steamers plowing insolently across the Strait of Georgia between Yokohama and Vancouver, proved too much to ignore. The era of a large-scale Puget Sound-Far East trade opened in May 1892, with formation of the Northern Pacific Steamship Company. NP Steamship contracted with London shipping agent Dodwell-Carlill Co. to provide steamers on regular sailings between Tacoma and Yokohama, Kobe, and Hong Kong. On July 23, a brass band played "Yankee Doodle" as the steamer *Phra Nang* docked in Tacoma with 158 Japanese and four Chinese passengers, and over 2,000 tons of tea, silk, sugar, hemp, fireworks, curios, and sake.

The Asian trade grew swiftly, and perhaps the proudest moment in Tacoma's maritime history came on January 2, 1893, as a stout black steamer sidled up to a Commencement Bay pier. Mill whistles shrieked and eyes grew misty as her name—*Tacoma*—caught the rays of the sun. First of a three-ship fleet owned by the NP, the *Tacoma* was joined by the *Victoria* (the ex-Cunarder *Parthia*), and, in 1896, the *Olympia.* By the turn of the century, the Northern Pacific flotilla was enlarged by the *Glenogle,* and Boston Steamship Co.'s *Hyades, Pleiedes,* and *Tremont,* along with additional contract ships, on a circuit to Vladivostock, Port Arthur, Shanghai, Hong Kong, Yokohama, Singapore, Manila, and other Pacific ports. Somewhere, Isaac Stevens and James Swan nodded in approval.

By 1904, however, the Asiatic trade had become problematic. The NP's fleet was by then largely obsolete—too small and too slow to compete with the new foreign flag ships crowding the Pacific. In March, they were sold to Seattle ship owner John Rosene's Northwestern Commercial Company, for service to Alaska. Contract steamers such as *Shawmut* and *Pleiedes* continued to offer NP ocean service in conjunction with Jim Hill's Great Northern Steamship Co., but the Northern Pacific fleet was no more.

America was more alive than ever before to the promise of the future when, in April 1893, the World's Columbian Exposition opened in Chicago. Among the millions of visitors to the great "White City" on Lake Michigan was Northern Pacific chief engineer Edwin H. McHenry. Stopping in at the Korean pavilion, McHenry was intrigued by a round emblem enclosing teardrops of red and blue, said to represent Nature's duality—a traditional Korean symbol called a monad. Pleased by the shape and its meaning, McHenry suggested to passenger agent Charles Fee that the Northern Pacific adopt it as an ensignia. The monad, its colors altered to black and red and encircled by the legend, "Northern Pacific—Yellowstone Park Line," was duly appropriated, and soon became a Pacific Northwest icon.

But world's fair gaiety and record traffic levels were not enough to keep the Northern Pacific unaffected by the coming depression. U.S. gold reserves had been depleted by European investors and the country as yet had little faith in its new "silver certificates." Credit grew tight, money markets dried up, and another of the 19th century's dreary round of financial slumps set in. President Oakes instituted a regimen of economizing, curtailing all improvements and laying off hundreds. It was not enough; in July, NP defaulted on $1,500,000 in bond interest payments, and on August 15, entered receivership.

Seattle's diversified economy, her status as a regional mercantile center, and the timely arrival of the Great Northern Railway all softened the blow of the panic of 1893. The manufacturing of such items as bicycles, boxes, bottles, clothing, cream, spices, firearms, building materials—and coffee—flourished and gave Seattle the edge.

Tacoma's cushion was thinner, and the terminal city followed the Northern Pacific into hard times. The Tacoma Land Company foundered, work on the Tourist Hotel stopped, and even the Tacoma Hotel, pride of Charles Wright, went broke. Seventeen of the city's twenty-one banks closed, and once-wealthy citizens found themselves picking berries and digging clams for sustenance. Deep in debt, NP land department manager Paul Schulze embezzled a million dollars from the railroad, then succumbed to conscience. Informing his Chinese cook, "I am going on a long trip," Schulze retired to his study and blew his brains out.[22]

Another casualty of the panic of 1893 was Henry Villard. He had spent five grueling years trying to bring about peace among the NP, OR&N, and other competing lines in eastern Washington, and working to modernize and expand the Northern Pacific. The fight was bitter and unyielding, and the once-sanguine empire builder grew more and more pessimistic over the ability of the railroad industry to survive the cutthroat competition and rate wars that were sapping the strength of even seemingly healthy companies.

Villard was particularly distressed by the incursions of James J. Hill's Great Northern; with its superior grades and lower operating costs, he recognized the GN as the "gravest danger" to the Northern Pacific. Hill proved him right, and with low rates and an interchange agreement with the OR&N at Spokane and Portland, the GN began siphoning off a substantial portion of eastern Washington's wheat traffic.

Early in 1889, Villard began probing the availability of Manitoba road stock, only to be brought up short by Hill, who, upon learning of Villard's movements, rushed to Villard's New York sickbed and disabused him of the notion. Hill then informed his ailing challenger that he would not hesitate to pit the Manitoba against the

Northern Pacific in a head-to-head rate war, and that he had bought up a large bloc of Oregon & Transcontinental stock in company with Elijah Smith. Villard had no stomach for the fight, and took the message to heart.

Three years later, however, the aging railroad king felt well enough to make another run at his rival. Apparently encouraged by disgruntled Hill associates who indicated that a controlling interest in GN stock would be made available to him, Villard enlisted the support of his ever-loyal German backers for a $20,000,000 assault on Hill securities.

In his memoirs, Villard gave a poignant description of waiting like an anxious suitor at Hill's New York office, only to learn that "Mr. Hill had slipped away again." It is highly doubtful that Hill ever held any intentions of letting his hard-won property fall into anyone else's hands, let alone Villard's—whom he regarded with a certain disdain as "a very sanguine man, full of his own importance." For Villard, the next year's plunge into receivership, with all its dismal feeling of *deja vu*, was a bitter blow.[23]

Once again, Henry Villard's eyes had proven bigger than his stomach. He blamed NP's financial embarrassment on the expense of completing the Seattle Lake Shore & Eastern, the Chehalis Valley expansion, and costly line improvements—programs that were largely his doing and probably unavoidable, if the company wished to remain competitive. Faced with stockholder criticism and yet another round of "discredit, calumny, and abuse," Villard resigned from the Northern Pacific board in August 1893 and retired to Dobbs Ferry, New York, "never again to be responsible for the use of other people's money, directly or indirectly."[24]

Henry Villard made his final Puget Sound appearance in July 1899, during an Alaska cruise aboard the venerable *Queen of the Pacific* (now renamed simply the *Queen*). Stopping at the Tacoma Hotel, he chuckled: "The Tacoma people were wont in the past to charge me with working against their city, but I always tried to favor them."

In Seattle, he reminisced fondly. "I have always had a fatherly feeling toward Seattle, and have watched its rapid growth with pride . . . It is, without doubt, the most prosperous and promising city in the Northwest."

Eugene Semple, president of the Seattle & Lake Washington Waterway Co., tried to enlist the aid of the veteran capitalist in backing his "south canal" between the lake and Elliott Bay. Opposition was strong, however, and this time Villard decided to obey his better judgment and stay clear: "If any one in Seattle is foolish enough to oppose a project that is so beneficial to the city, I am too old to go to war."[25]

On November 12, 1900, Villard died at Dobbs Ferry, New York. Seattle paid tribute to her old friend:

"Henry Villard was the first man who, after Ben Holladay, made an impress on the Pacific Northwest as a transportation magnate and brilliant financial exploiter. He was broad-gauged, which most of the coast people were not, and he created hopes and aspirations among the people of this new country such as had never been experienced before . . . He gave to the Pacific Northwest an energy the effects of which are still felt."

Cousin Troilus Tyndale reflected: "He always liked Seattle better than Tacoma . . . largely due to his personal friendship for certain of our citizens—Arthur Denny and Dr. Thomas T. Minor among the number—who frankly laid the grievances of the community before him and appealed to his sense of justice to help right them."[26]

With the resignation of the great harmonizer in 1893, the remaining elements of the Northern Pacific "old guard"—Brayton Ives, Charlemagne Tower, Charles Wright—turned to James Jerome Hill to put their bankrupt road back on track. The Great Northern chief had had his eyes on the NP since the 1880s, but his ambitions were tempered by the road's high operating costs and roundabout, roller coaster profile. Nevertheless, the NP tapped rich markets and had fine potential.

"If the Northern Pacific could be handled as we handle our property," Hill told a friend, "it could be made a great property. Its capacity to earn money is good, and with all unnecessary expenses and train service abolished, it would, I think, astonish even its friends."

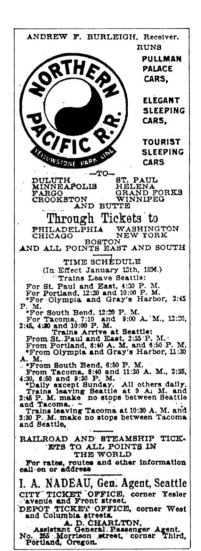

ANDREW F. BURLEIGH, Receiver.

NORTHERN PACIFIC R.R.
YELLOWSTONE PARK LINE

RUNS
PULLMAN PALACE CARS,

ELEGANT SLEEPING CARS,

TOURIST SLEEPING CARS

—TO—

DULUTH   ST. PAUL
MINNEAPOLIS   HELENA
FARGO   GRAND FORKS
CROOKSTON   WINNIPEG
        AND BUTTE

Through Tickets to

PHILADELPHIA   WASHINGTON
CHICAGO   NEW YORK
        BOSTON
AND ALL POINTS EAST AND SOUTH

TIME SCHEDULE
(In Effect January 12th, 1896.)
Trains Leave Seattle:
For St. Paul and East, 4:30 P. M.
For Portland, 12:20 and 10:00 P. M.
*For Olympia and Gray's Harbor, 2:45 P. M.
*For South Bend, 12:20 P. M.
For Tacoma, 7:10 and 9:00 A. M., 12:20, 2:45, 4:30 and 10:00 P. M.
Trains Arrive at Seattle:
From St. Paul and East, 2:35 P. M.
From Portland, 8:40 A. M. and 6:50 P. M.
*From Olympia and Gray's Harbor, 11:30 A. M.
*From South Bend, 6:50 P. M.
From Tacoma, 8:40 and 11:30 A. M., 2:35, 4:30, 6:50 and 9:30 P. M.
*Daily except Sunday. All others daily.
Trains leaving Seattle at 9 A: M. and 2:45 P. M. make no stops between Seattle and Tacoma.
Trains leaving Tacoma at 10:30 A. M. and 3:30 P. M. make no stops between Tacoma and Seattle.

RAILROAD AND STEAMSHIP TICK-ETS TO ALL POINTS IN THE WORLD

For rates, routes and other information call on or address

I. A. NADEAU, Gen. Agent, Seattle
CITY TICKET OFFICE, corner Yesler avenue and Front street.
DEPOT TICKET OFFICE, corner West and Columbia streets.
A. D. CHARLTON,
Assistant General Passenger Agent.
No. 255 Morrison street, corner Third, Portland, Oregon.

NP's MONAD FIRST APPEARED IN THE SEATTLE *Post-Intelligencer* ON FEBRUARY 24, 1896.

In April 1894, Hill took up the challenge, and two years later he and master-financier J.P. Morgan met in London and signed the "London memorandum" binding the NP and GN in a "permanent alliance, defensive and in case of need offensive, with a view of avoiding competition." From Dobbs Ferry, Henry Villard wired his approval.[27]

The charter of the Wisconsin's Superior & St. Croix Railroad was dusted off and on July 1, 1896, renamed the Northern Pacific Railway. On the morning of the 25th, the Northern Pacific Railroad was auctioned off on the steps of the courthouse in Superior. Edwin Winter, president of both the old and new companies, entered the winning bid of $10,000,000, then he and six Pullman loads of officials and bankers headed west, stopping at successive state-houses long enough to transfer the land grants of the respective states to the new Railway.

On August 3, the entourage presided over the largest real estate transaction ever to take place in the state of Washington. The new Railway was sole bidder on the Northern Pacific Railroad's Washington land grant; for $1,705,200, the title changed hands. Back in St. Paul, Hill began chatting with his neighbor, midwestern lumber baron Frederick Weyerhaeuser, over the profit potential of the land grant's immense timber stands. Weyerhaeuser was cautious about investing, but he had practically stripped Wisconsin and Minnesota clean of usable timber, and needed a new supply. After enduring several long evening harangues by Hill, he caved in and, in November 1899, purchased 900,000 acres of Northern Pacific timber land in Washington, at $6 an acre.

The transaction would have profound economic and environmental consequences for the Pacific Northwest. It also may have been illegal; under the terms of the land grant act of 1864, all grant lands not otherwise disposed of were to be opened to homesteaders within five years of the completion of the railroad, and, in the event that the corporation failed to do so, the lands were to be placed on public auction. It has been argued that neither provision was met—that no auction followed the bankruptcies of 1873 and 1893, and that selling the land to a large corporation rather than opening it to individual settlers was in fundamental violation of the terms and intent of the land grant act.

Subsequent government inquiries into the Northern Pacific land grant found a multitude of additional violations by the company: Among others, that it had not sold stock on the open market; it had not finished construction within the allotted time period; it falsely classified some tracts as mineral land (not included in the grant) and claimed in its place prime timber land; it wrongfully claimed over 13,000,000 acres included within Indian reservations; and it took more acreage than it should have in Washington. As it had since the 1880s, though, Congress remained disinclined to take any action. The Weyerhaeuser sale opened the door for the large-scale corporate logging of Washington's forests, with very visible and far-reaching consequences, and the great checkerboard swath of the NP land grant remains today, frustrating all attempts at forest land use planning—a perplexing and unintended legacy of the railroad-building era.[28]

Despite the depression, the NP's Puget Sound passenger offerings enjoyed steady improvement during the 1890s. Vancouver, British Columbia, was added to the map in 1893, as joint NP/CPR through service was inaugurated between there and Seattle via Mission, B.C., and Sumas, Washington. Seattle and Tacoma were brought closer together on November 10, 1894, as a twice-daily "flyer" service was instituted on a nonstop, seventy-five-minute timing that is barely outpaced a century later.

"It is a grand success, which has set everybody talking," the *Times* said of the flyers, which offered riders a luxurious new innovation—reclining seats.

The new schedule was a direct challenge to another *Flyer*, the popular, 50¢ steamer on the Seattle-Tacoma run. Charging a dime more, the NP flyer nonetheless proved an immediate hit and a lively rate war was on. The *Flyer, Multnomah, City of Aberdeen, Bay City*, and *Cricket* all cut their fares to 25¢, and, while probably doing themselves more harm than the Northern Pacific, gave Puget Sound a good show.

Eight hours were lopped off the transcontinental running time, and double summer season trains returned—Numbers 1 and 2, the Puget Sound Mail and Twin City Mail, offered a sixty-four-hour Tacoma-St. Paul schedule over the Butte line, which opened in 1890; Numbers 3 and 4, the Oregon Express and Twin City Express, maintained a seventy-seven-hour timecard via Helena. All sported the latest vestibuled equipment and ran through to Portland.

Welcome though these improvements may have been, Seattle still dreamed of a grand union depot. Due to the ongoing squabble over who got what on Railroad Avenue, however, Thomas Oakes had been unable to deliver on his 1890 promise of a new station. Instead, the Northern Pacific moved passenger operations from the broad gauge strip into the Seattle Lake Shore & Eastern's Columbia Street depot in April 1892. Things were peaceful until late in 1896, when Lake Shore successor Seattle & International canceled its express contract with the Northern Pacific in favor of Canada's Western Express Co. In a huff, the NP picked up and moved into makeshift digs across Columbia Street, and word spread that the offended railroad would blockade the S&I depot with coaches.

The Klondike gold rush shoved this niggling to the background. Word of a "ton of gold" arriving on the Seattle waterfront in June 1897 ignited gold fever across the country. Seattle's chamber of commerce wasted no time in promoting the city as the Klondike gateway, and publicist Erastus Brainerd deluged the East Coast with Seattle advertising, with spectacular results. Retail trade exploded, and much of the $200,000,000 in gold that landed on Seattle's docks during the decade stayed, giving the city the final push it needed to attain a true metropolitan status. Northern Pacific's traffic doubled, and both NP and GN found themselves with more business than they could handle. Passenger trains in multiple sections arrived daily in Seattle and Tacoma, and endless strings of boxcars were backed up the length of the White River Valley, stuffed with supplies for would-be sourdoughs. Tacoma, Portland, even San Francisco ate Seattle's dust in the great race to the north.

The waterfront was where the money was, and in 1896 the Northern Pacific began quietly taking possession of much of it. During the ensuing two years, and right under the nose of James J. Hill, the NP acquired eleven blocks between Yesler Avenue and University Street. In July 1899, President Charles Mellen came to town and declared himself pleased with the city's growth. Seattle offered the railroad more business than Tacoma and Portland combined, he exclaimed, and immigration to Washington far outstripped that to any other state on the line. Though irked at the lack of progress on the depot question, the city reveled in its ascendance over its old rival.

"Mr. Mellen has informed the City of Destiny that it will be treated on its merits," gloated the *Post-Intelligencer*.[29]

Though offering but a single daily transcontinental train, the Great Northern had garnered much first class passenger trade by consistently besting Northern Pacific's overland time by six to ten hours. NP took up the gauntlet in March 1899 with a fast, seven-car express, the Atlantic and Pacific Mail. For the first time, the Mail would run in 59 hours to and from the Twin Cities and Seattle. Alas, receipts were disappointing, and the lightning Mails were annulled after four months. Seattle was sidetracked again, but service aboard the cars of the Atlantic and Pacific Expresses made up for the snub. The varnished new dining cars offered 75¢ dinners of such items as boiled ox tongue, Kromekiss of Lobster a la Russe, roast English snipe, whortleberry pie, and curacoa punch.

Not that everyone availed themselves of luxury travel; the Northern Pacific joined the Great Northern that March in offering greatly reduced "homeseeker" fares in second class tourist cars, prompting an unprecedented stampede to Puget Sound. Many of these settlers rode the Chicago Burlington & Quincy from Kansas City to Billings, Montana, a major Northwest passage that opened in 1894:

"They are every one of them well to do men and women, nearly all in families, who have investigated the resources of Washington, sold their interests in the East and South, and come here with their money to invest,"

enthused the *Post-Intelligencer*. "They are unusually substantial, and will make the best class of citizens for a growing state."[30]

A Burlington official testified that travel was four times what it was at the height of the gold rush, with Washington getting more new settlers than any other three states put together.

The booming Seattle traffic prompted the Northern Pacific to announce, in May 1899, the construction of a twenty-two-mile shortcut linking the Cascade and Pacific divisions, as envisioned years earlier by Henry Villard—

the common point connection at last. This would run from Palmer Junction to Auburn, cutting thirty miles off the distance to Seattle, and five miles to Tacoma, and would bypass the original corkscrew alignment through Orting, Buckley, and Enumclaw. On August 19, 1900, the cut-off opened, and the old main line was gradually relegated to branch status.

Throughout the winter and spring of 1900, Northern Pacific track gangs were hard at work sprucing up roadbed, tightening up joints, and straightening curves in preparation for an astonishing new entrant in the booming Northwest travel market: the North Coast Limited. This incomparable "train de luxe" made its debut runs from Portland and St. Paul on April 29, and raised American railroad travel to new heights. The eight-car Limited carried not only new, vestibuled first and second class Pullmans, reclining seat coaches, a baggage car with a complete, steam dynamo electric lighting plant, and of course those exquisite diners, but a novel new "observation car" as well. These glistening, varnished seventy-foot carriages contained within their brocaded and oak-encrusted precincts a library, bath chamber, barber shop, buffet, smoking and card room, and parlor lounge. Seated in folding camp chairs, Pullman passengers could view the receding panorama from the spacious, brass-railed observation platform, which was adorned with a big, electrically lit monad.

Never had the Northwest seen such a conveyance. The first North Coast Limited schedule gave Seattle a 7:35 PM departure for St. Paul, and an 8:48 PM arrival. Unfortunately, in order to maintain its sixty-hour schedule, the North Coast would not swing up through Seattle. The city would have to content itself with "stubs" to and from East Auburn. In its first two years, the train ran only during the summer season, leaving the off-season to the Atlantic and Pacific expresses. The popularity of the North Coast Limited was such that year-round operation commenced with the October 1902 timetable.

As running mates for its new flyer, the Northern Pacific's 1902 offerings comprised the Twin City Express, and the Northern Pacific-Burlington Route's Portland Express and Kansas City Express to and from Kansas City via Billings, all on year-round schedules and terminating in Portland. Four trips a day between Seattle and Tacoma were run, at a roundtrip fare of $1.50, as well as three to Portland, and twice-daily locals to Olympia and Grays Harbor. One train a day visited Everett, Whatcom, Sumas, and Vancouver, B.C., making connection at Woodinville for Issaquah and North Bend.

Perhaps it was best that the North Coast Limited shunned Seattle at first, for in 1900 the city still had no depot worthy of such a train. In October of the previous year, NP president Mellen presented Seattle with plans for a stupendous stone depot it proposed erecting on its waterfront property, a proposition that ignited a furious public debate. The opposition was led, predictably enough, by Thomas Burke, who trotted out NP's ancient hostility to Seattle as reason enough to forbid construction. GN's Hill backed the judge with characteristic bluntness: Mellen's scheme would amount to civic suicide, cutting the city off from its waterfront. Hill, who wanted all rail facilities moved off the waterfront and onto the tideflats, warned that he would not stick around to watch this disaster unfold—he would simply move his terminus to Everett or Mukilteo, and run stub trains into Seattle.

Mellen found himself outnumbered and backed down red-faced, not a little miffed by the rejection of what he supposed was a good turn: "With all due deference to the good people of Seattle—among whom I count many valuable friends—I am utterly at a loss to know what they want, and at times doubt if they know themselves."[31]

Mellen would sulk for another four years before finally caving in under Jim Hill's relentless pressure. On August 11, 1902, the two signed a compact for the financing and operation of a grand new station and tunnel under the city. Until then, stopgap improvements had to suffice. Freight traffic had climbed beyond the pioneers' wildest imaginings, and there was never enough room. Local agents begged headquarters for more track, while loaded boxcars filled the sidings between Seattle and Tacoma and shippers howled at delays. In 1900, the railroad shoehorned more track onto the broad gauge strip, along with a four-stall roundhouse and a stockyard at the south end of the strip. On the waterfront, the monad appeared on new Northern Pacific wharves.

Modernization accelerated in the early years of the new century. In 1901, the Northern Pacific established a separate track into town—taking the west side while the Columbia & Puget Sound took the east half of their old joint right of way from Black River Junction. To create more storage room, an eight-track yard was developed that

SEATTLE & INTERNATIONAL
SCHEDULE, SUMMER 1898.

summer at Argo, in south Seattle. In the following February, this was linked to Railroad Avenue by a new mainline
along Colorado and South streets—all on pile trestle, as
the filling-in of the tideflats, begun in 1895 by the Seattle
& Lake Washington Waterway Co., was still far from
complete. The Argo yard was quickly swamped, thus in
the following year another facility along the west side of
Colorado Street was begun, to become the Northern
Pacific's main Seattle freight yard. (Today, this Seattle International Gateway Yard remains the main city terminus
of the Burlington Northern & Santa Fe Railway.)

The tideflats became the focus of new railroad and industrial development. As early as 1890, the Northern Pacific had started to build its trestle to the West Seattle
grain terminal and a new main line across the flats, but
was brought up short by tortuous litigation over appor-
tionment of Railroad Avenue and tidelands ownership.
Finally, in October 1901, the NP obtained a joint franchise to the grain terminal with the bankrupt Seattle &
San Francisco Railroad, which had inherited the defunct
Seattle Terminal Railway & Elevator Company's right of
way in 1895. With the dissolution of the Seattle & San
Francisco in 1903, NP inherited the long trestle. Gnawed
by worms and obstructing navigation, the structure had
by this time become a nuisance.

President Mellen found the cross-bay line "in such a legal tangle that it is hard to make head or tail of it."[32] The
trestle passed over a warren of disputed ground, he observed; the mess had to be straightened out and the track
brought into conformance with government harbor line
plans then being formulated. The following year, the railroad condemned the teredo-riddled structure and with
the city's encouragement began construction of a new
West Seattle line along Spokane Avenue, one that contin-
ues to serve the busy industrial area.

Other tidying-up proceeded as well. The first major
housecleaning in April 1898 saw the Northern Pacific
gathering into its fold the Green River & Northern,
Tacoma Orting & Southeastern, United Railroads of
Washington, and, at last, the Northern Pacific & Puget

Sound Shore. Absorption of the Seattle & International
on April 1, 1901, led off a second round of acquisitions,
most notably, the twenty-three mile Bellingham Bay &
Eastern in September 1902, which gave NP access to
Bellingham from the Sumas line at Wickersham, and
the Rockefeller-owned Everett & Monte Cristo. With
control of this strategic trackage between Snohomish
and Everett, the monad was planted in the mill town of
Port Gardner.

In January 1903, the Northern Pacific entered its last
major period of growth, and undertook a major push on
the virtually undeveloped Olympic Peninsula. Railroad
logging had made a first appearance near the south peninsula town of Shelton during the mid-1880s, with the creation of the Puget Sound & Grays Harbor and Satsop railroads, shortlines that would ultimately fall under Northern
Pacific and Simpson Timber Company ownership. Envi-
sioning a rich harvest of old growth timber, NP announced
it would build a belt line around the entire peninsula and
began gobbling up small local lines on the north end. First
was the Port Townsend Southern, whose two disjointed
limbs—the twenty-six mile Port Townsend-Quilcene line,
and the fifteen mile Olympia-Tenino leg—were leased
from the Pacific Coast Company in November 1902.

James J. Hill, who held controlling interest in both the
Great Northern and Northern Pacific, envisioned the
Olympic belt line as an integral part of an expanded "Hill
lines" network that would open virgin territory and tie
into a new east-west railroad he planned to build along
the Columbia River. Added impetus for development on
the peninsula was the ominous intelligence that the
Union Pacific and a newcomer, the Chicago Milwaukee
& St. Paul, were nosing about.

The Northern Pacific would not rush its peninsula
campaign. "We took the [Port Townsend Southern] out
of the wet," Charles Mellen explained, "and some day it
will probably be extended along Hood Canal to connect
with the Olympia road. However, at the present time
such an extension is not a necessity, and what money we
have to expend will be used in the improvements at

Seattle and other places in the state where work has already been started."

This was not what the long-isolated residents of Port Townsend wanted to hear. In November, a town deputation informed Mellen's successor, Howard Elliott, that the interests of the region demanded prompt completion of the Port Townsend-Olympia line and offered assurances that the freight in timber alone would make it a paying proposition. Expanded military installations near the town and other opportunities for developing the peninsula were further reason for alacrity.[33]

Elliott promised Port Townsend he would think about it, then turned his attention elsewhere on the peninsula, forming the Olympic Peninsula Railway in July 1903, to build up the west side through ninety miles of wild and heavily forested country from Moclips to the Strait of Juan De Fuca. There, it would join the Port Angeles & Pacific, which was born in September 1902. The PA&P managed to survey its own line to Moclips before going bust, but NP stuck to its plans and petitioned the government to allow it to build through the Quinault Indian Reservation.

Charles Mellen had previously noted that the "shutting up" of much of the timber tracts within the Quinault and Clallam reservations would render any railroad extension useless: "It is not very probable that the belt line will be completed until after the reservations have been opened."

Two more paper railroads were taken in, the Port Angeles & Peninsular and the Port Angeles & Olympia, the latter headed by Seattle streetcar and real estate magnate Jacob Furth.

"We incorporated and started preliminary work in the interests of eastern capital," stated Furth in July 1906, "but the whole project has now been sold to the Northern Pacific, which will go ahead with the work."

In September, the NP prepared to let the first twenty-five mile contract from Port Angeles to Lake Crescent, and paid the Quinault tribe $10,000 for right of way through their reservation.[34]

Nothing happened. Another dark cloud of economic

depression loomed over the nation as 1907 began, and railroad companies pulled in their horns. Recovery was not long in coming, but, despite years of "rumor on the very best authority" that the Port Townsend Southern and other Olympic components would be tied together, conditions never ripened. Chronic labor shortages, high demands of property owners for right of way compensation, and the urgent need for major capital improvements elsewhere on the Northern Pacific doomed the great peninsular belt line. The NP, UP, and Milwaukee would continue to rattle sabers on the peninsula until the eve of World War I, but they built only limited mileage. After four years of arduous effort, the Northern Pacific reached the seaside town of Moclips, at the southern boundary of the Quinault Reservation and twenty-eight miles northwest of Hoquiam, in July 1906. There, it stayed.

Another belt line would rise from the dead and become a profitable reality for the Northern Pacific, that around Lake Washington. The Northern Pacific, the Lake Washington Belt Line Company, and Peter Kirk's grand plan for integrated steel milling at Kirkland all went up in the financial conflagration of 1893. Mill buildings and machinery rusted in place and the rails of the Kirkland spur were removed. A decade later, however, Railroad Avenue had become congested to near-impassability, and the belt line plans were dusted off as a means of diverting heavy, Sumas-Tacoma freight traffic—as many as 150 cars a day—around the city and saving a day or more in transit time. Grading on the new right of way over the twelve miles between Renton and Woodinville began in April 1903, and the last spike was driven on October 22 of the next year. Freights had exclusive use of the Lake Washington belt line at first, but were joined in 1905 by passenger trains for Bellingham, Sumas, and North Bend.

Seattle received its full due on May 3, 1903, when the North Coast Limited came to town. Tacoma was not pleased; the crack train still passed through the terminus on its way to and from Portland, but sensitive Tacoma patrons were given the option of riding a connecting "stub" to East Auburn rather than suffer the indignity of a detour through Seattle.

The Tacoma Chamber of Commerce gnashed its teeth over this insult for three years, then filed suit in July 1906 to force the railroad to restore its through trains to the former itineraries. In a turnabout of supreme irony, the chamber charged the Northern Pacific with discrimination against Tacoma, claiming that it was difficult to buy tickets for Tacoma in eastern agencies, that the city's passenger service was not as good as Seattle's, that Tacoma did not get equal treatment in freight rates, that the city's depot was not what it deserved, and that Tacoma was slighted in favor of Seattle in Northern Pacific advertising! In district court, the suit was dismissed.

Tacoma's feelings were not soothed when Seattle's new King Street Station opened on May 10, 1906. Laying to rest more than a decade of complaints, the Great Northern/Northern Pacific station looked every inch a grand terminus, with its soaring clock tower. To Tacoma, though, it seemed a veritable dagger thrust at her vitals, and the suit was reopened in July 1907, this time claiming that valuable land had been deeded to the railroad in return for making Tacoma the terminal city. Since the building of the Palmer cut-off, it was alleged, the railroad had betrayed its compact with Tacoma by "practically making Seattle the terminus."

Again, Tacoma was denied satisfaction, and in 1909 took its case to the state supreme court. The justices noted that Seattle, with half-again the population of Tacoma, had for the past three years given the Northern Pacific more than twice as much business. Case closed.[35]

Tacoma was then thrown a meaty bone. Like Seattle, the terminal city had long complained of its dingy depots. The makeshift 1891 Pacific Avenue station had been no great improvement over the old Villard depot, and it doubly galled to see Seattle get the grand edifice Tacoma felt was her prerogative. The city finally received satisfaction in September 1907, when the Northern Pacific unveiled drawings for a monumental, copper-domed union depot

to rise on Pacific Avenue. Designed by New York architects Reed and Stem, who had just finished Seattle's new building, this temple of transportation outshone Seattle's in many respects, and achieved added distinction as one of the few domed depots in the country.

Mayor George Wright dampened things only somewhat when he groused, "I am glad to say that in all my experience I have never yet bought a gold brick or been taken in by a shell game," and vowed that "not a foot of city property" would be vacated for the new station. Too much, including the Tacoma waterfront, had already been "frittered away on hot air promises that have for the most part never been carried out by the Northern Pacific," declared the mayor.[36] Nevertheless, Tacomans beamed with pride on May 1, 1911, as Union Station opened its doors.

Still more improvements were in store for Tacoma. The original mainline into town from the south, with its stiff 2.2 percent mountain grade, had always been an operating nuisance, so in May 1906 plans were laid to begin construction of a water-grade line into Tacoma along Puget Sound, extending subsidiary Port Townsend Southern from Tenino to Tacoma via Steilacoom. During the summer, surveys were made for this route, which would come to be known as the Point Defiance line. But, financial considerations and right of way litigation took years to resolve. Not until 1914 would the "point line" be completed through the Nelson Bennett Tunnel, a 4,400-foot bore begun by Bennett and completed, after his death, by his wife.

Another sticking point was the ferry crossing at Kalama. Though deckhands had honed the art of hustling cars on and off the *Tacoma* to a twenty-minute interlude, heavy traffic now demanded a bridge. In January 1906, the NP bit the bullet and submitted to the War Department plans for a massive, seventeen-span truss structure over the Columbia River, Oregon Slough, and Willamette River between Portland and Vancouver; construction began that fall. Between Vancouver and Kalama, NP trains would use subsidiary Washington & Oregon Railway, later the Washington Railway & Navigation Co.

The first Northern Pacific train crossed the great bridge, touted as the longest double-track railroad bridge in the world, on December 26, 1908, and the venerable *Tacoma* sailed into a new career as a barge.[37] Isaac Stevens' "great thoroughfare" between the Columbia River and Puget Sound was now a reality. It was a timely improvement; the Northern Pacific hauled 15,000,000 tons of freight and nearly 6,000,000 passengers during 1906, and Washington State accounted for almost half that volume. The Stampede Tunnel was handling trains every twenty minutes, and the railroad was operating to the limits of its motive power, signal systems, and crews.

The Northern Pacific experienced its third and final outbreak of belt line mania in 1909, with the inception of the Lake Union branch. James J. Hill, in one of his many Seattle speeches, observed that, with the tidelands already occupied, future commercial growth must take place on the city's inland waters. Mill owner J.S. Brace agreed, and led business interests in planning a new commercial center south of Lake Union. Assuring the railroad they would build new warehouses there, the Brace and Hergert Mill Co., Metropolitan Press, Ernst Brothers Hardware Co., and others encouraged the Northern Pacific to build a spur off the old Seattle Lake Shore & Eastern line at Fremont, and gird the lake.

In December, property owners and the city deeded the NP right of way and approved a perpetual franchise from Salmon Bay along the south bank of the proposed government ship canal and down the west side of Lake Union along Westlake Boulevard, and around the south and east shore as far north as Hamlin Street; further rights were granted from Valley Street to Denny Way along Terry Avenue, where the NP erected a freight depot convenient to the expanding city center. A drawbridge over the east end of Lake Union at Latona Avenue was considered, to allow direct access into the heart of the city off the Sumas line, and a "common user" clause was inserted, giving other railroads trackage rights; neither of these elements became reality, nor was rail ever laid along the east shore.

"This line will work a revolution in the distribution of

freight to more than one half the city,"[38] declared the press as the population of Seattle edged toward a quarter-million. Construction began in 1911, and the Lake Union branch provided decades of useful service to the busy south lake commercial district, then in the 1950s began a long decline in the face of truck and suburban competition. In the early 1990s, the line was abandoned.

Full acknowledgment of Seattle's importance to the Northern Pacific came on October 31, 1909, when the railroad formed a new Seattle Division. This comprised the Sumas line as well as the Cascade Division as far east as Ellensburg. Tacoma was now head of the Tacoma Division, encompassing lines to Portland, Buckley, and Grays Harbor. "This marks the definite and final abandonment of the one-time policy of hostility to Seattle" beamed the *Post-Intelligencer*.[39]

Old enemies had become friends. ∎

LOUNGERS TAKE IN THE ACTIVITY AT SEATTLE'S OLD UNION DEPOT, CA. 1903. THE PREVIOUS YEAR—AND ONLY AFTER REPEATED URGING BY THE CHAMBER OF COMMERCE AND CITY COUNCIL—THE RAILROADS AGREED TO ADD THE LARGE CANOPY OVER THE PLATFORM.

Museum of History and Industry

CHAPTER 11

Enter the Empire Builder

"We made Seattle." —James J. Hill

The year 1890 saw a truce between Seattle and the Northern Pacific. At last, and as Isaac Stevens and Arthur Denny had dreamed, the city could take pleasure in being included on America's main line railroad map. And, proving that feast follows famine, this happy development was all but eclipsed that year by the advent of a second major railroad, the Great Northern. President James J. Hill was greeted by many as a savior; others were less impressed. Whatever one's opinion, it soon became apparent that a potent new force for change had descended upon Seattle.

For James Jerome Hill, it had been a long journey. During the 1870s, the Ontario-born St. Paul clerk parlayed an intimate knowledge of upper Midwestern soil, crops, people, and trade into control of the down-at-the-heels St. Paul & Pacific Railway. At decade's end, Hill enlisted the support of English financiers—his cousin and closest confidant, George Stephen, and Sir Donald Smith—and reorganized the 600 unfinished miles of the St. Paul & Pacific as the St. Paul Minneapolis & Manitoba Railway. As general manager and one-fifth owner, Hill spent the 1880s securing for his property a plodding but steady growth. His knowledge and instincts were seemingly infallible, the territory ripe; wheat accounted for 3,000,000 bushels in the "Manitoba Road's" first year carloadings, and by 1886 grain traffic had grown tenfold.

Hill was not content to tie his road's destiny to a limited and seasonal commodity like wheat. Moreover, the expansion of rival lines, in particular the Canadian Pacific and Northern Pacific, urged Hill westward lest his road be strangled. The gold, silver, lead, and copper of central Montana were hard to overlook, too, and influential men like Great Falls rancher Paris Gibson deluged Hill with pep talks on Montana's business prospects and the need for a second trunk line to compete with the NP; local interests began forming short line railroads in hopes of inviting absorption by just such a road. Hill had no choice: Go west, or die.

Early in 1886, James J. Hill began his "long march forward" from Devil's Lake, Minnesota. In one of history's greatest feats of manual labor, 940 miles of track from Minot, Dakota Territory, to Great Falls were thrown across the northern plains by the end of 1887; in one Day—August 8—an incredible eight miles of track were laid. A year later, Hill was in Butte, and offering through service to Salt Lake City and Portland over the rails of the Oregon Short Line and Oregon Railway & Navigation Co. Puget Sound beckoned: The once-great timber stands of the upper Midwest were virtually exhausted; not so those of the Northwest. Across the Pacific, too, Asia waited, to give and to receive. The Northern Pacific was the only line to the Sound, and a circuitous, poorly engineered, and expensive to operate one at that. Hill could do better.

Albert Bowman Rogers was sent for. The leathery, tobacco-stained, and foul-mouthed little mountain man was well-known to Hill, having found the Canadian Pacific's Rogers Pass in the Selkirks a few years earlier. Rogers was pleased to be given another such opportunity. In April 1887, he and his 22-year-old son, John Garwood

A landmark day for Seattle, the new Great Northern liner *Dakota* arrives at Smith Cove in March 1905. Two years later the big freighter would sink off the Japanese coast.

Puget Sound Maritime Historical Society, #696-3

Rogers, and two companions rode the Northern Pacific to Ravalli, Montana, and took to horseback. Rogers picked out a likely railroad route between the flathead River and Lake Coeur d'Alene, and continued into eastern Washington. The main objective was a feasible pass over the north Cascades, something neither George McClellan nor Virgil Bogue believed existed.

Rogers reached the Columbia by the end of June and headed into the rough country around Lake Chelan, encountering government surveyor L.A. Navarre, who informed him that no pass would be found between the Methow and the Okanogan valleys, or between the headwaters of the Wenatchee and the Skagit, west of the divide. The only possible way was up the Wenatchee to Peshastin Creek, Navarre concluded, then over Swauk and Snoqualmie passes.

Rogers nevertheless determined to see the Wenatchee headwaters for himself, just in case, and on July 24 wrote Hill that the valley of the Wenatchee "seems to offer the only solution . . . and of this I am not very hopeful."[1]

Doggedly, as if on the trail of destiny, Rogers and his son rode up the Wenatchee toward the mountains, exploring side canyons and cul de sacs. Fighting pleurisy and living on starvation rations of bacon and hardtack, Rogers never faltered. On July 31, as the little party reached the head of the Lekho, or Little Wenatchee, trail, he spotted a low gap in the peaks looming straight ahead. Leaving the horses behind, Rogers and his companions began clawing their way upward, hacking toeholds in the snow and crawling on hands and knees along sheer ridges. On August 10, Rogers stood atop a 5,300-foot summit and peered down on the Skykomish River, flowing westward to Puget Sound.

The north Cascades crossing was found, he scrawled to Hill, one that had the advantage of "covering every harbor on the Sound north of Seattle."

Rogers descended the Skykomish Valley, then explored the Skagit, Sauk, and Suiattle valleys, and Ward and Indian passes. He found the stakes left by the Northern Pacific surveyors fifteen years earlier, but did not find any better pass than the Wenatchee-Skykomish.

Again he wrote his employer: "I have great hopes of the Skykomish route, it being the shortest and . . . the lowest summit, the best general direction, and so far as I have seen, promising the best route for construction, and being also much more exempt from snow slides than any of the others."

A provisioning stop in Seattle provided a welcome respite. There, too, Rogers "dropped, accidentally, on some information" of an even better eastern approach to his newly discovered pass. In the second week of October, Rogers and his son were confirming that the valley of the Chumstick River offered an easier and less rocky gateway.[2]

Optimistic reports aside, Hill remained skeptical over whether there was room enough in the West for a third transcontinental railroad. He entertained the thought of buying control of the Northern Pacific instead, but George Stephen, former president and bank-roller of the Canadian Pacific and later Lord Mount Stephen, bucked him up: "I have no doubt of our ability to build a line on our own and think I can see my way to finance the extension to the coast on very economical terms."[3]

Hill brooded into his late night fire, and, in 1889, made up his mind to strike for Puget Sound.

The decision taken, it was obvious that the St. Paul Minneapolis & Manitoba had "outgrown its clothes"; a new name, more fitting for a great transcontinental enterprise, was needed. That was easy: Great Northern. In 1883, the Northern Pacific had advertised itself as "The Great Northern Transcontinental Route," a billing that undoubtedly impressed Hill, a guest at Henry Villard's last spike celebrations. Great Northern was also the name of one of England's major railways.

On the eve of his thrust to the Sound, Hill dusted off an old property, the moribund Minneapolis & St. Cloud, which had broader charter powers than the Manitoba's, and on September 16, 1889, rechristened it the Great Northern Railway. The St. Paul Minneapolis & Manitoba's $20,000,000 capital stock issue was doubled, and on January 31 was placed under Great Northern control. The Manitoba became a paper road

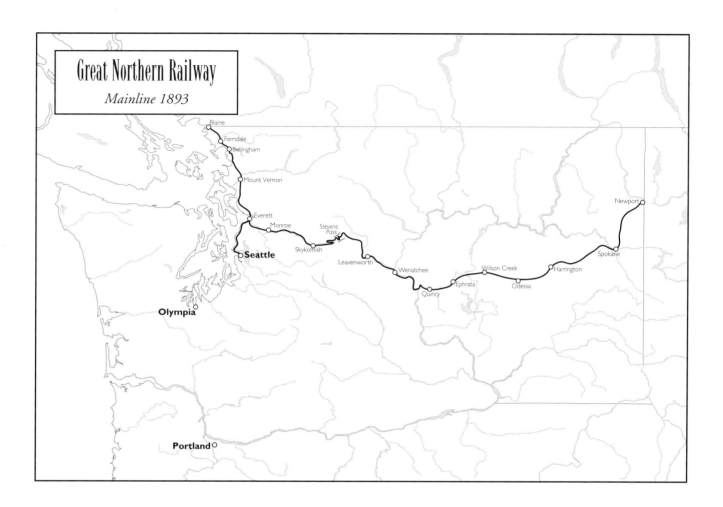

and financial engine for the Pacific extension, but the Great Northern would run the trains.

Hill whipped up his forces. Chief Engineer Elbridge Beckler was charged with getting the Great Northern from Fort Assiniboine, Montana, five miles west of present day Havre, to Puget Sound, and fast. No romantic, Hill's orders were blunt:

"What we want is the best possible line, shortest distance, lowest grades, and least curvature that we can build. We do not care enough for Rocky Mountain scenery to spend a large sum of money in developing it."

Hill did spend long hours pouring over the Isaac

Stevens survey, in particular Abiel Tinkham's explorations through the rugged northern Rockies along the Marias River. Tinkham had found a possible route, but, at almost 8,000 feet in elevation, this offered little promise for railroad use. Stevens, though, had held out his characteristic glimmer of hope:

"There are probably passages of the mountains connecting other branches of the Marias river with other tributaries of Flathead river, and giving, perhaps, opportunities for passing the divide with more ease than by the way explored."[4]

Beckler and his fifty-man expedition retraced Isaac

Stevens' path through Montana and decided that the gradient, snow pack, timber stands, and distance from the Northern Pacific line favored the northerly route that Tinkham and Saxton had mapped through the valleys of the Marias, Flathead, and Kootenai rivers. Following Stevens' intuition of a low divide, surveyor John F. Stevens (no relation) tramped through a blinding blizzard, and on the night of December 11, 1889, confirmed the existence of Marias Pass—at 5,200 feet one of the lowest in the Rockies.

Stevens hurried west, hoping to locate a similar easy crossing of the northern Cascades. The valleys of the Methow, Chelan, and Entiat rivers were probed, before Stevens confirmed the earlier estimations of Albert Rogers, and D.C. Linsley before him, that the best route was up the Wenatchee and Chumstick rivers. Stevens took the time to follow a small river that Linsley had observed only in passing during his 1870 exploration, a stream the Indians knew as Natopac but which whites later named Nason Creek. It soon became apparent that Nason Creek offered an ideal grade up to the Wenatchee-Skykomish divide. Assistant engineer Charles F.B. Haskell carved "Stevens Pass" on a cedar trunk, and it was official. Lines were run down the west slope, along the Skykomish and Snohomish rivers to Port Gardner, as well as through Cherry Valley to the north end of Lake Washington. Meanwhile, Great Northern general manager A.L. Mohler journeyed to the Sound on the Canadian Pacific for a covert look-see, slipping into Seattle on December 2, 1889. Pesky reporters sniffed him out at the Rainier Grand Hotel, but Hill's man remained tight-lipped. Mohler made some notes in a little black book, and ducked out for California.[5]

Scarcely had Hill taken his first step westward when terminal fever once again swept Puget Sound. In 1888, the Bellingham Bay towns of Fairhaven, Sehome, and New Whatcom rejoiced in newspaper reports that Hill had purchased 1,700 acres there, "on which he proposes to raise a future seaport city."

Beckler's crews further buoyed these hopes by running lines over the north Cascades through Cady and Indian passes. Tacoma, too, was hopeful, if only to witness the hu-miliation of her nemesis. "If Jim Hill's road goes to Bellingham," gloated the Tacoma *Ledger*, "Seattle, situated between the termini of two great transcontinental railways, will be ground to powder by the upper and nether millstones, so to speak."[6]

Seattle cheered the advent of competition to the "lazy old octopus," the Northern Pacific, and made much of rumors that the Great Northern would buy up its struggling local road, the Seattle Lake Shore & Eastern, to gain entrance to the city. But Hill kept mum. Then, in February 1890, Beckler and GN vice-president Colonel William P. Clough came to town. Clough looked over the hometown railroad, chatted with its officials, but admitted only that the two companies would establish harmonious relations. Lake Shore manager A.S. Dunham then ushered Clough into the offices of his friend, Judge Thomas Burke. The judge had created the Seattle road, Dunham attested, and had done much other good work; perhaps he could be of service to the Great Northern. Clough chose his words shrewdly: Mr. Hill was coming west; Fairhaven, Tacoma, Portland—they all had much to offer. What about Seattle?

Burke nodded eagerly: Mr. Hill would find all he required in Seattle—he would see to it! But time was wasting. The Canadian Pacific was doing a growing Puget Sound business, the Union Pacific was heading that way, even the Northern Pacific was cozying up to Seattle these days.

"Strike now!" Burke exhorted Clough—"Gain absolute control of the Sound."[7]

The Seattle Lake Shore & Eastern and Oregon Improvement Company were both down-on-their-luck and ripe for the plucking; they would secure for the Great Northern ready-made transportation facilities "unequaled on this continent." Lake Shore partner Daniel Gilman chimed in: The tidelands he and the judge owned north of Smith Cove would be ideal for yards and terminal facilities; Mr. Hill could have them at cost. These were the words Clough had been waiting to hear. He and Burke shook hands, and on March 7 the judge penned into life the paper railroad which would serve as the Great Northern's instrument on the Sound—the Seattle & Montana Railway.

The Seattle & Montana would build track eastward from tidewater, and deal with any local litigations that might crop up. Hill later explained:

"We find it more advantageous to have different corporations in different states. States, I have found, are sometimes very anxious to get railroads, and offer inducements for them to enter, and then, as soon as they do, they do all in their power to tear them to pieces. Having different state corporations limits to a great degree the influence of much undesirable action in its effect on the whole Great Northern company."[8]

While the ink dried on the Seattle & Montana charter, Burke drafted and presented to the city council a petition for a new ordinance granting the Seattle & Montana a sixty-foot-wide, four-track slice of Railroad Avenue immediately west of the Seattle Lake Shore & Eastern. A suitable passenger depot would be erected on the waterfront, and the new right of way would continue south, paralleling the broad gauge strip and following Ninth Avenue to the city limits.

Burke put the squeeze on the council: "Your petitioner would . . . beg leave to call the attention of your honorable body to the great importance of making this city the terminus on Puget Sound of the Great Northern . . . The consummation of such an event would confirm and emphasize the commercial predominance of this city in all the great region of country north of California."

Some objected to Hill's monopolizing the waterfront—as Burke himself had when the Villard franchise was granted in 1882. The judge quickly whipped them into line with the compelling argument that Bellingham, Port Gardner, and (shudder!) Tacoma would be only too happy to give Hill everything he wanted. Before a week had passed, the Seattle & Montana had its franchise.[9]

With "general rejoicing," the *Post-Intelligencer* revealed the Great Northern deal on March 8. Hill and company were lauded as "strictly business":

"The Great Northern road does not seek to set up, in the interest of a few grasping stockholders, an independent speculative townsite enterprise, but comes at once to the established commercial center and business headquarters of the Sound country."

Clough greeted reporters in his suite at the Rainier: Yes, Mr. Hill wanted to get to Seattle quick as possible; the work would be pushed from east and west, on a lower, shorter, straighter, cheaper line than anybody else's. He would probably spend between seven and eight million dollars at his terminal city, and that was just the beginning.

Seattle was "the coming city of the Northwest," declared the colonel. "If the citizens of Seattle show themselves as wise and public spirited as their official representatives, they will shortly possess railroad facilities unequalled by any now existing on the Pacific coast."[10]

In short order, Burke met with property owners and secured options for terminal grounds at Smith Cove, Salmon Bay, and on the lower Elliott Bay tideflats. Informed that the Great Northern needed their property to do great things for Seattle, most landowners were pleased to sell at cost. The few holdouts were swiftly and silently dealt with; Burke passed the hat among the Establishment, bought the malingerers out, and assured Hill all was well. In June 1890, the board of the St. Paul Minneapolis & Manitoba made a formal resolution to extend the Great Northern Railway from Fort Assiniboine, Montana, "to some suitable point on the waters of Puget Sound, at or near Seattle."

After his long and bitter struggle trying to keep the Seattle Lake Shore & Eastern afloat, Thomas Burke was elated by the development, and resolved to do his utmost to protect Hill's interests: "The city council of Seattle and the citizens . . . will be committing a blunder which will amount to a municipal crime, if they do not treat the Great Northern in a spirit of the utmost liberality," he gushed to his friend Daniel Gilman. "Hill is of the opinion that Seattle will be a larger city in fifteen years than San Francisco. What do you think of that?"[11]

Seattle & Montana surveyors quickly began running their lines northward from the city, through Gilman's Addition, across Salmon Bay, through the sawmill town of Ballard, and hard by the waters of Puget Sound to Port Gardner, where the track would turn east. A bit of a snag developed in Ballard where the Seattle & Montana found itself at odds with the Seattle Lake Shore & Eastern over the right of way. Beckler promptly shut down construction on the Salmon Bay trestle and penciled in an alternate route along the south side of the bay, crossing the outlet into Puget Sound by drawbridge and bypassing Ballard altogether. The dispute was soon resolved to Hill's satisfaction.

As Burke confided to Gilman, "Mr. Hill knows what he wants, isn't afraid to ask for it, and I may add, generally gets it."[12]

Still, skeptics persisted in doubting Jim Hill's good faith. The Seattle & Montana was "hogging the bed" on Railroad Avenue, they complained, and did not even bother to build an office building or depot.

To those who wanted a pretentious station, Hill offered his stock bromide: "He is a wise farmer who develops his farm before he builds a palace on it."

Such thinking failed to impress some. "If the demand for this depot would cause them to go to Everett or Podunk," carped one councilman, "then they are not the city's friend. And if they do so, Seattle would like to have the depot as a souvenir of their visit."[13]

As far as depots were concerned, the most the city would get out of Hill for the next half-decade was a modest ticket office next to the West Seattle ferry landing at the foot of Marion Street.

To silence the grumblers, Burke persuaded Clough that it would be a "good policy to have some work done without delay," and on July 20, 1890, a contract was let to Shephard & Company, of St. Paul, for seventy-five miles of railroad grading between Seattle and Fairhaven. In August, three dozen carloads of rails arrived in Seattle over the Northern Pacific, and, with the help of a revolutionary new track-laying machine, a thousand men began planting the Jim Hill road along the waters of Puget Sound. A mile-long freight yard was graded at Interbay, north of Smith Cove, and the GN's trestle curved gracefully across Salmon Bay.

All through the summer, surveyors combed the Cascades looking for the elusive "lower, shorter, straighter,

cheaper" route. They ranged through Suiattle, Indian, Cady, and Ward passes, but found no crossing better than John Stevens' divide at Nason Creek. Snoqualmie Pass, lowest and easiest of them all, was again bypassed, this time for a line that would give Hill no end of operating headaches.

"The Snoqualmie Pass is too near the Northern Pacific," Beckler explained, "and we should have to parallel that road for a considerable distance if we chose that route.[14]

On September 28, James J. Hill arrived in Seattle for the first time aboard his private car, Manitoba. With Chief Engineer Beckler and son-in-law Samuel Hill, the kinetic railroader spent four days in "prospection" at New Westminster, B.C., Bellingham Bay, Anacortes, Port Gardner, and Seattle.

At the Rainier Grand, he greeted reporters: "You have a fine town here . . . When a man gets in on the business streets, he feels that he is in a city . . . Yes, we will find a route over the mountains without a great deal of difficulty. There are four passes through which the line can come and we have practically decided upon one . . . The Snoqualmie Pass is the lowest one we have found, and we may adopt it. In that case, the line would cross the Columbia River at Moses Coulee, and come in from the south by way of Ellensburg . . . It is the determination of the Great Northern to run to Portland from Seattle, either by arrangement with the Union Pacific or without it . . . Undoubtedly, when you get the country subdued, and the Siwash [Native Americans] out of it, which will not be for many years, you will have a splendid agricultural country."[15]

Someone piped up: "Will you make Bellingham Bay your terminus?"

Hill coyly offered his standard equivocation: "It is always our policy to make our terminal facilities adequate for our business. They have a fine harbor there on Bellingham Bay, and so have you at Seattle. In fact, the whole Sound is a harbor which no man could turn his nose up at!"

Railroad building in undeveloped country such as the Pacific Northwest was risky, Hill reminded his listeners.

"We have to feel our way. If we build through a country which will not pay, we shall both the railroad and the country land in the mud! I may say that it will be our policy to build a road so as to carry on low grades at low rates. We must carry in large quantities, because most of your products are cheap stuff, which will only bear low rates."

No, Great Northern was assuredly not in the town-promotion business: "I do not believe in boom methods, nor will I countenance them in any respect. If we find anybody using our line or any portion of it, for real estate booming, they will speedily get a black eye!"[16]

Hill paid tribute to Judge Burke: "Whoever devised Railroad Avenue deserves a monument from Seattle."

The right of way squabble just then heating up in the city was unfortunate, but Hill was sure the people would see reason. "It is very difficult to settle the terminal question. When business has to be done at low margins, terminal facilities go a long way to settle the commercial importance of localities . . . Railroad terminals are a greater harbor than your ocean harbor, for the railroads carry many times more than all the ships on the ocean."

Was Hill being piggish on Railroad Avenue? "If we do our business in Seattle, and the country does not disappoint us, we shall need all the ground which has been given us within five years, and in ten we shall have to have more. Relatively, all business enterprises are selfish, and we have only asked for what we needed."[17]

Back in Burke's office, Hill detailed his grand plan: "I intend to have a road like a rake, with Seattle as the focal point and prongs that reach all the principal cities of the Northwest."

Hill would not be content to haul eastern merchandise west and empty cars east; western wheat and timber would be his primary traffic base and he would promote their development for eastern markets.

The Great Northern was not the recipient of a large federal land grant as was the Northern Pacific. It did, however, claim an 1857 Dakota grant held in trust by the federal government for any line that built across the territory. And because the Dakota lands in question had since been settled, the GN took as "in lieu" equivalent lands, in public timber acreage in Washington.

Pointing to a map of this tract, Hill informed Burke: "Unless I move that crop [timber], I might as well not have built the railroad. First, it is a natural product which is in demand; second, unless it is moved there will be no room for farmers. It must be moved at a low rate, lower than any such commodity was ever moved in the history of the world."

Hill asked Burke to sound out local lumbermen on what haulage rates would allow them to compete with midwestern and southern growers. With that, he departed for St. Paul, leaving a Seattle abuzz with excitement in his wake.[18]

With the 1891 spring thaw in the Rockies, Great Northern crews went to work in Marias Pass and fought their way westward down the Flathead and Kootenai valleys, averaging nearly two miles of grading a day. In August, Hill filed his line of definite location through the Cascades, over Stevens Pass, with the Department of the Interior.

On September 6, he was again in Seattle. "We are pushing the line right along," he told reporters. "I don't know yet where we will strike the Sound. It may be at Port Gardner, though the rumors that say I have bought up land there are all unfounded. If we can use a shorter route by coming down directly from Snohomish to Seattle, you can rest assured advantage will be taken, as railroad companies nowadays select the shortest routes . . . We will not use the Skagit [Indian] Pass, but probably Stevens."

Would Hill continue on to Portland? Throughout much of 1890, rumor had him throwing in with the Union Pacific's Portland & Puget Sound. In January 1891, he vowed that he would "most certainly" go to Portland, with or without the UP. That summer, though, he reversed himself: Great Northern did indeed own half-interest in the P&PS, and he declared: "We shall not build our own line to Portland, but shall wait for the construction of the Portland & Puget Sound."[19] It would be a long wait.

Possessing three major lines, the Northern Pacific, Union Pacific, and Southern Pacific, Portland was largely

indifferent about whether the Great Northern came or not. Tacoma, on the other hand, was anxious to gain a second transcontinental.

Of course the GN would come to Tacoma, breezed the *Ledger:* "The engineers are now secretly locating a line between Seattle and Tacoma, and Colonel Clough has arranged for the use of the Northern Pacific track on that portion of the line . . . The Great Northern doesn't care a rush or a railroad spike about Seattle as a terminus, but merely wants to tap that city and come on to Tacoma."

Hill made a flying visit in September 1890, and offered his patented nostrum that he was as likely to build in Tacoma as Seattle or any other place. A year passed without any further action, but the *Ledger* continued to take comfort in (or more probably fabricate) reports that GN surveyors were at work in Naches Pass: "[I]t is a well-known fact that Jim Hill stated publicly . . . that he deemed the Stevens, Snoqualmie, and Skagit passes impracticable."

The less well-known fact was that Hill had already been advised by Colonel Clough that "the Northern Pacific practically incloses [sic] all industries in this town," and that rumors of the impending arrival of the Union Pacific had inflated property values beyond reason.[20] Tacoma would also have to wait.

The focus of Jim Hill's western empire would remain the northern Sound. To the hopeful towns of Bellingham Bay—Fairhaven, Sehome, and Whatcom—he lectured: "[T]he plan of our enterprise secures you all the benefits that any other locality on Puget Sound can have from the railway . . . Your rates will be as low as those of any other locality on the Sound. That was the object we had in view when we planned a north-south line. Now, if with the advantage of . . . all the natural wealth you have, and your harbor, you cannot keep your end up, it will not be our fault. There is no reason in the world why you cannot have here not only a large city, but an imperial city!"[21]

This one-size-fits-all note of cheer was vintage Hill, and the wily railroad-builder put the Bellingham towns and their local railroads to good use. The Fairhaven & Southern

had been incorporated by Nelson Bennett, E.L. Cowgill, and Charles and Samuel Larabee on November 27, 1888, and Eugene Canfield formed his New Westminster Southern the same year—both in time to make handy stepping stones for the Great Northern.

Hill concluded a pact with Bennett, whereby the Great Northern provided funds to complete the Fairhaven & Southern between Whatcom and the Skagit Valley, and in 1890 Hill purchased controlling interest in both the Bennett and Canfield roads. Final absorption into the GN would take place only upon their completion. This followed Hill's policy of using regional entities as shock absorbers for the Great Northern, thereby localizing litigation and minimizing "undesirable action" against the parent company. As the Fairhaven & Southern's trestle began inching across the Bellingham tideflats in the summer of 1890, the bay towns cheered. The fever peaked in the summer of 1891, with reports that the Great Northern was surveying from Lake Osoyoos, in north central Washington, along the Simillkameen River and over the north Cascades to Bellingham Bay.[22]

Then Stevens Pass emerged as Hill's chosen mountain crossing, and, at the foot of that pass, lay not Bellingham, nor Tacoma, nor Seattle, but Everett. The village on Port Gardner Bay had its beginnings in 1888, when Henry Hewitt came to Puget Sound looking for grand possibilities. Convinced that the Northern Pacific would soon have company on Puget Sound, he scouted the harbors for a promising townsite, just as Morton Matthew McCarver had twenty years earlier. Port Gardner quickly impressed Hewitt as The Place, all the more likely since Jim Hill's railroad was by all evidence headed straight for it. With Charles Colby, he created the Everett Land Company in 1891, platted the city, and busily began selling lots. Mills sprouted up, and newly arrived townspeople settled in to await the Great Northern.

"Jim Hill and Providence have pushed the button," crowed the Port Gardner *News,* "and the Everett Land Company and the News are doing the rest."[23]

JAMES J. HILL DESIRED EASY GRADIENTS, BUT WAS STUMPED WHEN CONFRONTED WITH THE SHEER WALL OF THE CASCADE RANGE. THE GREAT NORTHERN'S STEVENS PASS CROSSING WAS MUCH TOUGHER THAN THE NP'S STAMPEDE PASS. THIS VIEW AT THE MARTIN CREEK LOOP, BARELY HALFWAY UP THE HILL FROM SKYKOMISH, GIVES STARK EVIDENCE OF THE GRUELING CLIMB BEDEVILING THE GREAT NORTHERN UNTIL COMPLETION OF THE NEW CASCADE TUNNEL IN 1929.
Warren W. Wing collection

Colby and Hewitt's land company incorporated the grandly named Snohomish Skykomish & Spokane Railway & Transportation Company, known locally as the "Three S Road," and managed to lay eight miles of line between Everett and Snohomish. The Three S Road was acquired by John D. Rockefeller's Everett & Monte Cristo, whose rails gave Hill entrée into Everett from Lowell. Throughout 1891-1892, 3,000 men (Chinese and Italians not wanted) swarmed over Stevens Pass and the Snohomish and Skykomish valleys, working twelve hours a day, at two dollars a day, seven days a week, to get the Great Northern finished by January 1893. Until a summit tunnel could be bored, the impatient Hill was forced to resort to a switchback over Stevens Pass; six levels of track were pinned to the mountainside and zigzagged over the top on four-percent grades. Stevens Pass would always be the Great Northern's toughest haul.

Seattle suffered Everett's terminus pretensions with ill grace, and Seattle & Montana secretary Thomas Milner assured Burke and his neighbors that the city would not "be left out in the cold" and that Port Gardner was "merely a convenient junction for our eastern and northern lines."[24]

The appearance of a GN car shop and eight-stall roundhouse at Interbay, close by the south end of the Salmon Bay trestle, further assuaged Seattle's fears.

The last spike in the Fairhaven & Southern was driven at Blaine on a snowy February 14, 1891, and on the 27th, Nelson Bennett's road was transferred to Hill ownership. Great Northern cars began running between Seattle and New Whatcom on March 10, but, until the Seattle & Montana main line south of Everett was done, were compelled to use the Seattle Lake Shore & Eastern between Seattle and Sedro. On April 18, the New Westminster Southern was opened from Blaine into South Westminster, on the south bank of the Fraser River directly across from New Westminster. Jim Hill had his toehold in western Canada.

One obstacle remained in his path: Elijah Smith's Seattle & Northern. This was under lease to the Northern Pacific, and lay squarely across the Great Northern right of way at the Skagit Valley town of Burlington. As Hill's track-layers approached, a Seattle & Northern locomotive took up sentry duty to block his trespass. After one late-night vigil, the picket engine's crew assumed all was well and retired to Anacortes. The wide-awake Seattle & Montana foreman quickly pressed his men into action, and the Seattle & Northern crew returned later that morning to find Hill's crossing firmly and irrevocably in place. The Seattle & Montana and Fairhaven & Southern were joined at Stanwood on October 12, 1891. The northern arm of the rake was virtually complete.[25]

At 8:30 AM, November 27, 1891, GN locomotive 202 departed the Seattle Lake Shore & Eastern's Columbia Street depot leading a baggage car and nine rented NP passenger cars bearing much of the Seattle Establishment and the 100th Regiment band. The excursionists laid over for the night at Blaine, then continued to South Westminster the next day, before returning to Seattle.

Fairhaven celebrated the event with wry good humor: "Seattle has done much under adverse circumstances. She wriggled out from the Anaconda curl of the Northern Pacific. She went out in a blaze. She rose up as if by magic. Her pluck is invincible . . . We welcome these live people to our city. Fairhaven needs to imbibe some of their enthusiasm. They are toned up with American grit. In ten years we hope to welcome them to Bellingham Bay, to the imperial city of Washington, the greatest city on Puget Sound."[26]

Regular service began on December 1, with a through connecting car off the Canadian Pacific running to Seattle on the single daily passenger train. It would not be until January 1904, with completion of the Fraser River drawbridge, that Great Northern trains would finally enter Vancouver, B.C. The Canadian Pacific did its best to shut Hill out, and filed suit against GN crossing its line. In characteristic injunction-be-damned style, the Hill forces rammed a crossing frog over the CPR in the dead of night on January 2, and in the guise of subsidiary Vancouver Victoria & Eastern established the Great Northern in western Canada's commercial center.

Arriving in Seattle on February 15, 1892, Hill assured the city in his backhanded fashion that it was indeed his first among equals. "Seattle will be the terminal. That is settled once and for all. Every point where the Great Northern road touches the Sound will be a terminal."

Always full of surprises, Hill then announced that when his road was finished, and to compete with the Canadian Pacific, he would put on a line of steamships between Seattle and Japan. At a Rainier Hotel banquet, Hill cautioned the Seattle business elite against chasing the "gilded butterfly" of real estate speculation rather than getting down to the real business that guaranteed the city's future greatness—harvesting timber. To this end, he declared that he would carry Puget Sound lumber east for 40¢ a ton. This was an astonishing figure, an upshot of Judge Burke's assignment to query the timber growers. George Stetson, Seattle's leading lumberman, indicated in response that 60¢ per 100 pounds might do the trick.

"They're crazy," Hill told the judge. "At that rate they couldn't compete with southern pine. I think I'll have to make the rate fifty cents, and perhaps I'll cut it squarely in two." Whatever the future might bring, Hill went on, "nothing can ever divide the interests of Seattle and the railway, because what will injure one will injure both."

Hill's 40¢ bombshell electrified his listeners and had the desired effect; scores of new mills sprouted around the Sound, and the era of large-scale logging in western Washington began.[27]

The last spike on the Great Northern was driven without ceremony at Deception Creek, thirteen miles west of Stevens Pass summit, at 8 o'clock on the evening of January 7, 1893. John F. Stevens and a smattering of local officials and laborers looked on. The officials then rode to Seattle aboard a two-car special, serenaded en route by the sawmill whistles of Snohomish, Lowell, Everett, and Ballard. Through freight service began a month later.

The New York *Mail and Express* noted the event: "The completion of the Great Northern to . . . its terminus as the great seaport city of the Evergreen state . . . means much for the Pacific coast and particularly for Seattle. There are those who predict for this city speedy rivalry not only with Portland, but also with San Francisco itself."[28]

Jim Hill, however, was getting peeved with his western terminus. The continuing Railroad Avenue conflict with other railroads was proving an intolerable and seemingly insoluble delay to his terminal building plans, which now centered around his property on Jackson Street at the southern fringe of the lower business district.

"We want to get into shape to do business, and we can't do it without terminal facilities," he complained to the chamber of commerce in February. "The matter was begun before our road reached Spokane and it is still unsettled."

Judge Burke squirmed as Hill bore the customary provincial grilling with ill-concealed exasperation: Yes, Seattle was the terminus—"Well, is it not the end of the line? What is at the end of a line, except its terminus?" But what kind of a terminus was it that offered its chief patron nothing but trouble? The Great Northern would only do business where it was wanted.

The point was well taken and the city council hastily voted an $11,650 subsidy to buy additional Great Northern right of way. Pacified, Hill took his leave with a promise to bring with him on his next visit "300 or 400 leading people from the eastern states, to show them the country through which we run."[29]

GN's first through passenger train, nameless No. 1, stole quietly into Seattle early on June 22. The press was wide-eyed at "the composition of the train, the originality of its design, the fullness of its equipment, the convenience of its many diversions from the older style."

Chief among its wonders was a parlor-observation car sporting silk curtains, a barber shop, commodious bathrooms, a well-stocked library, and a "pretty drinking fountain." Twenty-five dollars bought a first class fare from Seattle to St. Paul.

The trains arrived just in time to carry throngs of passengers to the Chicago World's Fair—the GN, NP, and CPR all offered equal rates to Chicago: $129.50 for a first class round trip ticket with Pullman berth. Dining car meals ranged from 50¢ to 75¢ each, and, lest travelers forget, "the porter needs attention, to get attention."[30]

But Hill's trainload of millionaires never showed up. In the gathering economic gloom, 1893 was a year for tending strictly to business. Three years before, Hill had predicted that the nation would be hit by a "panic that it will take five years to get over." Now, the panic of '93 was on in earnest. The Northern Pacific and Union Pacific both entered receivership, but not the closely held, conservatively managed Great Northern. The Hill formula—low rates, low train-miles, maximum tonnage—had paid handsome dividends, abetted by a record Dakota wheat crop and helped by the declining costs of labor and materials. Hill took no ease, however, and plowed his earnings back into improving his properties. When the current slump ended, he knew, traffic would only get heavier. As recession bit down on the nation, Hill instituted sweeping economy measures, including thirty-five percent wage reductions.[31]

The men out manning Hill's cabooses and pounding his spikes watched the long trains roar past, full of freight and passengers, and wondered why their pay was being cut. In March 1894, Great Northern coach cleaners at Seattle saw their $2-a-day wages sliced in half, and they promptly walked out on strike.

The American Railway Union appealed to the Seattle Chamber of Commerce: "These men are all men of a family, citizens, voters, and taxpayers . . . Such wages might be enough for an unmarried wanderer, and it was such men, or men who preferred slavery to crime, who had taken their places, for such wages were slavery . . . We appeal to the Seattle Spirit, the rule to stand together which has made this city famous the country over. All we want is a return to our former wages."[32]

Neither Hill nor the laborers would budge. The case was far from isolated, and as national unemployment reached twenty percent, Jacob S. Coxey, a Massillon, Ohio, quarry owner and scrap dealer, demanded that Congress institute reforms and called upon the nation's unemployed to march on Washington to deliver "a petition with boots on." The *Post-Intelligencer* assailed Coxey as a demagogue, but thousands of jobless men heeded his call and began making their way east.

Puget Sound Coxeyites came together in the Northwest Industrial Army, and at noon on April 13 all crafts struck the Great Northern. Hill, who took a paternalist view of his employees and refused to recognize Eugene Debs' American Railway Union, stood his ground. Scabs and officials took over hauling the mail and such other trains as could be made up. In Tacoma, Frank P. "Jumbo" Cantwell rallied that city's militants, and, joining the Seattle contingent in Puyallup, threatened to steal a train and run it straight through to the nation's capital: "We're going out of Puyallup tonight, and we ain't going to walk, and dat ain't no josh, neither!"[33]

The press largely dismissed the Northwest Industrial Army as an unorganized body of tramps, but the more than 1,000 men—cold, hungry, worn, but defiant—cadged meals, rides, and sleep wherever they could, and pushed on toward Washington, D.C. In Cle Elum, a group hopped aboard a coal car, released the brakes, and coasted as far as Ellensburg. Others appropriated a Northern Pacific freight train at Butte, decked it out with flags, and headed east, obligingly stopping to repair a caved-in Bozeman Tunnel en route, before running out of water at Forsyth, Montana. Many were carried by sympathetic engineers and train crews, who refused to eject them from their trains.

On April 30, Coxey's Army began pouring into Washington, D.C., and 10,000 men laid siege to the capitol. Then the great Pullman strike erupted in Chicago and spread across the land. Congress promised an investigation, then dithered as the militants slowly ran out of steam. On August 5, after forty days, the great ARU strike ended; Eugene Debs' union was permanently broken. The economy continued its slump, and on Puget Sound mills fell silent, more men were thrown out of work, and the press complained of the "tramp nuisance."[34] Hill, though, conceded to the car cleaners' demands, and turned to more pressing matters.

Getting his desired piece of Seattle was one. Trying to resolve the unending right of way dispute among all the local roads in his favor, the city council approved a November 1892 Hill plan for freight and passenger depots south of Jackson Street. If anyone thought that City Engineer R.H.

Thomson would rubber-stamp the plans however, they were mistaken. Amid an angry outcry, Thomson put the brakes on Hill's scheme until such fundamental issues as street grades and drainage could be resolved.

Hill and Thomson reached accord the following year, but it would be another two years—August 1895—before GN's franchise demands were granted. At last, on January 3, 1896, Great Northern crews began filling in a right of way to the Jackson Street site. Sidewalk superintendents cheered as the first trains rumbled down from Interbay loaded with a pungent mixture of clay and loam. The process was a doubly efficient one, as the fill taken from Interbay cleared the level grade for the big GN yard there; 120,000 cubic yards of earth would have to be moved to fill in the terminal site to a depth of eighteen feet, and a dense carpet of reinforcing pilings was hammered into the mud.

In March, the Great Northern took up co-tenancy at the Columbia Street station with the Northern Pacific and Seattle & International, and by October the big new freight depot was finished. This block-long structure ran east-west along Jackson Street, with loading bays on the north side and three spur tracks on the south. State-of-the-art technology was one of Jim Hill's hallmarks, and that fall he gave Seattle a memento of big-time eastern railroading, its first mechanical interlocking tower. The two-story, sixty-eight lever installation controlled the spaghetti-like junction of the Great Northern, Northern Pacific, and Columbia & Puget Sound at Railroad Avenue and King Street. This application was unique in controlling dual-gauge track, and its complex set of levers and rods was buried beneath the planking of intermingled city streets and rail lines. Thus began Hill's grand transformation of the southern business district, and the eclipse of the notorious Whitechapel tenderloin district. Sundry sporting houses, cribs, and the Never Touched Me Saloon were expunged from the landscape, to minimal lamentation.

Above all else, 1896 was the year James J. Hill brought Seattle and Asia together. The first step in Hill's overseas venture was taken in August 1893, when he arranged with Samuels & Samuels of Boston to forward Great Northern

ORIENTAL LIMITED ADVERTISEMENT, 1909.

Express Company traffic to and from the Far East in ships of the Pacific Coast Steamship Co. On October 16, the steamer *Crown of England* docked in Seattle, bearing tea, silk, curios, and other goods from Shanghai and Yokohama destined for inland points over the Great Northern.

The deal drew the attention of Japan's major steamship line, Nippon Yusen Kaisha. Subsidized heavily by a government which had lately adopted numerous western conventions, the NYK Line had by 1893 come to dominate Asian shipping lanes with a fleet of 400 ships, aggregating

169,000 tons. Late in 1894, NYK began eyeing Australia, Great Britain, and the U.S. Requesting trade, harbor, and manufacturing statistics from West Coast cities, the shipping company began negotiations with the Great Northern, Northern Pacific, Union Pacific, and Southern Pacific railroads for interchange. The Seattle Chamber of Commerce and press made maximum use of the fact that their city was 300 miles closer to Japan than San Francisco, and that the Great Northern was the shortest line across the continent. Behind the scenes, Jim Hill courted NYK officials in his solid, reassuring manner, and Thomas Burke entertained Japanese shipping men in Seattle.

Japan could not have found a better partner. Hill had long been convinced of the value of Asian trade: "Lying to the west of us is one-third of the population of the globe. That one-third is not an ignorant, barbarous people, but a learned people . . . The nation that has controlled the trade of the Orient has held the purse strings of the world."[35]

Well before the driving of his last spike, Hill met in Chicago with NYK's American agent and agreed in principle to interchange traffic. With notions of weaning Asia off rice in favor of bread made with Washington and Dakota wheat, he sent Captain James Griffiths of Port Townsend to Japan and China to make further contacts. Early in 1896, NYK informed Hill that if sufficient outgoing freights could be guaranteed, it would begin service at once. Hill and the Seattle Chamber of Commerce nodded eagerly, asking only that NYK guarantee a market for the goods in Japan. More nods and bows were exchanged, and, on July 17, Hill signed the contract with NYK for the forwarding of freight between Seattle and Yokohama.

"Seattle scores again!" trumpeted the *Post-Intelligencer*, and civic leaders praised the development.

"I fully believe this is the turning point in Seattle's history," cheered chamber of commerce shipping committee chairman J.S. Goldsmith. "The only thing hitherto lacking in our statements to the world at large has been our dearth of ocean steamers."[36]

Another businessman suggested, "Jim Hill has treated Seattle pretty badly, and he has a good many shortcomings.

But I forgive him everything for giving us an ocean line."

Happiest of all was Thomas Burke: "I believe that this is one of the best things that could have come to us as a city. It means far more than it appears on the surface."

Pop Wagner's big brass band blasted out Sol Ryner's "Miike Maru March" on a bright August 31, as the *Miike Maru* sidled up to the Smith Cove pier with a heavy load of bulbs, paper goods, umbrellas, curios, wool samples, books, clothing, raw silk, tea, sulphur, and sake. On September 6, the NYK steamer stood out from Elliott Bay, loaded with 1,820 tons of flour, 3,000 tons of lumber, electrical machinery, hardware, nails, twenty crates of bicycles, and four cabin and twenty steerage passengers. *Kinshiu Maru, Riojun*, and *Yamaguchi Maru* followed in quick succession.

In anticipation of the coming trade, Hill began enlarging his Smith Cove terminal, and for the next several years mulled over the wisdom of building his own high seas fleet. He was wise to be cautious; Japan's subsidized ships boded ill for any American presence on the Pacific.

"We found their subsidy about equal to the cost of their coal and the wages of their sailors," Hill noted in 1897. "They pay their sailors five dollars a month Mexican, or $2.50 in gold, enabling them to hire twelve good sailors for the wages of one American."

A year later, his outlook had not brightened. "The Oriental commercial trade is very slow in increasing, and I don't look for much of an improvement until such time that Congress makes provisions for the establishment of a merchant marine."

Hill prodded Congress to take the lead; a world of markets awaited American producers, he lectured, but the nation was paying some $300,000,000 annually to ship goods in foreign vessels, many of them subsidized and all manned by low-paid crews. Hill urged passage of the Hanna bill granting subsidies to American ships, and ridiculed a perennial pork barrel staple—river and harbor improvements. Supporting a U.S. merchant marine, Hill grumbled, would do "far more good than to lath and plaster the bottoms of rivers called navigable, on which there has not been a steamboat floated in ten years." Should the

Hanna bill pass, he vowed, he would put his own ships on line at once. That time was not long in coming.[37]

Hill found himself involved in two "lath and plaster" projects in Seattle. With the Northern Pacific, he lent his support in the state legislature for a bill to create a canal between Lake Washington, Lake Union, Salmon Bay, and Puget Sound. He was strongly abetted (perhaps put up to it) by Thomas Burke and Daniel Gilman, both of whom had high hopes for their Salmon Bay Railway & Development Company and its substantial holdings on the small inland harbor. Gilman indicated that Hill was ready to make Salmon Bay his principal terminus, if the canal were built.

"[NP attorney] Mr. McNaught is doing all he can," Daniel Gilman wrote Judge Burke, "and . . . Mr. Hill . . . was much taken with the project and . . . told me he could, and would, do a good deal among the Democrats—where we are weakest—to push the bill through."[38]

Hill soured on the deal in 1898, when the city council refused to guarantee that it would indemnify him in the event that the GN property on Salmon Bay had to be condemned for the canal.

"We have been compelled to apply to the authorities in Washington [D.C.] to stop the entire work," Hill informed Burke in 1898. "Railroads are just as necessary to Seattle, very much more so, and unless we can feel safe in our ownership of property and our right to permanently improve it . . . it would be a great mistake for us to attempt locating in Seattle anything more than is barely necessary to transact what business we may have."[39]

The Great Northern and the Northern Pacific (after its connections with the Kirkland steel mill venture dissolved in the panic of 1893) would continue to work against the north canal well into the 20th century, and in 1909 lobbied hard for their preferred alternative, the development of rail-steamship facilities handy to their property in the Duwamish River basin. In this matter, Judge Burke found his interests in opposition to Hill's, but he was by now conveniently retired from railroad affairs and content to leave the hard fighting to City Engineer Thomson and north canal advocate Hiram Chittenden. Despite railroad opposition, overwhelming popular and business sentiment in favor of the north canal saw it through to completion in 1917.

On the southern tideflats, another canal scheme drew Hill's attention. For a decade, between 1894 and 1904, former governor Eugene Semple labored to garner support for his Seattle & Lake Washington Waterway Company's "south canal" linking Elliott Bay and Lake Washington through Beacon Hill. Just as Semple appeared to have secured eastern capital, Hill filed suit in 1901 to block the project, claiming that it would slice in two his planned rail yards on the flats. Semple formed the illusion that a truce could be worked out, and the railroads be enlisted as allies. Hill had no such idea, and in 1902 Burke suggested to John F. Stevens that GN buy Semple out and put the whole business to rest. This expedient proved unnecessary; by this time most of the Establishment, the press, and the public were leaning toward acceptance of building a north canal and allegations of corruption sealed the fate of Semple's south canal.[40]

At Stevens Pass, the boring of the 13,000-foot Cascade Tunnel began in August 1897 and kept 800 men busy drilling an average of ten feet a day over the following three years. The tunnel was holed through on September 22, 1900, and in December trains began running through the mountain.

Some lamented the passing of the switchback—"one of the most impressive and beautiful features of railroad travel in this country," according to one official, who predicted the old roadbed might someday become a bicycle path.[41] Even without the switchback, the scenic wonders of GN's Cascade crossing, including the dizzying Martin Creek trestles and Windy Point, outdid those of NP's Stampede Pass.

The safety-conscious Hill feared that the long, confined Cascade Tunnel, with its two-percent eastbound grade, would be a potentially noxious death trap for steam locomotive crews and in 1899 he began considering the use of electric locomotives. This technology was still in its infancy, however, and it was not until December 1907 that the

FORMER TERRITORIAL GOVERNOR EUGENE SEMPLE FAILED IN HIS ATTEMPT TO BUILD A "SOUTH CANAL," LINKING ELLIOTT BAY AND LAKE WASHINGTON THROUGH BEACON HILL.

Washington State University Libraries, #85-022

Great Northern placed an order with General Electric for four 1,300-horsepower, three-phase electric locomotives. The first such machines in the Northwest, the "motors" were placed in service between Wellington at the west portal, and Cascade Tunnel at the east, in the summer of 1909.

The Great Northern's surfside line along Puget Sound between Seattle and Everett was a continual operating headache, subject to wave erosion on one side and slides on the other. To bypass this sore spot, an inland "Cherry Valley cut-off" between Monroe and Seattle had been considered since GN arrived on the Sound.[42] The scheme may have had additional utility to Hill as a Sword of Damocles to dangle over Everett in order to extract land concessions. In June 1893, the plan took a step toward reality with local incorporation of the Seattle & Northeastern, envisioned as a GN subsidiary to link Lake Washington and Everett by the inland route. By the end of the decade, this scheme had evolved to include an entrance to Seattle along the west side of Lake Washington as far as Union Street, thence by tunnel into Rainier Valley and another tunnel under Beacon Hill to a tideflats depot.

However, the Great Northern—if it had ever seriously considered the cut-off in the first place—scrapped the plan, and opted to fortify the shore line. John Stevens drew up plans for moving the right of way seaward from the worst slide zones and building a massive rock wall along the route's entirety. Stevens then left Hill's employ to take charge of the Panama Canal Company, but in 1906 his improvements were begun. Large granite boulders from the railway's Stevens Pass quarry at Halford were painstakingly puzzled together to create twenty miles of seawall, line was relocated, curves eased, water cannon sluiced down the most bothersome hillsides, and the whole was double-tracked.

A major line change was made in 1902 as the GN moved off its original alignment over Chuckanut Mountain between the Skagit Valley and Bellingham and was rerouted around Chuckanut Bay to the west, eliminating a helper grade and speeding trains, which was always a Hill priority. That February, too, the Great Northern gathered in the formerly hostile Seattle & Northern between Anacortes and Hamilton; Elijah Smith's line previously was under lease to the Northern Pacific. With Hill's characteristic Midas touch, GN extended the line east to Rockport and turned a white elephant into a lucrative hauler of marble, concrete, and lumber.

Jim Hill liked his passenger trains to make good time; thus in January 1899 ten hours were cut off the GN's best time by its new Flyer, on a 58-hour Seattle-St. Paul run. This prompted much derision from the Northern Pacific, since the Flyer, inadvisably launched in the dead of winter, seldom lived up to its name. Still, with its shorter route and consistently faster times, the Great Northern garnered the St. Paul-Seattle U.S. Mail contract that June, which it would hold for the next seventy years.

Hill was not nearly as interested in high-speed antics, though, as he was in colonizing and enriching his domain. That February, the Great Northern spurred a new era of Pacific Northwest growth by instituting semi-monthly "home-seekers" rates—half the minimum first class fare plus $1 to any point on the line. In March, Hill went further, dropping the $40 fare in second class immigrant sleepers between the Twin Cities and Puget Sound to $25. Since many prospective immigrant families numbered four or more, transporting a household of belongings was a substantial investment. The first Great Northern home-seekers' train left St. Paul that month with 800 souls bound for the Northwest. Hill-controlled Northern Pacific joined in, and a flood of new settlement swept the northern states.

As the 19th century drew to a close, James J. Hill was being hailed as the man of the age, a leading apostle of trade and political economy.

"He is a calculating machine," editorialized the *Post-Intelligencer* in August 1897. "He knows nothing of sentiment in business. Susceptible as he is to appeals to his own pocket, he never permits an invested nickel to be diverted from its duty of making more nickels . . . His system becomes a series of moving figures evolving new designs and multiplying themselves under his fascinating mind."

The *Wall Street Journal* praised the Great Northern's large net earnings, strict economy, low rates, and resultant benefits to both stockholders and the public.[43] In Seattle, Hill was now generally recognized as the greatest force in the city's phenomenal growth.

The "calculating machine" approached the new century with dreams of empire ever greater. With the backing of J.P. Morgan & Co., Hill gained control of the Northern Pacific and the Chicago Burlington & Quincy, following the scare of a nearly successful 1900 raid on the NP by Edward H. Harriman, chairman of the Union Pacific. Chastened, Hill and Morgan acted to fortify their properties against hostile takeover, and in 1901 formed the Northern Securities Company to manage the NP, GN, and CB&Q as a "community of interest."

"No merger or consolidation of the Northern Pacific and the Great Northern is contemplated," Hill explained. "Each company will be operated separately in the future as in the past . . . The Northern Securities Company is organized to deal in high class securities; to hold the same for the benefit of its shareholders, and to advance the interests of the corporations whose securities it owns. Its powers do not include the operation of railways."[44]

Hill and Morgan, however, would in fact retain final word in management and operating affairs for all three lines, and Northern Securities was very much a "merger" in the public mind. Seattleites were mixed in their reviews of the daring venture.

"There is as yet no evidence that the proposed merger will be detrimental in its effects," editorialized Seattle *Times* owner, Alden J. Blethen, a great Hill admirer.

The *Post-Intelligencer*, also a Hill ally, agreed: "The harmonious operation of the three great railroad systems included in the community of interest will build up this section as nothing else could do."

Others were not so sure. "Mr. Hill wishes to dominate," ventured the left-leaning Seattle *Star*, "and the desire has oft-times been productive of disastrous results to communities and to nations. Taking for granted as true the claim that Mr. Hill would not willingly injure the great Northwest if allowed imperialistic sway over the country, how will it be when Mr. Hill passes away and a new hand takes the sceptre?"[45]

Washington's Populist Party governor John R. Rogers was very much alarmed by Northern Securities and conjured up the dread specter of "trusts." Against such a foe, even the unthinkable—nationalization—might be preferable:

"Government ownership is the only and final end of the tremendous concentration of wealth which, so far, has proceeded without let or hindrance. Whether this is in truth a good remedy may possibly be an open question, but that it is the only effective one, no intelligent man can deny."

Rogers met with his Idaho and Montana counterparts to debate strategy against this new railroad octopus; Rogers died soon thereafter, but his anti-trust philosophy did not. On March 10, 1902, Attorney General Philander C. Knox brought suit in St. Paul against Northern Securities as a violation of the Sherman Anti-Trust Act of 1890. Washington attorney general Stratton filed a similar injunction with the state supreme court to prevent any consolidation of the NP and GN, and to dissolve Northern Securities. Governor Rogers' successor, Henry McBride, excoriated "the evils of the railroad lobby," and urged creation of a state railroad commission, the dream of public activists at least since statehood in 1889.[46]

An incredulous Hill erupted in outrage. "Why should I favor a state which brings suit against me?" he stormed. "It was the exceedingly low rate on lumber made by the Great Northern that made it possible for the lumbermen of Washington to do business in the East. Do the people of the state think I am compelled to continue that rate? Operating expenses in Washington last year were $2,500,000, with receipts so low that the business is no inducement to the Great Northern company. If the people of Washington do not desire a continuation of the efforts which the Great Northern has made in behalf of immigration and low lumber rates, but prefer that the railroads shall adopt a course which would always result in a profit, then the people will certainly be accommodated . . . I do not hesitate to let anybody from Washington know that I am thoroughly disgusted with the conduct of your people and feel that but very few, if any, know how Washington has been favored in railroad rates as compared with other states . . . I regard the present movement as an evidence of ingratitude."[47]

Among the ingrates were Puget Sound lumbermen. Beneficiaries of the 40¢ rate, but hard-pressed by overproduction and inefficient facilities, logging company and sawmill owners feared a Hill monopoly and were prominent in calling for state railroad regulation. In 1907, the Washington Lumbermen's Association would file suit against the Great Northern for restraint of trade. Hill could only shake his head in bewilderment, though it has also been claimed that he created a spurious freight car "shortage" in retaliation against the fractious mill owners. Hill's anger availed him not.

President Theodore Roosevelt, whom industrialists dubbed the "Boss Lunatic," threw the weight of government against the "trusts" and the railroads, and Hill was outgunned. After a three-year court battle, the U.S. Supreme Court ruled against Northern Securities on March 14, 1904, and ordered it dissolved. For Hill, it was a stern lesson in the new public mood. The following January, the U.S. Court of Appeals allowed Hill to retain his Northern Pacific and Burlington stock. However, he would henceforth find Uncle Sam in the fireman's seat.[48]

Northern Securities and the first five years of the 20th century marked the flood tide of railroad power in Washington. With the aid of Judge Burke and GN lobbyists such as John D. Farrell, Hill had his way with the Republican-dominated state legislature, and without breaking a sweat fended off virtually all railroad legislation until well into the 1900s. Free passes over the Hill roads kept many a lawmaker in line, and Hill had good relations with the leading voices in the Seattle press, throwing substantial financial support behind both *Times* publisher Blethen and the *Post-Intelligencer's* John Wilson, a former state senator.[49]

Hill was not without influential critics. Seattle *Argus* editor Harry Chadwick led the pack in charging him with monopolizing the waterfront, blocking out other railroads, pocketing state and local government, and engaging in economic imperialism.

"JIM HILL . . . is doing good work at building up the state," Chadwick editorialized wryly, "because whenever he settles a family in the territory adjacent to his road he has a mortgage on them for life. Everything that they consume that does not grow at home has to pay a tribute to Mr. HILL . . . And all of the produce which they raise over and above what they consume must pay tribute to him in order to reach a market."[50]

Despite growing doubts about the Far East trade, Hill took his long-pondered maritime plunge in August 1900 and formed the Great Northern Steamship Company. He then opened a bidding contest among marine architects for two new freighters; characteristically, it was 23-year-old William Fairburn's bold proposal to build the largest freighters in the world that won Hill's enthusiastic endorsement. The Eastern Shipbuilding Company was formed especially to construct the new monsters at Groton, Connecticut, and the 28,000 ton, 622-foot *Minnesota* and *Dakota* quickly took form. The revolutionary new GN monsters took the maritime world by storm, boasting the latest in refrigeration and other mechanical appliances, shell plating two inches thick, luxurious staterooms for 250 first-class passengers, accommodations for 68 "intermediate" and 1,500 steerage passengers, and, for "Asiatic" patrons, opium dens.

The *Minnesota* was launched on April 16, 1903. Thomas Burke regaled the crowd with tributes to Hill: "Twenty five years ago, he found the Northwest practically a wild, uninhabited, and inaccessible country . . . Yet, largely owing to his superior knowledge of the real character and capabilities of this new land, and through his wonderful energy and ability in providing for it, even in advance of population, the most judiciously planned, the most economically constructed, and the most wisely managed line that has ever served a new country has, in less than fifteen years, given four new states to the Union with an aggregate population of more than 1,500,000 people!"

Under a canopy of signal flags, the great liner departed Seattle on her maiden voyage to Yokohama on January

23, 1905, and was soon joined by the *Dakota*, along with leased Boston Steamship Company freighters *Shawmut* and *Tremont*. Together with the NYK ships, which remained under GN contract, this gave Hill a ten-ship fleet, and should have made him, and the United States, a major force on the Pacific.[51]

Sadly, it did not. Great Northern Steamship was, by Hill's own admission, an "experiment," and for good reason. Even as his ships made their maiden voyages, he was complaining bitterly to the Senate Interstate Commerce Committee that protectionist policies and rate-setting regulations lately enacted by the Interstate Commerce Commission made Pacific trade hopeless. Unless the government backed off, Hill declared, he would be forced to give up his "philanthropic endeavor" to secure foreign markets for the United States:

"It takes considerably more power to promote commerce than it does to suppress it. I am in the promotion business, and the government is in the suppression business! I undertook to find a market for Minneapolis flour in the Orient, and offered a forty-five-cent rate to Hong Kong. Then along came the Interstate Commerce Commission, and directed us to set new rates, so I simply withdrew, and the flour market was closed so far as China is concerned. Last year, these flour shipments were 10,000 tons—this year they are nothing whatever."[52]

Hill asked Thomas Burke to testify against the new ICC requirements that railroads make their rates public, advising him that Puget Sound might be faced with rate hikes, car shortages, and service deterioration as a result. The judge, by this time retired as Hill's western counsel, nonetheless submitted a strong deposition supporting Hill's effort to build up foreign trade, noting the beneficial effects to the Pacific Northwest. It did little good.

To the *Wall Street Journal*, Hill vented his growing frustration: "I do not believe this country will ever have a merchant marine under its own flag, under existing laws. It costs us five times as much to dock a ship at one of the Pacific ports as it does at Nagasaki . . . In some respects, this country, industrially, is going the way of England, where

the labor unions have dominated business with the result that there is no town in England of over 15,000 inhabitants where you cannot buy almost any important article to better advantage than by selecting one of foreign make . . . If labor finds itself beaten in this country, and many think it is beaten now, it will have itself to blame. It will have killed the goose that laid its golden egg!"

As if to prove Hill right, Congress passed the Hepburn Act in March 1906. This required thirty-day advance publication of tariffs and gave the ICC authority to set maximum rail rates upon application from shippers. There was no right of appeal and the act effectively transferred railroad rate-making authority from private enterprise to the federal government.

Hill, believing his life's work had been a gift to the nation, was stunned: "We feel that we are sort of outlaws!"[53]

To add insult to injury, the bulky *Minnesota* and *Dakota* were proving slow and expensive to operate. After some adjustment, however, they were capable of a respectable fifteen knots, and on a record-breaking passage Captain Thomas Garlick brought the *Minnesota* into Smith Cove on June 3, 1910, with a passenger list of 320 and a manifest of over 3,000 tons, after lopping a full thirty hours off the run from Yokohama. Still, the liners lost money and became known as "Hill's white elephants."

On March 3, 1907, the *Dakota* plunged recklessly into known shallows forty miles from Yokohama and ran its bow onto a reef. Heart-broken, *Dakota*'s master watched as his great ship settled deeply by the head. A few weeks later, the sea had broken the vessel to bits.

Passage of the LaFollette Act, requiring American ships to be manned by American crews, further hobbled Hill's maritime efforts, and in 1915 the *Minnesota* was sold to the Morgan-controlled International Mercantile Marine Co. for use as a munitions carrier between the East Coast and England. With its steam siren sobbing a bovine farewell, the great vessel made its last sailing from Seattle on November 14, 1915.[54]

Jim Hill was a man not given to frills, but he was also loath to see his passenger offerings bettered by the

A Great Northern crew at Seattle's King Street Station obliges the photographer with a classic train portrait.

Warren W. Wing collection

skyline. The great clock mechanism and dials, manufactured by the Howard Clock Company of Boston, arrived at the end of December and were hoisted into place.

Requisite for all this grandeur was a new main line through the city—rather, under it. Hill and City Engineer Thomson had agreed in 1893 that a tunnel was the best solution to Seattle's railroad problems. Years had passed—and much hashing about, over tidelands ownership and right of way franchises—but in April 1903, water cannon were trained on a hillside at the foot of Virginia Street and the Great Northern tunnel began burrowing under Seattle. By the close of 1904, the bore was complete.

As his grand terminus at last became a reality, Jim Hill paid a warm tribute to Seattle. "When we came to the Pacific coast we had many things to consider," he reminisced at a Rainier Club banquet. "There were other harbors certainly as good as this to the north of you. [But] the crowd of people in Seattle even in those days impressed me, and I thought that it would be cruel not to give them a chance to work out their own salvation . . . We have received loyal support here . . . but we have put more money into Seattle than we ever took out in profits . . . Today there is no city of your size anywhere that has the terminal facilities you will have within the next six months. It is only your hope and inflexible pluck that saved your lives."[55]

The imperial age of Seattle railroading opened with the doors of the towering new Union Depot—soon to be renamed King Street Station—on May 10, 1906. The Great Northern now hosted two daily transcontinental trains, the Oriental Limited and the Southeast Express, which offered connection with the Chicago Burlington & Quincy line to Kansas City via Great Falls and Billings. Four trains each way linked Seattle with Bellingham, and three with Vancouver, the latter joined in November by the overnight Owl.

In 1909, a Great Northern institution was born—the Fast Mail. The Mail inaugurated a record-breaking 47-hour time between St. Paul and Seattle, beating the old

competition. Thus, in November 1905, he gave the Great Northern a train to rival the Northern Pacific's North Coast Limited. On time to the minute, the new Oriental Limited slid into Seattle Union Depot at 8:50 in the evening of November 21, after a 59-hour trek from St. Paul. The Oriental drew much admiration for its luxury coaches and sleepers, diner, and library-observation car, complete with English oak card room, green leather upholstery, and afternoon high tea.

Likewise, the farmer was ready to build his palace. Hill had chosen famed New York architects Reed and Stem to design Seattle's new depot, and in May 1904 ground was broken at Hill's terminal site on Jackson Street. Throughout 1905, the spire of the new Union Depot, modeled on the bell tower of St. Mark's in Venice, crept slowly into the champion, Northern Pacific's North Coast Limited, by twelve hours and shaving sixteen hours off GN's previous best time. Long the fastest, regularly scheduled, long distance train in the world, Numbers 27 and 28 blazed proudly across the northern states for over 60 years.

An even more spectacular railroad phenomenon had already begun burning the Great Northern rails: The silk express. By 1904, silk had become the Far East's most important export, and naturally enough the Hill road was the favored stateside connection. Bales of the temperature-sensitive material were rushed in trains of baggage cars on timings not exceeded even by the Fast Mail—Smith Cove to Hoboken in an astonishing three days. Though the NP, Canadian Pacific, and Milwaukee Road all won a share of the silk trade, Hill's expresses consistently made the best time.

Tacoma looked on in envy. After the abortive joint GN/UP Portland & Puget Sound venture of 1891, Hill lost interest in extending south of Seattle and labeled recurrent rumors of an imminent move south "stupid rot":

"The Great Northern has never contemplated such a foolish move as going to Tacoma . . . There is no business between Seattle, Tacoma, and Portland that the Northern Pacific cannot handle, and the publication of such a story is nothing but pure, unadulterated slush!"

Smarting at the snub, the City of Destiny indulged in spite. "If any man doubts the hypnotic power of President James J. Hill, let him witness the cataleptic condition of Seattle," intoned the *News*, ridiculing the "phantom depot" Hill was forever promising and never building: "The phantom is fixed upon the minds of those who gave themselves up to the occult influences of this prince of the black art."[56]

Tacoma was at last received into the fold in June 1908, when the Great Northern purchased thirty acres of tidelands adjacent to the Northern Pacific's head-of-the-bay yard. Freight trains ran into Tacoma for the first time on December 14, and Tacoma enjoyed full rate parity with Seattle. Great Northern passenger trains, though, would not come to town until November of 1909.

Portland was next, and last, to get Great Northern service

when St. Paul-Portland trains 3 and 4, the Oregonian, were inaugurated in May 1910 over the Spokane Portland & Seattle (with a connecting Seattle-Spokane stub). Also, three Vancouver, B.C.-Portland schedules began June 19: the Owl, Seattle Express, and Vancouver Express, and the daylight Portland Limited and Vancouver Limited.

Following Hill's "back to the farm" philosophy, the Great Northern also sent farmers' demonstration specials across its system. Loaded with displays, implements, livestock specimens, and agricultural experts, these trains toured the Hill roads and brought to growers the latest farming methods.

GN's Seattle tunnel was the unlikely setting for a shocking event in 1908. Early in the morning of May 12, as Vancouver train 272 pulled out of King Street Station and plunged into the tunnel, two masked men looted the mail car strongbox of over $5,000 and beat the express messenger "into insensibility." The bandits jumped off at Smith Cove and disappeared into the city. This was not the first such incident; in 1905, a train had been relieved of $12,000 just north of Ballard. But the novel tunnel robbery caused a sensation. Detectives combed the rooming houses, barrooms, and alleyways, and, though a "tough looking pair" had been spotted lurking about the tunnel mouth shortly before the holdup and were later seen running from the train, the desperadoes were never caught.[57]

James J. Hill retired from the Great Northern presidency on April 2, 1907: "I don't retire; instead of two men's work, I shall now do one."

He passed day-to-day leadership to his able son, Louis. Where Hill the elder was an unvarnished pragmatist more concerned with ton-miles than mountain scenery, Louis was a romantic who put the beauty and mystique of the American West to work drawing vacationers to Great Northern "vacation land." He adopted "See America first" as a corporate motto, employed Native American images in GN advertising, and lobbied Congress to create a national park in the Rocky Mountain paradise adjoining the mainline. Glacier National Park became a reality in 1910, and for decades Glacier Park and the Great Northern Railway were virtually synonymous.

The elder Hill remained board chairman and was lionized as one of the great men of the age. In November 1908, he rode the first train down the Spokane Portland & Seattle "North Bank Road" and across the new Columbia River bridge at Vancouver. Hill had long borne such nicknames as the "Little Giant," "One-eyed Scotsman," and other, sometimes less-printable, epithets. In Portland on the evening of the 6th, however, he was greeted with thunderous applause and toasted as the "Empire Builder." Hill had come far since the 1890s, when the railroad Establishment laughingly dismissed the Great Northern as a "junk line" and its leader as "chimerical in his ideas."

Next day, he rode to Seattle, and was feted at a dinner at the New Washington Hotel. The great man expounded upon his personal philosophy of economy:

"Your commerce, your manufactures, everything, goes back more to the cultivation of the soil than to all the conditions in the world, and it always has been so at all times, and it always will be so . . . Next to the cultivation of the soil itself, in the amount of money invested and in the importance to all the people, is the railway property of this country."

Seattle *Times* publisher Colonel Alden Blethen paid Hill the warmest tribute: "Through the far sightedness of Mr. Hill, the wonderful development of the Pacific Northwest has been made possible . . . I believe that the coming generations will write as the epitaph of James J. Hill that he was not only the shrewdest businessman of his day, but that he was the greatest empire builder that the United States has ever known."[58]

Hill returned to Seattle in May 1909 for the Alaska-Yukon-Pacific Exposition. He gleefully led his breathless entourage on a tour of the fair, and on June 1 gave the opening address:

"This exposition may be regarded as the laying of the last rail, the driving of the last spike, in unity of mind and purpose between the Pacific coast and the country east of the mountains," he declaimed. "Never again can the Pacific coast draw into itself; never again can it know any slackening of the tide of life that sweeps through all the nation's veins when it crosses the great divide!"

With his high-pitched voice shrilling into the amphitheater, the stubby, grizzled man everyone now called the Empire Builder held a huge crowd in thrall. A "federation of the world," Hill thundered, would do much to ease international tensions: "We must meet all the rest of the world on [the] ground of common competition, including the awakened, competent, and highly competitive Japanese and Chinese."

The great agent of change begged his countrymen, almost wistfully, to pause and reflect. "It seems to me that this is especially a time for turning to the old things that have justified themselves by experience and grown strong and efficient through the centuries . . . the craving, the passion and striving after novelty for its own sake, the wild flight from experiment to experiment, the toying with untried ventures in social conduct . . . has gone dangerously far; there must be this balance of steadying forces, this respite from the incessant onward rush, as well as from the reactionary collapse."

Hill also preached the new and controversial doctrine of conservation. "The first and most imperative word . . .

is conservation! [This] particularly needs to be repeated and emphasized among the people of the North Pacific coast . . . Take care of your soil before it is too late, and it will take care of you . . . If no flake of gold had ever been found in Alaska, its fish products would have made it a rich possession . . . What are you doing to keep the salmon and the other fish of this coast not merely from extermination, but as a permanent source of wealth?"[59]

Hill would suffer a serious blow in the coming year. The construction of snow sheds and other improvements in Stevens Pass during 1904 had prompted some to observe that slides on the heavily snowed line were practically a thing of the past. This hopeful prognostication was shattered in the early hours of March 1, 1910, when an avalanche roared down on the tiny railroad town of Wellington, at the west portal of the Cascade Tunnel. Some structures, four steam locomotives, four electric motors, a rotary snowplow, and fourteen mail and passenger cars of the Fast Mail and Spokane Local were swept into the ravine and smashed to pieces. This, Washington's worst railroad disaster, claimed the lives of forty-four people.

Long in dread of just such a disaster, a crestfallen Hill visited the scene. "We must make the mountain district of the system impregnable against snow slides at any cost," he grumbled.

An assistant demurred at the expense, but Hill rapped out orders to begin building concrete snow sheds at once and mulled over the feasibility of a tunnel five or more miles long under the mountain. Others considered even more radical action: Hiram M. Chittenden, a brigadier general in the U.S. Army Corps of Engineers, proposed a thirty-two-mile bore between Skykomish and Leavenworth, to be constructed and shared by all railroads crossing the Cascades. Prophetically, Chittenden's plan had been first published only the previous June, 1909.[60]

By 1910, James J. Hill remained widely recognized as the dean of American railroading and one of the legends of American enterprise. He stood in austere grandeur, a symbol of an age of industrial giants and laissez faire economics that already was fast receding. The Empire Builder contin-

EMPIRE BUILDER—A PATRIARCHAL JAMES J. HILL HOLDS FORTH AT THE OPENING CEREMONY OF THE ALASKA-YUKON-PACIFIC EXPOSITION ON JUNE 1, 1909.

University of Washington, Special Collections, # 3012

ued to raise his voice tirelessly in praise of free enterprise, cheap transportation, and efficient agriculture, and against "political adventurers who have never done anything but pose and draw a salary," bureaucrats, and "doctrinaires [and] college tack-head philosophers and preachers."

Hill more than anyone else has been credited with creating the modern Pacific Northwest. Certainly, he was the greatest single agent of change—and obstacle to it—in Seattle's first half century of existence.[61]

On August 3, 1909—Minnesota Day at the Alaska-Yukon-Pacific Exposition—Jim Hill's friend Thomas Burke dedicated a large bronze bust of the Empire Builder on the University of Washington campus.

There it remains today, proud, implacable, imperious, peering into a future of infinite possibilities. ■

CHAPTER 12

RAILROAD MANIA

"Through trains to Seattle [is] the ambition of every connecting or trunk line this side of the Missouri River." —Seattle *Post-Intelligencer*

Seattle's mantra during the 1880s was "Railroads, railroads, and more railroads." The hated Northern Pacific thumbed its nose insolently from Commencement Bay, but other lines offered a hope of salvation. In the decade's nationwide "railroad mania," many of these boasted grandiose names and auspicious beginnings, only to get no further than their articles of incorporation. Other major players, though, gave every sign of answering Seattle's prayers.

With its November 1885 completion from Montreal, Quebec, to Port Moody, British Columbia, the Canadian Pacific Railway was the first major trunk line to offer serious competition to the Northern Pacific on Puget Sound. On June 22, 1891, over-enthusiastic greeters with fire hoses almost started an international incident as the first through CPR train to the Sound steamed into the Bellingham Bay town of New Whatcom, over the rails of Pierre B. Cornwall's Bellingham Bay & British Columbia from Sumas. Connection to Seattle was furnished by the steamer *Premier*.

By this time, however, the Northern Pacific was firmly entrenched at the border and offered the only direct, all rail line into Seattle. The Canadian Pacific and Northern Pacific both weighed the prospects of interchanging through St. Paul-Seattle trains, and NP president Oakes briefly considered selling the Canadian Pacific half-interest in the Seattle Lake Shore & Eastern.[1] Ongoing litigation between the NP and the SLS&E prevented this from taking place.

The Great Northern soon appeared on the scene, and it was over Jim Hill's line, on March 14, 1892, that Canadian Pacific sleeping cars began serving Seattle via South Westminster and Blaine. In August of the following year, GN dropped out of the deal, and the Canadian Pacific and Northern Pacific began joint operation of through Seattle-Vancouver trains via Sumas. In 1896, these trains began forwarding through CPR tourist sleepers from Toronto and Boston into Seattle, a pattern that would continue until the end of 1917.

The Canadian Pacific made a bid to purchase the Seattle & International outright in 1898, but was blocked by the Northern Pacific. President Mellen declared: "The Northern Pacific does not want to shut the Canadian Pacific out of this territory," but the NP nevertheless retained its firm grip on the erstwhile Seattle road.

Closer relations between Seattle and the CPR were evinced on December 26, 1902, when Seattle interests led by banker-street car magnate Jacob Furth incorporated the Seattle & Canada Railway to run from Tacoma to Sumas. A line was surveyed east of the former Seattle Lake Shore & Eastern to gain access to the mineral deposits of the Index, Monte Cristo and Mt. Baker districts.

Furth stated: "The line known as the Seattle & Canada . . . is a Canadian Pacific proposition . . . Their purpose is to connect with the Puget Sound country over their own tracks."[2] Apparently, however, CPR had no real interest in the scheme and nothing came of Furth's road.

THE COLUMBIA & PUGET SOUND STATION AT WASHINGTON STREET, ADJACENT TO PIERS A AND B—LATER PIER 98.

Museum of History and Industry, #19156

Seattle assumed the great Canadian road would come. However, CPR president Thomas Shaughnessy stated in September 1906: "It is against the policy of the company to build into American territory, and we are not going to extend to Seattle." Shaughnessy continued: "There is no reason why our traffic arrangements with the Northern Pacific should not be continued for a number of years."

This did not jibe with statements made by Jefferson Leavy, head of the Canadian Pacific financial interests on Wall Street—that the road was even then surveying line into the city. Nor did it square with mysterious reports from farmers east of Lake Washington, who during the fall and winter of 1906-1907 claimed to have encountered Canadian Pacific surveying parties on their property. A Deming farmer had several such questionable characters hailed into court for trespass and they too claimed to be in CPR employ. The Canadian Pacific denied everything, and in the end kept to its side of the line.[3]

Its trains did make it to Seattle, however. The year 1900 witnessed the introduction of summer season "Soo-Pacific" through trains between St. Paul and the west over the rails of the Canadian Pacific and its American subsidiary St. Paul Minneapolis & Sault St. Marie, the "Soo Line." Stimulated by booming Seattle traffic and the Alaska-Yukon-Pacific Exposition, wine red CPR trains made their first appearance in King Street Station on June 6, 1909, with inauguration of the Soo-Seattle-Pacific. This was a summer- and peak-season only service that continued over the next five years, known also as the Soo-Pacific Express and the St. Paul-Seattle Express. The Canadian Pacific terminated this service in September 1914, and connection to Seattle was made thereafter by the company's elegant "Princess" steamers between Seattle and Vancouver.

Another Canadian line would find the lure of Seattle irresistible. "Seattle's record speaks for itself," declared Charles M. Hayes, president of the Grand Trunk Pacific, during a visit in August 1909. "The Grand Trunk is going to have terminals in Vancouver and in Seattle, beyond any shadow of a doubt."[4]

Mr. Hayes' plans had their beginnings in 1902, when "to get a share of the Oriental business," he made the decision to take his Montreal-based Grand Trunk to the Pacific. During a West Coast visit that December, Hayes was properly impressed with both Seattle and Vancouver, but proceeded with plans to establish his own new terminal city—Prince Rupert—on the west coast of British Columbia. The Grand Trunk Pacific would ultimately enter Seattle, but not by rail. Passengers and freight instead travelled between Puget Sound and Prince Rupert by ship. The handsome, three-stack turbine liners *Prince George* and *Prince Rupert* were built in 1909-1910 by Fairfield, of Govan, Scotland, and in June 1910 inaugurated the Seattle-Prince Rupert sailings. The Princes berthed at the foot of Marion Street until December 3, when the ornate GTP dock, largest on the West Coast, opened its doors. The service was elegant, but handicapped by the lagging completion of the main line across Canada, recession, World War I, and too little business through its remote northern terminus. The Grand Trunk steamers were nonetheless a distinguished international presence on Puget Sound.

Standard Seattle newspaper fodder for the 1880s and well into the early 1900s was the recurrent rumor that any or all of the big "granger" roads of the Midwest—the Chicago & North Western, Chicago Milwaukee & St. Paul, Chicago Burlington & Quincy, and Chicago Rock Island & Pacific—were on the verge of a Puget Sound extension.

The Burlington was the most frequent candidate; summer 1890 saw contracts supposedly let for an extension from Newcastle, Wyoming, to Butte, Montana and grading underway. Three years later, "Q" engineers were reported to be surveying lines via the Snake River and White Pass to Seattle-Tacoma. Late in 1894, however, the Burlington completed what would be its westernmost extension from Omaha to Billings, Montana, via Lander and Cody, Wyoming. On October 28, the Billings gateway opened and proved an immediate success. Traffic between the southern Midwest and Puget Sound was heavier than estimated, despite the national depression, and the CB&Q

played up the appeal of breaking the tedium of a transcontinental journey on the Northern Pacific:

"After a two days' ride, it is refreshing to step into a clean, bright, sweet smelling train, as you do if you go east via Billings and the Burlington route. No dust on the car seats; no litter on the car floors; no foul air; nothing to remind you of former occupants."[5]

Another perennial paper contender in the race to Puget Sound was one of the Midwest's oldest lines, the Chicago & North Western. The C&NW got as far west as Lander, Wyoming, in 1905. Railroad pundits were not content to let it rest there, but insisted it must continue to the Sound to remain competitive. New North Western bond issues in 1906 and 1910, and alleged mysterious acquisitions of terminal grounds in Bellingham, Seattle, and Tacoma by shadowy characters, fueled speculation that the C&NW was coming. The reports made for interesting reading, but the North Western stayed in Lander.

Despite its title, the Chicago Rock Island & Pacific would also ignore the blandishments of Seattle rumor-mongers. "No, we do not intend to come this way," stated Rock Island president B.L. Winchell on a visit in September 1908. "We have our lines built from the Twin Cities to the Gulf of Mexico, and as is well known, where there are so many roads running lengthwise of the town, it is good to have a cross town line. We have lines which cut down the Mississippi Valley and cross every road running east and west. That is enough for us."[6]

Seattle also looked south for smoke. In 1887, Collis P. Huntington's giant Southern Pacific acquired Henry Villard's Oregon & California Railroad, which ran down the Willamette Valley into the Siskiyou Range. Last spike in the O&C was driven at Ashland, Oregon, that November, and a great steel crescent united Portland with San Francisco, Los Angeles, and New Orleans. The previous spring, Huntington and partner Charles Crocker were seen poking about Seattle and Port Townsend "armed with maps and survey plots."

Something was obviously up, and sure enough, on August 12, 1888, Southern Pacific director W.A. Brown and

SEATTLE ADVERTISEMENT, DECEMBER 1895.

local men formed the Seattle & Southern to build from Seattle to Portland and connect there with the Southern Pacific. A year later, a survey was reported complete between the two cities in December, with a line from West Seattle down the west bank of the Duwamish and White rivers, and a Columbia crossing north of Vancouver, Washington. Nothing more happened, prompting charges that the promoters were nothing more than "real estate sharks."

Another year passed, and Collis Huntington denied all Southern Pacific interest in the S&S and Seattle: "We will not build to the Sound if other roads treat us fairly";

interchange agreements and respect for the "territory of other lines" would be his policy. Southern Pacific would forever remain south of the Columbia.[7]

A more likely contender for a new Seattle-Portland line was the Oregon Railway & Navigation Company. Throughout the mid-1880s, OR&N leader Elijah Smith chafed under Northern Pacific hegemony in the Northwest, beholden as he was to the NP for through traffic from the East and, from 1887 on, watching a growing share of OR&N's wheat business defect to the Cascade Division. In November 1888, he made up his mind to establish a Puget Sound presence, and with Oregon Improvement Co. superintendent Thomas J. Milner formed the Seattle & Northern, to link Portland, Seattle, and Vancouver, B.C. A branch would cross Skagit Pass to Spokane, and the company would develop a new terminal city at Ship Harbor, on Fidalgo Island.

To complete Smith's pincers around the Sound (and foil a rumored Union Pacific incursion), the Oregon Improvement Company purchased the Port Townsend Southern in January 1889. This local road had been organized in August 1887 by Port Townsend citizens in hopes of building to a connection with the Northern Pacific at Olympia. Oregon Improvement took over the subscription of $1,000,000 in cash and land which Port Townsend had pledged to its road, and ground was broken in Port Townsend on March 23, 1889. Ultimate plans were to tie the Port Townsend Southern to the Seattle & Northern by ferry between Port Townsend and Ship Harbor—just as Thomas Canfield had envisioned twenty years before. The town of Anacortes was platted that spring, and by December rails had been laid between Sedro and Ship Harbor, and were creeping southward from Port Townsend toward Hood Canal.

To nail down the southern end of its envelopment, Oregon Improvement paid $300,000 for the narrow gauge Olympia & Chehalis Valley in September 1890, and converted it to standard gauge, forming the Olympia Division of the Port Townsend Southern. This home-grown line had begun life in 1871 as the Olympia Branch Rail-road, the capital city's bid to connect with the Northern Pacific. The Branch Railroad was renamed Olympia & Chehalis Valley, and in an "old fashioned working bee" on April 3, 1874, the townspeople began construction. Isaac Stevens' son, Hazard, spearheaded the early phase, and four years later Judge Obadiah McFadden completed the O&CV to a junction with the Northern Pacific at Tenino. After several marginal years, the road was purchased by a group that included old NP stalwart John W. Sprague, and it earned a modest living hauling lumber and Northern Pacific interchange freight.

Elijah Smith hoped to build up a solid carrying trade on the Olympic Peninsula and in the Skagit and Chehalis valleys, but in the deepening financial gloom of the early '90s, the bid failed. By February 1891, the Seattle & Northern had only made it as far east as Hamilton, by which time "Lijer" threw in the towel and leased the road to his nemesis, the Northern Pacific. Construction on the Port Townsend Southern continued, however, with 500 men grading between the Key City and Quilcene. In March 1891, the Port Angeles Southern was formed, to link the Port Townsend road with Port Angeles. On June 6, the first Port Townsend Southern train ran between its home terminus and Quilcene, twenty miles south, near Hood Canal. There, the Port Townsend Southern was to remain, and in August 1892 the Oregon Improvement Company sued delinquent subscribers for their subscription pledges. The laggards argued that they had signed up for a railroad to Olympia, and in the absence of same, they were no longer obligated for payment. Under this brutal logic, OIC's suit came to naught, and over the next several years the Port Townsend Southern passed through varied ownership, enduring a hand-to-mouth career primarily as a logging railroad.[8]

The 1890s were hard on the Oregon Improvement Company and Seattle's old road, the Columbia & Puget Sound. As early as 1884, civil engineer George Morison had inspected the narrow gauge and found it to be dangerously decrepit—its track of thirty-six-pound rail in pitiful condition, trestles wobbly, and most of its locomotives "of no value." With Henry Villard's resurgence in 1887, the company revived his 1881 plan to convert the C&PS to standard gauge and extend it to the "common point" junction with the NP. Surveys were made and thousands of tons of rail shipped west aboard, fittingly enough, the bark *Henry Villard*. The iron wound up elsewhere, though, and the Columbia & Puget Sound struggled on.

Great Northern vice-president William P. Clough advised James J. Hill that the Oregon Improvement Company might be a worthy investment, and "in competent hands could be so handled as to pay well."

Hill ultimately turned thumbs down, and in November 1890 the OIC landed in receivership. Early the following year, the company emerged from bankruptcy, moved its operating headquarters from Portland to Seattle, and continued its hand-to-mouth existence. The Newcastle and Franklin mines were plagued by fires and explosions that killed dozens of men, necessitated extensive repairs and new diggings, and prompted large lawsuits. This, along with growing labor disaffection, all compounded the OIC's troubles. Line improvements, preparations for conversion to standard gauge, and new surveys to the common point were made in 1893, just in time for the depression to bring everything to a halt.[9]

On October 4, 1895, Oregon Improvement was again bankrupt, and two years later the once-great Villard enterprise was reorganized as the Pacific Coast Company. Pacific Coast purchased the Columbia & Puget Sound Railroad and the mines at Newcastle and Franklin, and moved its headquarters to New Jersey.

The Columbia & Puget Sound was converted to standard gauge over the weekend of November 14, 1897, a change that seemed to rejuvenate the rickety old coal road. Two new Baldwin 2-8-0s and a switcher came to the property, joined by three hand-me-downs from the Port Townsend Southern and the Seattle & Northern, and a new fleet of coal cars was constructed as fast as the King Street shops could turn them out.

Three of the old narrow gauge locomotives and several cars were purchased by the new White Pass & Yukon Rail-

road and shipped north in the summer of 1898. Two of these engines have been preserved: No. 3 at Whitehorse (displayed as White Pass & Yukon No. 52), and 2-8-0 No. 8, at Dawson City.

Between 1901 and 1910, five additional standard gauge 2-8-0s, a 4-4-0 passenger engine, and an 0-6-0 switcher were placed in service, for a fleet ultimately totaling eleven locomotives.

The Columbia & Puget Sound fought valiantly through the storms of change. The Newcastle coal fields declined into oblivion, its dwindling product losing ground to more plentiful and easily extracted British Columbia and California coal. In 1910, Newcastle shut down, to be supplanted by digs at Coal Creek, two miles east. The Columbia & Puget Sound was renamed the Pacific Coast Railroad in 1916, and, in spite of the general

DUAL-HEADLIGHTED PORT TOWNSEND SOUTHERN NO. 6 WAITS AT AN UNIDENTIFIED STATION, POSSIBLY OLYMPIA, JUST BEFORE CONVERSION OF THE OLYMPIA DIVISION—FORMERLY THE OLYMPIA & CHEHALIS VALLEY ROAD— TO STANDARD GAUGE IN 1890.

Jefferson County Historical Society

decline in U.S. coal consumption, persevered, as if the spirit of James M. Colman himself were watching over it. The Coal Creek mine closed in 1929, the branch from Renton was abandoned in 1933 and pulled up four years later, but the Black Diamond mines kept the Pacific Coast Railroad afloat until well after the Second World War. In 1951—sixty years after Jim Hill refused to rescue it—the descendent of the Seattle & Walla Walla was bought by the Great Northern, which continued to operate the Pacific Coast as an independent entity until ultimate absorption within Burlington Northern in March 1970.

Direct competition to the Columbia & Puget Sound loomed on March 23, 1899, with the formation of the Seattle & San Francisco Railway & Navigation Company. Late in the 1890s, Seattle lawyer John Leary went after eastern capital to build a railroad from the city to his coal holdings near Black Diamond. He attracted the interest of William E. Guerin, a Philadelphia investor, and the Seattle & San Francisco was launched.

Rosy predictions were made for the line's future—followed by rumors of financial embarrassment and secret deals with the Northern Pacific. Leary vowed he would build his own road, only to be contradicted by Guerin and Northern Pacific president Mellen, who announced that the NP and S&SF would split the cost of building a cut-off from Palmer Junction to Auburn, and share running rights into Black River Junction. The Seattle & San Francisco got a right of way franchise on Railroad Avenue and Colorado Street in May 1900, and in October bought out the old Seattle Terminal Railway & Elevator Company.

Seattle Terminal had hoped to make Seattle a grain port. Thanks, however, to the city's limited facilities and the panic of '93, Seattle lagged far behind Tacoma and Portland in wheat shipment. In 1895, the STR&E went bankrupt and was reorganized as Seattle Warehouse & Terminal. Not until well after the turn-of-the-century would Seattle become an important grain port. Both the trestle across the bay and the West Seattle elevator passed to the Seattle & San Francisco, along with exclusive access to the new businesses on the tideflats—most notably Moran Iron & Shipbuilding Co. and the Centennial Flour Mill Co.

In November 1900, however, the Seattle & San Francisco was itself in default of its bond interest payments and under suit by stockholders who, in a dreary reprise of the Seattle Lake Shore & Eastern melodrama, complained of irregularities between the railroad and its allied Green River Construction Company. By October 1903, the Northern Pacific had absorbed the Seattle & San Francisco and all its assets.[10]

Other schemes fluttered about—and sputtered out. As early as 1883, efforts were made to build a railroad from Seattle to the Pacific, starting in September with the Seattle Puget Sound & Grays Harbor. It was hoped this road would open the Chehalis Valley and the prime farm and timber land to the west.

"A number of New York capitalists" had reportedly signed on, and local spearhead Frank Osborn appealed to Seattleites: "I have put what little means I own into it, and surely you who are now interested in it as a local institution will not fail to help us."[11] Fail, they did, as did the Seattle Puget Sound & Grays Harbor.

Duplicating the Northern Pacific between Seattle and Portland seemed to be a special obsession, beginning with the stillborn Portland Seattle & Northern of November 1889, and the Union Pacific's abortive Portland & Puget Sound of 1890-1892. One of the region's more colorful railroad schemers, Tacoma promoter Frank C. Ross, built his little Tacoma & Lake City from Union Avenue to American Lake in 1889, in hopes of fobbing it off on a major system. The Union Pacific obliged him and bought the ten-mile line, and Ross then tried to interest both the UP and NP in a road from Tacoma to Port Townsend through Gig Harbor and Bremerton. Both big companies went broke in 1893, but Ross would not give up, and he went to work grading a right of way through the Puyallup Indian Reservation, an activity not strictly within the bounds of the law.

When the Northern Pacific first arrived on Commencement Bay in 1873, it took up government tideland west of the Puyallup reservation, which occupied the greater portion of the tideflats, without infringing on tribal land. Building its branch line to the Wilkeson coal mines three years later was another matter, and the railroad was obliged to pay the tribe $848.55 for damages (later raised to $2,000 per acre) and provide a depot.

Ross appeared on the scene, promised the Puyallups that his new railroad would bring them prosperity, and, without obtaining the necessary congressional approval, put the Indians to work as laborers so as to be able to demonstrate that it was a Puyallup undertaking. Indian agent Rev. Myron Eells objected to this tactic and called on the government for help, which arrived in the form of the U.S. Army. A bloodless skirmish ensued, during which Ross acquired the title of "Colonel," but he lost his right of way in federal court.

Stymied in one direction, the indefatigable Ross persuaded the state legislature to give him a right of way franchise along Puget Sound from Seattle to Tacoma in September 1897, and he threatened to bypass Tacoma with a new Portland railroad if he did not get free right of way through town. Ross got his way, then dropped from sight. Years later, he surfaced and tried to revive his Tacoma-Port Townsend scheme. The colonel announced that he had lined up the money to begin construction, and that was the end of that.[12]

Seattle-Portland schemes multiplied in the 1890s. Two New Yorkers, Henry Braker, head of the East India Chemical Works, and attorney Austin Fletcher, thought they would give it a try, and in March 1898 incorporated the Seattle & Pacific Coast Railway to run from Portland through Seattle to the Canadian border.

SEATTLE & NORTHERN ENGINE NO. 2 AND COLUMBIA & PUGET SOUND CABOOSE NO. 815 AT BURLINGTON IN THE 1890s. NO. 2 WAS BUILT BY THE ROME LOCOMOTIVE WORKS IN 1890; BECAME SEATTLE & MONTANA NO. 139, THEN GREAT NORTHERN NO. 139 IN 1907.

Warren W. Wing collection

The *Post-Intelligencer* was suitably intrigued: "It has, or appears to have, back of it the great railroad interests of the Vanderbilts, and is in supposed furtherance of their purpose to control the ownership and operation of a continuous line of railroad from New York to Puget Sound."

Thoroughly jaded by railroad flummery, the Seattle *Times* dismissed the whole story as "another of the PI's Jim Jam fakes . . . somebody wants a valuable franchise from the city council and the grand and glittering spectacle of a Vanderbilt-Union Pacific-Canadian Pacific Railroad centering in Seattle is intended to temporarily blind the people while the steal is being worked through the city council."

Braker and Fletcher assured the council that they were in earnest, that non-Vanderbilt eastern capital was behind them, and that they intended to prosecute their line immediately. They got their right of way, and disappeared.

The Braker deal was resuscitated in February 1899 by two "New York millionaires," William G. Tiffany and former Seattle realtor William Llewellyn, who, like their predecessors, were earnest in their assurances of "no fettering alliances" with the Vanderbilts or anyone else, and promised that the Vancouver-Seattle-Portland line would be built by Mr. Tiffany and his "syndicate of friends." Tiffany paid a call on Seattle, pronounced it to have a wonderful future, shook hands with the city council, and was never seen in town again.[13]

Other, more fanciful schemes bubbled and broke: The Seattle Sydney & Grays Harbor of May 1893, aiming to operate a line of ferries and trains from Seattle to the Pacific by way of Hood Canal; the Midland Pacific, of 1894, to tap the Wyoming coal fields on the way from Sioux Falls, South Dakota, to Seattle; the Denver Yellowstone & Pacific Railroad, of 1905; the Denver Laramie & Northwestern, of 1907; the Willapa Harbor & Coast Railroad, of October 1910, to run from Portland to Tacoma by way of South Bend; the Seattle Boise & Salt Lake Railroad; the Puget Sound Southern; the Washington Southern; the Washington & Northern; the Seattle & Southeastern; the Seattle & Northeastern!

Paper railroads, all.

Still they came, railroad visions tiny and titanic: James Shute's twelve and one half inch gauge miniature railroad linking the Seattle suburbs of Leschi and Madrona; and M. de Lobel's world-girdling Transalaska Siberian Railway, via Paris, Moscow, the Bering Strait, Seattle, and New York. Both amused; neither ran.[14]

Perhaps the oddest of all Seattle railroad schemes saw the light of day in September 1891, when D.N. Baxter, Herman Chapin, Josiah Collins, and Frank H. Osgood formed the Seattle & Tacoma Air Line Railway Company. The Air Line (so-called for its direct route) would be built on the model of the "Boynton Bicycle" system, of which Osgood, a prominent Seattle street railway developer, was a vice president. The Boynton Bicycle, prototype of which was then in operation at Coney Island, embodied steam locomotives and coaches riding on centered, in-line wheels upon a single rail, stabilized by an overhead guide beam. The object of this contrivance was to reduce friction and fuel consumption while increasing speed. A line was surveyed along the highlands between South Seattle, Des Moines, Milton, and Tacoma, and Osgood claimed:

"We can make the trip from Seattle to Tacoma, a little over thirty miles, in little over twenty minutes . . . We can make better time and lower rates than any other road, the system being so economical that we can run a locomotive all day on half a ton of coal. We shall carry not only through freight and passengers, but also do considerable local business, as our line will run through a section which is more thickly settled than we expected."

Glowing prognosis to the contrary, the Air Line remained just that.[15]

Magnet for failed railroads though it was, Seattle could nevertheless boast by the turn of the century: "Through railroad trains to the Pacific coast is the object aimed at, and through trains to Seattle the ambition of every connecting or trunk line this side of the Missouri River. . . There is not a railroad connecting line east of St. Paul that is not straining every nerve to perfect a traffic arrangement with the Great Northern, Northern Pacific, or even the Central Pacific, to run at least one through car to Seattle."

Steel fingers reached toward the city and none aroused more controversy than the mysterious enterprise headed by Robert E. Strahorn. A former Union Pacific publicity agent and Spokane real estate developer, Strahorn incorporated the North Coast Railway Company on September 28, 1905, to bridge Spokane, Walla Walla, and Seattle. Mystery surrounded the Strahorn road from the outset, and observers were quick to perceive the Union Pacific/Southern Pacific "Harriman system," or the Missouri Pacific/Denver & Rio Grande "Gould system," or some other giant lurking furtively in the background.[16]

Happy to play along, Strahorn affected a Sphinx-like silence, which only added to the desired impression that his enterprise commanded great resources. The press reported several surveying parties ranging from Wallula to Yakima and up the Tieton River and over White Pass to both a connection with the Tacoma Eastern at Ashford, and a Cowlitz River outlet at Toledo. The main line would run over White Pass to Yakima, thence over the Rattlesnake Mountains into the Columbia Basin north of Pasco and on to Spokane. Branches would strike south to Walla Walla and Tekoa.

Strahorn applied for a Seattle right of way in December, only to be confronted by a wary city council which demanded to know who was behind him.

North Coast attorney James Kerr informed the gentlemen: "The North Coast Railway is to be the Pacific Division of a transcontinental line that intends to make Seattle its terminus."

Which line?

"I am not in a position now to give the name," Kerr rejoined; "we will build here if we are admitted. If not, we will go elsewhere." A poker-faced Strahorn sat silently in the corner.[17]

Ten days later, Kerr announced that the North Coast had obtained $25,000,000 in cash with which to begin con-struction, that the line had been definitely located from Walla Walla to Seattle, that a pass had been chosen, and that options had been taken on terminal grounds in Tacoma and Seattle. Insisting that it would be "suicidal" to disclose the identity of the North Coast's backer, he stiffened his veiled threats:

"There seems to be a disposition on the part of the city council and citizens, to compel the North Coast Railway to disclose its transcontinental connections before any action is taken on the franchise . . . But if the company is unable to secure a franchise from this city that gives it an equal chance with competing lines, I do not hesitate to say that the plans may be changed and Tacoma made the terminus."

Coyly letting slip that "either the Gould or the Vanderbilt system" backed the North Coast, Kerr promised that the "eastern representatives" would soon make their appearance in Seattle. Should the council see fit to grant an immediate franchise, trains would be running within two and a half years.[18]

Others told a different story. An engineer for the North Yakima & Valley, a Northern Pacific-controlled short line that had been contending with the North Coast for right of way through Union Gap and into Tieton Canyon, dismissed all claims of a surveyed line and big backing as balderdash: "Despite the claims that it is to have transcontinental connections, the North Coast Railway has not operated in such a way as to give credence to this statement."

There were no big surveying parties, and no surveys, he asserted—only a handful of Yakima men making a poor attempt to disguise the fact that they were building not a through railroad but a streetcar line. It did not take a genius to see through the hokum.

"The statement has been made that these small and poorly-equipped parties have made a definite location of line from Walla Walla to Seattle in three months," continued the NY&V man, "that under ordinary circumstances, would occupy four railroad parties an entire season from spring to fall."[19]

In February 1906, Strahorn spoke: "The project will stand on its own bottom. It is backed by powerful interests, but

MYSTERY MAN, NORTH COAST RAILROAD PROMOTER ROBERT STRAHORN. AS A JOURNALIST IN THE 1870S, STRAHORN PARTICIPATED IN THE PLAINS INDIAN WARS, AND LATER TURNED TO RAILROAD PUBLICITY AND PROMOTION.
Oregon Historical Society, #CN104468

Seattle train times, February 1910.

must be considered as an independent, local traffic proposition." Grading would commence within ninety days.

A show of work was made in the Yakima Valley that summer, but things soon petered out. Strahorn had a ready excuse:

"The real and only reason for our not building our road is that we have been hindered and delayed in every conceivable way by the Northern Pacific. That corporation has a transportation monopoly in the Yakima country, and proposes to keep it!"[20]

Strahorn's "powerful interests" ultimately turned out to be the Union Pacific. Chairman Edward H. Harriman had in the early years of the century become engaged in a bitter battle with James J. Hill for territory in eastern Washington and Oregon, and he perceived in Strahorn's road a handy and covert means of outflanking Hill in the Columbia Basin. Harriman's instincts told him that Hill might suffer lightly the presence of a small-timer like Strahorn in his territory, but would doubtless tender Harriman a rather different reception. The Union Pacific bought the North Coast Railway in February 1906 for $100,000, and reincorporated it as the North Coast Railroad. Strahorn was sworn to secrecy and stayed on as president and general manager, keeping up the smoke screen to distract the press from the truth. With Harriman behind him, Strahorn surveyed and completed fifty miles of track between Benton City and Yakima during 1906-1909, alternately hinting at and denying big backing and insisting he would push through to the Sound on his own. Secrecy remained air-tight, credit to the wiles of both Strahorn and Harriman.

"I consider that Mr. Strahorn has done something no other railroad man on earth has been able to accomplish, that is to let no one know who is back of him!" exclaimed Francis Clarke, president of Hill's newly completed Spokane Portland & Seattle in December 1908.

The publicity-minded Strahorn only heightened the intrigue when he declared that most of the shares of his company were actually held by his stenographer.[21]

Harriman had no intention of building a costly and re-

dundant line over the Cascade Range, but the fiction was maintained that the North Coast would.

"The North Coast is coming to Seattle," Strahorn told reporters in the fall of 1909. "We intend to make a terminal in this city, for the business is here!"

Relishing his role of "railway Sphinx," Strahorn laughed: "While the North Coast may seem a mystery to many persons, it need not worry them, for we are building a line in this state to get business, and are tapping the districts that furnish tonnage. Every road here is doing the same thing."

Strahorn promised a web of eastern Washington branch lines, main lines up both sides of the Columbia, and easier grades and lower operating costs than Jim Hill himself enjoyed. Electric operation of the railroad was considered, along with a vast grid of North Coast power stations, transmission lines, dams, and irrigation systems covering central Washington.

As late as fall 1910, Strahorn played out his part: "We will bring the North Coast to Puget Sound in a year and a half, and I do not see why Tacoma should not be one of its terminals."

But he never showed up, and the "road of mystery" succeeded only in laying a few miles of track down the Yakima Valley, and laying the way for Union Pacific entrance into Yakima and Spokane. The mystery ended on November 24, when it was revealed that the North Coast Railroad had been absorbed into the Spokane District of the Oregon-Washington Railroad & Navigation Co., a Union Pacific subsidiary. Robert Strahorn was appointed vice-president of the new district, his days of notoriety over.[22]

One "Seattle" railroad actually did become a reality, and enjoyed a profitable existence, while never coming closer than 170 miles from the city limits. This was the Portland & Seattle, built jointly by the Northern Pacific and Great Northern between Vancouver and Pasco in 1905-1908. From its inception, the Northern Pacific had planned to build down the Columbia, and in 1887, after years of frustration, the directors considered a new bond issue for construction along the north bank. Only eighteen years later, though, did the NP finally move. Menaced in the

Columbia Basin by the Union Pacific, Jim Hill began laying rail between Vancouver and Pasco, to contain E.H. Harriman and get his own line into Portland.

"[B]efore we stop, the Portland & Seattle will have a direct line from Elliott Bay to the Willamette River," promised President C.M. Levey.

As if to make good his word, the Portland & Seattle bought the old, aborted Portland & Puget Sound right of way from NP subsidiary, the Northwestern Improvement Company, and began new grading work at Chehalis in June 1906.[23]

The panic of 1907 stalled forever the Portland & Seattle's northward move, if indeed it was ever anything more than an anti-Harriman feint—certainly Hill was not in the business of building patently redundant line. Upon completion to Pasco in March 1908, the Portland & Seattle was renamed the Spokane Portland & Seattle, and the following February it reached Spokane. The superbly engineered "North Bank Road" provided much needed relief to the congested NP and GN mainlines, and with its gentle curves and almost non-existent grades became popular with travelers.

The last railroad to enter Seattle was, after a fashion, the Western Pacific. An 800-mile Salt Lake City-Oakland road, WP was, in 1910, the last to reach the Pacific, bringing to a close the age of transcontinental railroad-building. Seattle became a Western Pacific terminus in November, under interchange arrangements between the Gould system (Western Pacific/Missouri Pacific/Denver & Rio Grande) and the Pacific Coast Steamship Company. Passengers bound for Puget Sound via the Gould system's circuitous but scenic route could make a convenient ferry transfer between the Western Pacific terminal pier in Oakland and the steamer dock in San Francisco.[24]

By the first decade of the 20th century, virtually all of the major U.S. lines maintained agencies in the Queen City. Said the *Post-Intelligencer* on October 4, 1906:

"'All roads lead to Rome' once was said. It begins to appear now as if it might be said with truth: All railroads lead to Seattle." ∎

COLUMBIA & PUGET SOUND ENGINE ROSTER; STANDARD GAUGE.

No.	Type	Builder	Dates/notes
1	4-4-0	Norris	1866—Ex-Seattle & Northern, acquired 1897.
4	4-6-0	Baldwin	10/1890—Ex-Port Townsend Southern No. 4, acquired 1897. Sold to Copper River & Northwestern, 1906.
5	4-4-0	New York	7/1890—Ex-Port Townsend Southern No. 5. Scrapped 3/1943.
7	2-8-0	Baldwin	7/1897—Sold to McKenna Lumber Co., 1916.
8	2-8-0	Baldwin	7/1897—Scrapped 1938.
9	4-4-0	New York	7/1890—Ex-Port Townsend Southern No. 2. Scrapped 1910.
10	0-6-0	Baldwin	9/1897—Sold to Port of Seattle, 1941. To U.S. Army No. 4032, 1942.
11	2-8-0	Baldwin	7/1901—Scrapped 1938.
12	2-8-0	Baldwin	8/1903—Scrapped 1950.
14	2-8-0	Alco-Rhode Is.	2/1907—Scrapped 1951.
15	2-8-0	Alco-Rhode Is.	2/1907—Scrapped 1953.
16	2-8-0	Alco-Brooks	7/1910—Scrapped 1953.
17	0-6-0	Alco-Brooks	7/1910—Scrapped 1951.
18	4-4-0	Alco-Brooks	7/1910—Scrapped 1939.

CHAPTER 13

The Wonderful Interurban

"As the population of this section increases, there will be no distinguishing mark of where one town ends and the other begins." —Seattle *Post-Intelligencer*

With the perfection of the electric trolley by Frank Sprague in 1887, the street railway craze swept the nation. Seattle was not immune from trolley fever, and by 1889, men such as Thomas Burke, Jacob Furth, and Frank Osgood were busily creating a web of urban lines. A multitude of schemes to run the swift and smokeless cars beyond the city limits was quick to appear.

Fred Sander, a Seattle real estate and street railroad promoter, was first off the mark. In the fall of 1892, he began testing the waters for an electric line between Seattle and Kent (quickly changed to Tacoma). Before a gathering of White River Valley farmers in Kent, he promised that construction would begin just as soon as men and money could do it; the only catch was, men and money—$100,000, for starters—would have to be provided locally. Feet shifted.

Then Judge Orange Jacobs rose and assured the audience that Mr. Sander meant business. John Hancocks were signed, surveys begun, and the region's first interurban was born. Too many held back, however, and the panic of '93 finished off this pioneer interurban scheme.[1]

The interurban movement emerged slowly from the depression, gathered speed, and, by the end of the decade, no fewer than four Seattle-Tacoma electric railway propositions were being floated by Henry Bucey, John Collins, Malcolm MacDougal, and Fred Sander. Collins made the weightiest offer of eastern capital and in February 1899 won franchises from Seattle and Tacoma.

The Seattle land developer began planning a line using overhead rail instead of wire for power, with trains of elegantly equipped, vestibuled cars on hourly schedules, at a maximum fare of $1, as well as night freights. The line would not run down the White River Valley, but along the ridge above Puget Sound. The press predicted the interurban would be a "veritable bonanza."[2]

John Collins' electric road was formally incorporated on March 6 as the Seattle & Tacoma Electric Railroad Company. Squabbling among the partners led to reincorporation on April 11 as the Seattle & Tacoma Railway Co. A route was surveyed and in February 1900, work began at both ends of the system—a trestle across the Seattle tideflats, and track on Tacoma's Pacific Avenue. Partner Henry Bucey announced that rolling stock was on order and by August would be whizzing between the cities at sixty miles an hour.

At this point, the financial floor collapsed under Bucey and Collins, and they sold their assets and franchises to Boston's Stone & Webster Company, a nationwide operator of street railway and utility corporations. Stone & Webster was already firmly established in the area as owner of the Seattle Electric Company, the city's dominant traction and power concern. Jacob Furth, president of the Puget Sound National Bank and Seattle Electric, took over the development and management of the Collins line. Right of way was relocated from the ridges down to the floor of the White River Valley, and things moved ahead swiftly.[3]

The crew of a Puget Sound Electric poses at Renton Junction (now Tukwila).

University of Washington, Special Collections, PSE#512

Having invested three years of time and money in his own interurban study, Fred Sander was not content to take all this lying down. On January 17, 1901, he organized the Seattle & Tacoma Short Line Railway, to virtually duplicate Stone & Webster's line. Sander wired from New York the following month that he had a million dollars of eastern capital lined up and ready to go: "The very name 'Seattle' appeared to magnetize money men in the East, and all are looking this way for investments!"

Rolling stock was coming, Sander promised; his cars would be zinging down the valley in six months: "If men and money can do it."[4]

In the end, however, Furth, and Stone & Webster, emerged victorious. The right of way quickly took shape during the summer of 1901, and power poles were dropped beside the line as fast as loggers could supply them, followed by rail and spools of copper trolley wire. A third rail would carry the current in the open country, reverting to overhead wire only in populated areas and at grade crossings. The public was assured that touching the third rail would induce nothing more than a mild shock, but occasional hapless souls discovered otherwise. For right of way across the Puyallup Indian Reservation, the interurban paid the tribe over $7,000.

On the eve of the Seattle & Tacoma's opening, the press anticipated an exodus to the suburbs in the wake of the fast and frequent new service: "Enthusiastic friends of the interurban trolley declare that the White River Valley will within a few years become the home of thousands of city toilers, who will own small country places along the electric road. Even now, the influence of the road is being felt in an increasing demand for small farms, which has resulted in the subdivision of many of the smaller dairy and hop ranches along the river."

Along with improved transportation, the interurban carried on its transmission lines electricity to homes and farms that previously had had none, pioneering rural electrification.[5]

The swift and stylish cars of the Seattle & Tacoma Railway began running on August 26, 1902. A branch to Renton opened in September, and another to Puyallup was added in 1908. Business surpassed all expectations, and the anticipated development of the White River Valley took off.

"Though the Interurban line has been open for business but a short time," observed the *Post-Intelligencer*, "it fitted so nicely into the needs of the two cities that the people of Seattle and Tacoma have come to look upon it as a matter of course, and to wonder how they managed to get along without it for so many years . . . The day the first car was run, the people of [the] towns were lifted from the country right into the suburbs. . . and as the population of this section increases, there will be no distinguishing mark of where one town ends and the other begins."[6]

In February 1903, the company merged with Stone & Webster's Tacoma Railway & Power Co. and was reorganized as the Puget Sound Electric Railway Co.

Outfoxed to the south, Fred Sander turned his ambitions northward. He organized the Everett & Interurban Railway Company in May 1900, enlisted eastern capital in the form of Chicago steel millionaire James MacMurray, and in December 1902 reshaped the company as the Seattle-Everett Interurban Railway. The venture met with immediate opposition from Everett merchants, who feared loss of trade to Seattle, but, by the fall of 1906, Sander was running hourly cars over the twelve miles between Ballard and Hall's Lake.

Giant Stone & Webster was not to be denied its vision of a West Coast interurban empire, however. In June 1907, the Boston traction firm acquired the Everett Electric Co. and formed the Puget Sound International Railway & Power Company to link Everett and Vancouver, B.C. Fred Sander's interurban was gobbled up in November 1908, and reincorporated as the Seattle-Everett Traction Company. Track was quickly extended to Everett, the last spike was driven on February 23, 1910, wire went up, and on May 2

regular service commenced. The Seattle-Everett inter-urban quickly became a major artery of King and Snohomish county development.[7]

Another Seattle-Everett interurban scheme materialized in early 1904, to run via Issaquah, Fall City, Cherry Valley, Monroe, and Snohomish—the Snohomish & Cherry Valley and the Seattle Renton & Tolt electric railroads. These companies were combined in September as the Seattle Everett & Skagit Electric Railway Co., backed by a consortium known as the "Silver Lake syndicate." Despite the involvement of weighty names and the placement of bonds with London and New York firms, nothing came of the "Silver Lake road."

JANUARY 1904.

NOVEMBER 1910.

Seattle real estate leader James A. Moore tried his hand at the traction game, incorporating the Seattle & Vancouver Electric Railway in February 1904. This was followed in April 1908 by the Seattle Snohomish & Everett Railway, whose primary aim was to promote real estate development in north Seattle, Bothell, and Snohomish. The Seattle & Eastern, formed in 1911, had high hopes of linking Medina, on the east side of Lake Washington, with Factoria and Lake Sammamish, and of carrying heavy traffic from the dormant coal mine at Issaquah (formerly Gilman), which German entrepreneurs aimed to re-open. None of these propositions panned out.[8]

It was inevitable that someone would try to link Seattle and Portland by interurban. In June 1906, the Seattle & Portland Railway was formed by interests supposedly allied with James J. Hill, and by the following year surveys had been made roughly along the line of the old Portland & Puget Sound grade, only to go up in smoke.

The Seattle & Tacoma Short Line name was revived in October 1907, along with John Collins' old route through the south King County highlands, by a syndicate that based its prospectus on New York subway statistics proving that "an increase of traveling facilities developed more than a corresponding amount of new business."[9] Contracts were let in the spring, assurances were mouthed that construction would be rushed, and the second incarnation of the Seattle & Tacoma Short Line evaporated.

Those interurban lines that actually did run all but supplanted the steam railroads as the wonder of the age, and served as a potent agency of development.

"The improvement in social conditions in the villages, towns, and in the adjacent farming country along the lines of the interurban roads has been remarkable," noted the *Post-Intelligencer*.

"Commercial opportunities which have hitherto lain dormant have become possible . . . New markets have been created, and the reciprocal relations between city, town, and country have taken on new features."[10] ∎

Parlor car patrons take the air as a Seattle-Tacoma Interurban
train awaits departure on Tacoma's Pacific Avenue.

Mendenhall collection

CHAPTER 14

RAILROAD MUDDLE

"Fight, fight, there is nothing but an everlasting fight all the time."
—Thomas Burke

B Y 1889, SEATTLE was outgrowing her pioneer clothes. The city's irregular street pattern had become a nuisance, and its commercial facilities were cramped and ramshackle. The railroad scene was especially noisome; freight and passengers were descending upon Seattle in record numbers, but terminal facilities had not been significantly expanded since the completion of the broad gauge strip in 1884. Mountains of goods piled up in the open air, passengers were dumped out in the rain at shack-like depots, and locomotives played Dodge 'em on tangled yard tracks. The creation of Railroad Avenue in 1887 as the city's railroad thoroughfare had done little to alleviate the chaos. On the contrary, it precipitated a decade of "railroad muddle."

The opening battle and prelude to the main event took place in December 1888, as the Puget Sound Shore and the Columbia & Puget Sound butted heads over room on the already cramped broad gauge strip. Anxious to upgrade its inadequate freight facilities, the Puget Sound Shore had contracted with the Seattle Transfer Company to build a big freight depot and stock yard on the strip. Thomas J. Milner, general manager for both the Puget Sound Shore and the Columbia & Puget Sound, decided the narrow gauge road deserved equal access, and began laying a third rail on the Puget Sound Shore track to accommodate the smaller trains.

The Shore line superintendent, J. C. Haines, mustered his forces and barricaded the right of way with ties and timbers, which narrow gauge heavies promptly heaved into the bay. Milner's gang then hauled in a small shack, set it down on the track, and hunted up a "tenant," one Captain Farnham, to occupy the house and hold Haines' men at bay with a shotgun.

The arrival of sheriff and writ quieted things for a time, but on May 3 the battle was again joined. Opposing armies of railroad laborers—estimated at over 400 men—pitched into each other with shovels, crowbars, and brickbats.

"Come on and have your throats cut!" yelled a narrow gauge man.

"Where do you bury your dead?" an opponent jeered back.

A large crowd gathered to offer encouragement, and railroad fisticuffs as a Seattle spectator sport was born. Trains halted at the city line, consignments mildewed in the rain, and an exasperated chamber of commerce begged the parties to settle their differences.[1]

Puget Sound Shore president Tyndale met with Oregon Improvement Company president Elijah Smith, but both refused to budge.

"The claim of the C&PS Railroad Co. to the ownership of all the tide flats of Elliott Bay has long since been exploded and laughed to scorn," Tyndale told reporters. "The real and obvious animus of all this high-handed violence is simply that Elijah Smith, John L. Howard, and the Oregon Improvement Co. do not intend to loosen their grip upon the traffic of Seattle, nor intend that the city shall have any terminal facilities other than those controlled by them."

CRINOLINES MEET COWCATCHERS. FOR YEARS, RAILROAD AVENUE WAS SEATTLE'S "GRAND RAILROAD HIGHWAY," SHARED BY THE GREAT NORTHERN, NORTHERN PACIFIC, AND SEATTLE LAKE SHORE & EASTERN (LATER THE SEATTLE & INTERNATIONAL). VIEWED FROM SOUTH OF YESLER WAY, A NORTHERN PACIFIC TRAIN DEPARTS FROM THE OLD UNION DEPOT ABOUT 1905. TO THE RIGHT, COAL CARS FOR THE SEATTLE STEAM CO. OCCUPY THE STUBBY REMNANT OF THE RAM'S HORN, ON AN ALIGNMENT STILL VISIBLE A CENTURY LATER.

University of Washington, Special Collections, #1675

The disputed property belonged without question to his line, Tyndale affirmed: "We claim title by first occupancy, by long, undisputed, and undisturbed possession, and on account of the money and labor expended on the property. I have been officially connected with the various Villard enterprises in one capacity or another for 11 years—I am one of the veteran barnacles and stand-bys of the system."[2]

"Mr. Tyndale is only one of a large class of people who object to being met with forcible resistance when they attempt to acquire other people's property by his methods," countered Oregon Improvement Co. general manager H.W. McNeill.

Tyndale was out of bounds, McNeill declared—"as a veteran barnacle, he knew, or should have known" better. The Columbia & Puget Sound, McNeill promised, fully intended to build new facilities of its own, and needed access to the strip accordingly.

Puget Sound Shore general manager Ira Nadeau dismissed McNeill's assertions as "all bosh"; the narrow gauge had failed for years to build a promised terminal at the foot of Pike Street, had opposed all other efforts to bring improvements to the city's miserable railroad situation, and now wanted a free ride at his company's expense. What use had a coal road for warehouses, anyway? The Puget Sound Shore was Seattle's real friend, Nadeau declared, and both were the victims of "constant depredations" by a greedy Columbia & Puget Sound. The courts held for the standard gauge, the coal road was kept at bay, and work on the new warehouses resumed.[3]

Overshadowing this and all other such waterfront disputes was the question of tidelands ownership. Seattle's 3,000 acres of tideflats were held in trust by the federal government until such time as the territory should attain statehood. This technicality had been consistently overlooked during the city's early years, and various devices had been employed by territorial and local governments to give something that was not theirs to give: the Oyster Act of 1867; granting of riparian rights; issuance of Valentine and McKee land scrip; and the Seattle & Walla Walla donation of 1873.

The Villard boom of 1880-1883 enticed a big wave of "jumpers" to challenge railroad pre-eminence on the tideflats; individuals and corporations alike drove pilings, planted oyster beds, anchored derelicts and crudely prefabricated buildings, and made sundry other "improvements" for the purpose of staking claims on "no man's land." Rivals exchanged gunfire and pulled each others' pilings in the dead of night. When the Oregon Improvement Company indicated in 1888 that it would not act against a new wharf built by Henry Yesler, a fresh spate of squatter squabbles flared. A shanty town sprouted on the Columbia & Puget Sound right of way at the foot of Pike Street and its inhabitants refused to budge. The issue would dominate the Seattle scene well into the '90s.[4]

Flames, not crowbars, made the next move. On June 6, 1889, the great Seattle fire erupted from an overturned glue pot. The titanic conflagration swept through the dense wooden blocks of the lower business and waterfront district, and in one afternoon leveled the entire southern portion of downtown and destroyed virtually all of the city's railroad complex. Chaos reigned only briefly, however, and the following day many businesses, "burned out but still on deck," hoisted tents at their accustomed stands. By the 10th, huge gangs were at work rebuilding the railroad yards, and civic leaders were quick to see in the disaster a golden opportunity to transform the rickety pioneer town into a modern city.

"No More Wood!" was the cry, as plans were made to rebuild for the ages in stone and marble. At a mass meeting held the day after the conflagration, a committee was formed to replat the city and systematize the street system. As far as the railroad mess was concerned, district court judge Cornelius Hanford offered a resolution to eliminate the old twisting Villard right of way along the waterfront as an eyesore and an impedance to the city's growth. By unanimous vote, Hanford's motion was adopted and the business of creating a new Seattle commenced.[5]

Mayor Robert Moran backed the resolution and suggested concentrating all of the railroads on an expanded Railroad Avenue. The thoroughfare was widened to 180 feet and plans were made to create new extensions: Railroad Avenue West, to cross Elliott Bay to West Seattle; South Street, running due south across the tideflats; and Railroad Avenue Y, connecting South Street with Railroad Avenue West. To abolish the Villard right of way, the city used as legal argument the fact that the franchise holders—Columbia & Puget Sound, and Puget Sound Shore—had never lived up to terms: Track had been laid only from King to Pike streets, had never been extended to the common point in the Cascades, or widened to standard gauge. Within days of the fire, city crews set to work raising the grade of Columbia Street eighteen inches, dumping dirt on the Villard right of way in the process.

For a time, all was quiet. Then the realization dawned on the managers of the Columbia & Puget Sound that, once moved to Railroad Avenue, their road would be barred from accessing its old customers by the Seattle Lake Shore & Eastern, which held rights to the inside track. The Lake Shore informed Oregon Improvement's McNeill that it would be happy to switch his cars into the loading docks—for $5 each.

McNeill threw his hat down and refused to budge.

Aggravating the predicament was the fact that, after the fire, waterfront property owners had received assurances from the city that the old track would be removed; with this understanding they had begun putting up buildings on the right of way. Down the road apiece, Henry Yesler stubbornly refused to deed his waterfront property to Railroad Avenue. That did it. The Columbia & Puget Sound notified all and sundry that it would reoccupy its franchise forthwith; anything in the way, buildings and streets included, would be torn down.

Suits and counter suits flew, and the press chuckled: "The disputed line is now so thoroughly covered with injunctions there is scarcely room left for a pile driver."[6]

James J. Hill's Great Northern clumped stolidly into town in March 1890, under the name of the Seattle & Montana, and asked for a right of way. Judge Burke portioned out sixty feet of Railroad Avenue, summoned his considerable powers of persuasion, and impressed upon the

city council the necessity for giving Hill this and everything else he asked for. Eager for a second major railroad, especially one that would call Seattle its terminus, the city granted the Seattle & Montana its sixty feet in short order. Then the Northern Pacific showed up.

By now thoroughly seasoned in the quirks and crochets of doing business with Seattle, doughty President Thomas Oakes confronted the city council. The NP was now a Seattle road, Oakes told the city leaders on March 25; it was prepared to give the city all it needed in the way of transportation facilities. But Seattle should not make the mistake of signing away the waterfront to Hill or anyone else not actually on the scene and transacting business, as the NP was. Railroad Avenue should be managed by the city, he continued, with free and equal access for all lines; it would be a grave error to give one line a virtual monopoly.

"If the city should ever have 100,000 of a population, you do not want to have half of Railroad Avenue shut up by one company," Oakes concluded.

IN ITS FINAL INCARNATION, THE OLD UNION DEPOT SPORTED A BROAD CANOPY.

Museum of History and Industry, #83.10.6939

Attorney James McNaught seconded his boss, and suggested rescinding all individual railroad franchises in favor of a municipally controlled terminal company. The Northern Pacific's arrival in his native city was "one of the happiest days of my life," the veteran railroad lawyer attested, and its well-earned rights must not be thrown "into the maw of a paper railway" (the Seattle & Montana) whose only substance was "gall and wind."[7]

Faced with the demands of rival railroad companies, the city council froze like a deer in headlights. It had promised sixty feet of Railroad Avenue to the Great Northern, and thirty feet to the Lake Shore. What to do with everybody else?

The councilmen threw up their hands, with Mr. Niesz uttering the rather startling declaration: "The council did not feel competent to originate an ordinance for the control of the avenue."

Most seemed to agree that a municipal terminal company was a good idea, and McNaught stated that the Northern Pacific was prepared to convey right of way at cost, even hold the city harmless against any ensuing litigation, if a terminal company were adopted and all roads received equal treatment. Jim Hill would have to give.[8]

Not if Thomas Burke could help it. Next day, the judge sternly lectured the city council on their moral obligation not to give in to the "wicked men"—Oakes and McNaught—who would ask the city's new benefactor to sacrifice its rights. Mr. Hill and the Great Northern were the city's true friends and it was only due to their "prompt and businesslike movement" that the NP and other roads had any interest in serving the city at all. Burke flatly rejected the idea of a municipally owned terminal company; it would be "entirely too expensive." He then conveniently produced a telegram from Great Northern vice-president William P. Clough: A locating party would arrive within a few days and work would begin at the earliest possible date.[9]

The Union Pacific, in the guise of the Portland & Puget Sound, was next to pile into Railroad Avenue's crowded bed. General counsel Zera Snow expressed dismay that the city would assign most of the remaining space to the Northern Pacific without first consulting his company, which had completed surveys from Portland to Seattle and was ready to begin work.

Burke assured him that there was plenty of room, thanks to Railroad Avenue's common user clause—a "liberal" provision that, in fact, stipulated payment of tolls to the Seattle Lake Shore & Eastern. The judge promised Snow that the UP would not be shut out by the Northern Pacific, and appealed to the city council to string along:

"When I prepared this franchise ordinance for the Seattle Lake Shore & Eastern, I drew that instrument with an eye to the future. All I own is in this city!"

He informed the council that Clough had been shocked to hear that Seattle would even consider reneging on her "solemn obligations" and give part of GN's franchise to the NP. Seattle must remember who its true friends were: "Mr. Hill is the best railroad man, and his road was the first to come here and treat the city in a frank and fair manner!"

Clough made it clear there would be no compromise on GN's sixty feet. "We won't be pigs," he wired Daniel Gilman. "Northern Pacific can arrange with us for trackage on an equable basis."

A more pointed message soon followed: "Of course the [city] council will not listen to any proposition revoking any of the space on Railroad Avenue granted to us should they do so we would throw up everything and stop where we are so far as Seattle is concerned."[10]

Burke shuddered; one 1873 was enough. Hill had made it very clear that his western terminus must have plenty of good, cheap land, water, drainage, a large harbor, and "live, energetic people"; Seattle had no monopoly on those. As Great Northern crews surveyed lines from Spokane to Bellingham Bay in the late spring 1890, Fairhaven, Sehome, and Whatcom gleefully proclaimed their harbor was the Great Northern terminus. The judge bit his lip, and assured Clough that the city would "stand by the Great Northern against all comers."[11] It helped that a majority of the chamber of commerce consisted of men—John Leary, banker E.O. Graves, Burke, and Gilman—who also served on the board of the Seattle & Montana.

The opposing forces turned out en masse on April 3. Lights in the city council chambers burned late, and battle lines were drawn: James McNaught, his law partner John H. Mitchell, and Ira A. Nadeau for the NP, allied with Andrew Burleigh and J.B. Metcalfe, for the Puget Sound Shore, and Henry W. McNeill and John C. Haines for the Oregon Improvement Company, arrayed against Thomas Burke and Daniel Gilman representing James J. Hill. Commodore James Smith appeared for the Seattle Lake Shore & Eastern, and Colonel Thomas Ewing stood for the Seattle & Southern, a local road with pretensions of building to Portland. The Union Pacific's men sat silently in a corner, and others, prominent and not so prominent, filled the room to capacity.

McNaught led off, repeating his assertion that only a terminal company with track open to all on equal terms would serve everyone's needs. The Great Northern and Northern Pacific shared such a scheme in St. Paul, and it worked very well. Yet Seattle was ready to hand its waterfront over to one man, James J. Hill:

Surely, "in good conscience you should give the old companies that have been here for years the same rights and facilities you give these companies that only promise to come here!" Burke was not the only one with deep ties to his community: "[I]t is my hope and expectation . . . to return to Seattle and remain here until I have my bones laid away upon the hills between the lakes, and . . . I hope I have heard for the last time that I have come here as an obstructionist or to do anything against the interests of Seattle."

The Great Northern was being unreasonable—"I know that Mr. Burke and Mr. Gilman know and believe that the position they assume is not for the best interests of the city. They assume this position because they were smart enough to get in here and get valuable rights which they now wish to maintain."[12]

Oregon Improvement's McNeill was next on his feet, declaring that his company was one of the largest taxpayers in Seattle and that much of those taxes were paid out on 4,000 feet of waterfront property adjoining Railroad Avenue. If the city would take any of its existing franchise away, it must offer something of equal value in return. This did not mean the isolated middle tracks of Railroad Avenue, which would cut the Columbia & Puget Sound off from its old customers and its own docks. He would gladly go along with McNaught's very reasonable terminal company proposition. But he would not give a foot of right of way to the Seattle & Montana.

Where the Northern Pacific was concerned, Thomas Burke was incapable of reason. "The very moment the Great Northern came in, the Northern Pacific came after like blackbirds after wheat," he blustered.

McNaught and Oakes knew perfectly well that Mr. Hill needed four tracks, the judge continued, and he scoffed at a terminal company as "the thing which now seems to be necessary to human existence!" Seattle's old nemesis was working its customary wiles:

"The Northern Pacific is determined to choke every road that comes to Seattle's aid! More than three officials of that company have openly announced that the Canadian Pacific would not be allowed to carry a pound of freight into Seattle . . . It is this enemy of years' standing that now asks you to take it in and is preaching the doctrine of confiscation that would cover the city with ignominy and shame!"

Certainly, Hill would never consent to be partners with the NP in any terminal company: "Sooner than do it, it would seek a terminus elsewhere. We want nothing to do with a company so wholly lost to decency and honor."

Again, Burke displayed a wire from Clough: Great Northern's needs in Seattle would be "greater than those of all others combined," and that it must therefore have four tracks. The road would share its sixty feet with all others on reasonable terms, but if the city intended to give in to its foes and reduce this franchise, "it will be well for us to know it in time to take such steps as the protection of our interests shall secure." The colonel's meaning could not have been plainer.[13]

Burke tried to convey to Jim Hill's right-hand man the Byzantine complexity of the Seattle situation. The "cloven hoof" of the Northern Pacific was behind it all, he wrote Clough, and "trying to provide a muddle and to confuse the situation in every way they can." Oakes had revealed his contempt for the Great Northern and had been complaining to the city council that the GN was "always scurrying around where it has no business to be"; he had charged that Burke and Hill were scheming to shut everyone else out of Seattle in order to line their own pockets. And then there was McNaught, throwing up a blind with the nebulous issue of a terminal company:

"This . . . seems to be a very attractive thing to a great many people," the judge noted wryly. "They do not know just what it is, nor what office it can perform . . . but the less they know about it the more virtue they think it has."

The judge hoped that Clough might pull a few strings and bring the Oregon Improvement Company into line; this would be advantageous if the GN wanted to cross the Columbia & Puget Sound right of way and gain access to the tideflats, where Hill envisioned future freight yards. Otherwise, Burke warned the colonel, "an ugly fight" lay ahead."

Burke tried to talk Clough out of four of GN's sixty feet. A small compromise "would have relieved the tension here very much, without any sensible diminution of your franchise." It would also rob the Northern Pacific of ammunition in its battle for the hearts and minds of the city. Seattle was certainly "willing to treat the Great Northern as a special favorite," Burke grumbled, but had the right to expect "more patriotic action" in return.

The answer was still No. But "patriotic action" manifested itself that summer, in the form of surveying crews and the first grading gangs.[14]

The opposition did its best to turn the council against Burke and Hill. Northern Pacific's John Mitchell accused the UP and GN of ganging up against his company with Burke's connivance, and OIC's tart-tongued McNeill had little patience for the judge's "sawed-off eloquence" and his ramrod tactics in accommodating the other roads at his company's expense:

"I like to see this," he chuckled wryly, "this council sitting here in the gravity of its great wisdom, while these two railroads, one with bare knuckles and the other with sixteen-pound gloves, are pounding away, dividing up what neither one owns. It has never occurred to any one of this tripartite combination, or to your honorable body, that they are dividing up the clothes that belong to ME!" He repeated his willingness to deed right of way through Oregon Improvement property for a terminal company, but not to another railroad.

The debate was taking its toll. "We have been called together here day after day and night after night for the past six weeks," huffed Councilman Hall, " to hear the attorney of one railroad company tell what we ought to do for his company and what we should not do for the other roads . . . We ought to prepare these franchises ourselves and see that the city's interests have some protection!"[15]

Burke succeeded in making peace only with the Union Pacific, talking them into sharing the remaining twenty-two feet of Railroad Avenue with the NP. In exchange for this concession, he would see to it that the UP got its desired terminal grounds on the southern tideflats. The Union Pacific drove a few pilings, then cut short its Puget Sound venture. The remaining contestants would provide a lively show for years to come.

Clouding the possibility of a settlement on Railroad Avenue was its shaky legal underpinnings. Any claim to tideland and harbor line property, which until statehood remained vested in the federal government, was of dubious validity. The judge was well aware of this and had hoped "to avoid raising the question." Like the Villard roads and the squatters, though, Burke trusted in the right of occupancy and the lethargy of the law, and hoped the bottle would not come uncorked.

Burke's law partner, Thomas Shepard, confided to Hill that the Railroad Avenue dedication "has always been more than doubtful, in the judgements of the courts and the bar here generally . . . the question has always been avoided by all concerned."[16]

With Washington's evolution to statehood on November 11, 1889, tidelands jurisdiction passed from Washington, D.C. to Olympia. On March 22, 1890, the state legislature passed a bill giving the state preeminent rights to determine harbor lines and sell or lease tidelands. A State Board of Harbor Line Commissioners was appointed and immediately got to work. On Elliott Bay, they set the harbor line well inland of existing pier ends and ran a corridor of public land smack down the middle of Railroad Avenue.

"Confiscation!" screamed Judge Burke. In his sixteen years at Seattle, he had seen enough of hard times. In his eyes, the mere threat of government interference with property would scare away investment capital and cripple the commerce of the city. The harbor lines commission must be stopped.

"From the beginning, their actions have been of a secret and Star Chamber character," he barked. "If there is any justice in the State of Washington, the City of Seattle cannot at this time be plundered and pillaged in this fashion."

Testimony on the proposed harbor legislation was heard in town meetings, and Burke was loud in his demands that the shore lines be drawn to exclude waterfront improvements; otherwise, he declared, the future commerce and very greatness of Seattle—indeed, the entire state!—would be forfeit.[17]

The harbor lines controversy was only part of a larger battle. Burke had had an alarming taste of things to come in July 1889, as statehood approached and various committees drew up proposed legislation for the new state constitution. These included a raft of new controls on corporations—restrictions on absentee ownership, prohibitions against state subsidies and grants, stiff new definitions of eminent domain, and the stipulation that railroads were common carriers and subject to state jurisdiction. A state railroad commission was also proposed.

The judge blanched in horror; the package, especially those sections concerning railroads, was, he declared, "utterly unfit to become a part of the fundamental law of the land." Development of the state's resources required large investments of outside capital, he wrote an associate;

these laws would scare this away, and turn the state into an economic wasteland.[18]

Burke fell to with a vengeance. Acting with various boards of trade, chambers of commerce, and of course railroad lobbyists, he succeeded in expunging or eviscerating much of the proposed legislation, including the provision for a state railroad commission.

And, in October 1890, Burke filed suit in Judge I.J. Lichtenburg's district court to overturn the "monstrous outrage" of the harbor lines commission. Plaintiffs included the Seattle Lake Shore & Eastern, Seattle Terminal Railway & Elevator Co., Stinson Mill, Henry Yesler, Schwabacher Brothers & Co., and, for Burke, some strange bedfellows—John C. Haines, representing the Oregon Improvement Company, and the Northern Pacific's James McNaught. One additional plaintiff was unseen but very much felt: James J. Hill. Lichtenburg was friendly to Burke and slapped an injunction on the commission. Its term was set to expire in 1893 and Burke planned to litigate it to the bitter end. With $20,000 in seed money from Hill, Burke acquired his own newspaper, the *Telegraph*, and dug in for the "ugly fight."[19]

Things were heating up, too, along the old Villard right of way, which, by the end of 1890, the press began calling the "ram's horn" for its twisting shape.

At Burke's prodding, the city filed suit to abolish the ram's horn and on December 22, city and franchise-holders squared off, again before Judge Lichtenberg. No one bargained for what ensued. Orange Jacobs, the aging barrister who had taken Seattle's anti-Northern Pacific grievances to Congress in 1878, represented the city as corporation counsel, and to the general dismay, he moved to dismiss the city's suit.

Jacobs' motion roused a storm of indignation.

"The city is most shamefully victimized," howled the *Post-Intelligencer*, citing "overwhelming public sentiment" against the ram's horn. Even more scandalous, Judge Jacobs was "not in the possession of his sober senses" when he handed down his decision! "It is hard to say it of an old man," the *PI* ventured, "but it is the truth and must be stated that Judge Jacobs was under the influence of liquor."

Jacobs stoutly defended his actions. The ram's horn franchise had never been lawfully cancelled after the fire, he asserted, and, in fact, Columbia Street was not even a legally-constituted public thoroughfare. Jacobs swore before the Almighty that he had not touched a drop for forty-eight hours prior to the hearing, and that only afterwards did he take "about a teaspoonful of gin."[20]

With the law on its side, the Columbia & Puget Sound wasted no time. On the evening of December 22, a large force of laborers assembled on the railroad crossing at West and Columbia, and proceeded to tear up the street. Railroad officials stood nearby, chuckling among themselves, and a crowd gathered.

At ten o'clock, police captain Henry Sheehan huffed up: "I want this work stopped!"

Railroad attorney J.C. Haines dared Sheehan to present a warrant or stand back.

Sheehan retorted: "You have no right to do railroad work inside the city between 7 o'clock at night and 6 o'clock in the morning!" With the growing crowd egging him on, the officer continued: "You must stop, or I shall arrest the lot of you. The mayor said for me to stop this work, and I'm going to stop it!"

"Now, now, Henry," piped up Haines. "You had better be darned right in what you are saying. After all, we have the corporation counsel's verdict. The city might have a big suit for damages on its hands, if you are not careful."

Red-faced, Sheehan stammered, "I'll see about this!" To jeering from the crowd, the police captain beat a retreat.

As the gandy dancers tore into their work, the railroad officials, friends, and lawmen adjourned to a nearby saloon. After consulting his superiors uptown, Captain Sheehan was compelled to allow the work to proceed.

A voice in the crowd hooted: "Was the corporation counsel sober, Henry?"

The case was promptly bumped up to the state supreme court, which held for the NP and the C&PS. The ram's horn would not go quietly.[21]

Thomas Burke remained ever-vigilant of any attempt to reapportion Railroad Avenue. In May 1891, the city council unwisely drafted an ordinance lopping thirty feet off the Seattle & Montana's franchise, and was promptly slapped down: "It is a damnable outrage," cried the judge, who knew where to place the real blame.

"The manner in which this measure has been carried through is characteristic of the Northern Pacific . . . I should like to know what they have done for Seattle, that we should be robbed for their benefit! They won't even give us the through train they said they were going to give us long ago, and many a passenger is carried to Tacoma because he won't get up at midnight to change cars at Puyallup. The Great Northern on the other hand is . . . pouring money into the city and state just when they most need it, and this is the return which is proposed for it!"[22]

Tut tut, remonstrated Alderman George Kittinger: "The time is past and the city has grown too large, to still keep in mind the action of the Northern Pacific heretofore. "Others on the council were coming to regret having rushed Hill's sixty-foot franchise through as hastily as they did.

Burke promptly swore out an injunction to keep the Northern Pacific off Railroad Avenue, and the council meekly backed down. The judge also made ample use of the *Telegraph* in ensuring that Seattle hewed to the Hill line.

"We jumped on them with both feet and raised a tremendous popular storm and the other papers feebly followed our lead," Burke crowed to an associate in the midst of yet another holding action against the NP. At the same time, he was compelled to remind Hill of his utility and seek continued financial assistance for his struggling paper. "It is but fair that other beneficiaries should help us bear the burden," Burke muttered to Gilman.[23]

Things were still not moving fast enough to suit Hill. By December, he was thoroughly fed up, and gave the screw another turn.

"We cannot do our terminal business with less than four tracks," he wrote Burke, "and the time will come when that will be insufficient, resulting in business going elsewhere . . . I am heartily tired of the fast and loose manner in which this matter has been treated."

Hill came to town the following February and submitted his own plan for solving the muddle. The Great Northern would sacrifice thirty feet on Railroad Avenue south of Yesler Avenue, in exchange for which the Northern Pacific would vacate the ram's horn and straighten out the bulging "bow" in its track between Yesler and the broad gauge strip, eliminating the multiple crossings that hindered the GN from reaching the terminal site it planned to develop on Jackson Street. Hill was confident he could come to terms with Oakes, and asked the city to be patient until rapprochement could be made.

Hill informed a banquet audience that he considered the interests of the Great Northern and the city irrevocably intertwined, and warned that the city must not constrain its future trade by lack of proper rail facilities: "The time may come . . . when you will be far more crowded than you think."[24]

Burke law partner Thomas Shepard advised Hill that favorable public opinion had been "pretty thoroughly aroused by your addresses here." Still, the Northern Pacific was doing all it could to thwart his good work, "bringing all possible business pressure to bear" in Seattle and Olympia. Northern Pacific and Great Northern lobbyists were scuttling through the capitol, buttonholing lawmakers, currying favor in the press, and working to appoint and defeat aldermen and delegates. Shepard had observed one other thing; the day of blunt threats was past: "It seems to do no good with this [Seattle] council to intimate that if they antagonize railroad interests the development of commercial interests will go elsewhere."

By March 1892, Shepard claimed "complete victory" over the NP. "Our fight for control of the House of

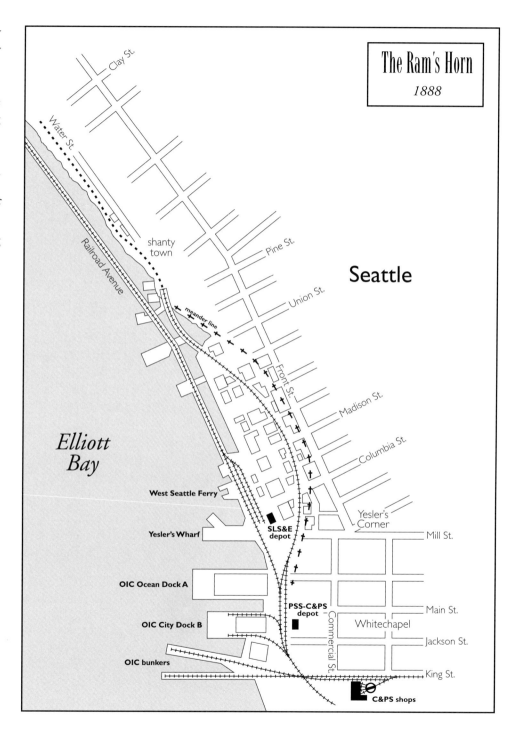

Delegates has cost us just $100," he informed Hill. "Every string available" had been pulled, and the attorney had "succeeded in getting public opinion worked up to quite a fever on the subject, even . . . the Post Intelligencer . . . whose proprietor, Mr. Hunt, as you know, is so dependent as to his Kirkland interests upon the friendly disposition of the Northern Pacific."

Burke's *Telegraph* had staunchly helped Hill's cause, as did certain "expense" payments to the local Democratic committee. The Northern Pacific forces, Shepard exulted, "have met their Waterloo."[25]

The Oregon Improvement Company was not so easily dealt with. As Burke pressed condemnation proceedings against the OIC to force an entry to GN's Jackson Street terminal grounds, Columbia & Puget Sound general manager Charles Smith accused him of throwing dust in the air to blind the public while stealing the city's birthright for Jim Hill:

"The judge's feelings are like paint on an actor's face—it can be put on or off with equal facility . . . The fact is, the judge has an old campaign speech he made against the Northern Pacific Railroad some years ago, which he occasionally brings out at council meetings . . . and he has revamped it now by inserting the name of the Oregon Improvement Company."

Oregon Improvement had stood by Seattle, said Smith, since "a time when to have faith in Seattle required money and endurance, not words and boasting." It had been the city's salvation, as all old Seattleites would testify. Oregon Improvement had run the Orphan Road at a loss and invested much in the city. Now here came the judge; was nothing safe from "the bottomless gulf of his desires"? Smith would be happy to go in on a terminal company, but only if Hill would do likewise.[26]

Burke cursed the "Oregon Obstruction Company," and another round of injunctions papered the waterfront.

Meanwhile, things on the ram's horn were seldom dull. The city and railroad squared off again early in the morning of May 14, 1892, when a Columbia & Puget Sound gang attempted to lay rail into West Street (later Western

Avenue). Mayor John T. Ronald hastened to the site, and ordered the work halted. The track-layers only laughed at him and kept working. A crowd assembled, the mayor sent for the police, and the railroad men blockaded Yesler Avenue with a locomotive and coach.

"Get your car out of here, or we'll take the track up on either side!" demanded Mayor Ronald.

"No, sir!" retorted Superintendent Bush.

"Alright, up goes your track!" rejoined the mayor.

Bush experienced a sudden change of heart, and did as ordered. Then another engine began backing a plug of boxcars toward the crowd. Planks were tossed under the wheels, derailing the rear car. A thoroughly annoyed mayor ordered the train moved and the track pulled up after it, and the police and numerous spectators pitched in gleefully to carry out the directive. Again the locomotive backed toward the crowd; engineer and fireman were carted off to jail, and dust settled over the ram's horn.[27]

If the ram's horn and Railroad Avenue were a nuisance, Seattle's squalid depots were an insult. The Northern Pacific's post-fire Weller Street station was little better than a frame shack, more appropriate to an eastern Washington cow town than the Queen City of Puget Sound, and stifling with cigar smoke and frequented by drunken ruffians.

Seattle's friend, James J. Hill, did no better with his miserly little digs next to the West Seattle ferry slip; for years, he was content to fend off criticism with homilies ("He is a wise farmer . . . ") and low freight rates. Then, early in 1893, a thick envelope from the Great Northern Railway Engineering Department arrived at Thomas Burke's law office. This contained plans for freight terminals on the flats south of Jackson Street, a truncated ram's horn, and a union depot on Railroad Avenue.

The city council was examining Hill's proposals with delight, when City Engineer R.H. Thomson rudely intervened.

Reginald Heber Thomson had come to Seattle from northern California in 1881, and went prospecting for coal with W.H. Whitworth. Three years later, he had become city surveyor and locating engineer for the Seattle

Lake Shore & Eastern. In 1892, Thomson was appointed city engineer, just in time to come face to face with James J. Hill.

Having thoroughly studied the Great Northern plans, he informed a stunned city council on May 18 that they spelled certain disaster. The resultant chaos of grade crossings and overhead bridges "would permanently retard the development of the most available portion of our city for manufacturing purposes." The mean tideflats street grade, or datum, proposed by GN was too low for proper drainage; and the proposed Jackson Street freight yard would throw a wall across the lower business district. Thomson condemned the kind of piecemeal, short-sighted development the railroads seemed to be imposing, by saying it would leave the city a legacy of "blight and cursing." He urged that a committee of experts—ex-Northern Pacific civil engineer Virgil Bogue, "Terminal" Johnson of Portland, and Andrew Rinker of Minneapolis—be appointed to consider the entire problem in depth before any action was taken.[28]

The city exploded. "The only surprise is that Engineer Thomson did not recommend C.B. Wright and T.F. Oakes while he was about it," griped one prominent citizen. Virgil Bogue? He was a "Tacoma man"! Hadn't he "steered the Northern Pacific over two ranges of hills, instead of down Green River, that Seattle might be left thirty-two miles on its side-track"?

Thomson's mailbox bulged with poison pen letters. Then he was rescued by an unlikely savior—Jim Hill. Hurrying west, Hill looked over his tideflat site with Thomson, and became more convinced than ever that the flats were the only place for Seattle's rail facilities, and equally, if grudgingly, was convinced that Thomson was right. They adjourned to Thomas Burke's office. "That Mr. Thomson is no damned fool," Hill informed the judge. He conceded Thomson's logic, and asked the city engineer why he had not offered suggestions as to what the Great Northern should do?[29]

"I did not think it was for me to advertise my view of the route which I think the city's position demands," Thomson

replied. "Had I done so, I would have been accused of trying to sell property." The response earned Hill's immediate and lasting respect.

What, then, did Thomson suggest? Move all but a few industry tracks off Railroad Avenue, for starters. Nothing should be allowed to obstruct movement to and from the tidelands, which one day would be filled and heavily developed.

Hill frowned: "And how can those things be avoided?"

"Easily enough," replied Thomson, "if you will cut a tunnel under the city reaching from a block or more north of Pike Street to the tideflats somewhere near south Third Street. This outlet is suggested on the theory that you will presently extend your line to Tacoma and to Portland. Your tracks will then be in a line to allow the city ample freedom in planning its streets north and south across the tidelands."

Hill brooded awhile, then faced Thomson. "I am under heavy bonds to purchase much property at a high price along Jackson and King streets if this franchise is granted any time soon," he declared. "If we can let the matter rest until I am released from the necessity of making payment on that property . . . and if I can adjust other property and railroad matters, I will do as nearly as possible just what you want. It will take considerable time, but when I can clear the air I will send my engineers to you."

Thomson and Burke smiled, and as Hill intoned, "We jointly form this agreement," the three shook hands on a compact to radically change the face of the city.[30]

A decade would elapse before the grand scheme could triumph over railroad rivalry, and the tidelands and harbor lines dilemma. In the meantime, Judge Lichtenburg upheld Hill's two ram's horn crossings in November 1892, and Hill quickly presented an updated tideflats union depot plan.

The city took its own ram's horn case to the state supreme court, arguing now that it was voided by the "nonexistence" of the Oregon & Transcontinental Co., which in 1890 had been reorganized by Henry Villard as the North American Company. The justices were unimpressed: They overturned Lichtenburg, denied GN's right to cross the ram's horn, and, as Burke had long feared, declared Rail-

REGINALD H. THOMSON, WHO FACED DOWN JIM HILL AND WON.
Author's collection.

road Avenue an illegal dedication. In their May 1893 ruling, the court asserted that it was "no part of the functions of cities to provide facilities for railroads."

"Fight, fight, there is nothing but an everlasting fight all the time," a disgusted Thomas Burke complained to his wife.[31]

Once more, the Northern Pacific and Oregon Improvement vowed to reoccupy the ram's horn. "We expect to commence laying track very soon," promised NP lawyer Andrew Burleigh. "We have been four years fighting to gain possession of this right of way, and we are not going to give it up for nothing."

The unsuspecting Burleigh then chose to go on vacation, however, and the city took advantage of his absence to run Post Street over the right of way.

The railroad lawyer was not amused: "On my return from a fishing trip, I was very much surprised to learn that some respectable Christian gentlemen in this community, together with the authorities, have so far forgotten their position and standing in the community as to get in in the night time . . . and undertake to confiscate $1,000,000 worth of property from these railroad companies."

Early in 1894, the ram's horn roads made their move. Crews began clearing the grade north of Pike Street, and General Manager Smith swore he would push his track through anything in his path, including the West Street Hotel and a business block owned by Seattle & Walla Walla benefactor James M. Colman. As another excited crowd gathered at West Street and Columbia, Smith's boys ran their rail up to the Colman Building and began tearing up the sidewalk, oblivious to the arm-flailing protestations of hotel proprietor William F. Butler.

"As the occupants of the building were making no preparation for moving, it became an interesting question as to how the line would be extended through the building," the press mused. The workers leaned a ladder against Colman's building in preparation for demolition, and hatchets were poised in mid-chop when a deputy hurried down with another restraining order.[32]

The ever-inventive Colman proposed scraping eight feet from Railroad Avenue along with whatever additional space the other property owners could afford, deeding it over to the contentious railroads, and being rid of the ram's horn once and for all. Again, the canny Scot's arguments carried the day, and a great sigh of relief came when, on April 17, 1894, a refinement of Colman's compromise was ratified as city ordinance 484. Like Banquo's ghost, however, the ram's horn was loath to completely dematerialize, and head-butting continued for another year over the Great Northern crossings at the Jackson Street "bow." At daybreak on February 6, 1895, Columbia & Puget Sound men ripped up GN's crossing frogs and several lengths of rail as spectators gathered at the disputed intersection in gleeful anticipation of fisticuffs. Hopes for yet another railroad slugfest were dashed by police reinforcements, and on March 5 the warring parties settled their differences, shook hands, and repaired to the theater, "the best of friends."[33]

As the railroads edged closer to a truce, the harbor line and tidelands controversy also approached resolution. The way had been considerably cleared when, on March 31, 1891, the state supreme court confirmed state ownership of all tidelands and navigable waterways. The old Seattle & Walla Walla dedication was nullified, and those parties who occupied or improved any tideland prior to March 1890 were given right of first refusal on their claims.

The court also upheld the harbor lines commission against Judge Lichtenburg's injunction. Thomas Burke immediately began a two-year delaying action in federal court, hoping to outlast that troublesome body. In this he was successful; the board's term expired in January 1893. When a second commission was convened in October of the following year, Burke saw to it that this board was comprised of men who were more sensitive to the needs of the community—and James J. Hill. Blithely declaring that the first commission's data was "missing," the second re-drew the harbor lines so as to minimize intrusions upon private property. To its credit, however, the second board took

R.H. Thomson's advice and appointed Virgil G. Bogue to draw up a tidelands master plan.[34]

A seasoned civil engineer, veteran builder of the Northern Pacific and Union Pacific, and discoverer of Stampede Pass, Bogue made a whirlwind tour of San Francisco, Chicago, Buffalo, Boston, Manhattan, Brooklyn, Philadelphia, and Baltimore to gather data. He coupled this with what he already knew of Venice and Glasgow, and in February 1895 submitted his plan. Bogue's handiwork was a milestone—an acknowledgment that comprehensive, government-sponsored, long-range city planning was now to be held on equal terms with town booming and haphazard growth.

"Unless all human history is at fault, unless the progress of the race is to cease," Bogue declared, "there will be a change, and when it comes it will bring a great extension of commerce . . . It is imperative, therefore, that any action taken under the law providing for improvements upon the harbor strip, or in the direction of construction of wharves, piers, etc. by the state, municipality, or by private parties, should conform to a wise, conservative, but nevertheless comprehensive plan which should be progressive in its features."

Bogue's vision for the 3,240 acres of Seattle tidelands embraced wide streets, spacious and uniform city blocks, and a series of interconnecting "railroad avenues" stretching from Ballard around West Point and along a proposed Puget Avenue, down the waterfront, onto the flats, and beyond to West Seattle.

Railroad Avenue was condemned as a "blot on the city and a menace to the lives of its citizens," and would be moved as far as possible from the water, to make room for wharves. The existing chaos of crossings and unresolved rights of way would be tidied up and confined to the middle ninety feet of the avenue, and the remainder of the thoroughfare (widened to 214 feet) would be dedicated to wagon and pedestrian traffic. Overhead bridges would speed traffic to and from the docks. On the southern tideflats, what eventually became Harbor Island was first mapped out along with east and west channels of the Duwamish River.

"Based upon the desire of the people of Seattle," Bogue called for a single terminal railroad to facilitate the interchange of cars among lines and ensure equal access, while avoiding congestion and duplication of facilities. A union passenger depot would be located on West Street between Columbia and Marion, and a 148-acre parcel south of King Street—roughly the same as the Great Northern's planned freight terminal site—was commended as an ideal location for union freight yards. All lines would share a common right of way into town. This grand plan, claimed Bogue, would ensure that "the railroad opportunities of Seattle will be ample for the transaction of the business of a New York, Philadelphia, or Chicago."[35]

Bogue also voiced a sentiment which could hardly have been welcome in certain quarters: "[I]n general, the greatest commercial success has resulted where there has been, either in part or in whole, municipal ownership or control of dock frontings."

The engineer confidently declared that his plan would give the city "a perfect railway system," and noted that it

WHAT MIGHT HAVE BEEN, THE NORTHERN PACIFIC'S PROPOSED WATERFRONT DEPOT AS RENDERED IN THE SEATTLE *Post-Intelligencer*, OCTOBER 25, 1899.

had already received wide railroad support. "The prominent officials of the railways interested, except President Hill . . . have expressed their approval of the general features of the plan presented and their willingness to favorably consider the idea of forming a terminal company. It is hoped that President Hill may have similar views."

Hill's views remained his own. He remained stubbornly opposed to a privately operated terminal company ("We cannot come out here 2,000 miles and then allow someone to run this end of the road for us"), and was inflexible in his attitude toward giving up even one inch in Seattle. The first Bogue plan sank from sight, to resurface in 1911 as part of a second and far more comprehensive proposal advanced by the visionary engineer. Meanwhile, Burke succeeded in getting a useful friend, Secretary of War Russell Alger, to set the harbor line to coincide with the end of the pier lines. This wiped out virtually all the public waterfront access the first harbor lines commission attempted to create. The railroads would remain in charge on Railroad Avenue.[36]

July 29, 1895, dawned bright and hot on the Seattle tideflats, where an ungainly black contrivance loomed like a monstrous water-strider. This was the Seattle & Lake Washington Waterway Company dredger *Anaconda*, ready to begin the filling-in of lower Elliott Bay. At 11:25 AM, the first Regiment band struck up, a chorus of whistles shrieked, and hundreds of white handkerchiefs fluttered, as the city entered a fifteen-year era which would see millions of cubic feet of earth moved and the flats transformed into a vast plain of commerce.

As the "Greatest undertaking in the West," the first phase was predicted to require five years and seven million dollars. Jim Hill's great tideflats vision was becoming reality. The loose strands of the Great Northern's Jackson Street franchise were tied together in August, and at the end of October the warring railroads all agreed to share four tracks on Railroad Avenue—with Hill keeping his sixty feet. City Engineer Thomson gave his blessing, and lest the imp get out of the bottle, a city ordinance making the new dispensation law was hurriedly signed.

Great Northern track gangs pitched into the Jackson Street approaches with a vengeance, and the "famous and historical ram's horn" was lopped off once and for all at Columbia Street. When at last the severed northern limb of the old track was removed in October 1900, the press took nostalgic note: "Its destruction is one of the last steps in the changing of the old order of things in Seattle."[37]

Virtually all that remained now was for Seattle to get its grand union depot. The Northern Pacific had been steadily tightening its grip on the waterfront since 1896, buying up one lot after another, but never enough to attract attention. President Edwin Winter promised in August that, in return for vacating Marion Street, the city would receive a new station of suitable distinction. The street was vacated and, by 1898, the NP held title to no fewer than eleven blocks; but still, no depot materialized.

Charles Mellen succeeded Winter, and came to town that summer boasting that Seattle was doing heavier business than either Tacoma or Portland. It was good to hear. Words were not depots, however, and not since the days of Robert Harris had a railroad executive been subjected to such withering fire as greeted Mellen.

"People leaving trains arriving here step into a public street without even a shingle over them!" griped a councilman.

Mellen reddened: "This company has large interests, and its movements are necessarily slow . . . It would not be policy for the Northern Pacific to construct a passenger depot here for its own exclusive use."

Only a union depot would serve the city's needs, Mellen concluded, and that would have to wait until all the roads agreed on a terminal company to operate it. The NP president left town visibly miffed, and a councilman gloated: "Mr. Mellen will probably entertain the same deference for Seattle that a farmer's boy has for the business end of a mule."[38]

Mellen stewed for a year, then in August 1899 took the beast in hand. The Northern Pacific, he announced, would erect large wharves, warehouses, and a fine new depot on the waterfront. The Great Northern was welcome to use the station: "We have no quarrel with Mr. Hill." If Hill demurred, though, the NP would go it alone.

Hill did more than demur. Getting wind of Mellen's effrontery, he leaped aboard one of his customary breakneck specials and rushed west in high dudgeon. Pausing in Spokane, he barked: "We made Seattle. We went in there when the town was in the throes of a panic, and gave them a rate east that made shingles legal tender in Seattle for two years. If some of the d——d asses there will only let us, we will make a town of Seattle."[39]

The tornado swept down on Puget Sound, and Hill's terminus felt his strongest blast yet. "The waterfront must be kept open as a thoroughfare, or the Great Northern will have to pull out of Seattle!" he raged at the city council:

"This we will surely do, as I will not submit to having my line cut in two! The future prosperity of this city and the degree to which the Great Northern will contribute to it depends entirely on how the city takes care of its waterfront . . . At one time it could have been my privilege to secure the Seattle waterfront. But this was not in accordance with my plans, which were to preserve the waterfront for the use of the immense and increasing Mosquito fleet, and to make the entrance or docking place for Oriental steamships at some point fully as accessible as the present waterfront, but clear from disturbing these smaller vessels . . . if a union depot is built, it must be on the south side at some point at or near King Street."

Hill acceded to the idea of a terminal company, but not on the waterfront. If Mellen got his way, he thumped, he would move to Mukilteo.[40]

The eruption sent a shock wave through the city. Editors and civic leaders fretted over whether or not he would make good on his threat, but after sober consideration agreed that Hill had too much at stake in Seattle to cut and run.

Chamber of commerce secretary Thomas Prosch called the threats "buncombe," and merchant W.D. McCarthy seemed to speak for most when he stated: "Mr. Hill cannot stop Seattle's growth . . . No corporation can stop it . . . Se-attle is too large and is too far on the road to commercial supremacy of the Pacific coast to be hindered in its growth by the opposition of a railroad company."

They were right; Hill remained loyal. On September 18, he gathered the leading businessmen at the Butler Hotel. After kicking out the reporters (who were "apt, sometimes, to do more harm than good"), he unrolled a map showing his latest proposals for arranging the railroads, centered, naturally enough, around his tideflats and Smith Cove holdings. He promised a giant stone union depot at Occidental and Jackson, and extended a generous olive branch to Mellen, offering half the Jackson Street property at cost.

"If the Northern Pacific people ask you where they can go, tell them right here!" he declared, slapping the map vigorously. Under no condition must Mellen's scheme be approved—it "would be suicide, and Seattle would be committing suicide to permit it!"[41] Hill's plan received immediate praise. But Charles Mellen had one more surprise up his sleeve.

THREE RAILROADS OCCUPY RAILROAD AVENUE IN A CA. 1900 PANORAMA—A TWO-CAR SEATTLE & INTERNATIONAL LOCAL READIES TO LEAVE FOR WOODINVILLE AND POINTS NORTH, WHILE A GREAT NORTHERN FLYER PREPARES FOR DEPARTURE TO THE EAST, AND IN THE BACKGROUND A NORTHERN PACIFIC TRAIN HAS RECENTLY ARRIVED.

Museum of History and Industry, #8904

On October 25, 1899, Seattle opened its morning papers to a startling apparition; a rendering by the noted New York architectural firm of Cass, Gilbert, of a huge, pinnacled chateau-like edifice—Northern Pacific's proposed waterfront depot. Soaring, "massively beautiful," and stretching the full city block between Madison and Columbia streets, here at last was the very incarnation of Seattle's railroad dream. Large reproductions were placed in store windows, to be rapturously exclaimed over by parasol wielding ladies. The city only had to vacate a few streets, President Mellen declared, and the depot would be put under contract at once.

The Northern Pacific leader came to town a few days later, confident of a much warmer reception than his last. He was, however, fully versed in Hill's latest efforts to torpedo his grand scheme. And this was Seattle, after all; his guard was up. Since 1896, Hill had shared overall control of the NP with J.P. Morgan & Co., and Morgan (who had an exasperating habit of appointing Northern Pacific presidents without informing Hill) had installed Mellen as chief executive officer. Both Hill and Mellen were blunt, opinionated executives jealous of their prerogatives; Hill considered Mellen to "have no business judgement more than a child," and Mellen resented Hill's know-it-all overlordship.[42]

Mellen truculently made it clear his offer was the last the city could expect: "The public is making a great mistake if it thinks the Northern Pacific is going to plead with it for the privilege of spending several hundred thousand dollars . . . We have planned the best we know how, and in accordance with a well-defined sentiment on the part of the local public, which seems to think that we should take the initiative in the matter, though for what reason I do not know. The company has never been accused of being the 'Father of Seattle,' and other roads are under just as much obligation as mine to provide such facilities!"

Mellen would have nothing to do with Hill's Jackson Street plan: There was not enough room, and the proposed stub-ended yard would oblige trains from the south—NP trains—to back in. "Northern Pacific is now offering you what for years you have been clamoring for," Mellen

concluded. Seattle could take it or leave it—"to us it is a matter of supreme indifference."[43]

The full significance of Mellen's scheme was revealed in December when the NP submitted its full plan to the city council. Along with the passenger depot were a large freight station and a seven-track, stub-ended yard north of Madison Street. Even a cursory look at the plan showed that Railroad Avenue would bloat into a fifteen-track Chinese wall between the city and its harbor. No fewer than four city streets were to be vacated, and the only direct access to eight blocks of waterfront from downtown was to be through a narrow culvert at the end of Marion Street.

It was Jim Hill's nightmare in spades. An apoplectic Thomas Burke accused the Northern Pacific of dangling the depot as a blind while going about its real business of gobbling up the waterfront.

"There are so many solid and substantial objections to the whole scheme that one is at a loss in the statement of them where to begin," he sputtered.

The waterfront would be ruined, walled off and taken over by long cuts of idle boxcars and trains shunting back and forth day and night. Mellen would have the city reach its harbor, its gateway to the world, through a "rat hole"!

"I think that it is clear that a passenger station at the foot of Marion Street would, inside of five years, be a nuisance to the commercial interests of the city." Burke cautioned: Giving in to Mellen would be to sign over to the NP "absolute, uncontrollable monopoly over the commerce of the city."[44]

Mellen's Chambord-on-the-Duwamish divided the city in rancorous debate. Many were excited by the plans, and wryly noted that Jim Hill's objections to the NP's bottling up of the waterfront were exactly the same ones R.H. Thomson had leveled against Hill six years earlier. Burke and friends had spent years fighting the Northern Pacific, however, and were not about to relent.

Northern Pacific ships did all their business at Tacoma, lectured Judge John J. McGilvra, Burke's father-in-law, at a heated town meeting on December 26: "Why, then, do they want this waterfront? It is for one of two reasons: either to throttle the commerce of the city, or to lay it under tribute!"

Forfeiture comrade "Warhorse Bill" White chuckled: "[The Northern Pacific] has changed its skin several times, and to me, it's the same old rattlesnake it has always been!"

Orange Jacobs protested that the waterfront would be "hermetically sealed," and reminded the audience that he had been one of the few objectors to the Villard right of way seventeen years earlier: "When I got up to state my opposition, I heard cat calls and hisses . . . But the supreme court subsequently, when the grant was contested, and I had gone on record as against it, said I was the only sober man in the city of Seattle! You seal up the waterfront and you present a commercial absurdity to a city of 250,000, as this city will be in a few years."

The assembly passed unanimously a resolution requesting the city council to vote Nay on the Northern Pacific plan as a "bold and bare-faced" attempt of "an old, bitter, malignant, and uncompromising enemy" to steal the waterfront.[45]

The Great Northern took its licks, too. In an editorial titled "President 'Yim' Hill," Seattle *Argus* publisher Harry Chadwick took vigorous umbrage at Hill's "We made Seattle" outburst, and spoke for the growing number who had come to resent Great Northern bullying:

"Mr. HILL did what any schoolboy might have been expected to do. He got mad. He not only talked, but he talked too much. He told Spokane people that he made Seattle, all unmindful of the fact that Seattle was just as good a town when he came here as it is today . . . It is a well-known fact that an employee of his system does not dare think in the presence of this great man, and so accustomed has he become to thinking for them, that he has apparently forgotten that the people of Seattle are quite accustomed to thinking for themselves. They will take Mr. HILL'S threats at just what they are worth. They are willing to give that gentleman anything in reason. But when he says, 'Either drive out the Northern Pacific, or we will leave,' he will be told, promptly and effectually, to go to Jericho, and take his road with him."

Though the *Argus* waxed increasingly vocal in its criticism of Hill—for monopolizing the waterfront, for gouging local shippers, for acting like he owned both city and state and proving it—there is no evidence that Mr. Hill learned humility from Mr. Chadwick.[46]

The debate raged on into the new century. The newspapers were full of pro and con letters, and behind the scenes Judge Burke and his council ally, Will Parry, fought hard to win over the fence-sitters. Burke brandished a letter from Hill assailing the Mellen plan as "utter madness."

The city should not get down on its knees to any corporation, Councilman Henry Clise agreed, and that included the Great Northern! Hill had broken a few promises of his own, had asked for and gotten street vacations for a new depot, but reneged and took the land for other purposes.

"Yes," erupted Burke, "and the proceeds used for building up Seattle's Oriental trade!"

On January 18, Hill presented the city council with his own petition for union depots and yards south of King Street.

Two days later, the council voted overwhelmingly to embrace Hill's vision. The Northern Pacific street vacations were vetoed, and the chateau that might have been, wasn't. Hill sent Burke his thanks: "I do not know anyone else who could or would have worked so long and so intelligently as you have done in this matter."[47]

Again, a Northern Pacific president had come to grief in Seattle. Fine with him, Mellen peevishly told a *Post-Intelligencer* reporter in New York—it would save his company a lot of money:

"Railroads are not in the habit of spending millions of dollars to improve their terminal facilities in cities that are antagonistic to such improvements . . . The people of Seattle, it appears, still adhere to the belief that the new management of the Northern Pacific Co. intends to continue the policy of the old management, but they have been misled. It is undoubtedly true that the old management imposed on the city, but we want fair treatment and expect to give fair treatment in return."

There would be no reconsideration, Mellen vowed, and there would be no partnership in depots or anything else with Hill.

Still the dominant presence on the Seattle waterfront, the NP applied itself to enlarging its Yesler and other wharves, while Hill applied himself to putting his franchise application through. After a thorough review by City Engineer Thomson, the Great Northern franchises were granted in August 1900. It would be Hill's way, or no way, in Seattle. Hill also applied himself to changing Mellen's mind, and all summer long worked his relentless wiles on the NP chief. Mellen resisted the Hill treatment as long as he, or anyone could, but when the two rivals again came face to face in Seattle that October, something like rapprochement was in the air.

"Contrary to the general belief, the views of Mr. Mellen and myself are not so very divergent," Hill purred.[48]

The Pacific Coast Company, which by this time had supplanted the Oregon Improvement Company, would not stand in the way, either. President J.D. Farrell, a friend of Hill's, affirmed that his company had no differences with either the NP or GN, and would accommodate them and the interests of the city in transferring its King Street property. This removed another stumbling block, as Mellen had doubted that Hill could procure the PC's land. He should have known better.

During his next visit in March 1901, Mellen announced that his company had acceded to Hill's plan, but not without lingering bitterness: "For the sake of harmony, we fell in with the views of the majority, and agreed to a union depot down on King street . . . We entered into an agreement with the Great Northern on the proposition, and that practically took the matter out of our hands, leaving us in a secondary position. We have a grand site for a depot, one that cannot be improved upon, and within easy reach of every leading hotel in town. Your council thought differently and turned us down at every turn, and there you are. We are now left with a lot of real estate on our hands . . . I think the citizens have made a mistake."[49]

Mistake or not, the pair met in Seattle on August 11, 1902, and signed the letter of agreement on the Jackson Street union freight and passenger terminals. Twelve years of railroad war were over.

In the interim, the Northern Pacific moved back into the old Seattle Lake Shore & Eastern/Seattle & International Columbia Street depot on August 13, 1900, joining the S&I and Great Northern (which had moved over from the ferry dock in March 1896). Seattle had a union depot at last, if not exactly of the desired style. Railroad Avenue entered its last and busiest phase, and limiteds, locals, and freights all jostled with innumerable horse-drawn vehicles and wary pedestrians in a tableau of steamy, aromatic commerce.

Hill and Mellen were not Seattle's only railroad visionaries. In January 1895, businessman Henry Dearborn and his Commercial Circle Improvement Club began a newspaper campaign to promote their own grandiose terminal plan. Over the next several years, the Commercial Circle Club put forth a succession of schemes which evolved to include elevated streets over block-wide rail yards, a mile-long stretch of finger piers along the southern waterfront, rail spurs running directly into factory and warehouse basements (with freight cars to be hoisted to the desired floor by elevator), and all to be built upon landfill washed down from Beacon Hill.

Seattle's railroad and shipping activities would thus move south of downtown to a dedicated transportation district, forming the kind of unified intermodal terminal that the city, a century later, is still struggling to create. Dearborn's grand depot would be sited two blocks south of the GN site on, naturally enough, Dearborn Street, and anchor a new commercial district. The centerpiece of all this was to

be a monumental plaza—the "Circle of Fame"—highlighted by an illuminated, 25-foot globe.

Hill was not to be derailed, though, and, in the spring of 1902, the Great Northern and city engineers made a final agreement and the way was clear for construction.[50]

Thomas Burke had worked long and hard. He was pleased to consider that his dogged labors in the interest of James J. Hill had born rich fruit for Seattle, and in January 1902 the judge departed for a well-earned European vacation. He got as far as St. Paul. President Hill greeted his friend warmly in the Great Northern offices, then told Burke that the time had come to start drilling his tunnel under Seattle. Elated, the judge dashed off breathless letters to his prominent friends back home—"radical change" was coming, and a vision "never before thought of by anyone in Seattle" would soon transform the city. Aborting his vacation, Burke hastened home to implement this last and greatest Hill work.[51]

The tunnel plan, for some time the subject of rumor, was made official and by the end of March the bore was fully surveyed. On April 17, the Seattle & Montana filed application for authority to build a two-track tunnel fifty feet in width between Washington and Virginia streets. "World's longest tunnel, between Washington and Virginia," people joked. The railroad would provide overhead viaducts "of permanent and substantial character" for surface streets, and at least $200,000 would be invested in a union depot and "proper facilities for handling the passenger traffic of all railroads now running trains into Seattle."

In city council and public meetings, stubby Judge Burke took ruler in hand, mounted a chair, and, gesturing at large maps, introduced the city to its railroad future. To alleviate fears of cave-ins, Burke produced diagrams showing tunnel ceilings ranging from twenty-seven feet beneath ground level at Stewart Street to 125 feet at Fourth and Seneca—plenty deep enough.[52] This would be the judge's last major campaign for Hill; the following year, Burke retired as Great Northern's western general counsel.

The year 1902 saw the railroad muddle become railroad musical chairs, as preparations for the Hill transformation began. The Columbia & Puget Sound ceded its old King Street right of way to the GN, and in return got the right to run between South Street (now Alaskan Way South) and Railroad Avenue through the spit of land known as the "Mackintosh strip" (which had been Dr. David Maynard's pioneer donation claim and was later acquired by banker Angus Mackintosh). Thus were the long-separated portions of Railroad Avenue united. The Pacific Coast Company erected new coal bunkers and yards at the foot of Dearborn Street, and its Columbia & Puget Sound also won trackage rights over the NP's Colorado Street line. The Northern Pacific got a new main line into Hill's depot along Second Avenue, and in trade for its concession on Colorado gained the old Seattle & Walla Walla/C&PS shore line along the foot of Beacon Hill. To make way for the new depot, this pioneer Seattle track was by the end of 1905 truncated at Seventh and Plummer. In August, the NP assumed equal rights with the GN in the tunnel and depot grounds. Joint "team tracks" for freight-loading would go in on newly established Railroad Way, a diagonal linking the new terminal grounds to Railroad Avenue. Several tracks, ostensibly for restricted use, would remain on Railroad Avenue, and the rest of it given over to a continuous public thoroughfare from Smith Cove to the East Waterway.

Thomas Burke happily surveyed his handiwork. "I thoroughly believe," he told the city council, "that you have passed some of the best ordinances, from the standpoint of the city of Seattle, that the council has ever passed. They will mean much for the development of this city."[53]

Ground was broken for the Great Northern tunnel in the first week of April 1903, and, by summer, excavators were well into the north and south portals, working in the relative comfort provided by electric ventilation and illumination. In accordance with his large locomotive policy, Hill stipulated that the tunnel be extra-generous in its proportions. The clay strata was hard to work and progress slow, but by October six hundred men working in two shifts had advanced a thousand feet at either end. An electric narrow gauge construction railroad removed the diggings, which were used to fill in the depot site and the Railroad Avenue trestle.

Like so many of his plans, Jim Hill's big depot kept getting bigger. The city marveled as the station blossomed into a twin-level structure, "metropolitan in its dimensions," filling the block between King and Jackson streets. Thankfully, too, the depot had been moved further from the Whitechapel "disorderly district," and safely out of view of that offense.

South of King Street, the GN's half-mile by two-block-wide tideland parcel would soon be carpeted with a network of tracks, loading docks, and freight houses, "giving the locality an appearance like that of Eastern railway centers."

Hard-working muckers and their clattering dredges were making fast work on the flats, and first Avenue South reached out well beyond the old King Street shore line. On what had been only recently a waste of water and mud, a new commercial city was sprouting—large brick warehouses, factories, and new industries along the margins of the flats as far south as Georgetown. On Second and Third avenues, the city's first major regrading projects were well underway, and the epic leveling of Denny Hill was soon to commence.

By this time, Seattle's rail facilities were working to capacity. "At no other point on the Pacific coast have the railroads been interested in so much terminal improvement work," asserted Northern Pacific Express agent M. G. Hall, "nor is there any other point on the coast where so many railroads are preparing to do their terminal business." His road's Seattle traffic, he added, was fifty percent greater than that of Portland or the Twin Cities.[54]

The tunnel burrowed relentlessly forward and fears that it would cause a cave-in were gradually forgotten. Then, in December 1903, tenants of the York Hotel at First and Pike, sixty-six feet above the tunnel roof, began hearing an ominous creaking. Cracks yawned in the walls, as engineers quickly determined that a spring beneath the structure had impregnated and softened the ground; the tunnel vented water from the porous clay beneath the hotel, with predictable results. The York was promptly vacated, purchased by the railroad, and demolished.

Settling also was observed in the foundations of the new Carnegie Public Library, under construction at Fourth and Madison; the stonework was raised on jacks until the earth stabilized under the completed bore. (Today, the tunnel roof is 125 feet beneath the Carnegie library's 1958 successor, and the rumble of trains is plainly audible in the reading rooms.) Tunneling progressed well in advance of the depot construction, and the bore was holed through at 11 PM on the night of October 26, 1904.

The Johnson Construction Company of Chicago took charge of the station, and all through the summer pile drivers banged away, hammering a carpet of fifty-foot pilings deep into the bedrock of the newly filled site. These were then covered by a ten-foot concrete mat. The papers of July 31 introduced Seattle to its new Union Depot; a handsome three-story structure of red brick, capped by a steep peaked roof and dominated by a soaring, 250-foot clock tower inspired by the Campanile of St. Mark's in Venice. Designed by the prestigious New York firm of Reed and Stem, the depot's estimated cost was half a million dollars, far beyond earlier estimates.

Amid the excitement, another depot, less pretentious but no less up-to-date, took form. After years of discharging its patrons at the foot of Washington Street without offering so much as a lean-to, the Columbia & Puget Sound was goaded into building a proper depot by the new president of the Pacific Coast Company, Henry Cannon.

Cannon himself had been among the hapless riders one day, and he demanded of the conductor: "Why don't these people get off at the depot?"[55]

"Because there is no depot to get off at," the trainman replied.

"How long has there been no depot?" pursued his boss.

"It has never had a depot. The other fellows thought no depot was necessary, and we just dumped the people into the street."

"The Columbia & Puget Sound must keep abreast with this era of depot building!" barked the executive. "Let the

chief engineer begin plans immediately on a new passenger station for Seattle—a station that will be large enough and that will be in keeping with the dignity of the Columbia & Puget Sound!"

Thus, in January 1905, the trim new Columbia & Puget Sound depot, made of Denny Clay pressed brick and sporting a red tile roof, opened its doors at the southwest corner of Railroad Avenue and Washington Street.

All the while, things at the old Union Depot were seldom dull. "Every nation in the world is represented, and every class in the social scale," observed a reporter. "A rich Japanese merchant fresh from the Orient is politely lifting his hat to the station master, who has just told him when his train for the East departs. A group of emigrants are hurrying by with blankets strapped to their shoulders. An Alaskan miner is dragging a protesting pair of huskies to the baggage car. English tourists are in deep conversation with a cowboy from eastern Washington. A Chinese woman in the costume of her land is clasping a gorgeously dressed child in her arms and giving her hand to another a little older. Baggage trucks are steered in and out of the crowd, the newsboys are everywhere. In color and motion, the scene is kaleidoscopic."

THE GREAT NORTHERN'S ORIENTAL LIMITED EASES OUT OF KING STREET STATION ON A WARM AFTERNOON WITH PASSENGERS ANTICIPATING A SCENIC RIDE ALONG PUGET SOUND.

University of Washington, Special Collections, #20017

The depot was also home to a "large class of the un-washed gentlemen of leisure," as well as the "dope fiend and the plain drunk."

Even stranger things could be seen. A trunk left unattended in the baggage room one afternoon emitted such a pungent odor that employees feared there was a "stiff" inside. A policeman kept watch on the trunk all night, but no one showed up to claim it. Next morning, police and customs officers gathered around and, fearing the worst, ordered the case opened, only to find that the "stiff" was a roll of Limberger cheese. A disgusted officer penciled on the box, "Never place any more cheese in your trunk. By order of the Seattle Board of Health."

On another occasion, a large crate consigned to the Ivers Pond Piano Company of Boston aroused suspicion by leaking. "Did you ever hear of a piano leaking water?" the baggage clerk asked the freight agent. The crate was jimmied, to reveal a smiling Mr. and Mrs. A.F. Tyler, amply provisioned with bread, fruit, soda crackers, several onions, and a water jug—cheerfully anticipating a confining but cut-rate journey to Boston.[56]

On March 9, 1906, a nine-hour-late Burlington-Great Northern Southeast Express was the first train to enter new Union Depot. "The opening of the fine new union depot marks the passage of the old and the beginning of the new in this city," celebrated the *Post-Intelligencer*.

Old familiar station masters H.H. Smith and J.A. McBean belted out train announcements as heartily as ever, and matron Mrs. Sue E. Stine became a fixture at the station, attending to the needs of newly unescorted ladies: "Ask any honorable conductor on the train. He will tell you what temptations girls traveling alone have to meet."[57] The police promised to keep the city's new pride and joy orderly, and no longer would hotel crimps and hack men be allowed to scream in passengers' ears or grab their valises.

Union Depot soon became more commonly known as King Street Station, and an electric sign facing Jackson Street made it official.

The opening of King Street Station was not quite the end of the railroad muddle. Even as the finishing touches were being put on, the Chicago Milwaukee & St. Paul and the Union Pacific railroads were knocking on Seattle's door. In November 1905, the Milwaukee asked for right of way on Colorado Street and pier frontage on Whatcom Avenue. The city and railroad came to loggerheads over who should provide overhead street bridges. A year passed before the Milwaukee, which had met no such obstacles in Tacoma, prevailed.

Concurrently, and after a fifteen-year absence from the Puget Sound railroad scene, the Union Pacific made its bold new push toward the city. In the guise of the Washington Northern Railroad, the UP applied to the city council in February 1906 for a franchise along Colorado, Whatcom, and Railroad avenues as far north as Salmon Bay, and another route along Fourth Avenue as far as Jackson, where a big passenger station would be built on the site of the old municipal gas plant. Alternate routes to the depot site were surveyed, including a line from Renton down Rainier Valley and cutting through the north end of Beacon Hill. The Harriman road also planned its own tunnel under the city, parallel to Great Northern's, to extend its reach to Salmon Bay and possibly even as far north as Everett.

In the course of the Hill terminal expansion, Fourth Avenue South had at Judge Burke's instigation been designated a major arterial through the tideflats, and the council was understandably loath to give it to the Union Pacific. Property owners along Fifth Avenue made liberal offers of at-cost land for the right of way, but the railroad stuck to its guns.

"We have found many people ready to advance plans for the handling of our $14 million dollar terminals in Seattle," grumped UP attorney John Hartman, "but have no intention of retreating . . . If we accept the proposal to enter this city by Fifth Avenue south, awaiting the opening of the street before construction is commenced, it will take five years to secure an entrance to Seattle. Every month's delay means an added expense and we want to come into Seattle now."[58]

Predictably, Jim Hill jumped in. Deep in a fierce rivalry

with Union Pacific president Edward H. Harriman in eastern Washington and Oregon, Hill rushed to Seattle to repulse the Harriman invasion. On July 16, the city council and assorted railroad lawyers cowered under an hour-long Hill harangue. He had not been so worked up since Charles Mellen dared attempt to build his waterfront chateau, and now he raged against one more scheme that would "kill Seattle":

"The minute a track is placed on either Fourth or Fifth avenues . . . the city will commence to regret its action . . . [This] will destroy the value of the only section now left open for the enlargement of the wholesale district, and will mean that Seattle must stop growing pretty soon."

Hill had acquired hundreds of acres on the flats between Fourth and Ninth avenues in anticipation of that enlargement and he had no intention of making room for the interloper. Hill and the city had the perfect partnership, he reminded his listeners—don't blow it:

"There has never been a time in its history when Seattle needed the support of its friends, as it does now . . . Don't make us regret that we have ever expended a cent in the improving of our terminals here, and do not prevent such future improvements as we may desire to make!"

Hill was not the least bit shy in telling the UP where to go—along First Avenue, Whatcom Avenue, or Colorado Street, with the Milwaukee, and out Railroad Avenue to Salmon Bay. The rest was off-limits: "If these people want a right of way, let them buy it!" blustered the Empire Builder. "The granting of [this] franchise would be placing a club in the hands of the Union Pacific railway with which to beat us over the head, and we do not propose to stand for the beating!"[59]

"The Union Pacific officials also have their opinions in the matter," counselor D.H. Farrell dryly responded, and that was Fourth Avenue or nothing.

In the end, though, Harriman blinked. In January 1907, he and Hill came to terms on reciprocal trackage rights in Portland and Seattle; Harriman accepted a compromise which gave the Union Pacific Fifth Avenue South, and Great Northern switching rights over the new right of way.

STATIONMASTER J.A. McBEAN PRESIDED OVER THE MAIN WAITING ROOM OF THE KING STREET STATION IN ITS FIRST YEARS OF SERVICE.

University of Washington, Special Collections, #20.011

Said one UP official: "No franchise has ever been granted that involved so much detail and so many complications anywhere on the Pacific coast, if anywhere in the United States."[60]

By June 1908, the Union Pacific and Milwaukee tracks were fast taking shape on trestles along Fifth and Whatcom avenues. In September 1909, both companies agreed to joint use of the Harriman road's $500,000 station, then under construction at Fifth and Jackson. Prior to completion, their passenger trains would share the Union Pacific freight depot at First and Dearborn, running over Columbia & Puget Sound rail. When it opened on May 15, 1911, the magnificent Oregon-Washington Station was a fitting climax to almost forty years of Seattle railroad development.

"Railroad muddle" was Seattle's first major city planning controversy, and its first big contest between private and public interests. Thomas Burke and James J. Hill

LADIES WAITING ROOM AT THE
OREGON-WASHINGTON STATION.
Museum of History and Industry, #83.10.9332

Time, however, and the relentless trend toward government regulation of commerce and industry were against Mr. Hill. In January 1905, governor-elect Albert Mead made it known that one of the first acts of his new administration would be the launching of a three-man state railroad commission, charged with full powers to set rate ceilings and correct abuses. Judge Burke scored a few more victories, however. In 1907, his Seattle Economic League repulsed an attempt by progressive state senator George Cotterill's Municipal Ownership League to legislate public waterfront improvements, and, four years later, the railroad-backed Seattle Harbor Improvement Association obfuscated to death a similar effort. By then, the public, press, and even the normally conservative, pro-business element had had enough, and Judge Burke was enjoying retirement. On September 5, 1911, the Port of Seattle was born. The old days of railroad overlordship were over.

Railroad Avenue remained, for decades the ineradicable symbol of railroad power. Despite ordinances forbidding daytime movement, strings of boxcars clogged the waterfront, prompting city council president Hiram Gill to quip: "Have a few engineers thrown into jail without bail, like the Socialists and the saloon men who keep open one minute after 1 o'clock, and there will be no more trains!"

Seattle's chamber of commerce and the Commercial Club ordered a study of the situation in 1910, and to no one's surprise found a mess: "For each of the five railroads now entering the city to . . . maintain a separate system unrelated to any other[,] . . . operates to the great disadvantage of facility and economy in handling terminal freights. The time has come for the establishment of one common system."[62]

It never happened, and to the curses of generations of ferry patrons and teamsters, the mile-long freights and poky switch engines of Seattle's assorted lines held the waterfront in thrall. Only after a century had passed was the judge's great railroad highway finally abolished, and in 1988 the waterfront was handed back to the city.

But in the pavement of Western Avenue, north of Yesler Way and in the shadow of the old steam plant, lurk two shining rails: The undead ghost of the old ram's horn. ∎

fought hard for the former, molding the waterfront to their liking and for sixteen years holding state railroad legislation at bay.

Seattle *Argus* publisher Chadwick, Hill's most vehement Seattle critic, pronounced harsh judgement on what Hill and his friend had wrought: "Mr. HILL has grabbed everything in sight . . . His franchise here was granted in an underhanded way. Not only was Hill given everything that he could think to ask for, but the franchise was granted in such a way that certain members of the city council secured options on property and made themselves wealthy before the average citizen knew what was doing . . . Seattle needed Hill, and Hill needed Seattle. And Hill drove as cold, hard, and unsympathetic a bargain . . . as it was possible to drive."[61]

ORNATE WALL SCONCES AND POTTED
PLANTS ACCENTUATE THE GRANDEUR
OF THE NEW OREGON-WASHINGTON
STATION.

Museum of History and Industry, #83.10.9334

CHAPTER 15

THE HARRIMAN ROAD

"I shall always think that the mission of the Union Pacific Railroad is not fulfilled until it builds . . . to the Pacific Ocean." —Grenville Dodge

FOR DECADES, SEATTLE dreamed of a connection with America's pioneer transcontinental railroad, the Union Pacific. Lurking tantalizingly over the southern horizon, the Union Pacific was the city's handy antidote to the Northern Pacific during the troubled years of the 1870s and 1880s.

As early as 1867, the Union Pacific was making surveys along the Oregon Trail. "I shall always think that the mission of the Union Pacific Railroad is not fulfilled until it builds this branch to the Pacific Ocean," declared Chief Engineer Grenville Dodge.

More exploration followed under Assistant Engineer J.O. Hudnutt, who was impressed by the volume of wagon traffic laboring over the old Oregon Trail, and the high tariffs commanded by teamsters. Over the ensuing two decades, "reliable reports" of the UP's imminent extension to Puget Sound were a perennial Seattle newspaper staple—not without reason. Late in the 1870s, Union Pacific president Sydney Dillon was said to be planning a northwest move, declaring: "We . . . are like an apple tree without a limb . . . Unless we have branches, there will be no fruit."

In 1879, he reviewed the Dodge-Hudnutt surveys, and joined in tentative partnership with Henry Villard to build a branch up the route of the Oregon Trail and through the Columbia Gorge to Portland. The deal soon fell through, killed by the jealousy of Central Pacific's Collis P. Huntington, the UP's transcontinental partner, along with the high cost of construction and the reluc-tance of Congress to approve additional subsidies for the railroad. Dillon bided his time.[1]

Struggling across the northern plains, the Northern Pacific was the Union Pacific's only obvious major rival, but was financially weak and seemed no immediate threat. Then Henry Villard took its helm and the picture changed drastically. Villard's ascendancy coincided with—some might say prompted—a sharp upswing in Pacific Northwest commercial activity, and movement into Oregon and Washington was heavy. With things stirring at the far end of the Oregon Trail, Dillon was spurred to action. Early in 1881, the Union Pacific began its Northwest passage.

Dillon incorporated a subsidiary, the Oregon Short Line, to build and operate its new "limb." Field engineers updated the 1867 survey from Granger, Wyoming, to Baker City, Oregon, and Short Line construction began at Granger that June. Seeking entry to Portland, Dillon approached Villard with an offer to buy the Oregon Railway & Navigation Company. Villard turned him down, but the two arrived at a concord in February 1883: UP and NP would share joint facilities in Montana, and the UP and OR&N would interchange freight at Baker City. In November 1884, the Union Pacific and Oregon Railway & Navigation Co. rails met at Huntington, Oregon, and the first trains from Chicago, Omaha, and Salt Lake City steamed into Portland.

The Union Pacific's foothold in the Northwest was enlarged in 1887 when the company took control of the

THE BRICK AND MARBLE OF RAILROADING'S GOLDEN AGE REPLACES THE WOOD AND PILINGS OF THE FRONTIER ERA. THE NEWLY COMPLETED OREGON-WASHINGTON STATION STANDS AT LEFT CENTER, WITH KING STREET STATION TO THE RIGHT, CA. 1911-1912. THE GHOSTLY OUTLINE OF THE BROAD GAUGE STRIP MAY STILL BE SEEN ON SEATTLE BOULEVARD (NOW AIRPORT WAY SOUTH) AT TOP, AND THE CURVED BUILDING ABOVE THE O-W STATION REVEALS THE OLD C&PS ALIGNMENT.

University of Washington, Special Collections, #555

OR&N in a 99-year lease. Rumors of a push to Puget Sound flew thick, but, at first, this took an unexpected form when, on August 23, 1889, the OR&N established the famous Union Pacific shield on the Sound through inauguration of steamer service between Seattle, Victoria, and intermediate points with the speedy *Olympian, Victorian, T.J. Potter*, and *North Pacific*. Then, on November 8, the Portland & Puget Sound Railroad was incorporated in Olympia to bring Union Pacific rails into western Washington. Initial projections were for a line east of the Northern Pacific's Kalama-Tacoma route, with a bridge over the Columbia and Willamette rivers between Portland and Vancouver, Washington. The new road would also build branches to Grays Harbor and Port Townsend.

UP's chief engineer Virgil Bogue announced that construction would proceed swiftly, and, in March 1890, company counsel Zera Snow arrived in Seattle to ask for a right of way through town. He refuted pronouncements by NP president Oakes that the UP would simply rent trackage rights between Portland and Seattle.

"The Northern Pacific and Union Pacific are not so friendly as President Oakes' statements would lead people to believe," Snow declared. "We will build here, and if given fair right of entry, will build the line here this summer."[2]

Thomas Burke assured Snow that the Northern Pacific, also clamoring for right of way on Railroad Avenue, would not be allowed to shut the UP out of Seattle.

With Burke guiding it through the city council, the Portland & Puget Sound franchise was granted in June, and UP crews began hammering pilings into the tideflats. West Seattle, the projected northern terminus, experienced a minor land boom and was expected to become "Seattle's Oakland." By November, 3,000 men were at work grading and filling along the Columbia and Cowlitz rivers; the roadbed between Vancouver and Kalama was ready that month, and sandhogs were sinking bridge footings in the Columbia River at Vancouver. Surveyor Frank Ross initially laid out a route following the east shore of Puget Sound between Olympia, Tacoma, and Seattle, but he and Bogue ulti-

mately decided that a water-level route would be subject to landslides, wave erosion, and cost much more than an inland route, so the projected right of way was moved into the White River Valley.

Tacoma was all excitement at the coming of the Union Pacific. "Tacoma rather than Seattle will be its real terminus," bragged the *News* in December 1889.

The following April, however, UP vice-president W.H. Holcomb wired the mayor: A direct line from Portland to Seattle had been surveyed—bypassing Tacoma. If Tacoma wanted the railroad, it should "offer inducements for such change of our line as to pass through your city."

Virgil Bogue and Tacoma leaders—developer-philanthropist Allen C. Mason, Tacoma Land Co. president Isaac Anderson, General Sprague, and Nelson Bennett—saw to the deeding-over of right of way land, and by October more than 100 property owners had come through. The city council reserved thirty-three acres on the tideflats for the railroad, provided it was running into Tacoma by January 1, 1892. Frank Ross set gangs of Native American laborers to work grading right of way through the Puyallup Indian Reservation, employing the ruse that the railroad was being built by the Puyallup Indians themselves, and therefore was legal.

Tacoma enjoyed its second great land boom in twenty years—"Sunday was eliminated and dickering had become a seven day itch," chuckled city historian Herbert Hunt.[3]

Olympia had her chance, too, when Bogue asked a town meeting (held, ironically enough, in Tacoma Hall) for an outright cash subsidy of $50,000, five miles of right of way, fifteen acres of terminal grounds, and 1,000 feet of the town's waterfront and tideflats. These inducements were granted by the eager townspeople upon condition that the Union Pacific had a locomotive in the capital by December 31, 1891.

Ten miles northeast of town, the ghost of a would-be metropolis, dormant since the Northern Pacific fever of the 1870s, came to life—Puget City. UP's activity beckoned a new rush of hopeful settlers to the Sound, and some made their way to this promising townsite on the planned right of way, which by 1892 boasted a post office, general store, schoolhouse, water tower, and 100 residents waiting anxiously for the Union Pacific to show up.[4]

The railroad industry was rocked in November 1891 when aging "robber baron" Jay Gould captured control of the Union Pacific, which had begun to find itself under severe financial strain. Word spread that the fiscally cautious Gould would halt the Portland & Puget Sound in its tracks. One thing might persuade Gould to keep going, however: James J. Hill. The Great Northern chief had previously asked the UP for trackage rights over the OR&N between Spokane and Portland. Fine, agreed President Dillon—if Hill would put up the money to finish the Portland & Puget Sound.

Great Northern engineers surveyed the route in June 1890, and Vice-President Clough reported to Hill that $6,000,000 would be required to complete the P&PS between Portland and Seattle. The cash-strapped Union Pacific proposed to split the cost fifty-fifty, and in October Hill agreed to advance the UP half a million dollars as a down payment on its share. However, a closer look at the partially completed Portland & Puget Sound roadbed convinced GN chief engineer Elbridge Beckler that it was far from meeting GN's standards. Hill agreed and decided to build his own line.

An optimistic Virgil Bogue, nevertheless, vowed that the UP would press on. The railroad's financial position was getting dangerously wobbly, however, and in January 1891 Bogue went hat-in-hand to Tacoma for a time extension on its subsidy. Before the city council could say No, construction ceased, and the stumps of the Columbia River bridge were left to the ospreys.[5]

It seemed a shame to stop now. Bogue rushed to New York and tried to change Gould's mind; he almost succeeded.

"Mr. Dillon, I am convinced that we have made a mistake in abandoning the line from Portland to Tacoma," Gould declared to his president. "What say you that we instruct Mr. Bogue to go back and resume work?"

"But how can we raise the money?" Dillon wondered.

"Give me the use of your name with mine, and I'll raise it in 24 hours!" Gould replied.

The venerable Dillon, worn out from decades of railroad fights, simply shook his head: "I am too old—I am too old!" And Union Pacific was too broke.

The company gave hundreds of employees pink slips and in March 1892 laid up its Puget Sound steamers. The Great Northern and Union Pacific made one last attempt to revive their partnership in October, but the depression intervened the following year. In October 1893, the Union Pacific went bankrupt, and the Portland & Puget Sound died.[6]

It was left to Edward H. Harriman to restore the Union Pacific to glory. In 1897, the walrus-mustachioed financial wizard, fresh from revitalizing the Illinois Central, captured control of the rickety pioneer transcontinental and began a stupendous $25,000,000 facelift which would ultimately transform it into a prosperous industry leader.

Harriman (known, like arch-rival James J. Hill, as the "Little Giant") came to Seattle in July 1899 and was keenly impressed by the lively, gold rush bustle of the city and the mountains of freight on Railroad Avenue. Harriman drew his private car alongside that of NP president Charles Mellen and asked if he would be willing to share his track between Portland and Seattle.

Mellen was favorable, and in October 1900 told reporters: "The Union Pacific people have said they want to come in, and we have offered them trackage. But large bodies move slowly, and the time of their coming is uncertain . . . I believe they will come to the Sound within the next year. This is a matter which I believe will move more quickly the less said about it."

Sporadic talks continued between Harriman and Hill, who had gained overall control of the Northern Pacific in 1901. Relations between Hill, Harriman, and Mellen (whom Hill disliked but was forced to tolerate) were prickly at best, so an agreement remained elusive.

In December 1903, Harriman promised that, one way or

Newspaper advertisement, December 1895.

another: "The Union Pacific will come to Seattle . . . I consider the question of the Union Pacific's extension to this city a live and very important question."

Harriman also warned Washingtonians against taking up the growing anti-railroad fad: "Drastic legislation should be avoided by the Northwestern states . . . Instead of hampering the railroads that are seeking to develop the country . . . the people should encourage railroad builders . . . I hope it is realized that the railroad's and people's interests are identical."[7]

Such a realization eluded the body politic, however, and a trackage agreement eluded Harriman and Hill. At UP headquarters in Omaha, the old plans of the Portland & Puget Sound were dusted off.

On February, 2, 1906, the Union Pacific incorporated the Washington Northern Railway, to build from Kelso at the confluence of the Columbia and Cowlitz, to Everett. Straw men quietly began taking options on terminal grounds in Tacoma and Seattle. The UP's first bite of Seattle was a million-dollar tideflats parcel ostensibly bought for a "large eastern packing house." No one was fooled, and that month, the Washington Northern applied for passage through town along Whatcom and Railroad avenues to Salmon Bay. After considering an elevated line along the waterfront, the railroad drew up plans for a tunnel under the city parallel to the Great Northern's. On April 17, the Washington Northern filed suit to condemn a block at Fifth and Jackson, at the projected south portal and adjacent to King Street Station, for use as a passenger depot.

Harriman came to town on April 29 and did his best to speed things along. "The Union Pacific will be extended to Seattle," he told reporters, "if this city is willing to let us enter on a basis that will assure it a chance to compete with the existing roads . . . It is our desire to reach this city as early as possible."

Declaring "This city has a future that can scarcely be realized at this time, and the extension of the Union Pacific will be one of the factors that will assist in its upbuilding," the UP executive promised the city steamer service to Alaska and the Far East.

Like his nemesis James J. Hill, Harriman wanted the best-engineered, most up-to-date rail facilities handling a maximum of tonnage at minimum cost. He and Hill shared the feeling that American railroads faced a major capacity crisis, and required a vast modernization program.

"We have got to increase the capacity of the railroads some way or another," Harriman observed at the Rainier Club. "We may have to electrify our road; perhaps some means will be adopted to construct tracks of wider gauge to enable us to use heavier and larger engines and cars. We have reached to limit of our present carrying capacity."

There could be no prosperity, Harriman lectured, if the climate of over-regulation and "anti-railroad conspiracy" were allowed to continue. "If you destroy the credit of the transportation companies, there can be no development."[8]

Publicly, Harriman stated that he would maintain independence and build his own line to Seattle. On May 12, 1906, the Oregon & Washington Railroad Company succeeded the Washington Northern. Everett was added to the route map and surveys proceeded quickly. That fall, it was determined that little of the old Portland & Puget Sound right of way was usable and new alignments were surveyed north of Portland, diverging well inland to the east of the Northern Pacific's Achilles heel, the steep helper grade of Napavine Hill. Three tunnels were in the works—the Seattle bore, a mile-long dig under the Willamette River north of Portland, and a two-track tunnel into Tacoma from the southwest. As for the problem of building across the Puyallup Indian Reservation—overruled by a federal court during the 1890s campaign—this had been resolved in 1899 when Congress gave blanket approval to railroad-building on Indian land, provided damages were paid to the tribes.

Privately, however, Harriman was reluctant to indulge in costly building sprees when he could use existing track. Blanching at the looming expense of duplicating the NP, he reopened his appeal for trackage rights, and at the same time began negotiating with Chicago Milwaukee & St. Paul president Albert J. Earling for joint use and ownership of the Milwaukee's forthcoming Tacoma-Seattle line down the White River Valley. Earling was himself a Union Pacific director and an agreement was soon forthcoming. NP's Howard Elliott, who had succeeded Mellen in 1903, prevaricated, and balked at allowing his rival to serve on-line industry, while Harriman doggedly kept pushing for "intelligent and lasting agreements whereby a saving can be made . . . which will be beneficial not only to [the railroads] but to the territory and public service as well."[9]

Harriman also found slow going in Seattle. Both the city council and the Great Northern offered strenuous objections to his favored right of way along Fourth Avenue South, and not until January 1907 was a compromise reached granting the UP and GN joint rights on Fifth Avenue. Other details, such as overhead bridges, remained to be ironed out, but the Union Pacific's tunnel was allowed to proceed. Mayor William Moore was afraid the bore would undermine the new municipal building, under construction at Fifth and Yesler, while City Engineer Thomson was more philosophical: "If the Union Pacific builds a tunnel under that building and wrecks it, let them. They will have to rebuild it!"

The municipal building was completed without mishap, and in March tunnel crews began burrowing into the hillside at Fifth and Washington. The 800-foot mark was achieved in November, and, to further ensure against the collapse of the municipal building, a permanent concrete tunnel roof was poured.[10]

Tacoma was next to feel the drill. In April, the Union Pacific applied to bore an 8,700-foot, two-track tunnel under the southern part of the city, from Prospect and Center streets to 25th and Jefferson. The object was to avoid large right of way condemnations, and steep South Tacoma hill. Also included in the franchise application were passenger and freight depots at 18th and Jefferson, a huge viaduct and drawbridge over Pacific Avenue and the City Waterway, and freight yards east of the waterway. Harriman privately hoped to avoid as much of this expenditure as possible, but to his vexation, the Northern Pacific continued to dither on Portland-Tacoma trackage rights.

The NP seemed to be doing its best to "keep us out of

Seattle," complained Oregon & Washington president J.D. Farrell. To goad his rival, Harriman set crews to work in November, grading right of way near Centralia and digging the South Tacoma tunnel approaches. Barely a month later, however, the panic of 1907 brought the national economy to a standstill and Harriman ordered the work stopped.[11]

The doldrums were short-lived, and by the spring of 1908 the Union Pacific had sunk more than $15,000,000 into Seattle and anticipated a total outlay in excess of $40,000,000, an astonishing sum that included the $500,000 depot, tunnel and wharves at Salmon Bay. After more than two years of negotiation, the city council approved the O&W franchise at an evening session on March 4. Construction crews lost little time, and the Fifth Avenue trestle across the flats was rushed to completion literally at

POISED FOR A FAST RUN TO OAKLAND, THE SHASTA LIMITED AWAITS THE HIGHBALL FOR DEPARTURE ON THE OPENING DAY OF THE OREGON-WASHINGTON STATION, MARCH 15, 1911.
Museum of History and Industry, #83.10.6758

the eleventh hour of its franchise deadline, July 1. Major servicing facilities were established at Argo, including an eleven-stall roundhouse, machine shop, car shop, and commissary. During September, the UP's separate main line over the eight miles between Argo and Black River Junction took shape immediately east of the NP. Early in 1909, the O&W resumed work in the Chehalis area, grading both main line and a branch from Chehalis to Aberdeen. That February, laborers for the Twohy Brothers Construction Company began drilling both portals of the Tacoma tunnel; the diggings were hauled to the tideflats to fill the O&W yard site.

On February 16, Harriman signed a 99-year agreement with the Chicago Milwaukee and Puget Sound (western subsidiary of the Chicago Milwaukee & St. Paul) for joint ownership of the right of way between Tacoma and Black River Junction, which the Milwaukee had begun in 1908. In true Harriman fashion, almost thirty miles of otherwise redundant construction and millions of dollars were saved. At the same time, ground was broken for the big depot at Fifth and Jackson. O&W and the Milwaukee both received running rights over the Columbia & Puget Sound from Argo into a temporary depot at First and Dearborn, which would later serve as Seattle's O&W freight station. No fewer than sixty-five condemnation suits were filed for terminal grounds on the north and south shores of Salmon Bay; Vice President Julius Kruttschnitt, a prime mover of the Puget Sound line, indicated that Salmon Bay would remain Harriman's northern outpost; there would be no Everett extension.[12]

Harriman was determined not to build if he could avoid it, and kept hammering away on the Northern Pacific for Portland-Tacoma trackage rights.

Jim Hill expressed himself amenable in 1908, slowly brought reluctant President Elliott around, and the deal was closed in March of the following year. The Union Pacific would pay annual rent and a share of maintenance costs, and get rights to conduct local as well as through freight and passenger business. Harriman also got entry to the NP's forthcoming new Tacoma depot and water-level

main line around Point Defiance. After half a mile had been drilled, the Tacoma tunnel was abandoned and sealed. Seattle's tunnel, too, was closed up, and the Union Pacific's big plans for Salmon Bay terminals quietly laid to rest. Like the other Seattle lines, UP trains would meet ships on the southern tideflats.[13]

Like the Northern Pacific, the Union Pacific had eyes on the Olympic Peninsula. In the summer of 1906, Harriman gained control of the Grays Harbor & Puget Sound Railway—which had been incorporated the previous May—and began surveying line to Cosmopolis, Aberdeen, and in Jefferson and Clallam counties bordering the Strait of Juan de Fuca. The Union Pacific sold half-interest in this line to the Milwaukee in January 1909, and construction began in March. On August 15, 1910, the joint line between Centralia and Grays Harbor opened. Neither the Union Pacific nor the Milwaukee ever extended north of Grays Harbor.

Eager to attain its northern outpost, the UP pressed its Seattle extension on at full speed during 1909. Julius Kruttschnitt, Harriman's capable operating vice president (who in 1902 had directed the building of the Southern Pacific's monumental Lucin cut-off across the Great Salt Lake), pushed hard on Twohy Brothers' 200-man crew to finish the Black River-Argo section that spring, so the O&W might get in on the heavy traffic to the Alaska-Yukon-Pacific Exposition. Capturing trackage rights over the NP and Milwaukee saved at least two years' time, but not until 1910 would Union Pacific trains enter Seattle.

After spirited bidding, the contract for the O&W station was let on October 15 to the Thompson-Starrett Construction Co. of New York, which bid $450,000 to execute the design of Harriman system architect H.J. Patterson. To be constructed of reinforced concrete faced with brick, Patterson's depot would be of monumental design featuring a lofty barrel-vaulted waiting room patterned after a Roman basilica.

That December, Seattle eagerly anticipated the arrival of Union Pacific trains. Most exciting was the O&W/Southern Pacific Shasta Limited, direct to and from

Oakland in thirty-four hours over the scenic but tortuous Siskiyou route.

"Seattle business men, after January 1, can work up to 11 o'clock in the morning, board the Shasta Limited at that hour and arrive in San Francisco at 9:15 o'clock the next night," promised a local official.

No through train to the East was scheduled, but the Owl, departing Seattle at 11:45 PM, would offer quick connections in Portland the next morning. A morning local on an all-stops, eight-hour run, and an overnight freight rounded out the timecard.

Slim-boilered locomotive no. 2300 drew seven heavily loaded coaches into Dearborn Street station at 6 o'clock on the evening of January 1, 1910, fulfilling Seattle's thirty-year dream. Brass bands met the train at several stops, and Tacoma tried to barricade its departure. The first Shasta Limited followed three hours later, and a hundred empty boxcars arrived in Seattle on the third, to begin freight service.

Patronage on the Oregon & Washington was brisk from the outset. With George Francis Train long-departed, the City of Destiny found a new booster in perennial railroad promoter Colonel Frank Ross: "Ever since I built the old line to American Lake in 1889, and sold it to the Union Pacific a year later, I have been waiting to ride out of Tacoma on a Union Pacific train!"

The jubilant colonel and his mother departed on the first southbound Shasta Limited, bound for Mexico City. In their luggage were 200 picture postcards of Tacoma, with which Ross intended to boom his city and promote through Tacoma-Mexico train service.

On May 20, 1911, the Oregon-Washington Station opened its doors, and the Harriman system had a fitting terminus on Puget Sound. Throngs of awed Seattleites gazed up at the great, skylighted vault, and seasoned travelers pronounced the depot the most impressive of its size in the country. Even today, the grand sweep of Union Station's interior remains among the most majestic of all of Seattle public spaces.

Sadly, Edward H. Harriman did not live to see it. On September 9, 1909, he died, having created the greatest railroad network in the United States, comprising the Union Pacific, Southern Pacific, Illinois Central, and Chicago & Alton. Given his way, he would have unified all American railroads into one—"But we would all be put in prison if we tried," he ruefully admitted.

The *Post-Intelligencer* eulogized: "The dollar loomed large in his life, but his passion was to merge into a common mass the energies and power and capital of great enterprises, and to introduce into the economic system of the country a harmony which would minimize the evil and often disastrous consequences of foolish business rivalry, and at the same time quicken and strengthen the constructive activities of the republic."

In Harriman's view, the Pacific Northwest held two keys to the future greatness of his Union Pacific—"Seattle, with its marvelous growth and remarkable geographic position; and the awakening of China."

In obtaining land on Puget Sound, he had instructed his officials to keep this in mind: "Prepare in one for the other. Look ahead fifty years and buy accordingly."[14] ∎

WITH BELL TOLLING, AN OREGON & WASHINGTON LOCAL PAUSES AT CASTLE ROCK ON A RUN FROM SEATTLE TO PORTLAND. NEW "TELESCOPE-PROOF" ALL-STEEL COACHES AND SWIFT HARRIMAN STANDARD OIL-BURNING LOCOMOTIVES MADE THIS STATE-OF-THE-ART TRANSPORTATION IN 1911.

Warren W. Wing collection

CHAPTER 16

Rails over Snoqualmie

"If the roadbed had thoughts, and could give them expression, it must have shouted with the pleasure of a satisfied ambition when it felt the weight of the first transcontinental train upon its shoulders." —Clarence Bagley

As early as 1881, railroad pundits were predicting that the giant, Midwest-based Chicago Milwaukee & St. Paul Railroad would extend to the West Coast. At 3,775 miles, the CM&StP was the longest railroad in the world, and one of the most profitable.

"The managers of this great concern are undoubtedly looking to the Pacific," declared the Seattle *Post-Intelligencer* on June 9. "Their lines are already in Dakota, and to push them across that Territory, and into Montana, Idaho, and Washington, would not be with them a very herculean task. If they do this . . . they will find, without twenty years' searching, an available pass through the Cascade Mountains, and their enormous system of railroads will be terminated on Puget Sound."

Of the era's many pie-eyed railroad predictions, this one would eventually come true.[1]

The 1890s were good to the Chicago Milwaukee & St. Paul, or "St. Paul Road" as it was known in its midwestern territory. With the addition of numerous branch lines, the St. Paul attained 6,500 miles by the turn of the century and was glutted with traffic, experiencing the same capacity crunch that was congesting the Great Northern and Northern Pacific. The road's connecting traffic to the West and Asia, particularly that through Puget Sound, was increasing along with its traditional "granger" staples of wheat and farm produce, and consignments for the CM&StP often languished for days in Seattle and Tacoma. The company got only the short end of the stick on overland traffic, collecting revenues for a paltry 490 miles, versus interchange partner Union Pacific's long-haul 1,848 miles. The St. Paul received even less satisfaction from connections with the NP and GN, and, with the inclusion of the Chicago Burlington & Quincy in the Jim Hill empire in 1901, saw much of its former Chicago-Twin Cities traffic diverted to the "Q."

Facing the dreary realization that the St. Paul would eventually be strangled into insignificance by the Hill lines, the desire of directors William Rockefeller and Roswell Miller for an independent western outlet grew.

"If we do not make it [a Pacific extension] we will be bottled up by a combination between the Union Pacific, the Great Northern, and the Northern Pacific," Miller complained to President Albert J. Earling.

Hubris stepped in, as the St. Paul managers were loath to find themselves relegated to second class status in the railroad fraternity. Miller relayed to Earling an edifying exchange of playground badinage with the Union Pacific's Harriman: "He said we could not build a line to the Coast as good as his, to which I replied we could build just as good a road as he could build. He said, 'Why don't you start it tomorrow?' I said we were not ready."[2]

In 1901, Rockefeller and his board swung into action. President Earling dispatched an engineer west to estimate the cost of duplicating the Northern Pacific; the verdict: $45,000,000. Next year, the St. Paul increased its common stock issue by $25,000,000, igniting speculation that it was preparing to build westward from South Dakota. Rumor had the St. Paul building to Los Angeles in

A WESTBOUND MILWAUKEE PASSENGER TRAIN PICKS ITS WAY CAUTIOUSLY DOWNHILL, ONE MILE WEST OF SNOQUALMIE SUMMIT IN CA. 1911.

Warren W. Wing collection

league with George Jay Gould's Missouri Pacific-Denver & Rio Grande system.

Behind the scenes, board chairman Miller was favoring a line to Eureka, California, and also being considered was a joint line with the Chicago & North Western to some unspecified Pacific terminus. For three years, Rockefeller, Miller, and the board debated. Then, late in 1904, Rockefeller made up his mind: There would be no joint line with Gould or anyone else; the St. Paul itself would build to Puget Sound. In November, Earling got the high-ball to start west.[3]

Once roused, the St. Paul Road moved with a swiftness that surpassed even Jim Hill's westward dash. There was a sense of urgency; the glut of traffic to and from the Pacific Northwest had become virtually indigestible by the Northern Pacific and Great Northern, and the time was definitely ripe for a third road to Puget Sound.

"The business has been so heavy that despite the utmost efforts it is impossible to furnish cars enough to meet the demand," observed the *Post-Intelligencer*. "It is a fact that the State of Washington furnishes more eastbound business to the transcontinental railroad lines than all of the other states on the Pacific coast"

His Great Northern and Northern Pacific all but paralyzed, even fiercely territorial James J. Hill welcomed company: "If the St. Paul or North Western would come to the Coast, I [would be] delighted, and would be disappointed if they did not come right here . . . I should be very glad to see them make their terminus at Seattle . . . The greater the number of lines entering Seattle, the more rapid will be the city's growth."[4]

In March 1904, President Earling came to Puget Sound for a look. Plat maps in hand, he tramped the tideflats of Tacoma and Seattle and met in long confidential sessions with John Bagley, general manager of the Tacoma Eastern Railroad, a local line running from Tacoma into the Mt. Rainier foothills.

Reporters were not long in detecting his presence, but Earling denied everything: No, his company (by this time more commonly known as the "Milwaukee Road") had no plans to come west; no, it was not buying terminal land.

In June, however, local "dummies" took options on 420 acres of Tacoma tidelands for mysterious "eastern people"; while in Seattle, one J.T. Woodward signed on for a like amount. The ill-concealed comings and goings of a plethora of Milwaukee officials were duly noted in the ensuing months, making ridiculous Earling's denials, and in September the Tacoma parties filed with the state land commission to make improvements on their tideflats holdings for "railroad terminal purposes." Plans for dredging the flats and the building of four large deep-water wharves were drawn up, and "dummy" L.R. Manning, a friend of Earling's, confessed that he was acting for John T. Woodward, president of the Hanover National Bank of New York, of which William Rockefeller was a director. More shadowy land deals followed, as Milwaukee lawyers came, went, and said nothing.[5]

On October 13, 1905, the Pacific Railroad of Washington was incorporated in King County, to build from Puget Sound to the Columbia. Henry R. Williams was named president, and duplicate Pacific Railroads were formed in Idaho, Montana, and South Dakota to prosecute construction and oversee matters of condemnation and litigation, in the same manner as James J. Hill by keeping the parent company beyond reach of local action. The J.T. Woodward holdings were transferred to the new railroad company, which the press promptly dubbed the "mysterious charter" and which president Williams insisted had nothing at all to do with the Milwaukee.

Railroad officials maintained the charade. "You may say unreservedly that the directors of the St. Paul road are not considering an extension to the Pacific coast at this time," puffed Second Vice-President McKenna; "the road has not purchased any land at either Seattle or Tacoma, and so far as I know, the directors have never even discussed the proposition." Perhaps the Union Pacific was behind all the activity, he mused.[6]

Nevertheless, Milwaukee Road officials continued to take "vacations" in Seattle and Tacoma.

By the end of October, multiple Pacific Railroad surveying parties were ranging through the Cascades under Milwaukee Chief Engineer A.J. Darling, who resolutely refused to name his employer. Once more, Snoqualmie,
Naches, and Cowlitz passes vied for the honor of being
the chosen route. Earling showed up again, fending off reporters, denying everything, and viewing the scenic
tideflats arm-in-arm with his friend, Pacific Railroad
president Williams.

The press was philosophical about Earling's stone-wall-
ing. "This denial is . . . technical, and will probably continue until such time as the Milwaukee is ready to consult
with the financiers as to the floating of bonds to pay for
the new line or to call for actual bids on construction,"
ruminated the *Post-Intelligencer*.

The existence of parallel Pacific Railroad companies in
Idaho, Montana, and South Dakota made a joke of secrecy,
but: "On the whole, this is rather more satisfactory than to
have blatant announcements by irresponsible people of
projected railroad lines which never materialize."[7]

Earling departed, and in his wake the Pacific Railroad
applied to the Seattle City Council for rights of way on
Colorado Street and Whatcom Avenue into terminal
grounds at Massachusetts Street. In November, as reports
came in of three surveying parties working east of
Issaquah, a franchise was granted by the King County
Council to one Robert S. Coe for a railroad right of way
through Snoqualmie Pass. Coe, like everyone else, refused
to say who was behind him.

Three days later, the game was up. The board of directors of the Chicago Milwaukee & St. Paul announced the
immediate construction of a 1,500-mile extension from
Evarts, South Dakota, to Puget Sound, at a cost now projected at $60,000,000. Work would be done on multiple
fronts, and Earling promised through trains between Chicago and Seattle-Tacoma within four years. The Milwaukee would wend a spectacularly scenic way west, crossing
the Bitterroots at Lolo Pass and traversing the rolling
Palouse country of southeastern Washington. Meeting the
Pacific Railroad at Wallula, the extension would turn

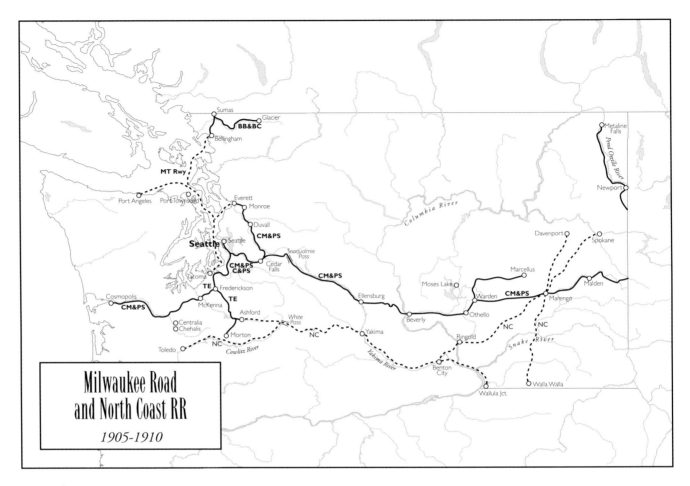

**Milwaukee Road
and North Coast RR**

1905-1910

northwestward through Pasco and cross the arid Columbia Basin, pass through Ellensburg, cross Snoqualmie Pass, and follow the Cedar River into Renton, Seattle, and Tacoma. Branch lines would tap Helena, Spokane, and Portland. The road was to be built to the most modern engineering standards, using ninety-pound rail, and would pierce the summits of the Cascade, Bitterroot, and Rocky mountains in long tunnels.

On January 10, the Pacific Railroad was renamed the Chicago Milwaukee & St. Paul Railroad Company of Washington.

Seattle celebrated the final vindication of Snoqualmie Pass: "There are reasons of sentiment which would make

it particularly pleasing to many old settlers to have a transcontinental railroad come into this city over Snoqualmie Pass, the route which the pioneers selected, and continue its way into this city over a railroad to the original construction of which every resident of Seattle in the early '70s contributed."[8]

Pleased as Seattle may have been over its new railroad, the city fathers could not bring themselves to give it a right of way into town. Fearing congestion on the flats, City Engineer R.H. Thomson demanded that the Milwaukee track be elevated.

Railroad officials protested, and the *Post-Intelligencer* angrily criticized the "occult influence" stalling the

Milwaukee franchise: "Here is the big city, the natural terminus; but the businessmen and property owners of this city should remember that there is a large and growing city not far away, which will be anxious to step into Seattle's shoes, and its name is Tacoma."[9]

Slowly, the council gave way and okayed most of the plans, but Thomson held firm on elevated tracks. Talks dragged on.

Not in Tacoma. As early as December 1905, the Milwaukee decided that Seattle would be its western headquarters, but Tacoma would be the actual terminus with the principal yards and shop facilities. The City of Destiny gladly accommodated every wish of its new railroad, and, the following March, Milwaukee director J.A. Hall laid it on the line to obstreperous Seattle:

"Tacoma has been far better inclined to us at all times than has Seattle. Seattle is too popular. Also, I guess, J.J. Hill has too many friends out there . . . I guess it would not cost us any more to work from Tacoma than from Seattle. Of course, in the long run, Seattle will be the more important point on the line, but the city does not seem to want to be a construction base."[10]

On March 26, Seattle ratified the Milwaukee franchise; there would be no elevated track.

The pace accelerated, and by the end of 1906 the Pacific extension was completely located. Pasco and Wallula Gap would be avoided in favor of a more direct east-west "air line" between Ellensburg and Lind via the desolate Saddle Mountains. Veteran Seattle railroad builder Horace C. Henry was awarded the contract for construction from the Cascades to the Bitterroots, and with startling swiftness began carving the Milwaukee Road into the landscape. Large crews slashed and grubbed along the Cedar and Snoqualmie rivers, down the White to Tacoma, and out onto the eastern Washington desert, followed by graders and finally the track layers, equipped with the latest in machinery.

In a reprise of the Puget Sound Shore/Columbia & Puget Sound agreement of 1882, the Milwaukee negotiated a 99-year trackage rights lease over the C&PS

between Renton and Seattle after surveying several alternate routes into the city, including one up the west shore of Lake Washington. A temporary "high line" over Snoqualmie summit would serve for the few years necessary to drive the mile-long tunnel.

Albert Earling kicked himself for not going west sooner: "I regret that the work of building the extension was not undertaken earlier and that the road is not here now to share in the general prosperity."

Still, he looked forward happily to booming traffic on a line that "promises to be almost swamped with the volume of business which it will have to handle."[11]

There was one slight problem with the Milwaukee's route along the Cedar River. The watershed was the primary source of Seattle's drinking water and there was concern that it would be contaminated by railroad construction and passing trains. "Dangerous pollution" dropped on the roadbed and the inevitable expectorations of "tramps" and train crews raised the frightful specter of plague.

The track was too close to the river, complained Thomas Burke, and the judge threatened to "use every influence to stop construction."

Railroad officials promised thorough safeguards— barbed wire fencing, warning signs, and the locking of lavatory doors on passenger trains—and agreed to move the right of way back from the riverbank.

Sanitation expert John Freeman gave his assent. "The risks . . . which will remain from the presence of the railroad after the prescribed safeguards are rigorously provided will, I believe, be of the microscopic and academic character that we continuously have to accept."[12]

The state board of public health, King County Medical Society, and Judge Burke, were satisfied.

As the national depression of 1907 tightened its screws, President Earling announced that the Milwaukee would have to "trim sails," maybe even halt work. "It seems to me there are plenty of squalls on every side for the railroads just now," he cautioned.

Moreover, radical new railroad legislation being

adopted by the federal government and "even those states which the construction of the road would most benefit" threatened to stop the Pacific extension in its tracks. Too much had been invested, however, and too much was at stake, so the Milwaukee Road pushed ahead at undiminished speed, buoying the sagging economy, employing thousands, and driving rails through a rich and undeveloped country.

Steam shovels and state of the art track-laying machines gave Milwaukee crews tools undreamed of by the builders of earlier railroads, not to mention convenient transport of materials over the nearby Northern Pacific and Columbia & Puget Sound. The rocky reaches of Snoqualmie Pass and the south shore of Lake Keechelus, though, were a challenge even to machinery. Skilled dynamite handlers—known as "coyote men"—were suspended from baskets to blast right of way into seemingly impassable granite faces. Simultaneously, bridge gangs erected dizzying timber trestles over Change, Hansen, and Hall creeks. The boomtowns of North Bend and Easton roared with all-night poker games and ragtime as the "horny handed sons of pick and shovel" blew their $2.50-a-day wages. The first of 125,000 tons of rail arrived in Seattle in July and track gangs headed toward the mountains. Keeping the labor force happy and up to snuff was a continual contractor's headache, especially when better pay lured men to the wheat fields in the summer.

Even so, the tempo hardly slowed, and Earling was building for the ages: "We are not acting hastily, or throwing our line together haphazard. Not a foot of it but that it is substantially built, the bridges are of steel, and the roadbed as perfect as it can be made."[13]

Early in 1907, hydraulic engineer C.B. Pride suggested to Earling that Idaho's St. Joe River be harnessed to power electric locomotives across the rugged Bitterroot grade. Great economies in operation would result. Pride estimated that 35 miles of river generated 180,000 horsepower (the equivalent of 500 steam locomotives) and was capable of pulling 20,000 boxcars—a train 100 miles long. Earling was convinced; that spring, the Milwaukee formed the subsidiary Idaho & Montana Power Company and took options on substation sites. The following year, the road signed a twenty-five year contract with the Great Falls Water Power Co. for 26,000 horsepower a year.

Not until 1915, however, would electric locomotives begin humming over the Milwaukee.[14] Meanwhile, Earling looked forward to capitalizing on the great scenic beauty of the Milwaukee route, and planned to build hotels in the Cascades and Bitterroots for vacationers and "scenery hunters"—a vision that was never realized.

The Milwaukee Road made its presence in Seattle official in December 1907 when it moved into the handsome new White Building, which for more than seventy years would be company headquarters west of Milwaukee, Wisconsin. The following May, operations began in Washington with an every-other-day mixed train between Lind and Othello. This was expanded in November 1908 to cover the 156 miles between the Columbia River and Rosalia. Winter 1909 saw completion of the mile-long Columbia River bridge at Beverly, along with the Johnson Creek Tunnel at the summit of the Saddle Mountains east of Ellensburg, and the St. Paul Pass Tunnel (also briefly known as Taft Tunnel) under the Bitterroots. By this time, the originally proposed Lolo Pass route had been discarded in favor of a more northerly crossing of the Bitterroots via the St. Regis and St. Joe watersheds.

President Earling and William Rockefeller made one of the first trips on the new Seattle-Tacoma line shortly after it was finished in September 1908. Rockefeller pronounced himself exceedingly pleased with the progress of the road, and found Seattle to be "situated in an ideal location for the making of a great city."

Earling promised the highest standards for Milwaukee passenger service. "We shall run local passenger trains into Seattle on July 1, next year, but so far as through passenger trains, we shall not send them over the road until the roadbed is in such condition as to guarantee the patrons of the line the comfort that we desire them to enjoy."

The Milwaukee's crack transcontinental train, he

WHERE GEORGE McCLELLAN FEARED TO TREAD, THE MILWAUKEE ROAD TRIUMPHED—THOUGH HIS GHOST MAY HAVE SAID "I TOLD YOU SO!" WHEN CRUSHING SNOWS STRUCK THE CASCADES IN THE EARLY 20TH CENTURY. LACONIA, THE MILWAUKEE'S STATION AT SNOQUALMIE SUMMIT, WAS A BUSY PLACE UNTIL THE SNOQUALMIE TUNNEL WAS FINISHED IN 1914. INTERSTATE 90 RUNS HERE NOW.

Warren W. Wing collection

announced, was to be a white-enameled, all-steel, all-Pullman express of the very latest design, complete with a New York through sleeper—the "White flyer."

On September 29, rails reached Snoqualmie summit. "From the time of the founding of Seattle," rejoiced the *Post-Intelligencer*, "the inhabitants of the little town looked upon the Snoqualmie Pass as the one inevitable route for any railroad . . . Seattle's long deferred hope is being realized."[15]

The Milwaukee Road soon began making aggressive moves on its well-entrenched Hill lines competition on Puget Sound. Shouldering its way into the Olympic Pen-

insula in the fall of 1906, the company began buying large timber tracts and surveying a peninsular belt line parallel with that planned by the Northern Pacific. This activity was due in part to a request from lumber interests for more rail service. At a dinner on February 2, 1906, the Lumbermen's Association of Washington feted President Earling, informed him and his executives that the present service provided by the Northern Pacific in southwest Washington was wholly inadequate, and begged him to extend his road to Grays Harbor.

Earling took up the challenge, and a "sensational race" among railroads on the peninsula was anticipated as the

Milwaukee and Union Pacific joined forces in planning a line from Centralia to Aberdeen, with the UP to occupy the west side of the peninsula, and Milwaukee the east, with Port Angeles as the meeting place. In 1909, the Union Pacific and Milwaukee divided equal interest in UP subsidiary Grays Harbor & Puget Sound, and laid rail from Centralia to the east end of Grays Harbor at Cosmopolis. To tie this extension into its main line, the Milwaukee ran a branch from Centralia to a junction with the Tacoma Eastern at McKenna.[16]

The Milwaukee Road's Olympic belt line, like the Northern Pacific's, was not to be. Though the company would periodically continue to entertain the scheme, the 1907 recession intervened and the Milwaukee found a less expensive way to serve the peninsula and other isolated Sound points. The numerous mills on the Sound and the many new towns opening along the Milwaukee main line were expected to furnish a large lumber business for the road. Thus, the Milwaukee Terminal Railway Company was incorporated in April 1908 to provide car ferry service on Puget Sound. Ferry slips and spur tracks were installed at Salmon Bay, Bellingham, Everett, Port Townsend, Eagle Harbor, Port Blakeley, Tacoma, and Port Angeles, and two large steel railroad barges were built at Hall Brothers' Eagle Harbor shipyard. On July 19, 1909, the Milwaukee fleet began plying between the Whatcom Avenue pier (later Pier 27) and Salmon Bay.

Service quickly expanded, and for decades the tug *Milwaukee*, with Captain Peter Shibles at the helm and boxcar-laden barges in tow, was a familiar sight on Puget Sound. The Milwaukee maritime venture was a highly economical means of projecting the railroad beyond the end-of-track and it proved very successful.[17] Milwaukee Road track finally appeared on the Olympic Peninsula in 1915, in the form of a branch between Port Angeles and Discovery Junction, connecting there with the Port Townsend Southern.

Neither would the Milwaukee leave the Far East trade to Jim Hill. The railroad opened negotiations late in 1906 with steamship agents in New York and Liverpool to provide steamer service between Seattle-Tacoma and Shanghai-Yokohama. Rumor made the rounds that the Milwaukee would build and operate its own ocean fleet, but Earling concluded that this would be "somewhat out of the line of endeavor of a railroad."

In the summer of 1907, therefore, he contracted with Japan's Osaka Shoshen Kaisha (OSK) Line to interchange at Tacoma. Two years later, OSK's first liner, the *Tacoma Maru*, was fitting out at Yokohama, and Milwaukee agents scoured Asia and the East Coast securing cargoes. An aggressive campaign touted the line as the fastest, most modern, most direct route to the Orient. On August 1, after a thirty-day voyage from Yokohama, the *Tacoma Maru* arrived in Commencement Bay with 1,700 tons of merchandise in its hold. Sister ships *Seattle Maru* and *Chicago Maru* followed in monthly succession, and the fleet ultimately numbered five. Radically low trans-Pacific rates were published by the Milwaukee, transgressing the prevailing "gentlemen's agreement" on ocean tariffs observed by the Great Northern, Northern Pacific, and Canadian Pacific. For the Milwaukee Road, with its superior sea-land terminus at Tacoma, partnership with OSK would be long and fruitful.[18]

Another Milwaukee metamorphosis occurred in January 1909, as the individual CM&StP companies of Washington, Idaho, and Montana were consolidated into the Chicago Milwaukee & Puget Sound Railway, a title which would hold only until 1913, when it was folded into parent Chicago Milwaukee & St. Paul. On Sunday, April 4, the first Milwaukee train from eastern Washington crossed Snoqualmie Pass and shuffled into Seattle, a humble work train consisting of engine 26, a coach, and a caboose. A rotary snowplow had to lead the modest procession over the snow-covered summit:

"It was a risky business," declared a crewman. "We had no idea where the track was, and we shut our eyes and let her go, hoping that some slide had not torn away the track."[19]

Though the Snoqualmie Pass high line would not prove nearly as malevolent as GN's Stevens Pass crossing during its five years of operation, it offered plenty of lurking dangers until the Snoqualmie Tunnel was finished in 1914. As if to vindicate George B. McClellan, some of the heaviest snow packs ever recorded in the state covered the track in those early winters.

Service over the 285 miles between Seattle-Tacoma and Malden, in eastern Washington, began on June 14, 1909, with one daily (except Sunday) passenger, and one thrice-weekly mixed. Passenger trains 1 and 2 left their terminals at 5:30 AM and ended their journeys at 11 PM. Jim Noble, a thirty-year veteran, had the honor of taking the first Number 2—two coaches and a combination car—east, and, after a crew change at the division point of Cle Elum, bringing Number 1 back the same day.

Early in 1911, this run was extended to Butte, Montana. Engineer Noble also brought the first through freight into Seattle on June 25, after a six-day run from Chicago. After months of negotiation, the Milwaukee and the Oregon & Washington agreed in September to share the O&W's forthcoming passenger terminal at Fifth and Jackson. Until the station's completion, the roads used O&W's temporary depot at First and Dearborn.

A small crowd of Milwaukee employees witnessed the driving of the last spike on May 19, 1909, at Gold Creek, Montana, near the spot where Henry Villard drove the Northern Pacific's final spike twenty-six years before. A steel fleet of 280 passenger cars and the latest in high-speed, oil-burning locomotives was assembled in Milwaukee in preparation for through service. The White flyer, with its New York sleeper, would, however, remain an Earling pipe dream; the forthcoming Milwaukee expresses

CM&StP Tacoma-Malden passenger train number 2 pauses for water at Rockdale, four miles west of Snoqualmie summit . The west portal of the Snoqualmie Tunnel, completed soon after in 1914, is located a few hundred yards east of this location.

Warren W. Wing collection

TIMETABLE, MAY 1911.

CHICAGO, MILWAUKEE & PUGET SOUND RY.

New Union Station
Jackson at Fourth and Fifth

Leave.	The Olympian.	Arrive.
9:00 a.m.	Ellensburg, Lind, Rosalia, Missoula, Butte, Miles City, Mobridge, Aberdeen, Minneapolis, St. Paul, Milwaukee, Chicago and East.	8:00 p.m.

	The Columbian.	
7:15 p.m.	Cle Elum, Ellensburg, Rosalia, St. Maries, Missoula, Butte, Three Forks, Harlowton, Forsyth, Miles City, Mobridge, Aberdeen, Minneapolis, St. Paul, Milwaukee, Chicago and East.	11:10 a.m.

	Kittitas Express.	
7:25 a.m.	Moncton, Easton, Cle Elum, Ellensburg.	8:40 p.m.

	Enumclaw Local.	
6:10 p.m.	Moncton, Enumclaw.	10:15 a.m.

would wear the road's standard but no less unique orange and maroon colors. The line produced handsome pictorial brochures promoting the Milwaukee Northwest as a "Veritable Garden of Eden," prompting a new generation of settlers and homesteaders to board Milwaukee trains and make their way into virgin sections of South Dakota, Montana, and eastern Washington. By the end of 1910, the main line was ready for full operation.

"I have been over every mile of the transcontinental road bed," grinned Traffic Manager R.M. Calkins, "and it is in perfect condition . . . there is not 1,400 miles of continuous track in the world that can equal it."

Management was well pleased with their investment. "If it had not been for our transcontinental extension . . . we would have had nothing from operation to add to our surplus last year," declared Vice President William Ellis.[20]

More Milwaukee tentacles sprouted in western Washington. Service to Mt. Rainier began on July 1, 1910, in conjunction with the Tacoma Eastern Railroad, which during 1902-1903 was built from Tacoma to Frederickson, Eatonville, and Ashford. Trains left Seattle daily at 8:30 AM, and arrived at National, gateway to Mt. Rainier National Park, at 1 PM; motor limousines took over for the ten-mile drive into the park. A branch from Cedar Falls to Everett, though Carnation and Monroe, was begun in 1910 and opened for service in the summer of 1911. More lines were added during 1911-1918—including the subsidiary Puget Sound & Willapa Harbor, between Maytown, Chehalis, and South Bend; Pierre Cornwall's old Bellingham Bay & British Columbia, from Bellingham to Sumas and Glacier; the Idaho & Washington Northern, between Newport and Metaline Falls; the Port Townsend & Puget Sound, between Discovery Junction and Port Angeles; a branch from Othello to Moses Lake, Warden, and Marcellus; and all 2.3 miles of the Seattle Southeastern, from Selleck to Bagley Junction.[21]

Earling and Miller were optimistic that the Pacific extension would garner a healthy share of the traffic to and from Puget Sound. Reality soon proved otherwise. The venture cost not the estimated $60,000,000, but $250,000,000, and business proved slim, especially after the opening of the Panama Canal in 1914. Earling's gamble traversed some of the emptiest country in the West, and even in the major cities its operations were modest in comparison with those of the well-entrenched Northern Pacific and Great Northern. The great boom of settlement and development that the Pacific Northwest had enjoyed since the late 1890s peaked in 1910, just as the first Milwaukee trains began rolling. From then on, save for a brief spurt during World War I, it was downhill. The recession-ridden early 1920s were hard on the Pacific Northwest and its railroads, and by 1925 the Milwaukee was bankrupt.

Financial analyst Max Lowenthal characterized the Pacific extension as "the great mistake" that trebled the Milwaukee's funded debt and plunged it into a financial illness from which it could never recover.

The Interstate Commerce Commission agreed. "The record leaves no doubt that first among the causes of the

receivership was the failure of that extension to earn any-where near a return sufficient to help the system carry the burden incurred in its construction."

The commission scored the railroad's failure to conduct adequate financial, engineering, or traffic studies before undertaking the extension, and observed pointedly: "The project was the result of rivalry between powerful groups."[22]

Earling and Miller had been sanguine; other insiders were not. Director John D. Ryan offered the bleak assessment that the Pacific extension would not attract profitable traffic until branch lines were built to feed it, but that the expense of building branch lines would not be justified until traffic improved. Three times between 1925 and 1977, the company endured bankruptcy. Loaded with Milwaukee Road office furniture and filing cabinets, the last freight pulled out of Tacoma on March 15, 1980, and the Pacific extension was abandoned, leaving behind rusting trestles and recreational trails in Snoqualmie Pass and the Bitterroots.

In 1911, though, the future looked good. Few moments in the company's history were brighter than the warm morning of May 28, when the shiny orange Olympian stood out from Oregon-Washington Station and began fifty years of continuous service over the last of the northern transcontinental railroads.

The pioneer dream of rails over Snoqualmie Pass had come true. ■

EPILOGUE

"New York, Alki~ New York, By and By." —Pioneer slogan

WHEN THE FIRST MILWAUKEE ROAD freight train steamed into Seattle in 1910, it arrived without ceremony and largely without notice. Thanks in large part to the railroads, Seattle had grown into a prosperous, comfortable middle age, with 237,000 residents. Four transcontinental lines now entered the city, meeting every hope of the anxious boosters of the 1880s and 1890s.

But the Iron Horse had become yesterday's news. The city was well-connected, and her ancient hungers and anxieties had been assuaged. Now, folks were titillated by picture advertisements for Maxwell and Apperson touring cars, thrilling stories of the Glidden Tours, and Bleriot's electrifying heavier-than-air flight across the English Channel. The prevailing trust-busting mood saw railroads as something to be controlled and regulated, not encouraged; motorists cursed the long trains at grade crossings, and Seattle wanted them off its waterfront and out of sight.

What a battle it had been. The city seemed possessed from the beginning with an unusual sense of introspection, and, with each painful stage in its growth, contemplated its many tribulations—isolation, Indian war, depression, and railroad rejection. It was pleased to discover its durability. Seattle, however, vented her frustration in town meetings, homegrown railroad building projects, and a civic booming vociferous even by frontier standards. "Seattle Pluck," the press first called it; or "Spirit of the city," or "old Spirit of Progress." Finally, in the early 1890s, someone hit on the happy alliteration—

"Seattle Spirit." By then, the city and the railroads had settled into a more or less peaceful and mutually beneficial partnership. At the close of the nineteenth century, the urban dream of Arthur Denny was a reality.

The city's attitudes towards the railroads it had so desperately wanted went through stages as well. As in the rest of the nation, pioneer idealism gave way to "robber baron" contempt, as the unintended and unforeseen consequences of the railroad miracle sank in—land ring venality, influence peddling, high rates, rude and unaccommodating service, and the importation of such unwanted new residents as the Chinese and the "degenerate scrubs" Arthur Denny so deplored.

As the boom of the late 1880s swelled, Denny and his pioneer neighbors watched in dismay as the old urban dream of the 1850s began spinning further and further beyond comprehension. Strangers from "back East" brought with them a new and sometimes unsettling cosmopolitanism, and strange attitudes, religions, and expectations, while women seemed to be growing more independent. Along with the boom came vice, crime, "tramps," anti-Chinese riots, labor strife at the Oregon Improvement mines, and even horse-drawn traffic congestion.

For decades, Railroad Avenue had bottled up the Seattle waterfront, and the vast checkerboard of the Northern Pacific land grant would continually bedevil attempts at land use planning in Washington forests. The bullying Jim Hill—who so baldly and brutally proclaimed "We made Seattle!"—was for many the last straw. It became possible to both revere the Empire Builder and revile him.

Today, with these historical byproducts and legacies so engrained in our consciousness, the robber baron view remains common currency. A good example is Seattle historian Roger Sale, who in *Seattle, Past to Present* (1976) condemned Northern Pacific "scoundrels" and Hill's "economic imperialism." Highlighting the demoralizing effect of eastern capital on local initiative, Sale asserts that Seattle's own innate "push" assured the city's prosperity, with or without the cooperation of James J. Hill or Henry Villard. Sale criticizes Judge Burke's "unblinking" search for eastern capital: "Whenever [Seattle] has looked elsewhere—to the east or to the government or to San Francisco—for its capital, its ideas, its essential definitions of its destiny, it has floundered."

Burke, he maintains, was wrongheaded in giving so much of the city's birthright over to James J. Hill: "If Seattle could have been impeded in its healthy growth, and if one person could have done it, Judge Burke would have been that person. The moment he became Hill's Seattle agent, he assumed unblinkingly that what was good for the Great Northern was good for Seattle, a frame of mind totally antithetical to all that had made the city what it was."

The judge, and probably most of his neighbors, would have blinked in incomprehension at such a remark. Seattle needed money, New York had it, so Seattle got it. What was wrong with that? Seattle had the gumption to put that money to good use, and look what happened— four railroads, 237,000 people!

Still, in the sobering spectacle of homegrown railroad building and Jim Hill tantrums, Seattle learned that neither eastern capital nor railroads in themselves "made" a city. By the 1890s, the press was calling loudly and persistently for more local manufacturing, a campaign that would be waged periodically for the next eight decades. Some have even suggested that the railroads—setting freight rates in collusion with Puget Sound's major producers, the lumbermen and farmers—stymied this cam-

paign. The producers received favorable commodity rates and opposed the lowering of railroad "class rates" for manufactured items out of fear that their commodity rates would be raised to compensate.

Many railroads came to Seattle, though, and no matter how low their rates were, they could not move the city any closer to the nation's manufacturing and consuming centers in the East and Midwest. However, as Edwin J. Cohn, Jr., points out in *Industry in the Pacific Northwest and the Location Theory* (1952), really the most important commodity moved in the years up to 1911 was people. It was as people movers that the railroads made the biggest mark on Puget Sound, importing great numbers of restless young men and families seeking new lives and creating a new civilization.

Through it all, Seattle Spirit has waxed, waned, and flowered anew. When the George Jetson wonders of the Century 21 Seattle World's Fair were unfolded in 1962, Seattle Spirit reached its zenith. Seattle was as glamorous as San Francisco, which was almost visible from the observation deck of the Space Needle! Seattle made the cover of *Life*! Again Seattleites rejoiced in having arrived, just as their descendents did when watching the *A.A. Denny* getting up steam. The boosters of the 1950s—Al Rosellini, Eddie Carlson—were as reassuring in their forward vision as Thomas Burke and Daniel Gilman had been 70 years earlier.

Then something strange happened. Secure in its connections and amid the postindustrial comforts of accumulated wealth and leisure, Seattle came to relish its once dreaded isolation. Boosterism was out, isolationism in! Seattle Spirit turned in righteous militancy against sprawl, pollution, and "Californication." Perhaps Arthur Denny would have understood—Thomas Burke never would have!

Such bleak parsimony could never last. In a new century, as fad succeeds fad in ever-shortening waves, Seattle will enjoy having it both ways. Seattle will continue to fear growth and loss of self, while the daily papers regale us, not with the latest anti-Northern Pacific diatribes, but rising trade statistics, Boeing's record sales, Microsoft's world dominance, and the "Seattle Sound." Sports franchises, not the Great Northern and Northern Pacific, vie for public resources, and the imperious stone visage of James J. Hill now is replaced by the unpretentious and unlikely features of a software magnate.

The equally unlikely descendents of the locomotive *A.A. Denny*—espresso machines—too have become the city's symbol. Seattleites sip home brewed coffee, pleased to know it also is being enjoyed in Manhattan. Perhaps a vestigial fear of isolation still lurks there just below the skin after all. For Seattle never tires of proving on her old motto, "New York, Alki," or "New York, By and By."

Railroads and railroad controversy—be it 1873, 1884, 1893, or 1910—compelled Seattle to look into her soul, and face hard and perhaps unexpected questions about what it wanted to be as a city. The implicit "quality of life" questions—ones that, variation on a theme, are still being asked a hundred years later—heralded Seattle's painful transition to maturity. ∎

Endnotes

Chapter 1: Isaac Stevens and the Northern Pacific Survey

1. Quoted in Thamar E. Dufwa, *Transcontinental Railroad Legislation, 1835-1862* (New York: Arno Press, 1985), p. 19.
2. Quoted in Enoch A. Bryan, *Orient Meets Occident: The Advent of the Railways to the Pacific Northwest* (Pullman, Washington: Students Book Corporation, 1936), p. 2. Dufwa, *Transcontinental Railroad Legislation*, pp. 23-26.
3. Edwin F. Johnson, *Railroad to the Pacific. Northern Route. Its General Characteristics, Relative Merits, Etc.* (New York: Railroad Journal Job Printing Office, 1854). Eugene V. Smalley, *History of the Northern Pacific Railroad* (New York: G.P. Putnam's Sons, 1883), pp. 69-76.
4. Canfield accused Jefferson Davis of conspiring to influence the outcome of the Pacific railroad survey in favor of a southern route. Thomas H. Canfield, *Life of Thomas Hawley Canfield: His Early Efforts to Open a Route for the Transportation of the Products of the West to New England, by Way of the Great Lakes, St. Lawrence River, and Vermont Railroads, and His Connection with the Early History of the Northern Pacific Railroad, from the History of the Red River Valley, North Dakota, and Park Region of Northwestern Minnesota* (Burlington, Vermont, 1889), pp. 17-18.
5. Kent D. Richards, *Isaac I. Stevens: Young Man in a Hurry* (Provo: Brigham Young University Press, 1979; reprint, Pullman: Washington State University Press, 1993), p. 160. Arthur A. Denny, *Pioneer Days on Puget Sound* (Seattle: C.B. Bagley, 1888; reprint, Fairfield, Washington: Ye Galleon Press, 1979), p. 23.
6. Quoted in Hazard Stevens, *The Life of Isaac Ingalls Stevens, by His Son, Hazard Stevens*, vol. 1 (Boston: Houghton Mifflin, 1900), p. 290.
7. United States War Department, *Reports of Explorations and Surveys to Ascertain the Most Practicable and Economical Route for a Railroad from the Mississippi River to the Pacific Ocean, 1853-1854. Made under the Direction of the Secretary of War, 1853-1856.* House Executive Document, 33rd. Congress, 2nd Session, 1855-1861 (Washington, D.C.: A.O.P. Nicholson, printer, 1855-1861), volume 1, Report of Explorations for a Route for the Pacific Railroad near the Forty-seventh and Forty-ninth Parallels of North Latitude from St. Paul to Puget Sound, by I.I. Stevens, Governor of Washington Territory, pt. II, ch. XVIII, p. 188: General Report of Captain George B. McClellan, Corps of Engineers, U.S.A., in Command of the Western Division, February 25, 1853 [*sic*]. Volume 1 of *Reports of Explorations and Surveys* contains five parts: Report of the Secretary of War, Examination of Reports of All Routes, Railway Memoranda, Letter from Major General Thomas Jesup, and Report of Governor Stevens. At 636 pages, Stevens' two-part report is by far the longest and most extensive of the subsections of *Reports of Explorations and Surveys*.
8. [Footpath:] Philip H. Overmeyer, "George B. McClellan and the Pacific Northwest," *Pacific Northwest Quarterly* vol. 32, no. 1 (January, 1941), p. 35. ["Improperly called the Snoqualme Pass":] War Dept., *Reports of Explorations*, vol. 1, Stevens report, pt. II, ch. XVIII, p. 623: Letter of Captain G.B. McClellan to Governor I.I. Stevens, January 31, 1854. Despite the distinction between Snoqualmie and Yakima passes, McClellan and Stevens would use the term "Snoqualmie" for both in subsequent correspondence. ["It should be stated":] War Dept., *Reports of Explorations*, Stevens report, pt. II, chapter XVIII, p. 194, paper C-7: General Report of Captain G.B. McClellan, February 25, 1853 [*sic*]. Arthur Denny noted during an 1865 Snoqualmie Pass journey: "We next turned in the direction of the Snoqualmie Pass, so-called at the time, but it was what in later times has been called Cedar River Pass. It was in early times used by the Indians and Hudson Bay men as a pack trail, and was sometimes called by them Green River Pass." Denny's trip through Snoqualmie Pass with J.W. Borst and William Perkins confirmed the existence of McClellan's tree-choked "possibility"; Denny, *Pioneer Days on Puget Sound*, p. 57.
9. War Dept., *Reports of Explorations*, vol. 1, Stevens report, pt. II, ch. XI, p. 117: Railroad Practicability of the Snoqualmie Pass; and *Ibid.*, ch. XV, p. 145: Estimate of Cost of Road.
10. Overmeyer, "George B. McClellan and the Pacific Northwest," pp. 48-49.
11. *Ibid.*, pp. 51-52.
12. War Dept., *Reports of Explorations*, vol. 1, Stevens report, pt. II, ch. XVIII, p. 623: Letter, Captain G.B. McClellan to Governor I.I. Stevens, January 31, 1854.
13. *Ibid.*, p. 617: Governor I.I. Stevens to A.W. Tinkham, December 12, 1853.
14. ["Would cause very little detention":] *Ibid.*, p. 631: A.W. Tinkham to Governor I.I. Stevens, February 1, 1854. ["Genial rains":] *Ibid.*, ch. XIV, p. 136: Meteorology of the Field Explored.
15. *Ibid.*, ch. XVIII, pp. 182-183, paper B-4: Railroad Practicability of the Cascades and of the Line of the Snoqualmie Pass, by Captain George B. McClellan, February 8, 1854.
16. Hazard Stevens, *The Life of Isaac Ingalls Stevens*, vol. 1, pp. 406, 410. Overmeyer, "George B. McClellan and the Pacific Northwest," pp. 35, 36, 42. The author deals at length with McClellan's "splendid faculty for superficiality." ["Not the slightest faith":] *Ibid.*, pt. I, p. 25: Captain G.B. McClellan to the Secretary of War, September 18, 1853.
17. ["The examination of the passes":] *Ibid.*, pt. II, ch. XVIII, pp. 182-183, paper B-4: Railroad Practicability of the Cascades and of the Line of the Snoqualmie Pass, by Captain George B. McClellan, February 8, 1854. [The cursory nature of his exploration:] *Ibid.*, p. 198, paper C-7: General Report of Captain George B. McClellan, February 25, 1853 [*sic*].
18. ["The major is crazy":] Hazard Stevens, *The Life of Isaac Ingalls Stevens*, vol. 1, p. 300. ["I was struck with the high qualities":] *Ibid.*, p. 410. ["Lying in their lodges":] War Dept., *Reports of Explorations*, vol. 1, Stevens report, pt. II, ch. XIV, p. 134: Meteorology of the Field Explored. ["As seldom as possible":] Stephen W. Sears, *George B. McClellan: The Young Napoleon* (New York: Tichnor and Fields, 1988), p. 41.
19. ["Lucid and able":] *Ibid.*, ch. XI, p. 117: Railroad Practicability of the Snoqualmie Pass. ["I have mentioned Seattle":] *Ibid.*, ch. XVIII, p. 183, paper B-4: Railroad Practicability of the Cascades and of the Line of the Snoqualmie Pass, by Captain George B. McClellan, February 8, 1854. ["Seattle combines the greatest number":] *Ibid.*, ch. X, p. 113: Resources and Geographical Importance of Puget Sound, and its Relation to the Trade of Asia.
20. *Ibid.*, pp. 113-114.
21. ["The department very much regrets":] *Ibid.*, pt. I, p. 72: Secretary of War to Governor I.I. Stevens, December 1, 1853. [The secretary then applied:] War Dept., *Reports of Explorations*, vol. 1, p. 29: Report of the Secretary of War.
22. ["The information now possessed":] *Ibid.*, vol., p. 29. ["The work upon this route":] *Ibid.*, p. 12. Hazard Stevens noted that Jefferson Davis was "astonished and deeply disappointed" at the favorable outcome of the northern survey, and had dealt his father "unworthy treatment." See Hazard Stevens, *The Life of Isaac Ingalls Stevens*, vol. 1, pp. 428, 430.
23. ["Our commerce doubles":] Charles M. Gates, *Messages of the Governors of the Territory of Washington to the Legislative Assembly, 1854-1889* (Seattle: University of Washington Press, 1940), p. 6. ["Within the mouth of the Columbia":] Johnson, *Railroad to the Pacific*, p. 173.
24. [Canadian Northern Pacific railroad scheme:] John L. Harnsberger, *Jay Cooke and Minnesota: The Formative Years of the Northern Pacific Railroad, 1868-1873* (New York: Arno Press, 1981), p. 7. [Washington's Northern Pacific project:] Olympia *Pioneer and Democrat*, February 6, 1857.
25. Isaac I. Stevens, *Address on the Northwest, before the American Geographical and Statistical Society, Delivered at New York, December 2, 1858* (Washington, D.C.: C.S. Gideon, 1858), pp. 9, 13.

Chapter 2: The New Northwest

1. Eugene V. Smalley, *History of the Northern Pacific Railroad* (New York: G.P. Putnam's Sons, 1883), pp. 114-115.
2. Isaac I. Stevens, *Address on the Northwest, before the American Geographical and Statistical Society, Delivered at New York, December 2, 1858* (Washington, D.C.: C.S. Gideon, 1858), p. 26.
3. Smalley, *History of the Northern Pacific Railroad*, p. 151.
4. Quoted in *Ibid.*, pp. 152-153.
5. Quoted in the Tacoma *Ledger*, September 18, 1891.
6. United States War Department, *Reports of Explorations and Surveys to Ascertain the Most Practicable and Economical Route for a Railroad from the Mississippi River to the Pacific Ocean, 1853-1854. Made under the Direction of the Secretary of War, 1853-1856.* House Executive Document, 33rd. Congress, 2nd Session, 1855-1861 (Washington, D.C.: A.O.P. Nicholson, printer, 1855-1861), vol. 1, p. 10: Report of the Secretary of War, February 27, 1855.
7. Quoted in the Portland *Oregonian*, July 14, 1869. Also, Port Townsend *Weekly Message*, July 14, 1869; and Olympia *Transcript*, July 17, 1869.
8. Thomas H. Canfield, *Northern Pacific Railroad: Partial Report to the Board of Directors, of a Portion of a Reconnaissance Made in the Summer of 1869, between Lake Superior and the Pacific Ocean . . . Accompanied with Notes on Puget Sound, by Samuel Wilkeson.* "For Private Circulation Only" (Northern Pacific Railroad, May 1870), p. 14.
9. *Ibid.*, pp. 16, 18-22, 28-31, 39-44, 47, 51.
10. *Ibid.*, pp. 50-52.
11. ["Intimated their intention":] *Ibid.*, p. 31. [Ben Holladay:] *Ibid.*, p. 58.
12. *Ibid.*, pp. 86, 89-91.
13. *Ibid.*, p. 9.
14. [Puget Sound & Columbia River:] Thomas W. Prosch, *McCarver and Tacoma* (Seattle: Lowman and Hanford, 1906), pp. 167-168. ["We find this very Territory":] Canfield, *Northern Pacific Railroad*, p. 92.
15. ["If judiciously located":] quoted in Peter J. Lewty, *To The Columbia Gateway: The Oregon Railway and the Northern Pacific, 1879-1884* (Pullman: Washington State University Press, 1987), p. 5. ["The biggest thing on earth":] quoted in John L. Harnsberger, *Jay Cooke and Minnesota: The Formative Years of the Northern Pacific Railroad, 1868-1873* (New York: Arno Press, 1981), p. 69.
16. Quoted in Smalley, *History of the Northern Pacific*, p. 176. Also, Samuel Wilkeson, *Wilkeson's Notes on Puget Sound: Being Extracts from Notes by Samuel Wilkeson on a Reconnaissance of the Proposed Route of the Northern Pacific Railroad Made in the Summer of 1869* (Northern Pacific Railroad, 1870).

Chapter 3: Terminal Fever

1. JoAnn Roe, *Stevens Pass: The Story of Railroading and Recreation in the North Cascades* (Seattle: Mountaineers, 1995), p. 52. Also, Harry M. Majors, "D.C. Linsley's Railroad Survey of the Sauk and Wenatchee Rivers in the 1870s," *Northwest Discovery* vol. 2, no. 4 (April 1981). Majors uses the term "Kaiwhat Pass" in his account, but the pass is not officially so named; see p. 262.
2. Olympia *Transcript*, October 29, 1870.
3. ["Olympia is no rival":] Seattle *Puget Sound Dispatch*, January 15, 1872. ["Deserted village":] Olympia *Washington Standard*, April 15, 1871.
4. According to the Port Townsend *Argus*, September 28, 1872, the Northern Pacific also purchased 20,000 acres of waterfront land on Whidbey Island, opposite to Port Townsend. ["Better than I had assumed":] W. Milnor Roberts, papers, University of Washington Library, Manuscripts and University Archives, Accession no. 4866-001, microfilm reel no. 2: Puget Sound journal, May 1871: vol. 1, p. 23.
5. *Harper's* magazine, April 1870. ["Terminus saloons and barrooms":] San Francisco *Chronicle*, December 31, 1871.
6. Quoted in Thomas G. Edwards, "Terminus Disease: The Clark P. Crandall Description of Puget Sound in 1871," *Pacific Northwest Quarterly* vol. 70, no. 4 (October 1979), p. 171. Crandall's articles originally appeared in the Portland *Oregonian*, August 4, 6, and 7, 1871.
7. *Ibid.*, p. 172.
8. *Ibid.*, pp. 165, 173.
9. Puget City ultimately became a modest reality fifteen miles northeast of Olympia. See Seattle *Puget Sound Dispatch*, January 15, April 4, 1872. Also, South Bay Historical Association, *South Bay: Its History and Its People, 1840-1940* (Olympia, 1986), p. 30. ["Where is the terminus?":] Kalama *Beacon*, November 10, 1871.
10. Olympia *Transcript*, December 30, 1871.
11. The general routes of the surveyors are recorded in the Seattle *Post-Intelligencer*, June 4, 1884.

12. Quoted in John L. Harnsberger, *Jay Cooke and Minnesota: The Formative Years of the Northern Pacific Railroad, 1868-1873* (New York: Arno Press, 1981), p. 138.
13. ["Thus virtually settling the point":] Seattle *Puget Sound Dispatch*, October 24, 1872. ["Indeed, it was high treason":] Edmund T. Coleman, "Puget Sound and the Northern Pacific Railroad," *Washington Historical Quarterly* vol. 23, no. 4 (October 1932), p. 245.
14. Quoted in Thomas W. Prosch, *McCarver and Tacoma* (Seattle: Lowman and Hanford, 1906), p. 111.
15. Philip Ritz, *Letter upon the Agricultural and Mineral Resources of the North Western Territories, on the Route of the Northern Pacific Railroad* (Washington, D.C., 1868). Much controversy surrounds the name "Tacoma." Theodore Winthrop popularized it in his best-selling account of travels in the Pacific Northwest, titled *The Canoe and the Saddle* (Boston: Ticknor and Fields, 1863), among whose readers was Philip Ritz. Puget Sound pioneer Ezra Meeker vehemently denied the name's authenticity; Seattle *Post-Intelligencer*, January 24, 1904. See also, Murray Morgan, *Puget's Sound: A Narrative of Early Tacoma and the Southern Sound* (Seattle: University of Washington Press, 1979), p. 152.
16. Prosch, *McCarver and Tacoma*, p. 33.
17. Herbert Hunt, *Tacoma, Its History and Its Builders: A Half-Century of Activity* (Chicago: S.J. Clarke, 1916), vol. 1, p. 192. James Montgomery always insisted, "I was unquestioningly the first one to suggest Tacoma" to Jay Cooke and the Northern Pacific; *Ibid.*
18. ["For two years":] Seattle *Puget Sound Dispatch*, February 13, 1873. ["No competent or experienced engineer":] *Ibid.*, July 10, 1873.
19. ["The monster swindle":] *Ibid.*, July 24, 1873. ["There is not":] quoted in Robert Sobel, *Panic on Wall Street: A History of America's Financial Disasters* (New York: Macmillan, 1968), p.172. [Ogontz meeting:] Seattle *Chronicle*, September 15, 1883.
20. [Advance clearing gangs:] Hunt, *Tacoma*, vol. 1, p. 188. Some believed this apparent cut-off was evidence that the NP would go to Seattle or even Bellingham, but Hunt maintained that it was only to permit an easy grade into Tacoma via the Puyallup Valley. ["The railroad company':] Mrs. J.B. Montgomery, "The First Railroad," in *Building a State: Washington, 1889-1939: Commemorative of the Golden Jubilee Celebration*, edited by Charles Miles and O.B. Sperlin (Tacoma: Washington State Historical Society, 1940), vol. 3, ch. XXIV, p. 534.
21. [Didn't anyone tell you?:] Kalama *Beacon*, June 30, 1873. ["As this company cannot locate":] Northern Pacific records, location no. 136.D.4.4F, vol. 3, pp. 292, 302: board minutes, March 1872. Another possible factor in the NP's bypassing of Olympia was presented by historian John C. Rathbun, who claimed that one Ira Bradley Thomas bought land for the railroad, then died, leaving the property in probate and effectively derailing Olympia's bid for the terminus. See John C. Rathbun, *History of Thurston County, Washington* (Olympia, 1895), p. 61.
22. [The secretary of the interior:] Bellingham Bay *Mail*, July 12, 1873. ["Mukilteo, Seattle, or Tacoma":] Northern Pacific records, location no. 136.D.5.1B, vol. 21, p. 172: executive committee resolution, May 6, 1873. Bellingham pioneer Edward Eldridge stated that the sabotage of Jay Cooke's European bond issue by the Franco-Prussian war, and his subsequent Wall Street debacle, ruined Bellingham Bay's chances for the terminus: "But for that war, the Northern Pacific would have been finished by the [U.S.] Centennial, and there would have been a city on Bellingham Bay of 100,000 inhabitants today." See Lottie R. Roth, ed., *History of Whatcom County* (Chicago: Pioneer Historical Publishing, 1926), vol. 1, p. 154.
23. Seattle *Puget Sound Dispatch*, July 3, 1873.
24. *Ibid.*
25. ["We must make":] *Ibid.*, July 17, 1873. ["Documentary evidence":] Seattle *Chronicle*, September 15, 1873. ["Judge Rice knows too well":] Seattle *Puget Sound Dispatch*, July 10, 1873.
26. ["Hold construction in check":] Northern Pacific records, location no. 136.D.5.1B, vol. 24, p. 185: minutes of executive committee, June 24, 1873. ["To carry out plan":] quoted in Glenn C. Quiett, *They Built the West: An Epic of Rails and Cities* (New York: D. Appleton-Century, 1934), p. 412.

Chapter 4: Digging In

1. ["Land Ring Triumphant!":] Seattle *Puget Sound Dispatch*, July 17, August 28, 1873. ["Bitter will be the disappointment":] Olympia *Washington Standard*, July 19, 1873.
2. ["Most liberal donation":] Herbert Hunt, *Tacoma, Its History and Its Builders: A Half-Century of Activity* (Chicago: S.J. Clarke, 1916), vol. 1, p. 191. ["The big men from Seattle":] quoted in Glenn C. Quiett, *They Built the West: An Epic of Rails and Cities* (New York: D. Appleton-Century, 1934), p. 411.
3. Northern Pacific Railroad, corporate records. Minnesota Historical Society. Location no. 137.H.1.0.6F, vol. 4, p. 239: letter of George W. Cass to Frederick Billings, July 12, 1873.
4. Clinton P. Ferry came to regret his intransigence: "We blundered in not selling . . . For years the town suffered from it . . . the trains ran direct to the wharf and no one passing through saw anything of the town except the Chinese shanties and the wharf, and they were invariably informed at other points that they had seen all of Tacoma." Ferry did concede that Old Town had less room for rail facilities and urban growth than the new site. Tacoma historian Herbert Hunt agreed that Old Tacoma was bound to fail: "It was McCarver and his partners who made the mistake, not the railroad company." Hunt, *Tacoma*, vol. 1, p. 188. Also, *The Northwest* magazine, October 1884, p. 2. The NP Tacoma land acquisition did not include the greater proportion of the tideflats, which was included within the Puyallup Indian Reservation.
5. Seattle *Puget Sound Dispatch*, August 7, 1873.
6. ["As I looked up":] Tacoma *Ledger*, March 24, 1898. ["Even to this day":] Seattle *Post-Intelligencer*, June 28, 1887.
7. Mrs. J.B. Montgomery, "The First Railroad," in *Building a State: Washington, 1889-1939; Commemorative of the Golden Jubilee Celebration*, edited by Charles Miles and O.B. Sperlin (Tacoma: Washington State Historical Society, 1940), vol. 3, ch. XXIV, p. 536.
8. ["The grand railroad terminus":] Seattle *Puget Sound Dispatch*, September 25, 1873. ["No Bottom at Tacoma":] Seattle *Press-Times*, July 21, 1893. ["The 'terminus' has affected":] Portland *Oregonian*, July 26, 1873.
9. Seattle *Post-Intelligencer*, June 4, 1884.
10. ["It over the unsophisticated":] Seattle *Puget Sound Dispatch*, August 28, 1873. ["These men entered";] *Ibid.*, November 27, 1873. [Last straw for Skookum:] *Ibid.*, December 25, 1873. The Kalama *Beacon*, July 14, 1873, took a contrasting view, hailing Sprague and Smith as "uniformly courteous and liberal in their intercourse and dealings with our people."
11. Thomas C. Cochran, *Railroad Leaders, 1845-1890: The Business Mind in Action* (Cambridge: Harvard University Press, 1953), p. 285: letter of G.W. Cass to James Gregory Smith, March 3, 1873. Jay Cooke also had been sharply critical of the railroad's and the land company's hostility-generating speculative practices; see John L. Harnsberger, *Jay Cooke and Minnesota: The Formative Years of the Northern Pacific Railroad, 1868-1873* (New York: Arno Press, 1981), p. 83.
12. Northern Pacific records, location no. 137.H.1.O.6F, vol. 6, pp. 15-21: correspondence between G.W. Cass and A.A. Denny, December 6, 1873-February 27, 1874. ["Seattle still lives!":] Seattle *Puget Sound Dispatch*, December 18, 1873.
13. Northern Pacific records, location no. 137.H.1.O.6F, vol. 6, pp. 15-21: correspondence between G.W. Cass and A.A. Denny, December 6, 1873-February 27, 1874.
14. W.A. Fairweather, a locomotive engineer during the early days of the Pacific Division, noted that it was incumbent upon crews going off duty to notify relieving crews of cars left standing at various points along the line: "So faithful to duty were the crews of these trains that in no case did they fail to give such notice, and no accidents ever occurred on account of the practice." W.A. Fairweather, "Early Day Railroading in Washington," in *Building A State: Washington, 1889-1939; Commemorative of the Golden Jubilee Celebration*, edited by Charles Miles and O.B. Sperlin (Tacoma: Washington State Historical Society, 1940), vol. 3, ch. XXV, p. 540.
15. Robin W. Winks, *Frederick Billings: A Life* (New York: Oxford University Press, 1991), p. 211.
16. Portland *Oregonian*, May 16, 1875.
17. Quoted in James B. Hedges, *Henry Villard and the Railways of the Northwest* (New Haven: Yale University Press, 1939), p. 27.
18. Seattle *Intelligencer*, March 6, 1878. United States Congress, *Argument of Hon. J.J. McGilvra before the Committee on Public Lands in the House of Representatives*, document 316117 (United States Printing Office, 1878).
19. [Mitchell bill:] Seattle *Puget Sound Dispatch*, April 6 and 24, 1878; Seattle *Post-Intelligencer*, October 2, 1890. [South Pass road:] Enoch A. Bryan, *Orient Meets Occident: The Advent of the Railways to the Pacific Northwest* (Pullman, Washington: Students Book Corporation, 1936), p. 133.
20. ["Objectionable and impracticable":] Seattle *Puget Sound Dispatch*, April 4, 1878. [Land Grant Act:] Derrick Jensen, George Draffan, and John Osborn, *Railroads and Clearcuts: Legacy of Congress's 1863 Northern Pacific Railroad Land Grant* (Sandpoint, Idaho: Inland Empire Land Council [Spokane] and Keokee Publishing, 1995), p. 122, and appendix 1, p. 111.
21. ["Fairly feasible":] W. Milnor Roberts, papers. University of Washington Library, Manuscripts and University Archives. Accession no. 4866-001, microfilm reel no. 3: Northern Pacific Railroad surveys for the branch from Tacoma across the Cascade range in 1878. ["This company is desirous":] Northern Pacific records, location no. 136.D.5.2, vol. 24, p. 285: resolution of board of directors.

Chapter 5: Seattle Spirit and the Seattle & Walla Walla RR

1. ["The railroad is the entering wedge":] Seattle *Intelligencer*, July 27, 1878. ["How could the prospects":] Rev. David Blaine, letters. University of Washington Library, Manuscripts and University Archives. Accession no. 4611: letter of November 20, 1854.
2. Seattle *Puget Sound Dispatch*, March 28, 1872.
3. ["Seattle marches right along":] *Ibid.*, April 4, 1872. ["Think of that":] Olympia *Transcript*, June 22, 1873.
4. ["The whole assemblage":] Seattle *Puget Sound Dispatch*, July 24, 1873. ["To build a line":] Thomas Burke, papers. University of Washington Library, Manuscripts and University Archives. Accession no. 1483-2, box 51, folder 1: Seattle & Walla Walla charter, articles of incorporation. The charter was amended on August 8, 1873, to specify Walla Walla as the eastern terminus. See also, Henry Villard, papers. University of Washington Library, Microforms and Newspapers. Box A133, reel 1: "Seattle & Walla Walla Railroad, 1879-1880."
5. Seattle *Puget Sound Dispatch*, July 31, 1873.
6. Clinton A. Snowden, *History of Washington: The Rise and Progress of an American State*, advisory editors Cornelius H. Hanford, Miles C. Moore, William D. Tyler, and Stephen J. Chadwick (New York: Century History, 1909), vol. 4, p. 234.
7. Seattle *Puget Sound Dispatch*, July 2, 1874.
8. [Poem, and "Seriously disabled":] Seattle *Press-Times* July 21, 1893. Richard K. McDonald and Lucile McDonald, *The Coals of Newcastle: A Hundred Years of Hidden History* (Washington: Issaquah Alps Trail Club, 1987), p. 118. According to the authors, the starting point of the Seattle & Walla Walla was 100 feet east of the present-day intersection of Airport Way and Spokane Street. Also, Roberta F. Watt, *The Story of Seattle* (Seattle: Lowman and Hanford, 1931), pp. 367-368.
9. ["Never, perhaps, were before seen":] Seattle *Puget Sound Dispatch*, May 7, 1874. ["Oh, the wailing":] Seattle *Press-Times*, July 19, 1893.
10. Seattle *Puget Sound Dispatch* July 24, 1873.
11. *Ibid.*, April 9, 1874.
12. ["Pretentious city-like appearance":] *Ibid.*, July 22, 1875. Frederick J. Grant, *History of Seattle, Washington: With Illustrations and Biographical Sketches of Some of Its Prominent Men and Pioneers* (New York: American Publishing, 1891), p. 294.
13. ["Selfish greed and personal jealousy":] Seattle *Puget Sound Dispatch*, April 20, 1876. ["Capital is sensitive":] *Ibid.*, April 6, 1876.
14. Accounts vary on the Colman deal. See *Ibid.*, February 10, April 20, 26, and November 11, 1876. ["Doing more for the permanent prosperity":] *Ibid.*, April 27, 1876. Also, C.H. Hanford, *Seattle and Environs, 1852-1924* (Chicago: Pioneer Historical Publishing, 1924), vol. 1, p. 183. McDonald, *The Coals of Newcastle*, p. 118. Snowden, *History of Washington*, vol. 4, p. 237.
15. Seattle *Puget Sound Dispatch*, March 31, 1877.
16. The Seattle *Intelligencer*, July 11, 1878, indicated that Colman and other major Seattle & Walla Walla backers were "preferred creditors" of the

Newcastle extension and garnered the first profits of that line. The Seattle *Post-Intelligencer*, December 14, 1906, stated that Colman never got back more than a fraction of his stake in the Seattle & Walla Walla.
17. Seattle *Puget Sound Dispatch*, March 13, 1878.
18. ["A railroad across the Cascade mountains":] Seattle *Intelligencer*, July 27, 1878. ["Receivable at par":] *Ibid.*, May 24, 1878.
19. ["A portion of our property":] Seattle *Puget Sound Dispatch*, August 24, 1878. ["The object of more personal detraction":] *Ibid.*, April 20, 1878.
20. ["Well, who will be injured":] *Ibid.*, June 22, 1878. ["The community is scanning the list":] Seattle *Intelligencer*, July 24, 1878.

Chapter 6: The Villard Boom

1. Seattle *Puget Sound Dispatch*, March 3, 1877.
2. James B. Hedges, *Henry Villard and the Railways of the Northwest* (New Haven: Yale University Press, 1939), p. 58.
3. ["On the Sound I believe":] *Ibid.*, p. 59. ["The mere threat":] Henry Villard, *Memoirs of Henry Villard, Journalist and Financier, 1835-1900* (Boston, New York: Houghton Mifflin, 1904), vol. 2, p. 296. Hedges, *Henry Villard*, pp. 58-59. Glenn C. Quiett, *They Built the West: An Epic of Rails and Cities* (New York: D. Appleton-Century, 1934), p. 365.
4. ["Absolute control":] Hedges, *Henry Villard*, p. 60. ["All the obtainable land":] *Ibid.*, pp. 77-78. ["I do not complain":] *Ibid.*, p. 85. Northern Pacific chief engineer William Milnor Roberts had made the recommendation to divide the mainline and Cascade branch at Wallula, the "common point" of equal distance to Puget Sound. See W. Milnor Roberts, papers. University of Washington Library, Manuscripts and University Archives. Accession no. 4866-001, microfilm reel no. 2: Puget Sound diary, April 28, 1871.
5. Henry Villard, *The Early History of Transportation in Oregon*, edited by Oswald G. Villard (Eugene: University of Oregon Press, 1944), p. 91.
6. Thomas C. Cochran, *Railroad Leaders, 1845-1890: The Business Mind in Action* (Cambridge: Harvard University Press, 1953), p. 260: letter of Frederick Billings to John W. Sprague, February 21, 1881.
7. ["I feel more confident than ever":] Cochran, *Ibid.*, p. 481: letter of Henry Villard to William Endicott, Jr., February 4, 1881. ["The very novelty and mystery":] Villard, *Memoirs*, vol. 2, p. 298.
8. L.A. Westerners Corral, *The Westerners' Brand Book*, vol. 9, edited by Henry Clifford, "Steamboating on the Columbia River: the Journals of Captain John C. Ainsworth" (Los Angeles, 1961), p. 156. Also, Peter J. Lewty, *To The Columbia Gateway: The Oregon Railway and the Northern Pacific, 1879-1884* (Pullman: Washington State University Press, 1987), p. 69.
9. ["His well-known financial ability":] Watson C. Squire, papers. University of Washington, Manuscripts and University Archives. Accession no. 4004, box 13, folder 6: letter of Watson C. Squire to Arthur Denny, March 16, 1880. ["Dreadfully complicated condition":] *Ibid.*, box 13, folder 5: letter of Henry Villard to Watson Squire, April 1, 1880. The S&WW board of trustees promised Squire a commission of $25,000 should he sell the first mortgage bonds. Despite his failure to do so, he claimed the commission in a suit against the S&WW and subsequently carried over to its purchaser, Henry Villard. In November 1881, Squire settled for $5,000; see *Ibid.*, box 13, folders 2, 3, 7, 14. Also, Seattle *Post-Intelligencer*, August 21, 1898.
10. Squire papers, box 13, folder 4.
11. ["For reasons of policy":] Hedges, *Henry Villard*, p. 67. ["An undoubted benefactor":] Seattle *Intelligencer*, October 10, 1880.
12. Oregon Improvement Company, corporate records. University of Washington Library, Manuscripts and University Archives. Accession no. 249, box 24, folder 29: preliminary study of Lake Washington canal.
13. Portland *Oregonian*, October 8, 1881.
14. *Ibid.*
15. Seattle *Chronicle*, March 10, 1882. Also, Frederick J. Grant, *History of Seattle, Washington: With Illustrations and Biographical Sketches of Some of Its Prominent Men and Pioneers* (New York: American Publishing, 1891), p. 165.
16. Portland *Oregonian*, October 8, 1881.
17. *Ibid.*
18. [Watson Squire had urged:] Squire papers, box 15, folder 15, unidentified newspaper clipping of March 19, 1880 letter from Watson Squire to Orange Jacobs. ["No matter how it affects Tacoma":] Robin W. Winks, *Frederick Billings: A Life* (New York: Oxford University Press, 1991), p. 228. [Roberts confirmed:] *Ibid.*, p. 243.
19. Portland *Oregonian*, October 8, 1881.
20. *Ibid.*, October 24, 1881.
21. Hedges, *Henry Villard*, p. 86.
22. Portland *Oregonian*, October 24, 1881.
23. *Ibid.*, October 4, 1881. Also, Seattle *Intelligencer*, June 30, 1881, September 20, 1883.
24. Seattle *Chronicle*, February 16, March 1, March 4, 1882. City ordinance 259, in *Ibid.*, March 9, 1882.
25. ["Tacoma will be effectively sidetracked":] *Ibid.*, February 11, 1882. ["A degree of opposition":] *Ibid.*, March 10, 1882. Also, C.H. Hanford, "The Orphan Railroad and Ram's Horn Right of Way," *Washington Historical Quarterly* vol. 14, no. 2 (April 1923).
26. Tacoma *Ledger*, April 22, 1883.
27. Seattle *Post-Intelligencer*, January 21, 1883.
28. Seattle *Chronicle*, April 1, 1882.
29. *Ibid.*, March 31, 1882.
30. Henry Villard, papers. University of Washington Library, Microforms and Newspapers. Box A133, reel 1: letter of A.A. Denny to Henry Villard, November 18, 1882.
31. Seattle *Post-Intelligencer*, April 13, 1883.
32. Villard considered the Puyallup-Stuck Junction branch to be part of the Cascade Division; see *Ibid.*, May 9, 1884. ["Stuck":] Robert Hitchman, *Place Names of Washington* (Tacoma: Washington State Historical Society, 1985), p. 292; Florence K. Lentz, *Kent, Valley of Opportunity* (Chatsworth, California: Windsor Publications, 1990), p. 10.
33. Seattle *Chronicle*, November 17, 25, 1882.
34. ["Mr. Villard has revolutionized":] Seattle *Post-Intelligencer*, December 2, 1882. ["People and capital":] Olympia *Transcript*, August 23, 1883.
35. Seattle *Post-Intelligencer*, April 21, 1883.
36. *Ibid.* Peter J. Lewty, *To The Columbia Gateway: The Oregon Railway and the Northern Pacific, 1879-1884* (Pullman: Washington State University Press, 1987), p. 105. According to the author, the construction and land patent freeze was imposed at the instigation of Collis P. Huntington and the "California railroad lobby." ["My paramount duty":] Seattle *Post-Intelligencer*, April 21, 1883.
37. *Ibid.*, April 21, 25, 1883.
38. ["The people of Yeslerville":] Tacoma *Ledger*, April 22, 1883. ["The future of your town":] *Ibid.*, April 21, 1883.
39. W.P. Bonney, "Naming Stampede Pass," *Washington Historical Quarterly* vol. 12, no. 4 (October 1921), p. 278. Also, Herbert Hunt, *Tacoma, Its History and Its Builders: A Half Century of Activity* (Chicago: S.J. Clarke, 1916), vol. 1, p. 330.
40. Seattle *Post-Intelligencer*, July 15, 1883.
41. ["The town was full of people":] *Ibid.*, September 2, 1883. ["I have visited Puget Sound":] Frederick J. Grant, *History of Seattle, Washington: With Illustrations and Biographical Sketches of Some of Its Prominent Men and Pioneers* (New York: American Publishing, 1891), p. 168.
42. *New York Times*, September 23, 1883.
43. Tacoma *Ledger*, September 14, 1883.
44. Seattle *Post-Intelligencer*, September 14, 1883.
45. *Ibid.*, September 15, 1883.
46. *Ibid.*
47. Francis Jackson Garrison, "Opening of the Northern Pacific Described by Henry Villard's Brother-in-Law Francis Jackson Garrison." Henry Villard papers, Harvard University, the Houghton Library. File bMS Am 1322-642.
48. Seattle *Post-Intelligencer*, September 15, 1883.
49. ["The crowning fact":] Tacoma *Ledger*, September 12, 1883. ["You now have all rail":] *Ibid.*, September 12, 1883.
50. ["The asylum for the insane":] *Ibid.*, September 12, 1883. ["Stale lies":] *Ibid.*, September 16, 1883.
51. Seattle *Post-Intelligencer*, September 20, 1883.
52. Villard, *Early History*, p. 81.
53. ["Strange fondness":] San Francisco *Chronicle*, November 7, 1881. [Three hundred settlers a day:] Vancouver (WA) *Independent*, July 6, 1882.
54. ["Turned into a marble statue":] Seattle *Post-Intelligencer*, November 13, 1900. In a subsequent statement to NP stockholders, Villard described the erroneous engineering department estimates as "the true key to and the sole cause of your and my disappointments." He did admit that, "justice requires me to say that I do not wish to attach undue blame to the engineering department. The estimates . . . were made in good faith and in the light of the best information to be had." *Ibid.*, September 17, 1884. Chief Engineer Adna Anderson vigorously rebutted Villard's statement; see Tacoma *Ledger*, November 8, 1884. Also, Villard, *Memoirs*, vol. 2, p. 307.
55. Villard claimed that German backers were "so much impressed with the vast regions" served by the NP as to support a $20 million dollar second mortgage bond issue. Villard, *Memoirs*, vol. 2, p. 313. Hazard Stevens was aboard one of the specials, and took a similar positive view: "I am sure that nearly all the parties were highly pleased with the country and the road and their resources. The real cause of the [Villard stocks] failure was the sudden fall in the stock market. At every stopping place the guests were hurrying to the telegraph station and found constantly falling quotations which recorded heavy losses for many of them and, of course, they were in no mood to invest in anything." See H.W. Fairweather, "The Northern Pacific Railroad and Some of Its History," *Washington Historical Quarterly* vol. 10, no. 2 (April 1919), p. 100: "Comment on Mr. Fairweather's Article, by Hazard Stevens." A contrary view was expressed by Villard's ordinarily upbeat son, Oswald Garrison Villard: "His guests of September 1883 were appalled at the long, empty stretches through which they passed from St. Paul to the Pacific . . . Hence they cabled home unfavorably and the resultant sales helped to bring about the disaster." Oswald Garrison Villard, "He Believed in the Pacific Northwest," Portland *Oregonian*, August 27, 1933, magazine section. [The *New York Times* hinted:] *New York Times*, August 26, 1883.
56. Villard, *Memoirs*, vol. 2, p. 314.
57. Seattle *Post-Intelligencer*, September 8, 1883.
58. ["No landed interests at Seattle":] *Ibid.*, December 23, 1883. ["Mr. Villard has not been a success":] *Ibid.*, January 4, 1884. Seattle historian Clarence Bagley claimed that "one of the presidents" of the Northern Pacific swore: "If I had it in my power, no locomotive would ever turn its wheels in Seattle"; Bagley, *History of Seattle*, vol. 1, p. 243. William Speidel attributes this oath to Wright in his delightful *Sons of the Profits; or, There's No Business Like Grow Business: The Seattle Story, 1851-1901* (Seattle: Nettle Creek Publishing, 1967), p. 165.
59. Seattle *Post-Intelligencer*, December 18, 1883.
60. ["Henry Villard has done more":] *Ibid.*, January 5, 1884. ["Instead of carrying out":] *Ibid.*, January 17, 1884.
61. ["We have been blamed":] Tacoma *Ledger*, April 8, 1884. The *Ledger's* antipathy to Villard dates at least from 1881, when Radebaugh charged him with unscrupulous and fraudulent business practices, including stock-watering, in an article that appeared in the New York *Sun* on May 25. Radebaugh later claimed that Villard had been infuriated by the article and had stormed, "I will burn that *Ledger* up; I will invite the coyotes to take possession of that town." Tacoma *Ledger*, April 20, 1884. Pioneer Tacoma historian Herbert Hunt likewise considered Villard to have been a "blight" on his city; see Hunt, *Tacoma*, vol. 1, p. 257.
62. N.B. Coffman, "When I Came to Washington Territory," *Washington Historical Quarterly* vol. 26, no. 2 (April 1935), p. 96.
63. *Ibid.*, p. 97.

Chapter 7: Orphan Road

1. ["Laborers swarm through the fields":] Seattle *Post-Intelligencer*, October 18, 1883. ["Railroad building in good style":] *Ibid.*, October 3, 1883.
2. ["Under a Black Cloud":] Seattle *Chronicle*, January 11, 1884. ["The call to action":] Seattle *Post-Intelligencer*, March 21, 1884.
3. Seattle *Post-Intelligencer*, March 23, 1884.
4. *Ibid.*
5. *Ibid.*, March 28, 1884.
6. ["A laborer does not demand":] *Ibid.* [Seattle Idea:] *Ibid.*, September 17, 1886.

7. *Ibid.,* March 29, 1884. During 1883 and 1884, the Northern Pacific's mouthpiece, *The Northwest* magazine, campaigned for restoring what many believed to be Mt. Rainier's "musical and significant Indian title," Mt. Tacoma. "There seems a perverse injustice in substituting the names of wandering foreigners, however worthy . . . for the old names born of love, and inspired by poetry we know not how many centuries ago; names sacred, moreover, as the only mementoes which, soon, will be left of a race that has died at our hands," March 1883, p. 9.
8. Seattle *Post-Intelligencer,* March 29, 1884.
9. *Ibid.,* April 4, 1884.
10. ["What a spectacle":] Tacoma *Ledger,* April 22, 1884. ["Some foolish people":] *The Northwest* magazine, June 1884, p. 11.
11. Tacoma *Ledger,* March 23, 1884.
12. Portland *Oregonian,* December 1, 1880; January 24, February 15, 1882.
13. James B. Hedges, *Henry Villard and the Railways of the Northwest* (New Haven: Yale University Press, 1939), pp. 139-140.
14. ["So many lies":] Seattle *Post-Intelligencer,* April 26, 1884. [Queen City:] O. Muiriel Fuller, *John Muir of Wall Street: A Story of Thrift* (New York: Knickerbocker Press, 1927), p. 169.
15. [Struggling to stay afloat:] Oregon Improvement Company, corporate records. University of Washington Library, Manuscripts and University Archives. Accession no. 249, box 22, folder 38: letters of John Muir to A.H. Holmes, April 16, 17, 1884; folder 46: John Muir to Elijah Smith, June 9, 1884. ["As there is not very much money":] box 23, folder 6: Muir to Smith, June 3, 1884.
16. *Ibid.,* box 22, folder 48: letter of John Muir to Elijah Smith, June 17, 1884; folder 49: telegrams between A.D. Edgar and J.H. Hannaford, June 19, 1884.
17. ["Villard's wild scheme":] Tacoma *Ledger,* April 14, 1884. ["It therefore behooves the merchants":] *Ibid.,* April 24, 1884.
18. *Ibid.,* June 19, 1884.
19. ["Mr. McNaught is the only loser":] Seattle *Post-Intelligencer,* June 18, 1884. ["At a moment's notice":] Tacoma *Ledger,* June 20, 1884.
20. ["It is highly objectionable":] Thomas C. Cochran, *Railroad Leaders, 1845-1890: The Business Mind in Action* (Cambridge: Harvard University Press, 1953), p. 356: letter of Robert Harris to Thomas F. Oakes, March 31, 1884. ["I have been warned":] Seattle *Post-Intelligencer,* July 18, 1884.
21. *Ibid.*
22. *Ibid.*
23. *Ibid.*
24. *Ibid.*
25. *Ibid.* Also, Fuller, *John Muir,* p. 169. According to the author, Charles Wright complained to Henry Villard of this slight to Tacoma in John Muir's 1883 promotional folder. Thus the 1884 edition was amended to recognize "Tacoma and Seattle, the two Queen Cities of the Sound."
26. ["The seat of President Harris":] Tacoma *Ledger,* July 19, 1884. ["The action of the demagogues":] *Ibid.,* July 1, 1884.
27. Seattle *Herald,* July 20, 1884.
28. Seattle *Post-Intelligencer,* July 25, 1884.
29. ["Rather poor picking":] Oregon Improvement Co. records, box 23, folder 5: letter of John Muir to Elijah Smith, July 16, 1884. ["As you have no facilities":] *Ibid.,* box 24, folder 27: J.H. Hannaford to John Muir, August 9, 1884.
30. ["It is our object":] *Ibid.,* box 23, folder 12: Muir to Smith, August 21, 1884. ["It has been reported":] J.H. Hannaford to John Muir, August 18, 1884. ["Fear of losing the hops business":] *Ibid.,* box 23, folder 18: Muir to Smith, September 6, 1884.
31. [Crew wages:] *Ibid.,* box 23, folder 21. ["Simply a terminating link":] *Ibid.,* folder 18: Muir to Smith, September 6, 1884. ["If it don't pay":] *Ibid.,* folder 30: Muir to Smith, December 15, 1884 (reference to Smith letter of July 25).
32. Seattle *Post-Intelligencer,* August 25, 28, 1884.
33. Lottie R. Roth, ed., *History of Whatcom County* (Chicago: Pioneer Historical Publishing, 1926), vol. 1, p. 277. Roth asserted that the Northern Pacific & Puget Sound Shore was a direct outcome of Harris' visit to Bellingham Bay.
34. *Ibid.,* box 24, folder 28: Robert Harris to Seattle Chamber of Commerce, October 28, 1884.
35. ["This would not do at all":] Oregon Improvement Co. records, box 23, folder 29: letter of John Muir to Elijah Smith, December 11, 1884. ["Freeze out":] *Ibid.,* folder 30: Muir to Smith, December 15, 1884. ["Nothing could be done":] *Ibid.,* box 23, folder 33: Muir to Seattle Chamber of Commerce, February 1, 1885. ["Almost any terms":] *Ibid.,* box 23, folder 36: Muir to Arthur Denny, March 23, 1885.
36. Seattle *Post-Intelligencer,* October 5, 1884.
37. Cochran, *Railroad Leaders,* p. 357: letter of Robert Harris to Thomas Oakes, October 7, 1884.
38. ["The citizens of Washington Territory":] Tacoma *Ledger,* July 26, 1884. ["Such firm reliance":] *Ibid.,* September 29, 1884.
39. Olympia *Transcript,* September 27, 1884.
40. Tacoma *Ledger,* November 23, 1884.
41. Seattle *Post-Intelligencer,* April 6, 1884.
42. N.B. Coffman, "When I Came to Washington Territory," *Washington Historical Quarterly* vol. 26, no. 2 (April 1935), p. 106.
43. ["Autocrat of Tacoma":] Hunt, *Tacoma,* vol. 1, pp. 315-316. The author remembered General Sprague as "a delightful man . . . fair and true," p. 296. ["I have felt a deep interest":] Tacoma *Ledger,* November 17, 1885.
44. Tacoma *Ledger,* July 3, 1884.
45. ["Stuffing a deluded constituency":] Seattle *Herald,* August 5, 1884. ["Some will swear":] *Ibid.,* July 20, 1884.
46. Art Chin and Doug Chin, "The Legacy of Washington State's Early Chinese Pioneers," *International Examiner,* March 4, 1987. Lucile McDonald, "Seattle's First Chinese Resident," Seattle *Times* magazine, September 11, 1955.
47. Robert E. Wynne, "Reaction to the Chinese in the Pacific Northwest and British Columbia, 1850-1910," Ph.D. dissertation, University of Washington, Seattle, 1964.
48. Seattle *Post-Intelligencer,* July 7, 1885.
49. *Ibid.,* September 27, 1885.
50. *Ibid.*
51. *Ibid.*
52. Seattle *Chronicle,* October 16, 1885.
53. Tacoma *Ledger,* October 28, 1885. Also, *Ibid.,* December 29, 1885.
54. Seattle *Post-Intelligencer,* March 17, 1886.
55. ["I made change recently":] Northern Pacific Railroad, corporate records. Minnesota Historical Society. Location no. 137.H.6.6F, special paper no. 59: telegram of Thomas Oakes to Robert Harris, March 22, 1886. ["Some assurance must be given":] *Ibid.,* letter of T.F. Oakes to Robert Harris, March 31, 1886. "Seattle screeching" is listed in the table of contents of a Northern Pacific executive committee meeting minute book: *Ibid.,* location no. 136.D.5.2., vol. 25. ["Public opinion will support us":] Cochran, *Railroad Leaders,* p. 360, letter of Robert Harris to Thomas Oakes, March 26, 1886.
56. Tacoma *Ledger,* January 20, 1887.
57. Seattle *Post-Intelligencer,* August 25, 1886.
58. ["This question might be":] Seattle *Post-Intelligencer,* February 8, 1887. ["If Seattle is determined":] Tacoma *Ledger,* January 23, 1886.
59. ["It would cost $150,000":] Seattle *Post-Intelligencer,* March 2, 1887. ["The time for subsidized railroads":] *Ibid.,* December 2, 1887. [Rail to close the gap:] *Ibid.,* December 14, 1888.
60. ["It is the policy of the N.P.R.R.":] *Ibid.,* January 3, 1887. ["You can say to the people":] Seattle *Times,* June 21, 1886.
61. *Ibid.,* June 9, 1886.
62. ["From this time on":] Seattle *Post-Intelligencer,* July 1, 1887. ["More liberal spirit":] *Ibid.,* July 1, 1887. [Behind the scenes:] Northern Pacific records, location no. 136.D.5.2, vol. 25, p. 238: undated board resolution.
63. ["The approaches to Tacoma":] Tacoma *Ledger,* August 11, 1886. ["It perches up":] Seattle *Times,* August 11, 1887. ["Persons who have traveled":] Portland *Oregonian,* August 12, 1886.
64. *The Northwest* magazine, February 1886, p. 1.
65. Seattle *Post-Intelligencer,* September 16, 1887.
66. [Seattle's latest list of demands:] Hedges, *Henry Villard,* p. 152. ["Have faith and be patient":] *Ibid.,* p. 153. ["To see if an arrangement":] Northern Pacific records, location no. 136.D.5.2, vol. 25, p. 238: executive committee resolution of November 2, 1887.
67. Tacoma *Ledger,* May 22, 1888. Murray Morgan, *Puget's Sound: A Narrative of Early Tacoma and the Southern Sound* (Seattle: University of Washington Press, 1979), p. 211. All Stampede Tunnel hands were given a turkey dinner; those who had stuck it out for three months or longer received a new suit of clothes, a box of cigars, and a free pass to any station on the Northern Pacific.
68. *The Northwest* magazine, April 1888, p. 1.
69. ["Degenerate scrubs":] Arthur A. Denny, *Pioneer Days on Puget Sound* (Seattle: C.B. Bagley, 1888), p. 16. ["Seattle is one of the great cities":] Seattle *Post-Intelligencer,* September 20, 1888.
70. *Ibid.,* December 7, 1888.
71. Seattle *Times,* August 29, 1889.

Chapter 8: City of Destiny

1. Tacoma *Ledger,* July 11, 1885.
2. ["I congratulate Tacoma":] *Ibid.,* February 25,1886. ["There should be prompt":] *Ibid.,* March 4, 1886.
3. ["Mediterranean of the Northwest":] Portland *Oregonian,* July 14, 1869. George F. Train, *My Life in Many States and in Foreign Lands, Dictated in My Seventy-fourth Year* (London: William Heineman, 1902), p. 299.
4. Tacoma *Ledger,* January 14, 1886.
5. *Ibid.,* February 23, 1886.
6. *Ibid.*
7. ["New Era Dawning":] *Ibid.,* July 31, 1886. ["CITY-of-DESTINY!":] *Ibid.,* April 22, 1886. [Julius Dickens:] Herbert Hunt, *Tacoma, Its History and Its Builders: A Half-Century of Activity* (Chicago: S.J. Clarke, 1916), vol. 1, p. 384.
8. ["The company has been promising":] Seattle *Post-Intelligencer,* March 22, 1887. ["I have been dying":] *Ibid.,* March 25, 1887. ["Repression":] *Ibid.,* March 23, 1887.
9. ["There is no [ill] feeling":] Tacoma *Ledger,* June 24, 1887. ["Add three people":] Seattle *Post-Intelligencer,* March 29, 1887. ["Any attack on Seattle":] Tacoma *Ledger,* March 26, 1887.
10. ["Rivalry will exist":] *Ibid.,* July 5, 1887. ["There are busy times ahead":] *Ibid.,* July 6, 1887.
11. [Radebaugh would let bygones be bygones:] *Ibid.,* September 23, 1887. ["Post Seattle wiregrams":] *Ibid.,* September 18, 1887.
12. Hunt, *Tacoma,* vol. 1, p. 543.
13. Tacoma *Ledger,* May 5, 1890.

Chapter 9: Burke, Gilman, and the Seattle Lake Shore & Eastern RR

1. Seattle *Post-Intelligencer,* March 29, 1884.
2. Daniel Hunt Gilman, papers. University of Washington Library, Manuscripts and University Archives. Accession no. 2730-2, box 1, folder 2: letter of D.H. Gilman to F.M. Jones, December 8, 1883.
3. *Ibid.,* box 1, folder 2: letter of D.H. Gilman to F.M. Jones, April 8, 1884.
4. [Oregon Improvement was a dead duck:] *Ibid.* ["There is no better or safer place":] *Ibid.,* Gilman to Jones, October 9, 1884.
5. SLS&E articles of incorporation: Seattle *Post-Intelligencer,* August 10, 1886.
6. *Ibid.,* April 2, 1884. ["A country of its own":] Gilman papers, box 1, folder 11: SLS&E draft route plan, July 3, 1885.
7. ["As you would readily see":] Gilman papers, box 1, folder 2: letter of D.H. Gilman to F.M. Jones, August 13, 1885. ["Your people could have":] *Ibid.,* Gilman to Jones, October 16, 1885.
8. ["How is the fishing":] Thomas Burke, papers. University of Washington Library, Manuscripts and University Archives. Accession no. 1483-2, box 33, letterpress book March-July 1886, p. 377: letter of Thomas Burke to D.H. Gilman, May 31, 1886. ["Like so many":] Tacoma *Ledger,* January 16, 1886.
9. ["A very bright railroad man" . . . "Still our own masters":] Burke papers, box 6, folder 1: letter of D.H. Gilman to Thomas Burke, November 25, 1886.
10. [Major changes:] Robert C. Nesbit, *"He Built Seattle": A Biography of Judge Thomas Burke* (Seattle: University of Washington Press, 1961), pp. 109-110. [Northern Division:] *Ibid.,* p. 118.
11. Clarence Bagley, *History of Seattle from the Earliest Settlement to the Present Time* (Chicago: S.J. Clarke, 1913), vol. 1, p. 249.
12. [John Howard blustered:] Seattle *Post-Intelligencer,* January 14, 1887. ["Scurry and his dudes":] *Ibid.,* January 8, 1887.

13. *Ibid.*, April 26, 1887. Also, Bruce B. Cheever, "The Development of Railroads in the State of Washington, 1860 to 1948," M.A. thesis, Western Washington College of Education, Bellingham, 1949, p. 164.

14. Seattle *Post-Intelligencer*, September 18, 1887; Tacoma *Ledger*, September 17, 1887.

15. ["Hurry up":] Nesbit, *"He Built Seattle,"* p. 112. ["If Kirk won't play fair":] *Ibid.*; Burke papers, box 6, folder 1: letter of D.H. Gilman to Thomas Burke, December 9, 1886.

16. ["Pacify Kirk and the Denny people":] Nesbit, *"He Built Seattle,"* p. 113. [Burke saw to it:] *Ibid.*, p. 115.

17. Seattle *Post-Intelligencer*, December 25, 1886.

18. *Ibid.*, January 26, 28, February 8, 1887. Burke papers, box 42, folder 49.

19. ["We shall be able":] Nesbit, *"He Built Seattle,"* p. 117. ["The matter has been kept":] Seattle *Post-Intelligencer*, January 26, 1887.

20. *Ibid.*, March 15, 1892.

21. ["Enemies":] Nesbit, *"He Built Seattle,"* p. 124. [Ugly rumors:] *Ibid.*, p. 133. [Schulze bragged:] *Ibid.*, September 16, 1887; March 15, 1892.

22. Burke papers, box 34, letterpress book November 21, 1887-March 30, 1888, p. 78: Thomas Burke to Joseph Foster, December 14, 1887.

23. ["The Lake Shore will not swerve":] Seattle *Post-Intelligencer*, April 1, 1888. ["Within two years":] *Ibid.*, March 15, 1888. ["We have two tables":] Nesbit, *"He Built Seattle,"* p.148.

24. Seattle *Post-Intelligencer*, May 17, 1888. Arline Ely, *Our Foundering Fathers: The Story of Kirkland* (Kirkland, Washington: Kirkland Public Library, 1975), p. 35.

25. Burke papers, box 20: letter of Thomas Burke to D.H. Gilman, April 22, 1888.

26. Bagley, *History of Seattle*, vol. 1, p. 250. The pioneer Seattle historian and friend of Thomas Burke presented a colorful verbatim recapitulation of the dialogue between the judge and sheriff.

27. Nesbit, *"He Built Seattle,"* p. 151.

28. Burke papers, box 20, letterpress book March 21, 1888-February 6, 1890, p. 12: Thomas Burke to F.M. Jones, April 4, 1888. Seattle *Post-Intelligencer*, August 24, 1888.

29. Was Daniel Gilman himself one of the welshers? Robert Nesbit observed that he "lived on . . . rosy prospects and borrowed cash," and subscribed to the entire $15,000,000 stock issue "without putting up a penny." Nesbit, *"He Built Seattle,"* p. 138.

30. Burke papers, box 35, letterpress book May 14, 1889-October 12, 1889, p. 187: Burke to Gilman, June 22, 1889.

31. *Ibid.*

32. Burke papers, box 20, letterpress book March 21, 1888-February 6, 1890, p. 180: Thomas Burke to D.H. Gilman, November 20, 1888.

33. Seattle *Post-Intelligencer*, December 15, 1888.

34. [West Coast Improvement Company:] Seattle *Press*, September 14, 1888. [Salmon Bay Development Company:] Seattle *Post-Intelligencer*, January 24, 1890. [Gilman attempted to rope James J. Hill:] Nesbit, *"He Built Seattle,"* p. 273.

35. Seattle *Press-Times* July 13, 1889. Also, Sophie Frye Bass, *When Seattle Was a Village* (Seattle: Lowman and Hanford, 1947), pp. 96-106.

36. Seattle *Post-Intelligencer*, July 11, 1889.

37. Burke papers, box 14, folder 66: Report to the Executive Committee of the Board of Trustees, Seattle Lake Shore & Eastern Railway Co., by William R. Thornell, General Manager, June 14, 1889.

38. ["The company is in sound financial condition":] Seattle *Post-Intelligencer*, October 13, 1889. [Burke begged Jones:] Burke papers, box 35, letterpress book March 21, 1888-February 6, 1890, p. 405: Burke to Jones, August 14, 1889.

39. ["Almost a business necessity":] Burke papers, box 20, letterpress book February 14, 1890-September 16, 1892, p. 26: Thomas Burke to W.P. Clough, April 25, 1890. ["Impracticable to fit that property":] Gilman papers, box 3, folder 10: Clough to Gilman, June 11, 1890.

40. Burke papers, box 21, folder 4: unaddressed draft letter of Thomas Burke, April 20, 1890.

41. ["What the bondholders want":] *Ibid.*, February 21, 1890. ["The Seattle Lake Shore & Eastern railroad is in exceedingly bad shape":] Tacoma *Ledger*,

February 20, 1890. The Northern Pacific held to its position that the Seattle Lake Shore & Eastern had been largely a speculative boondoggle: "The record is a disgraceful one," noted an 1896 NP evaluation report—"the enterprise appears to have been robbed by its promoters." Lorenz P. Schrenk and Robert L. Frey, *Northern Pacific Classic Steam Era* (Edmonds, Washington: Hundman Publishing, 1997), p. 25.

42. Spokane *Spokesman-Review*, February 22, 1890.

43. ["Most of the bonds" . . . "The Lake Shore road has never been stronger!":] Seattle *Post-Intelligencer*, February 26, 1890. ["A scheme worthy of the days of Fisk and Gould":] Burke papers, box 20, letterpress book December 13, 1889-March 6, 1890, p. 407: Thomas Burke to F.M. Jones, March 11, 1890.

44. Burke papers, box 3, folder 21: letter of James D. Smith to D.H. Gilman, June 30, 1890. Historian Glenn C. Quiett noted that NP bought the SLS&E "so that Hill could not acquire this western outlet to the sea." Glenn C. Quiett, *They Built the West: An Epic of Rails and Cities* (New York: D. Appleton-Century, 1934), p. 389. Also, Seattle *Post-Intelligencer*, June 12, 1890.

45. Northern Pacific Railroad, corporate records. Minnesota Historical Society, location no. 137.H.11.2F, vol. 47, pp. 34, 52: letters of Thomas Oakes to J.W. Bryant, March 11, 26, 1890. Seattle *Post-Intelligencer*, July 21, 1890.

46. Seattle *Post-Intelligencer*, August 6, 1890. Northern Pacific records, location no. 136.D.5.2, vol. 25, p. E25: executive committee minutes, June 5, 1890. Oregon & Transcontinental had purchased majority interest in the SLS&E "at the instance, request, and for the benefit of the Northern Pacific Co., which . . . is to operate said . . . railway." The committee passed a resolution that NP would finish construction to Sumas, guaranteeing construction bonds at a rate of $25,000 per mile.

47. ["The city council should now be":] Burke papers, box 21, folder 5: Thomas Burke to D.H. Gilman, June 17, 1890. ["The wonderful change":] Seattle *Post-Intelligencer*, June 12, 1890. ["The balm that assuaged":] *Ibid.*, January 1, 1891.

48. Arline Ely, *Our Foundering Fathers: The Story of Kirkland* (Kirkland, Washington: Kirkland Public Library, 1975). William R. Sherrard, "The Kirkland Steel Mill: An Adventure in Western Enterprise," *Pacific Northwest Quarterly* vol. 53, no. 4 (October 1962). [The Seattle press agitated:] Seattle *Press-Times*, March 24, 26, 1892.

49. Seattle *Post-Intelligencer*, May 22, July 30, 1893; November 20, 1895; Seattle *Times*, July 27, 1896.

50. Seattle *Post-Intelligencer*, July 14, 1895, January 21, 1898; Seattle *Times*, July 27, 1896.

51. Burke papers, box 51, folder 17: undated draft history of SLS&E.

52. Nesbit, *"He Built Seattle,"* pp. 96-97.

Chapter 10: Pax Northernia Pacifica

1. Seattle *Post-Intelligencer*, January 1, 1890.

2. ["Nadeau and I":] *Ibid.*, November 24, 1900. ["Seattle is at last":] *The Northwest* magazine, January 1890.

3. Seattle *Post-Intelligencer*, August 14, 1890.

4. *Ibid.*, March 25, 1890.

5. *Ibid.*

6. *Ibid.*

7. ["Unpopularity of the Northern Pacific":] Tacoma *News*, August 7, 1890. ["We are running a full train":] *Ibid.*, December 16, 1890.

8. David M. Buerge, *Seattle in the 1880s* (Seattle: Historical Society of Seattle and King County, 1986), p. 23. ["Our resources are unlimited":] Seattle *Press-Times*, September 22, 1890.

9. ["In view of all the schemes":] Northern Pacific Railroad, corporate records. Minnesota Historical Society. Location no. 137.H.11.2F, vol. 47, p. 43: letter of T.F. Oakes to Henry Villard, March 17, 1890. [United Railroads:] Seattle *Post-Intelligencer*, August 7, 1890. Interstate Commerce Commission: *Valuation Reports* (Washington: U.S. Printing Office, 1929), vol. 25 (February-May, 1929), p. 697.

10. Seattle *Post-Intelligencer*, March 25, 1890.

11. Northern Pacific records, location no. 136.D.5.2, vol. 25, p. E13: resolution of board of directors to build and operate Lake Washington belt line. ["The company has already acquired":] Seattle *Post-Intelligencer*, July 4, 1890.

Alexander G. Anderson, *The Lake Washington Belt Line. Lake Washington: Resources of the Region tributary to Its Eastern Shores and the Belt Line Railroad . . .* (Seattle: Lowman and Hanford, 1891). [Northern Pacific agreed:] Arline Ely, *Our Foundering Fathers: The Story of Kirkland* (Kirkland, Washington: Kirkland Public Library, 1975), p. 38.

12. Portland *Oregonian*, October 7, 1890.

13. ["The astonishment which we all feel":] Tacoma *Ledger*, September 18, 1891. [Villard and canal:] Seattle *Press-Times*, November 26, 1891.

14. ["If there were any great works":] *Ibid.*, January 29, 1892. ["Barrel of salt":] Tacoma *Ledger*, February 4, 1892.

15. ["We timidly suggest":] *Ibid.*, December 10, 1891. ["Tacoma is becoming weaned":] Seattle *Press-Times*, December 12, 1891.

16. Tacoma *News*, September 9, 1892.

17. ["I launched this magic town":] Tacoma *Ledger*, March 5, 1890. The picture of George Francis Train shaking hands with Job Carr is an appealing one, but during a May 1890 visit, Thomas Canfield recalled that the party did not actually go ashore (*Ibid.*, May 22, 1890). ["Chief Seattle was my father":] Seattle *Post-Intelligencer*, March 16, 1890.

18. Bellingham Bay *Express*, July 25, 1891.

19. ["No difficulty would be experienced":] Oregon Improvement Company, corporate records. University of Washington Library, Manuscripts and University Archives. Accession no. 249, box 23, folder 9: letter of John Muir to Elijah Smith (digest of reports of H.M. Kersey to Muir), July 25, 1884. ["Practically consummated":] *Ibid.*, folder 7: Muir to Smith, July 22, 1884.

20. ["To extend the interests of the Northern Pacific":] Tacoma *News*, August 17, 1889. ["If we loaded our boats full":] Seattle *Post-Intelligencer*, August 27, 1890. See also, Gordon R. Newell, *The H.W. McCurdy Marine History of the Pacific Northwest* (Seattle: Superior Publishing, 1966), p. 47.

21. Seattle *Times*, February 7, 1902, noted that Walter Oakes' marriage to one of Hill's daughters may have played a part in this arrangement.

22. Murray Morgan, *Puget's Sound: A Narrative of Early Tacoma and the Southern Sound* (Seattle: University of Washington Press, 1979), p. 278.

23. ["Gravest danger," Villard 1892 acquisition attempt:] Henry Villard, *Memoirs of Henry Villard, Journalist and Financier, 1835-1900* (Boston, New York: Houghton Mifflin, 1904), vol. 2, pp. 335-336. ["A very sanguine man," Villard 1889 acquisition attempt:] Albro Martin, *James J. Hill and the Opening of the Northwest* (New York: Oxford University Press, 1976), pp. 372-373.

24. ["Discredit, calumny, and abuse":] Villard, *Memoirs,* vol. 2, p. 365. ["Other people's money":] *Ibid.*, p. 372.

25. ["I always tried to favor them":] Tacoma *Ledger*, July 12, 1899. ["I am too old to go to war":] Eugene Semple, papers. University of Washington Library, Manuscripts and University Archives. Accession no. 174, 532, box 18, folder 1: "History of the South Canal, August 24, 1903."

26. ["Henry Villard was the first man":] Seattle *Post-Intelligencer*, November 13, 1900. ["He always liked Seattle better":] *Ibid.*, November 24, 1900.

27. Joseph G. Pyle, *The Life of James J. Hill* (Garden City, New York: Doubleday, 1917), vol. 2, p. 7.

28. [Largest real estate transaction:] Seattle *Times*, February 2, 1897. [Neither provision was fully met:] Derrick Jensen, George Draffan, and John Osborn, *Railroads and Clearcuts: The Legacy of Congress's 1863 Northern Pacific Railroad Land Grant* (Spokane: Inland Empire Land Council; Sandpoint, Idaho: distributed by Keokee Publishing, 1995), p. 3. [A multitude of violations:] *Ibid.*, pp. 16-17.

29. Seattle *Post-Intelligencer*, July 31, 1899.

30. Seattle *Times*, March 2, 1899; Tacoma *Ledger*, June 8, 1899.

31. Seattle *Post-Intelligencer,* March 3, 1901.

32. *Ibid.*, November 13, 1902.

33. [Peninsula plans:] *Ibid.*, January 22, 1903. ["We took the [Port Townsend Southern] out of the wet":] *Ibid.*, May 19, 1903. [A town deputation:] *Ibid.*, November 25, 1903.

34. ["It is not very probable":] *Ibid.*, May 19, 1903. ["In the interests of eastern capital":] *Ibid.*, July 7, 1906. Also, Bruce B. Cheever, "The Development of Railroads in the State of Washington, 1860 to 1948," M.A. thesis, Western Washington College of Education, Bellingham, 1949, pp. 45-46; John T. Labb and Peter J. Replinger, *Logging to the Salt Chuck: Over 100 Years of*

Railroad Logging in Mason County, Washington (Seattle: Northwest Shortline, 1990).

35. Seattle *Post-Intelligencer*, July 10, 1906; August 9, 1907; June 5, 1909.

36. *Ibid.*, September 3, 1907.

37. After conversion to a barge, the *Tacoma* was sold to the Chicago Milwaukee & Puget Sound Railroad in 1917. As the Milwaukee's Barge No. 6, the hull of the old ferry served until January 1950, when it sank off Elliott Bay. See Clark County Genealogical Society, *Kalama, Washington: A Centennial History*, edited by Violet A. Johnson (Kalama, 1990), p. 31.

38. Seattle *Post-Intelligencer*, December 5, 1909. Also, June 6, 1908; September 22, October 20, 1909.

39. *Ibid.*, November 4, 1909.

Chapter 11: Enter the Empire Builder

1. Albert Bowman Rogers, diary. University of Washington Library, Manuscripts and University Archives. Accession no. 642, folder 392A, p. 60: letter of Albert B. Rogers to James J. Hill, July 24, 1887.

2. ["Covering every harbor":] *Ibid.*, p. 76; ["I have great hopes":] *Ibid.*, p. 79; ["Dropped, accidentally, on some information":] *Ibid.*, p. 98. Also, John Garwood Rogers, diary. University of Washington Library, Manuscripts and University Archives. Accession no. 643.

3. Albro Martin, *James J. Hill and the Opening of the Northwest* (New York: Oxford University Press, 1976), p. 374.

4. ["The best possible line":] *Ibid.*, p. 366. ["There are probably passages":] *Ibid.*, p. 382.

5. [Linsley had observed only in passing:] Harry M. Majors, "D.C. Linsley's Railroad Survey of the Sauk and Wenatchee Rivers in the 1870s," *Northwest Discovery*, vol. 2, no. 4 (April 1981), p. 253. ["Stevens Pass":] JoAnn Roe, *Stevens Pass: The Story of Railroading and Recreation in the North Cascades* (Seattle: Mountaineers, 1995), p. 55.

6. [Bellingham Bay:] Lottie R. Roth, ed., *History of Whatcom County* (Chicago: Pioneer Historical Publishing, 1926), vol. 1, p. 283. ["If Jim Hill's road goes to Bellingham":] Tacoma *Ledger*, August 24, 1887.

7. Thomas Burke, papers. University of Washington Library, Manuscripts and University Archives. Accession no. 1483-2, box 20, letterpress book (March 21, 1888-February 6, 1890), p. 25: letter of Thomas Burke to W.P. Clough, April 25, 1890.

8. Seattle *Post-Intelligencer*, November 28, 1906.

9. ["Your petitioner":] *Ibid.*, March 8, 1890. Also, Clarence Bagley, *History of Seattle from the Earliest Settlement to the Present Time* (Chicago: S.J. Clarke, 1916), vol. 1, p. 255. Robert C. Nesbit, *"He Built Seattle": A Biography of Judge Thomas Burke* (Seattle: University of Washington Press, 1961), p. 214.

10. ["The Great Northern road does not seek" . . . "If the citizens of Seattle show themselves":] Seattle *Post-Intelligencer*, March 8, 1890.

11. [Burke passed the hat:] Burke papers, box 20, letterpress book (December 13, 1889-May 6, 1890), p. 458: letter of Thomas Burke to D.H. Gilman, March 20, 1890. ["Some suitable point":] Burke papers, box 46, folder 2: St. Paul Minneapolis & Manitoba board resolution, June 24, 1890. ["Municipal crime":] *Ibid.*, box 21, folder 5: Burke to Gilman, June 17, 1890. Also, Bagley, *History of Seattle*, vol. 1, p. 255.

12. Burke papers, box 21, folder 5: Burke to Gilman, June 17, 1890. The alignment on the west side of Salmon Bay would ultimately be adopted in 1910.

13. ["He is a wise farmer":] Bagley, *History of Seattle*, vol. 1, p. 258. ["Everett or Podunk":] Glenn C. Quiett, *They Built the West: An Epic of Rails and Cities* (New York: D. Appleton-Century, 1934), p. 461.

14. ["Good policy":] Burke papers, box 20, letterpress book (February 14, 1890-September 16, 1892), p. 26: Burke to Clough, April 25, 1890. ["The Snoqualmie Pass is too near the Northern Pacific":] Seattle *Post-Intelligencer*, August 23, 1890.

15. Seattle *Post-Intelligencer*, October 5, 1890.

16. *Ibid.*

17. *Ibid.* Also, January 1, 1891.

18. ["A road like a rake":] Quiett, *They Built the West*, p. 461. ["Unless I can move that crop":] Bagley, *History of Seattle*, vol. 2, pp. 257-258. [Great Northern land grants:] Derrick Jensen, George Draffan, and John Osborn, *Railroads*

and Clearcuts: The Legacy of Congress's 1863 Northern Pacific Railroad Land Grant (Spokane: Inland Empire Land Council; Sandpoint, Idaho: distributed by Keokee Publishing, 1995), p. 22. Great Northern also inherited from predecessor Minneapolis & St. Cloud a grant of odd sections of Minnesota "swamp land"; see Thomas Burke papers, box 54, folder 18: Minneapolis & St. Cloud articles of incorporation.

19. ["We are pushing the line":] Seattle *Press-Times*, September 7, 1891. [Portland extension:] Seattle *Press*, January 6, 1891. ["We shall not build our own line":] Seattle *Press-Times*, September 7, 1891.

20. ["The engineers are . . . secretly locating":] Tacoma *Ledger*, March 27, 1890. ["Rush or a railroad spike":] *Ibid.*, August 4, 1890. ["It is a well-known fact":] Tacoma *Ledger*, October 30, 1891. ["The Northern Pacific practically incloses":] Great Northern Railway, corporate records. Minnesota Historical Society. Location no. 132.E.19.1B: letter of W.P. Clough to J.J. Hill, February 26, 1890.

21. Seattle *Press-Times*, September 14, 1891.

22. Robert Nesbit stated that Hill used Bellingham solely as a lever to secure better terms from Seattle, and that "neither Hill nor his biographer, Joseph G. Pyle, left the impression that he had seriously considered any other terminus than the principal port city on the Sound"; *"He Built Seattle,"* p. 214. Also, Bruce B. Cheever, "The Development of Railroads in the State of Washington, 1860 to 1948," M.A. thesis, Western Washington College of Education, Bellingham, 1949, p. 92. Roth, *History of Whatcom County*, vol. 2, pp. 284, 293.

23. Port Gardner *News*, September 11, 1891.

24. Seattle *Post-Intelligencer*, August 14, 1891.

25. Seattle *Press-Times*, August 18, 1891.

26. *Ibid.*, December 8, 1891.

27. ["Seattle will be the terminal":] *Ibid.*, February 15, 1892. ["Gilded butterfly":] Seattle *Telegraph*, February 17, 1892. Clarence Bagley asserted "in a twinkling" the value of Washington timberlands had increased by an amount at least as great as the entire capital stock of the Great Northern Railway: "The result of this sweeping cut was magical; the woods became alive, and instead of the empty cars going eastward they were soon coming westward, for there was not enough westbound traffic to offset the enormous lumber shipments to the prairie states"; *History of Seattle*, vol. 1, p. 258.

28. Seattle *Post-Intelligencer*, January 19, 1893 (from the New York *Mail and Express*).

29. ["We want to get into shape":] Seattle *Press-Times*, January 21, 1893. ["Is this not the end" . . . "300 or 400 leading people":] *Ibid.*, January 23, 1893.

30. ["The composition of the train":] *Ibid.*, June 23, 1893. ["The porter needs attention":] *Ibid.*, May 17, 1893.

31. J. Kingston Pierce, "The Panic of 1893," *Columbia Magazine* vol. 7, no. 4 (winter 1993-94), p. 37.

32. Seattle *Post-Intelligencer*, March 15, 1894.

33. *Ibid.*, May 1, 1894.

34. *Ibid.*, December 26, 1894.

35. Martin, *James J. Hill*, p. 471.

36. ["Seattle scores again" . . . "This is the turning point":] Seattle *Post-Intelligencer*, July 18, 1896.

37. ["They pay their sailors":] *Ibid.*, April 9, 1897. ["I don't look for much":] *Ibid.*, May 30, 1898. [Hill urged passage:] *Ibid.*, January 13, 1899. ["Lath and plaster":] Martin, *James J. Hill*, p. 472.

38. Burke papers, box 6, folder 1: letter of D.H. Gilman to Thomas Burke, February 21, 1892.

39. *Ibid.*, box 8, folder 14: Hill to Burke, March 3, 1898.

40. Burke papers, box 6, folder 21: Burke to John F. Stevens, September 15, 1902. Eugene Semple papers, University of Washington Library, Manuscripts and University Archives. Accession no. 174, 532, box 18, folder 1: history of the Seattle & Lake Washington Waterway Company.

41. Seattle *Post-Intelligencer*, August 20, 1897. Mountain bikers now trek up the Iron Goat Trail, which was opened in 1993—the centennial year of the driving of the Great Northern's last spike in 1893.

42. *Ibid.*, June 6, 1893; June 24, 1899.

43. ["Calculating machine":] *Ibid.*, August 27, 1897. *The Wall Street Journal*, April 20, 1899.

44. Seattle *Post-Intelligencer*, December 22, 1901.

45. ["There is as yet":] Seattle *Times*, December 21, 1901. ["The harmonious operation":] Seattle *Post-Intelligencer*, March 28, 1902. ["Mr. Hill wishes":] Seattle *Star*, December 23, 1901.

46. ["The only and final end":] Seattle *Times*, December 23, 1901. ["Evils of the railroad lobby":] Seattle *Post-Intelligencer*, May 16, 1902. [State railroad commission:] Tacoma *News*, August 3, 1889.

47. Tacoma *Evening News*, May 20, 1902.

48. [Hill and lumbermen:] Martin, *James J. Hill*, p. 514. Norman H. Clark, *Mill Town: A Social History of Everett, Washington, from Its Earliest Beginnings on the Shores of Puget Sound to the Tragic and Infamous Event Known as the Everett Massacre* (Seattle: University of Washington Press, 1970), p. 70. The author claimed that Hill's withdrawal of freight cars imposed a "virtual embargo on Washington lumber" during the early 1900s.

49. [Hill and *Times*:] Sharon A. Boswell and Lorraine McConaghy: *Raise Hell and Sell Newspapers: Alden J. Blethen and The Seattle Times* (Pullman: Washington State University Press, 1996), p. 268. [Hill and *Post-Intelligencer*:] Richard C. Berner, *Seattle in the Twentieth Century*. Volume 1: *Seattle 1900-1920. From Boomtown, Urban Turbulence, to Restoration* (Seattle: Charles Press, 1991), p. 34. Seattle *Argus* publisher Harry Chadwick claimed that Colonel Blethen "owes his very business and financial life to Mr. Hill." *Argus*, March 13, 1909.

50. Seattle *Argus*, May 23, 1903.

51. ["Largely owing to his superior knowledge":] Quiett, *They Built the West*, p. 488. [Hill's ships:] Seattle *Post-Intelligencer*, February 7, 1904.

52. Seattle *Post-Intelligencer*, May 13, 1905.

53. ["I do not believe":] *Ibid.*, January 2, 1906. ["Sort of outlaws":] Martin, *James J. Hill*, p. 541.

54. ["Hill's white elephants":] Gordon R. Newell, *The H.W. McCurdy Marine History of the Pacific Northwest* (Seattle: Superior Publishing, 1966), p. 251. Robert Nesbit cited additional factors that doomed Hill's Asian venture: the growth of domestic markets, the California oil boom, heavy competition through Vancouver, B.C., and the growth of Japan's own industrial capacity; *"He Built Seattle,"* p. xiv.

55. Seattle *Post-Intelligencer*, September 30, 1905. Claiming that Hill had been so impressed from the outset by Seattle Spirit as to assure the city's terminal status, Welford Beaton attributed to him the following statement: "A people that showed such spirit and energy and love for their town are a good people to live among and do business with, and it would be a pity to turn them down." Welford Beaton, *The City that Made Itself: A Literary and Pictorial Record of the Building of Seattle* (Seattle: Terminal Publishing, 1914), p. 11.

56. ["Stupid rot":] Seattle *Post-Intelligencer*, December 5, 1898. ["This prince of the black art":] Tacoma *News*, August 21, 1900.

57. Seattle *Post-Intelligencer*, May 13, 14, 1908.

58. ["Empire Builder":] Portland *Oregonian*, November 7, 1908. ["Junk line":] *Ibid.*, November 6, 1908. ["Your commerce, your manufactures":] Seattle *Post-Intelligencer*, November 11, 1908. Occasional references to Hill as an "empire builder" may be found at least as early as 1905, but by 1908 he was certainly recognized by that name.

59. *Ibid.*, June 2, 1909.

60. *Ibid.*, May 1, 1910, December 25, 1910. [Chittenden plan:] *Ibid.*, March 5, 1910. See also, Itothe Pucher, *The Puget Sound and Inland Empire Railway. "Cascade Tunnel Route."* Undated publication (Seattle: A. Harriman).

61. [Political adventurers:] Martin, *James J. Hill*, p. 494. [Doctrinaires":] *Ibid.*, p. 539. Arthur Stilwell, a railroad executive, gave Hill credit for creating at least half a million jobs and adding over $6,000,000,000 to the nation's wealth since the opening of the Great Northern in 1893; Arthur E. Stilwell, "Confidence or National Suicide?" Seattle *Post-Intelligencer*, August 25, 1910. Robert Nesbit stated, "The selection of Seattle as its western terminus by the Great Northern was possibly the greatest single factor in the city's growth and subsequent prosperity"; *"He Built Seattle,"* p. 243.

Chapter 12: Railroad Mania

1. Northern Pacific Railroad, corporate records. Minnesota Historical Society. Location no.137.H.11.2F, vol. 51, p. 455: letter of T.F. Oakes to C. Van Horne, April 24, 1891.

2. ["The Northern Pacific does not want":] Seattle *Post-Intelligencer*, May 24, 1900. ["The line known as":] *Ibid.*, January 14, 1903.

3. ["We are not going to extend":] *Ibid.*, September 18, October 5, 1906. [Mysterious reports:] *Ibid.*, November 23, 1907.

4. ["To get a share":] *Ibid.*, December 5, 1902. ["Seattle's record speaks for itself":] *Ibid.*, August 13, 1909.

5. Michael Malone asserted in his biography of James J. Hill that the CB&Q's Billings gateway amounted to a "forced marriage" interchange arrangement with the Northern Pacific, extorted under threat of building to Butte or beyond; Michael Malone, *James J. Hill: Empire Builder of the Northwest* (Norman: University of Oklahoma Press, 1996), p. 204.

6. [Chicago & North Western:] Seattle *Post-Intelligencer*, August 25, 1906, November 28, 1909. Also, H. Roger Grant, "Seeking the Pacific: The Chicago & North Western's Plans to Reach the West Coast," *Pacific Northwest Quarterly* vol. 81, no. 2 (April 1990). ["We do not intend to come":] *Ibid.*, September 23, 1908.

7. ["Armed with maps":] *Ibid.*, April 7, 1887. [Seattle & Southern:] *Ibid.*, August 12, 1888, August 14, 1889; ["Real estate sharks":] *Ibid.*, September 2, 1889. ["We will not build":] Tacoma *Ledger*, April 9, 1890.

8. [Seattle & Northern:] Seattle *Post-Intelligencer*, November 20, 1888. [Port Townsend Southern and OIC:] *Ibid.*, September 9, 1890, April 18, 1891; Tacoma *Ledger*, April 16, September 16, 1890; April 16, 1891. Gerald M. Best, *Ships and Narrow Gauge Rails: The Story of the Pacific Coast Company* (Berkeley: Howell-North, 1964), pp. 131, 134. See also, Henry L. Gray, *Historic Railroads of Washington* (Seattle, 1971), p. 13.

9. [Columbia & Puget Sound plans:] Seattle *Post-Intelligencer*, December 13, 14, 1888. [George Morison survey:] Oregon Improvement Company, corporate records. University of Washington Library, Manuscripts and University Archives. Accession no. 249, box 75, folder 4. ["In competent hands":] Great Northern Railway, corporate records. Minnesota Historical Society. Location no. 132.E.19.1B: letters of W.P. Clough and J.J. Hill, July 21 and 27, 1890.

10. [Seattle & San Francisco, Seattle Terminal:] Seattle *Post-Intelligencer*, April 16, May 27, August 1, October 13, 1899; November 3, 1900; October 8, 1901. [Northern Pacific absorbs Seattle & San Francisco:] Northern Pacific records, location no. 136.E.1.1B.

11. ["A number of New York capitalists":] Seattle *Post-Intelligencer*, September 6, 1883.

12. [Frank C. Ross:] Tacoma *Ledger*, June 14, 1890; Seattle *Post-Intelligencer*, May 3, 1893, July 26, 1896, September 4, 1897. [Puyallup Indian Reservation:] Elizabeth Shackleford, "History of the Puyallup Indian Reservation," M.A. thesis, University of Puget Sound, Tacoma, 1918, pp. 24-26. Also, Herbert Hunt, *Tacoma, Its History and Its Builders: A Half-Century of Activity* (Chicago: S.J. Clarke, 1916), vol. 2, p. 308. Ross sold the little Tacoma & Lake City to the Union Pacific in 1891, which in turn sold the short line to local interests in 1896; the line was abandoned the following year. See Bruce B. Cheever, "The Development of Railroads in the State of Washington, 1860 to 1948," M.A. thesis, Western Washington College of Education, Bellingham, 1949, p. 67.

13. ["It has, or appears to have":] Seattle *Post-Intelligencer*, March 22, 1898. ["Jim Jam fakes":] Seattle *Times*, March 23, 1898. ["New York millionaires":] Seattle *Post-Intelligencer*, February 8, 9, 1899.

14. [James Shute, M. de Lobel:] *Ibid.*, May 15, June 1, 1903.

15. [Boynton Bicycle:] *Ibid.*, September 23, 1891. ["We can make the trip":] *Ibid.*, December 1, 1891. Tacoma *News*, February 19, 1892.

16. Seattle *Post-Intelligencer*, March 1, 1900.

17. ["The North Coast Railway is to be the Pacific Division":] *Ibid.*, December 7, 1905. Also, Jeff Asay, *Union Pacific Northwest: The Oregon-Washington Railway & Navigation Company: A History* (Edmonds, Washington: Pacific Fast Mail, 1991), p. 121.

18. ["There seems to be a disposition":] Seattle *Post-Intelligencer*, December 17, 1905. ["Either the Gould or the Vanderbilt":] *Ibid.*, December 20, 1905.

19. *Ibid.*, January 8, 1906.

20. ["On its own bottom":] *Ibid.*, February 1, 1906. ["Hindered and delayed":] *Ibid.*, November 10, 1906.

21. [North Coast and Union Pacific:] Asay, *Union Pacific Northwest*, p. 121. ["No other railroad man on earth":] Seattle *Post-Intelligencer*, December 8, 1908. [Stenographer:] *Ibid.*, June 12, 1909.

22. ["The North Coast is coming":] *Ibid.*, September 8, 1909. [Strahorn promised:] *Ibid.*, March 2, 1909. ["We will bring the North Coast to Puget Sound":] *Ibid.*, October 3, 1910. [North Coast and O&W:] *Ibid.*, November 24, 25, 1910; Asay, *Union Pacific Northwest*, p. 129.

23. [Northern Pacific Columbia River line:] *The Northwest* magazine, April 1887. ["Before we stop":] Seattle *Post-Intelligencer*, June 27, 1906.

24. *Ibid.*, November 26, 1910.

CHAPTER 13: THE WONDERFUL INTERURBAN

1. Tacoma *News*, September 12, 1892.

2. ["Veritable bonanza":] Seattle *Post-Intelligencer*, February 14, 1899.

3. *Ibid.*, February 1, 1900.

4. *Ibid.*, February 11, 1901.

5. ["Enthusiastic friends":] *Ibid.*, April 6, 1902. [Puyallup right of way:] Elizabeth Shackleford, "History of the Puyallup Indian Reservation," M.A. thesis, University of Puget Sound, Tacoma, 1918, p. 28. See also, Warren W. Wing, *To Tacoma by Trolley: The Puget Sound Electric Railway* (Edmonds, Washington: Pacific Fast Mail, 1995), p. 16.

6. ["It fitted so nicely":] Seattle *Post-Intelligencer*, November 23, 1902.

7. [Immediate opposition:] *Ibid.*, December 20, 1902. Also, Warren W. Wing, *To Seattle by Trolley* (Edmonds, Washington: Pacific Fast Mail, 1990).

8. Seattle *Post-Intelligencer*, February 19, September 23, 1904; November 22, 1905; April 25, 1908. Seattle & Eastern Railway, prospectus. University of Washington Library, Special Collections and Preservation.

9. ["An increase of traveling facilities":] Seattle *Post-Intelligencer*, October 13, 1907.

10. *Ibid.*, February 12, 1908.

CHAPTER 14: RAILROAD MUDDLE

1. [Milner's gang:] Seattle *Post-Intelligencer*, December 30, 1888. ["Come on":] *Ibid.*, May 4, 1889.

2. *Ibid.*, January 26, 1889. Also, *Ibid.*, January 1, 19, March 9, 1889.

3. ["One of a large class of people":] *Ibid.*, January 27, 1889. ["Bosh":] *Ibid.*, May 8, 1889.

4. *Ibid.*, November 25, 1888. [Tidelands controversy:] *Ibid.*, July 29, 1895, November 14, 1897. Also, Padraic Burke, *A History of the Port of Seattle* (Seattle: Port of Seattle, 1976), p. 13.

5. Seattle *Post-Intelligencer*, June 6, 1909.

6. ["Scarcely room left":] *Ibid.*, October 23, 1889. Also, July 31, August 9, 10, October 11, 1889. The Seattle *Press-Times* of February 15, 1892, noted: "The terms under which the original ram's horn franchise [Villard right of way] was obtained were never observed in good faith or any faith. Some track was laid down, but it was never operated. Not a single car nor pound of freight was ever hauled over it. It could not be used today if the companies held undisputed possession." For description of existing and "imaginary" portions of the right of way, see Seattle *Post-Intelligencer*, December 25, 1890.

7. *Ibid.*, March 25, 1890.

8. *Ibid.*

9. *Ibid.*, March 26, 1890.

10. ["All I own is in this city":] *Ibid.*, March 27, 1890. ["We won't be pigs" . . . "we would throw up everything":] Daniel H. Gilman, papers. University of Washington Library, Manuscripts and University Archives. Accession no. 2730, box 3, folder 10: letters of W.P. Clough to D.H. Gilman, March 25, 26, 1890.

11. *Ibid.*, p. 551: Burke to W.P. Clough, April 2, 1890.

12. Seattle *Post-Intelligencer*, April 3, 1890.

13. *Ibid.*

14. ["Cloven hoof":] Thomas Burke, papers. University of Washington Library, Manuscripts and University Archives. Accession no. 1483-2, box 20, letterpress book (December 13, 1889-May 6, 1890), p. 583: Burke to Clough, April 4, 1890. ["Trying to produce":] *Ibid.*, p. 548; ["Scurrying around":] *Ibid.*, p. 507; ["This . . . seems to be":] *Ibid.*, p. 549; ["An ugly fight":] *Ibid.*, p. 586; ["Would have relieved":] p. 658: letter of Thomas Burke to W.P. Clough, April 17, 1890; ["Special favorite":] *Ibid.*, p. 684.

15. ["I like to see this":] Seattle *Post-Intelligencer*, April 16, 1890. ["Day after day":] *Ibid.*, April 17, 1890.

16. ["To avoid raising":] Robert C. Nesbit, *"He Built Seattle": A Biography of Judge Thomas Burke* (Seattle: University of Washington Press, 1961), p. 117. ["More than doubtful":] Great Northern Railway, corporate records. Minnesota Historical Society. Location no. 132.E.19.1B: letter of Thomas Shepard to J.J. Hill, December 2, 1891.

17. Seattle *Post-Intelligencer*, October 30, 1890. Padraic Burke, *Port of Seattle*, p. 15.

18. [A raft of new controls:] Nesbit, *"He Built Seattle,"* p. 303. ["Utterly unfit":] *Ibid.*, p. 306.

19. *Ibid.*, p. 253. Also, *Ibid.*, chapter 11, "Satrap to the Empire Builder."

20. Seattle *Post-Intelligencer*, December 23, 24, 27, 1890.

21. *Ibid.*, December 24, 1890.

22. *Ibid.*, May 13, 1891.

23. ["The time is past":] *Ibid.* ["We jumped on them" . . . "It is but fair":] Burke papers, box 6, folder 14: letter of Thomas Burke to Daniel Gilman, March 2, 1892.

24. ["I am heartily tired":] Burke papers, box 40, folder 26: Hill to Burke, December 18, 1891. [Hill plans:] Seattle *Post-Intelligencer*, February 20, 22, 1892. ["The time may come":] Seattle *Telegraph*, February 17, 1892.

25. Great Northern records, location no. 132.E.19.1B: Thomas Shepard to Hill, February 24, March 4, 1892.

26. Seattle *Post-Intelligencer*, October 16, 1892.

27. *Ibid.*, May 14, 1892.

28. *Ibid.*, May 18, 1893.

29. ["The only surprise":] Seattle *Press-Times*, May 20, 1893. ["No damned fool":] Reginald H. Thomson, *That Man Thomson*, edited by Grant H. Redford (Seattle: University of Washington Press, 1950), p. 50.

30. Thomson, *That Man Thomson*, p. 50.

31. Nesbit, *"He Built Seattle,"* p. 227. Also, Seattle *Post-Intelligencer*, February 7, 1895.

32. ["We have been four years fighting":] Seattle *Press-Times*, July 21, 1893. ["Some respectable Christian gentlemen":] *Ibid.*, September 7, 1893. ["An interesting question":] Seattle *Post-Intelligencer*, February 13, 1894.

33. [Colman compromise:] *Ibid.*, February 14, April 17, 1894. ["The best of friends":] *Ibid.*, March 6, 1895.

34. *Ibid.*, November 14, 1897. Also, Nesbit, *"He Built Seattle,"* p. 339.

35. Seattle *Post-Intelligencer*, March 17, 1895.

36. *Ibid.*, January 20, 1895. ["We cannot come out here 2,000 miles":] Seattle *Press-Times*, June 6, 1892. [A useful friend:] Padraic Burke, *Port of Seattle*, p. 16.

37. Seattle *Post-Intelligencer*, October 4, 1900.

38. *Ibid.*, July 8, 1898.

39. *Ibid.*, September 18, 1899.

40. *Ibid.*, September 17, 18, 19, 1899. Glenn C. Quiett, *They Built the West: An Epic of Rails and Cities* (New York: D. Appleton-Century, 1934), p. 465.

41. Seattle *Post-Intelligencer*, September 19, 1899.

42. [NP depot:] *Ibid.*, October 25, 1899. ["No business judgement":] Albro Martin, *James J. Hill and the Opening of the Northwest* (New York: Oxford University Press, 1976), p. 458.

43. Seattle *Times*, October 30, 1899.

44. Seattle *Post-Intelligencer*, December 31, 1899.

45. *Ibid.*, December 27, 1899.

46. Seattle *Argus*, September 23, 1899.

47. ["Utter madness":] Burke papers, box 6, folder 17: Hill to Burke, January 19, 1900. [Pro and con letters:] Seattle *Post-Intelligencer*, January 4, 5, 6, 1900. ["I do not know anyone else":] Burke papers, box 6, folder 17: Hill to Burke, January 19, 1900.

48. ["Railroads are not in the habit":] Seattle *Post-Intelligencer*, January 21, 1900. ["Contrary to the general belief":] *Ibid.*, October 26, 1900.

49. *Ibid.*, March 3, 1901.

50. *Ibid.*, January 1, 1895; January 13, October 25, 1901; April 2, 19, 1902.

51. Burke papers, box 21, folder 16: letters to Blethen, Goldsmith, et al., January 7, 1902. Burke's written exclamations that the tunnel plan was a "complete surprise" and "never before thought of by anyone in Seattle" are at odds with R.H. Thomson's account of the tunnel agreement made between himself, Burke, and Hill, nine years earlier; see Thomson, *That Man Thomson*, p. 50.

52. Seattle *Post-Intelligencer*, May 15, 1902.

53. *Ibid.*, January 6, 1903.

54. *Ibid.*, January 23, 1904; also, November 15, 1903; April 10, 1904.

55. *Ibid.*, August 3, 1904.

56. ["Every nation":] *Ibid.*, July 3, 1904. [Cheese:] Seattle *Press-Times*, February 12, 1896. [Stowaways:] Seattle *Post-Intelligencer*, October 25, 1897.

57. *Ibid.*, July 23, 1906.

58. *Ibid.*, May 16, 1906.

59. *Ibid.*, July 17, 1906.

60. ["The Union Pacific officials":] *Ibid.*, July 18, 1906. ["No franchise":] *Ibid.*, March 7, 1908.

61. Seattle *Argus*, March 13, 1909.

62. ["Have a few engineers":] *Ibid.*, December 17, 1907. ["For each of the five railroads":] Nesbit, *"He Built Seattle,"* p. 242.

Chapter 15: The Harriman Road.

1. ["I shall always think":] Peter J. Lewty, *To the Columbia Gateway: The Oregon Railway and the Northern Pacific, 1879-1884* (Pullman: Washington State University Press, 1987), p. 31. ["Apple tree without a limb":] Robert G. Athearn, *Union Pacific Country* (New York: Rand McNally, 1971), p. 224. [Jealousy of Collis P. Huntington:] James B. Hedges, *Henry Villard and the Railways of the Northwest* (New Haven: Yale University Press, 1939), p. 34.

2. Seattle *Post-Intelligencer*, March 27, 1890.

3. ["Tacoma rather than Seattle":] Tacoma *News*, December 23, 1889. ["Inducements":] Tacoma *Ledger*, April 8, September 5, 1890. ["Sunday was eliminated":] Herbert Hunt, *Tacoma, Its History and Its Builders: A Half-Century of Activity* (Chicago: S.J. Clarke, 1916), vol. 1, p. 497.

4. [Olympia:] Tacoma *Ledger*, April 12, 1890. [Puget City:] South Bay Historical Association, *South Bay: Its History and Its People, 1840-1940* (Olympia, 1986), pp. 30-31.

5. [Great Northern and Union Pacific:] Seattle *Post-Intelligencer*, November 28, December 31, 1890; Tacoma *Ledger*, January 1, 1891; Seattle *Times*, January 6, 1891. Great Northern Railway, corporate records. Minnesota Historical Society. Location no. 132.E.19.1B: letter of W.P. Clough to J.J. Hill, June 30, 1890; letter of J.S. Cameron to J.J. Hill, August 27, 1890. See also, location no. 132.E.10.2F, folder no. 3722; location no. 132.E.14.10F, folder 4065; and branch line file, vol. 6, Portland & Seattle Railway. As collateral for its share in the building of the Seattle line, Union Pacific deposited certificates of indebtedness with J.P. Morgan & Co. Northern Pacific subsidiary Northwest Improvement Co. bought these in 1897, acquiring as well the uncompleted Columbia River bridge and Portland & Puget Sound roadbed, and in 1905 assumed full title from both the UP and GN. This in turn was transferred to the Portland & Seattle Railway in June 1906—ironically, a tactic to occupy the ground against a renewed Union Pacific threat to build to Seattle.

6. Glenn C. Quiett, *They Built the West: An Epic of Rails and Cities* (New York: D. Appleton-Century, 1934), p. 429.

7. ["Large bodies move slowly":] Seattle *Post-Intelligencer*, October 20, 1900. ["The Union Pacific will come":] *Ibid.*, December 11, 1903.

8. ["The Union Pacific will be extended":] *Ibid.*, April 30, 1906. ["We have got to increase":] *Ibid.*, May 1, 1906.

9. [Oregon & Washington Railway:] *Ibid.*, May 13, 1906. ["Intelligent and lasting agreements":] Jeff Asay, *Union Pacific Northwest: The Oregon-Washington Railway & Navigation Company* (Edmonds, Washington: Pacific Fast Mail, 1991), p. 106.

10. Seattle *Post-Intelligencer*, March 7, 14, 20, November 25, 1907.

11. [Tacoma right of way:] *Ibid.*, April 25, 1907. ["Keep us out of Seattle":] Asay, *Union Pacific Northwest*, p. 109.

12. [Milwaukee deal:] Seattle *Post-Intelligencer*, February 17, 1906; April 11, July 28, 1909. [Kruttschnitt indicated:] *Ibid.*, February 14, 1909.

13. *Ibid.*, April 16, 1909; May 19, 1910; Asay, *Union Pacific Northwest*, pp. 109, 112. See also, Hunt, *Tacoma*, vol. 2, p. 220. Hunt claimed that, in the opinion of railroad insiders, the UP's Tacoma tunnel was nothing more than a bluff to force the NP into granting trackage rights. Rapprochement with Hill and economic factors likely doomed the Everett extension, if indeed it was ever seriously considered. It, and the decision to abandon Salmon Bay,

remain a mystery; the relevant files in the Union Pacific archives in Omaha are no longer available and are presumed destroyed.

14. ["We would all be put in prison":] Seattle *Post-Intelligencer*, March 31, 1909. ["The dollar loomed large":] *Ibid.*, September 10, 1909. ["Seattle, with its marvelous growth":] *Ibid.*, September 11, 1909.

Chapter 16: Rails over Snoqualmie

1. Seattle *Post-Intelligencer*, June 9, 1881.

2. ["If we do not make it" . . . "He said we could not build":] Max Lowenthal, *The Investor Pays* (New York: A.A. Knopf, 1933), pp. 16-17.

3. [Duplicating NP, build to Eureka:] August W. Derleth, *The Milwaukee Road: Its First Hundred Years* (New York: Creative Age Press, 1948), p. 170. [Build to Los Angeles:] Seattle *Post-Intelligencer*, September 27, 1902.

4. ["The business has been so heavy":] Derleth, *The Milwaukee Road*, p. 171. ["I should be very glad":] Seattle *Post-Intelligencer*, September 30, 1905. [Hill expressed these further comments in 1906: "When the Chicago Milwaukee & St. Paul first considered plans for making connections with the coast and Puget Sound, an effort was made to secure such entrance by a traffic arrangement with the Northern Pacific. I told the officers [of the Milwaukee] that they should by all means build a line to Seattle. I told them there was a strip between the Yellowstone and the Platte rivers that was unoccupied, and that if they did not build a line by that route, we would!" Seattle *Post-Intelligencer*, July 17, 1906.

5. *Ibid.*, June 25, 26, August 7, September 2, 1904; February 28, April 13, 28, August 6, 1905.

6. ["You may say unreservedly":] *Ibid.*, October 19, 1905; also, October 14, 19, 21, 25, 1905.

7. ["This denial is":] *Ibid.*, October 25, 1905. ["This is rather more satisfactory":] *Ibid.*, November 14, 1905; also, October 28, November 3, 13, 21, 22, 25, 1905.

8. *Ibid.*, January 8, 1906.

9. ["Occult influence" . . . "Here is the big city":] *Ibid.*, March 3, 4, 1906; also, January 13, 30, February 8, 13, 1906.

10. *Ibid.*, March 18, 1906.

11. [Final route:] *Ibid.*, December 9, 1906. ["I regret":] *Ibid.*, January 14, 1907. ["Almost swamped":] *Ibid.*, September 20, 1907.

12. ["Use every influence" . . . "Microscopic and academic character":] *Ibid.*, August 15, 23.

13. ["Plenty of squalls":] *Ibid.*, February 27, 1907. [Boom towns:] *Ibid.*, August 5, 11, 1907, August 20, 1908. ["We are not acting hastily":] *Ibid.*, September 28, 1908.

14. *Ibid.*, July 21, September 1, 1907; July 21, November 17, 1908. Derleth, *The Milwaukee Road*, p. 188.

15. [Earling visit:] Seattle *Post-Intelligencer*, September 28, 1908. ["Seattle's long deferred hope":] *Ibid.*, October 1, 1908.

16. [Lumbermen's dinner:] *Ibid.*, February 3, 1906; ["Sensational race":] *Ibid.*, February 28, 1907, October 31, 1909.

17. *Ibid.*, April 10, 1908; Derleth, *The Milwaukee Road*, p.191.

18. ["Somewhat out of the line":] Seattle *Post-Intelligencer*, August 2, 1907. [Gentlemen's agreement:] *Ibid.*, August 8, 1909.

19. *Ibid.*, April 6, 1909.

20. ["It is in perfect condition":] *Ibid.*, November 15, 1910. ["If it had not been for":] *Ibid.*, September 23, 1910.

21. Bruce B. Cheever, "The Development of Railroads in the State of Washington, 1860 to 1948," M.A. thesis, Western Washington College of Education, Bellingham, 1949, pp. 85, 86, 88, 139. On January 2, 1909, the separate Milwaukee entities of Washington, Idaho, Montana, and South Dakota were consolidated into the Chicago Milwaukee & Puget Sound Railroad, which was independent of the CM&StP west of Mobridge, South Dakota. In December 1912, the Chicago Milwaukee & Puget Sound was absorbed by its parent. The Milwaukee gathered in its Puget Sound subsidiaries, and the Tacoma Eastern, on December 31, 1918. See also, Henry L. Gray, *Historic Railroads of Washington* (Seattle, 1971), p. 16.

22. ["The record leaves no doubt" . . . "The project was the result" . . . John D. Ryan:] Lowenthal, *The Investor Pays*, pp. 14, 18, 20.

BIBLIOGRAPHY

ARTICLES AND ESSAYS

Bonney, W.P. "Naming Stampede Pass." *Washington Historical Quarterly* vol. 12 , no. 4 (October 1921).

Chin, Art, and Doug Chin. "The Legacy of Washington State's Early Chinese Pioneers." *International Examiner*, March 4, 1987.

Coffman, N.B. "When I Came To Washington Territory." *Washington Historical Quarterly* vol. 26, no. 2 (April 1935).

Coleman, Edmund T. "Puget Sound and the Northern Pacific Railroad." *Washington Historical Quarterly* vol. 23, no. 4 (October 1932).

Edwards, G. Thomas. "Terminus Disease: The Clark P. Crandall Description of Puget Sound in 1871." *Pacific Northwest Quarterly* vol. 70, no. 4 (October 1979).

Fairweather, H.W. "The Northern Pacific Railroad and Some of Its History." *Washington Historical Quarterly* vol. 10, no. 2 (April 1919) ["Comment on Mr. Fairweather's Article, by Hazard Stevens"].

Fairweather, W.A. "Early Day Railroading in Washington." In *Building A State: Washington, 1889-1939; Commemorative of the Golden Jubilee Celebration*, vol. 3. Edited by Charles Miles and O.B. Sperlin. Tacoma: Washington State Historical Society, 1940.

Grant, H. Roger. "Seeking the Pacific: The Chicago & North Western's Plans to Reach the West Coast." *Pacific Northwest Quarterly* vol. 81, no. 2 (April 1990).

Hanford, C.H. "The Orphan Railroad and Ram's Horn Right of Way." *Washington Historical Quarterly* vol. 14, no. 2 (April 1923).

Hartman, John P. "The Coxey Army Invasion of Puyallup." In *Building a State: Washington, 1889-1939; Commemorative of the Golden Jubilee Celebration*, vol. 3. Edited by Charles Miles and O.B. Sperlin. Tacoma: Washington State Historical Society, 1940.

Majors, Harry M. "D.C. Linsley's Railroad Survey of the Sauk and Wenatchee Rivers in the 1870s." *Northwest Discovery* vol. 2 , no. 4 (April 1981).

Montgomery, Mrs. J.B. "The First Railroad." In *Building a State: Washington, 1889-1939; Commemorative of the Golden Jubilee Celebration*, vol. 3. Edited by Charles Miles and O.B. Sperlin. Tacoma: Washington State Historical Society, 1940.

Overmeyer, Philip H. "George B. McClellan and the Pacific Northwest." *Pacific Northwest Quarterly* vol. 32 , no. 1 (January 1941).

Pierce, J. Kingston. "The Panic of 1893." *Columbia Magazine* vol. 7, no. 4 (Winter 1993-94).

Russell, Pearl. "Analysis of the Pacific Railroad Reports." *Washington Historical Quarterly* vol. 10, no. 1 (January 1919).

Sherrard, William R. "The Kirkland Steel Mill: An Adventure in Western Enterprise." *Pacific Northwest Quarterly* vol. 53, no. 4 (October 1962).

Stevens, Isaac I. "Letters of Governor Isaac I. Stevens, 1853-1854." Edited by John S. Richards. *Pacific Northwest Quarterly* vol. 30, no. 3 (July 1939).

Westerners LA Corral. "Steamboating on the Columbia River: The Journals of Captain John C. Ainsworth." *The Westerners' Brand Book*, vol. 9. Edited by Henry Clifford. Los Angeles, 1961.

BOOKS AND MONOGRAPHS

Anderson, Alexander G. *The Lake Washington Belt Line. Lake Washington: Resources of the Region Tributary to Its Eastern Shores and the Belt Line Railroad; Kirkland: The Manufacturing City of the Puget Sound Region.* Prospectus. Seattle: Lowman and Hanford, 1891.

Asay, Jeff. *Union Pacific Northwest: The Oregon-Washington Railway & Navigation Company: A History.* Edmonds, Washington: Pacific Fast Mail, 1991.

Athearn, Robert G. *Union Pacific Country.* Chicago: Rand McNally, 1971.

Bagley, Clarence. *History of Seattle from the Earliest Settlement to the Present Time*, 3 vols. Chicago: S.J. Clarke, 1916.

Bass, Sophie F. *When Seattle Was a Village.* Seattle: Lowman and Hanford, 1947.

Beaton, Welford. *The City that Made Itself: A Literary and Pictorial Record of the Building of Seattle.* Seattle: Terminal Publishing, 1914.

Berner, Richard C. *Seattle in the Twentieth Century.* Volume 1: *Seattle 1900-1920. From Boomtown, Urban Turbulence, to Restoration.* Seattle: Charles Press, 1991.

Best, Gerald M. *Ships and Narrow Gauge Rails: The Story of the Pacific Coast Company.* Berkeley: Howell-North, 1964.

Binns, Archie. *Northwest Gateway: The Story of the Port of Seattle.* Portland: Binfords and Mort, 1941.

Boswell, Sharon A., and Lorraine McConaghy. *Raise Hell and Sell Newspapers: Alden J. Blethen and The Seattle Times.* Pullman: Washington State University Press, 1996.

Bryan, Enoch A. *Orient Meets Occident: The Advent of the Railways to the Pacific Northwest.* Pullman, Washington: Students Book Corporation, 1936.

Buerge, David M. *Seattle in the 1880s.* Edited by Stuart R. Grover. Seattle: Historical Society of Seattle and King County, 1986.

Burke, Padraic. *A History of the Port of Seattle.* Seattle: Port of Seattle, 1976.

Canfield, Thomas H. *Life of Thomas Hawley Canfield: His Early Efforts to Open a Route for the Transportation of the Products of the West to New England, by Way of the Great Lakes, St. Lawrence River and Vermont Railroads, and His Connection with the Early History of the Northern Pacific Railroad, from the History of the Red River Valley, North Dakota, and Park Region of Northwestern Minnesota.* Burlington, Vermont, 1889.

_____. *Northern Pacific Railroad: Partial Report to the Board of Directors, of a Portion of a Reconnaissance Made in the Summer of 1869, between Lake Superior and the Pacific Ocean . . . Accompanied with Notes on Puget Sound, by Samuel Wilkeson.* "For Private Circulation Only." Northern Pacific Railroad, May 1870.

Cheever, Bruce B. "The Development of Railroads in the State of Washington, 1860 to 1948." M.A. thesis, Western Washington College of Education, Bellingham, 1949.

Clark, Norman H. *Mill Town: A Social History of Everett, Washington, from Its Earliest Beginnings on the Shores of Puget Sound to the Tragic and Infamous Event Known as the Everett Massacre.* Seattle: University of Washington Press, 1970.

Cochran, Thomas C. *Railroad Leaders, 1845-1890: The Business Mind in Action.* Cambridge: Harvard University Press, 1953.

Cohn, Edwin J., *Industry in the Pacific Northwest and the Location Theory.* New York: King's Crown Press, 1952.

Denny, Arthur A. *Pioneer Days on Puget Sound.* Seattle: C.B. Bagley, 1888; reprint, Fairfield, Washington: Ye Galleon Press, 1979.

Derleth, August W. *The Milwaukee Road: Its First Hundred Years.* New York: Creative Age Press, 1948.

Dorpat, Paul. *Seattle, Now and Then.* Seattle: Tartu, 1984.

Dufwa, Thamar E. *Transcontinental Railroad Legislation, 1835-1862.* New York: Arno Press, 1985.

Ely, Arline. *Our Foundering Fathers: The Story of Kirkland.* Illustrated by William H. Conogue, edited by Betty Howe. Kirkland, Washington: Kirkland Public Library, 1975.

Fuller, O. Muiriel. *John Muir of Wall Street: A Story of Thrift.* New York: Knickerbocker Press, 1927.

Gates, Charles M. *Messages of the Governors of the Territory of Washington to the Legislative Assembly, 1854-1889.* Seattle: University of Washington Press, 1940.

Grant, Frederick J. *History of Seattle, Washington: With Illustrations and Biographical Sketches of Some of Its Prominent Men and Pioneers*. New York: American Publishing, 1891.

Gray, Henry L. *Historic Railroads of Washington*. Seattle, 1971.

Hanford, C.H. *Seattle and Environs, 1852-1924*, 3 vols. Chicago: Pioneer Historical Publishing, 1924.

Harney, Thomas P. *Charles Barstow Wright, 1822-1898: A Builder of the Northern Pacific Railroad and of the City of Tacoma, Washington*. Tacoma, 1956.

Harnsberger, John L. *Jay Cooke and Minnesota: The Formative Years of the Northern Pacific Railroad, 1868-1873*. New York: Arno Press, 1981.

Hedges, James B. *Henry Villard and the Railways of the Northwest*. New Haven: Yale University Press, 1939.

Hidy, Ralph, and Muriel Hidy, Donald Hofsommer, Roy Scott; Elizabeth A. Burnham, editorial assistant. *The Great Northern Railway: A History*. Boston: Harvard Business School Press, 1988.

Hilliard, George S. *The Life and Campaigns of George B. McClellan, Major-General U.S. Army*. Philadelphia: Lippincott, 1865.

Hitchman, Robert. *Place Names of Washington*. Tacoma: Washington State Historical Society, 1985.

Hunt, Herbert. *Tacoma, Its History and Its Builders: A Half-Century of Activity*, 3 vols. Chicago: S.J. Clarke, 1916.

Jensen, Derrick, and George Draffan, John Osborn. *Railroads and Clearcuts: The Legacy of Congress's 1863 Northern Pacific Railroad Land Grant*. Sandpoint, Idaho: Inland Empire Land Council (Spokane) and Keokee Publishing, 1995.

Johnson, Edwin F. *Railroad to the Pacific. Northern Route. Its General Character, Relative Merits, Etc*. New York: Railroad Journal Job Printing Office, 1854.

Johnson, Violet A., ed. *Kalama, Washington: A Centennial History*. Kalama: Clark County Genealogical Society, 1990.

Labb, John T., and Peter J. Replinger. *Logging to the Salt Chuck: Over 100 Years of Railroad Logging in Mason County, Washington*. Seattle: NorthWest Shortline, 1990.

Lentz, Florence K. *Kent, Valley of Opportunity*. Chatsworth, California: Windsor Publications, 1990.

Lewty, Peter J. *To The Columbia Gateway: The Oregon Railway and the Northern Pacific, 1879-1884*. Pullman: Washington State University Press, 1987.

Lowenthal, Max. *The Investor Pays*. New York: A.A. Knopf, 1933.

Malone, Michael. *James J. Hill: Empire Builder of the Northwest*. Norman: University of Oklahoma Press, 1996.

Martin, Albro. *James J. Hill and the Opening of the Northwest*. New York: Oxford University Press, 1976.

McDonald, Richard K., and Lucile McDonald. *The Coals of Newcastle: A Hundred Years of Hidden History*. Washington: Issaquah Alps Trail Club, 1987.

McKenzie, William A. *Dining Car Line to the Pacific: An Illustrated History of the NP Railway's "Famously Good" Food, with 150 Authentic Recipes*. St. Paul: Minnesota Historical Society Press, 1990.

Morgan, Murray. *The Mill on the Boot: The Story of the St. Paul & Tacoma Lumber Company*. Seattle: University of Washington Press, 1982.

_____. *Puget's Sound: A Narrative of Early Tacoma and the Southern Sound*. Seattle: University of Washington Press, 1979.

Nesbit, Robert C. *"He Built Seattle": A Biography of Judge Thomas Burke*. Seattle: University of Washington Press, 1961.

Newell, Gordon R. *The H.W. McCurdy Marine History of the Pacific Northwest*. Seattle: Superior Publishing, 1966.

_____. *Totem Tales of Old Seattle: Legends and Anecdotes, by Gordon Newell and Totemizer Don Sherwood*. Seattle: Superior Publishing, 1956.

_____. *Westward to Alki: The Story of David and Louisa Denny*. Seattle: Superior Publishing, 1977.

Palmer, Robert D. *The Northern Pacific Railroad and Its Choice of a Western Terminus*. Seattle: University of Washington Press, 1968.

Prater, Yvonne. *Snoqualmie Pass: From Indian Trail to Interstate*. Seattle: Mountaineers, 1981.

Prosch, Thomas W. *McCarver and Tacoma*. Seattle: Lowman and Hanford, 1906.

Pucher, Itothe. *The Puget Sound and Inland Empire Railway. "Cascade Tunnel Route."* Seattle: A. Harriman, n.d.

Pyle, Joseph G. *The Life of James J. Hill*, 2 vols. Garden City, New York: Doubleday, 1917.

Quiett, Glenn C. *They Built the West: An Epic of Rails and Cities*. New York: D. Appleton-Century, 1934.

Rathbun, John C. *History of Thurston County, Washington*. Olympia, 1895.

Renz, Louis T. *The History of the Northern Pacific Railroad*. Fairfield, Washington: Ye Galleon Press, 1980.

Richards, Kent D. *Isaac I. Stevens: Young Man in a Hurry*. Provo: Brigham Young University Press, 1979; reprint, Pullman: Washington State University Press, 1993.

Ritz, Philip. *Letter upon the Agricultural and Mineral Resources of the North Western Territories, on the Route of the Northern Pacific Railroad*. Washington, D.C., 1868.

Roe, JoAnn. *Stevens Pass: The Story of Railroading and Recreation in the North Cascades*. Seattle: Mountaineers, 1995.

Roth, Lottie R., ed. *History of Whatcom County*, 2 vols. Chicago: Pioneer Historical Publishing, 1926.

Sale, Roger. *Seattle, Past to Present*. Seattle: University of Washington Press, 1976.

Schrenk, Lorenz P., and Robert L. Frey. *Northern Pacific Classic Steam Era*. Edmonds, Washington: Hundman Publishing, 1997.

Sears, Stephen W. *George B. McClellan: The Young Napoleon*. New York: Tichnor and Fields, 1988.

Shackleford, Elizabeth. "History of the Puyallup Indian Reservation." M.A. thesis, University of Puget Sound, Tacoma, 1918.

Shapiro, Scott E. *Watson C. Squire, Senator from Washington, 1889-1897*. Seattle, 1992.

Smalley, Eugene V. *History of the Northern Pacific Railroad*. New York: G.P. Putnam's Sons, 1883.

Snowden, Clinton A. *History of Washington: The Rise and Progress of an American State,* 4 vols. Advisory editors: Cornelius H. Hanford, Miles C. Moore, William D. Tyler, and Stephen J. Chadwick. New York: Century History, 1909.

Sobel, Robert. *Panic on Wall Street: A History of America's Financial Disasters*. New York: Macmillan, 1968.

South Bay Historical Association. *South Bay: Its History and Its People, 1840-1940*. Olympia, 1986.

Speidel, William C. *Sons of the Profits; or, There's No Business Like Grow Business: The Seattle Story, 1851-1901*. Seattle: Nettle Creek Publishing, 1967.

Stevens, Hazard. *The Life of Isaac Ingalls Stevens, by His Son, Hazard Stevens*, 2 vols. Boston: Houghton Mifflin, 1900.

Stevens, Isaac I. *Address on the Northwest, before the American Geographical and Statistical Society, Delivered at New York, December 2, 1858*. Washington, D.C.: C.S. Gideon, 1858.

Thomson, Reginald H. *That Man Thomson*. Edited by Grant H. Redford. Seattle: University of Washington Press, 1950.

Train, George F. *My Life in Many States and in Foreign Lands, Dictated in my Seventy-fourth Year*. London: William Heineman, 1902.

United States Government. Interstate Commerce Commission. *Valuation Reports: Decisions in the Interstate Commerce Commission of the United States; Reports by the Commission*, vol. 25, February-May 1929. Washington, D.C.: U.S. Printing Office, 1929.

_____. War Department. *Reports of Explorations and Surveys to Ascertain the Most Practicable and Economical Route for a Railroad from the Mississippi River to the Pacific Ocean, 1853-1854. Made under the Direction of the Secretary of War, 1853-1856*, vol. I-XI. House Executive Document, 33rd Congress, 2nd Session, 1855-1861. Washington, D.C.: A.O.P. Nicholson, 1855-1861.

Villard, Henry. *The Early History of Transportation in Oregon*. Edited by Oswald Garrison Villard. Eugene: University of Oregon Press, 1944.

_____. *Memoirs of Henry Villard, Journalist and Financier, 1835-1900*, 2 vols. Boston, New York: Houghton Mifflin, 1904.

Watt, Roberta F. *The Story of Seattle*. Seattle: Lowman and Hanford, 1931.

Wilkeson, Samuel. *Wilkeson's Notes on Puget Sound: Being Extracts from Notes by Samuel Wilkeson on a Reconnaissance of the Proposed Route of the Northern Pacific Railroad Made in the Summer of 1869*. Northern Pacific Railroad, 1870.

Wing, Warren W. *To Seattle by Trolley*. Edmonds, Washington: Pacific Fast Mail, 1988.

_____. *To Tacoma by Trolley: The Puget Sound Electric Railway*. Edmonds, Washington: Pacific Fast Mail, 1995.

Winks, Robin W. *Frederick Billings: A Life*. New York: Oxford University Press, 1991.

Wynne, Robert E. "Reaction to the Chinese in the Pacific Northwest and British Columbia, 1850-1910." Ph.D. dissertation, University of Washington, Seattle, 1964.

MANUSCRIPTS AND SPECIAL COLLECTIONS

Blaine, Reverend David Edward. Letters. University of Washington Library, Manuscripts and University Archives. Accession no. 4611.

Burke, Thomas. Papers. University of Washington Library, Manuscripts and University Archives. Accession nos. 1483, 1483-2 [extensive records and correspondence regarding the Seattle Lake Shore & Eastern, Seattle & Montana (Great Northern), Railroad Avenue, and ram's horn franchise].

Columbia & Puget Sound Railroad. Corporate record books, 1880-1917; minutes, resolutions, titles, deeds, capital improvements, Railroad Avenue and ram's horn agreements, city ordinances. Museum of History and Industry, Seattle. Burlington Northern collection, accession no. 5375, boxes 1-8.

Gilman, Daniel Hunt. Papers. University of Washington Library, Manuscripts and University Archives. Accession no. 2730.

Great Northern Railway. Corporate records. Minnesota Historical Society History Center, St. Paul.

Northern Pacific Railroad. Corporate records. Minnesota Historical Society History Center, St. Paul.

Oregon Improvement Company. Corporate records. University of Washington Library, Manuscripts and University Archives. Accession no. 249.

Roberts, William Milnor. Journey from Portland to Puget Sound; Puget Sound diary, 1871; Northern Pacific Railroad surveys for the branch from Tacoma across the Cascade range in 1878. University of Washington Library, Manuscripts and University Archives. Accession no. 4866.

Rogers, Albert Bowman. Diary. University of Washington Library, Manuscripts and University Archives. Accession no. 642.

Rogers, John Garwood. Diary. University of Washington Library, Manuscripts and University Archives. Accession no. 643.

Seattle & Walla Walla Railroad. Corporate record book, 1880; inventory, mortgages, and liens, articles of indenture, tidelands titles, Villard transfer memoranda. Museum of History and Industry, Seattle. Burlington Northern collection, accession no. 5375, box 1. [Other Seattle & Walla Walla correspondence, inventories, minutes, transactions may be found in the Thomas Burke papers, University of Washington Library, Manuscripts and University Archives. Accession no. 1483-2.]

Seattle Lake Shore & Eastern Railroad. Thomas Burke papers, University of Washington Library, Manuscripts and University Archives. Accession no. 1483-2; and Daniel H. Gilman papers, University of Washington Library, Manuscripts and University Archives. Accession nos. 2730, 2730-2.

Squire, Watson C. Papers. University of Washington, Manuscripts and University Archives. Accession no. 4004.

Villard, Henry. Papers. University of Washington Library, Microforms and Newspapers. Box A133.

NEWSPAPERS

Bellingham Bay *Mail*
Kalama *Beacon*
Olympia *Pioneer and Democrat*
Olympia *Puget Sound Courier*
Olympia *Transcript*
Olympia *Washington Standard*
Port Gardner *News*
Port Townsend *Argus*
Port Townsend *Weekly Message*
Portland *Oregonian*
San Francisco *Chronicle*
Seattle *Argus*
Seattle *Chronicle*
Seattle *Herald*
Seattle *Intelligencer*
Seattle *Post-Intelligencer*
Seattle *Press-Times*
Seattle *Puget Sound Dispatch*
Seattle *Star*
Seattle *Telegraph*
Seattle *Times*
Spokane *Spokesman-Review*
Steilacoom *Express*
Tacoma *Herald*
Tacoma *Ledger*
Tacoma *News*
Vancouver (Wash.) *Independent*

Index